The Spirit of St. Francis de Sales

by Jean Pierre Camus

Translated by J. S.

Originally published in 1910.

PREFACE.

The Spirit of a Saint we may, perhaps, regard as the underlying characteristic which pervades all his thoughts, words, and acts. It is the note which sounds throughout the constant persevering harmony which makes the holiness of his life. Circumstances change. He grows from childhood to boyhood; from youth to manhood. His time of preparation is unnoticed by the world until the moment comes when he is called to a public activity which arrests attention. And essentially he remains the same. In private as in public, in intimate conversation as in writings or discourses, in the direction of individual consciences as in the conduct of matters of wide importance, there is a characteristic note which identifies him, and marks him off apart even from other heroes of sanctity.

We owe to a keen and close observer a knowledge of the spirit of St. Francis de Sales for which we cannot be too grateful. Let it be granted that Mgr. Camus had a very prolific imagination; that he had an unconscious tendency to embroider facts; that he read a meaning into words which their speaker had no thought of imparting to them. When all such allowances have been made, we must still admit that he has given to us a picture of the Saint which we should be loath to lose; and that his description of what the Saint habitually thought and felt has made Saint Francis de Sales a close personal friend to many to whom otherwise he would have remained a mere chance acquaintance.

The Bishop of Belley, while a devoted admirer, was at the same time a critical observer of his saintly friend. He wanted to know the reasons of what he saw, he did not always approve, and he was sufficiently indiscreet to put questions which, probably, no one else would have dared to frame. And thus we know more about St. Francis than about any other Saint, and we owe real gratitude to his very candid, talkative, and out-spoken episcopal colleague.

Many years ago a brief abridgment of the "Spirit of St. Francis de Sales" was published in English. It served its purpose, but left unsatisfied the desire of his clients for a fuller work. To-day the Sisters of the Visitation, now established at Harrow-on-the-Hill, give abundant satisfaction to this long-felt desire. Inspired by the purpose of the late Dom Benedict Mackey, O.S.B., which his premature death prevented him from accomplishing, and guided by the advice which he left in writing, these Daughters of St. Francis of Sales, on the occasion of their Tercentenary, give to the English-speaking world a work which, in its wise curtailment and still full detail, may be called the quintessence of the Spirit of their Master, the Founder of their Institute. We thank them for their labour; and we beg God's blessing upon this book, that it may be the means of showing to many souls that safe and easy way of sanctification and salvation, which it was the special mission of the saintly Bishop of Geneva to make known to the world.

FRANCIS, ARCHBISHOP OF WESTMINSTER.

May 18th, 1910.

SKETCH OF THE LIFE OF JEAN PIERRE CAMUS,

BISHOP OF BELLEY

Jean Pierre Camus came of an illustrious, and much respected family of Auxonne in Burgundy, in which province it possessed the seigneuries of Saint Bonnet and Pont-carré.

He was born in Paris, November 3rd, 1584.

His grandfather was for some years Administrator of the Finances under King Henri III. Though he had had the management of the public funds during a period when fraud and dishonesty were as easy as they were common, he retired from office without having added a single penny to his patrimony. On one occasion having received from Henri III. the gift of a sum of 50,000 crowns, which had been left by a Jew who had died intestate, and without children, this upright administrator sent for three merchants who had lost all their property in a fire, and distributed it among them.

The father of our Prelate, inheriting this integrity, left an honourable name, but few worldly goods to his children.

Faithful, and devoted to the interests of his king, Henri IV., he gave part of his fortune to the support of the good cause, the triumph of which he had the happiness of witnessing. He died in 1619.

The mantle of paternal loyalty and patriotism undoubtedly descended upon the young J. P. Camus, for second only to his love for God, and His Church, was his devotion to France, and its king.

On his mother's side, as well as on his father's, he was well connected. Her family had given to France chancellors, secretaries of state, and other distinguished personages, but noble as were the races from which he sprang their chief distinction is derived from the subject of this sketch.

"This one branch," says his panegyrist, "bore more blossoms and more fruit than all the others together. In John Peter the gentle rivulet of the Camus' became a mighty stream, yet one whose course was peaceful, and which loved to flow underground, as do certain rivers which seem to lose themselves in the earth, and only emerge to precipitate themselves into the waters of the ocean."

Books and objects of piety were the toys of his childhood, and his youth was passed in solitude, and in the practices of the ascetic life. His physical strength as it increased with his years, seemed only to serve to assist him in curbing and restraining a somewhat fiery temperament. His wish, which at one time was very strong, to become a Carthusian, was not indeed fulfilled, it being evident from the many impediments put in its way, that it was not a call from God.

Nevertheless, this desire of self-sacrifice in a cloistered life was only thwarted in order that he might sacrifice himself in another way, namely, by becoming a Bishop, which state, if its functions are rightly discharged, assuredly demands greater self-immolation than does that of a monk, and is indeed a martyrdom that ceases only with life itself.

If he did not submit himself to the Rule of the Carthusians by entering their Order, he nevertheless adopted all its severity, and to the very end of his life kept his body in the most stern and rigorous subjection.

This, and his early inclination towards the religious life, will not a little astonish his detractors, if any such still exist, for it is surely a convincing proof that he was not the radical enemy of monasticism they pretend. In his studies he displayed great brilliancy, being especially distinguished in theology and canon law, to the study of which he consecrated four years of his life.

After he had become a Priest his learning, piety, and eloquence not only established his reputation as a preacher in the pulpits of Paris, but soon even crossed the threshold of the Louvre and reached the ears of Henry IV. That monarch, moved by the hope of the great services which a prelate might render to the Church even more than by the affection which he bore to the Camus family, decided to propose him for a Bishopric, although he was but twenty-five, and had not therefore reached the canonical age for that dignity.

The young Priest was far too humble and also too deeply imbued with a sense of the awful responsibility of the office of a Bishop to expect, or to desire to be raised to it. When, however, Pope Paul V. gave the necessary dispensation, M. Camus submitted to the will both of the Pontiff and of the King, and was consecrated Bishop of Belley by St. Francis de Sales, August 30, 1609.

The fact that the two dioceses of Geneva and Belley touched one another contributed to further that close intimacy which was always maintained between the

Bishops, the younger consulting the elder on all possible occasions, and in all imaginable difficulties.

Bishop Camus had already referred his scruples regarding his youth at the time of his consecration to his holy director. The latter had, however, reminded him of the many reasons there were to justify his submission, viz., the needs of the diocese, the testimony to his fitness given by so many persons of distinction and piety, the judgment of Henry the Great, in fine the command of His Holiness. In consecrating Mgr. Camus, St. Francis de Sales seems to have transmitted to the new Prelate some of the treasures of his own holy soul. Camus was the only Bishop whom he ever consecrated, and doubtless this fact increased the tender affection which Francis bore him. John Peter was, what he loved to call himself, and what St. Francis loved to call him, the latter's only son. There was between the two holy Prelates a community of intelligence and of life. "Camus," says Godeau, the preacher of his funeral discourse, "ever sat at the feet of St. Francis de Sales, whom he called his Gamaliel, there to learn from him the law of God: full as he himself was of the knowledge of Divine things."

We must bear this in mind if we wish to know what Camus really was, and to appreciate him properly. He was by nature ardent, impetuous, and imaginative, eager for truth and goodness, secretly devoted to the austere practices of St. Charles Borromeo, but above all fervently desirous to imitate his model, his beloved spiritual Father, and therefore anxious to subdue, and to temper all that was too impetuous, excitable, and hard in himself, by striving after the incomparable sweetness and tenderness which were the distinguishing characteristics of St. Francis de Sales.

Mgr. Camus was endowed with a most marvellous memory, which was indeed invaluable to him in the great work to which both Bishops devoted themselves, that of bringing back into the bosom of the Church those who had become strangers, and even enemies to her.

His chief defect was that he was over hasty in judging, and of this he was himself perfectly well aware. He tells us in the "Esprit" that on one occasion when he was bewailing his deficiency to Francis, the good Prelate only smiled, and told him to take courage, for that as time went on it would bring him plenty of judgment, that being one of the fruits of experience, and of advancing years.

Whenever Mgr. Camus visited the Bishop of Geneva, which he did each year in order to make a retreat of several days under the direction of his spiritual Father, he was treated with the greatest honour by him.

St. Francis de Sales gave up his own room to his guest, and made him preach, and discharge other episcopal functions, so as to exercise him in his own presence in these duties of his sublime ministry.

This was the school in which Camus learnt to control and master himself, to curb his natural impetuosity, and to subjugate his own will, and thus to acquire one, in our opinion, of the most certain marks of saintliness.

The Bishop of Geneva was not contented with receiving his only son at Annecy. He often went over to Belley, and spent several days there in his company. These visits were to both Prelates a time of the greatest consolation. Then they spoke, as it were, heart to heart, of all that they valued most. Then they encouraged one another to bear the burden of the episcopate. Then they consoled each other in the troubles which they met with in their sacred ministry.

It never cost the younger Bishop anything to yield obedience to the elder, and no matter how great, or how trifling was the occasion which called for the exercise of that virtue, there was never a moment's hesitation on the part of the Bishop of Belley.

The latter, indeed, considered the virtue of obedience as the one most calculated to ensure rapid advance in the spiritual life. He tells us that one day at table someone having boasted that he could make an egg stand upright on a plate, a thing which those present, forgetting Christopher Columbus, insisted was impossible, the Saint, as Columbus had done, quietly taking one up chipped it a little at one end, and so made it stand. The company all cried out that there was nothing very great in that trick. "No," repeated the Saint, "but all the same you did not know it."

We may say the same, adds Camus, of obedience: it is the true secret of perfection, and yet few people know it to be so.

From what we have already seen of the character of John Peter Camus, we may imagine that gentleness was the most difficult for him to copy of the virtues of St. Francis de Sales; yet steel, though much stronger than iron, is at the same time far more readily tempered.

Thus, in his dealings with his neighbour he behaved exactly like his model, so much so, that for anyone who wanted to gain his favour the best plan was to offend him or do him some injury.

I have spoken of his love of mortification, and a short extract from the funeral discourse pronounced over his remains will show to what extent he practised it.

Godeau says: "Our virtuous Bishop up to the very last years of his life, slept either on a bed of vine shoots, or on boards, or on straw. This custom he only abandoned in obedience to his director, and in doing so I consider that he accomplished what was far more difficult and painful than the mortifications which he had planned for himself, since the sacrifice of our own will in these matters is incomparably more disagreeable to us than the practising of them."

This austerity in respect to sleep, of which, indeed, he required more than others on account of his excitable temperament, did not suffice to satisfy his love for penance, without which, he said, the leading of a Christian and much more of an episcopal life was impossible. To bring his body into subjection he constantly made use of hair-shirts, iron belts, vigils, fasting, and the discipline, and it was not until his last illness that he gave up those practices of austerity. He concealed them, however, as carefully as though he had been ashamed of them, knowing well that such sacrifices if not offered in secret, partake more of the spirit of Pharisaism than of the gospel. This humility, notwithstanding, he was unable to guard against the pardonable curiosity of his servants. One of them, quite a young man, who was his personal attendant during the first years of his residence at Belley, observing that he wore round his neck the key of a large cupboard, and being very anxious to know what it contained, managed in some way to possess himself of this key for a few moments, when his master had laid it aside, and was not in the room.

Unlocking the cupboard he found it full of the vine shoots on which he was accustomed to sleep. The bed which everyone saw in his apartment was the Bishop's; the one which he hid away was the penitent's. The one was for appearance, the other for piety. He used to put into disorder the coverings of the bed, so as to give the impression of having slept in it, while he really slept, or at least took such repose as was necessary to keep him alive, on the penitential laths he had hidden.

Having discovered that through his valet the rumour of his austerity had got abroad, he dismissed the young man from his service, giving him a handsome present, and warning him to be less curious in future. But for his failing, however, we should have lost a great example of the Bishop's mortification and humility.

The latter virtue John Peter Camus cultivated most carefully, and how well he succeeded in this matter is proved by the composure, and even gaiety and joyousness, with which he met the raillery heaped upon his sermons, and writings.

Camus, like the holy Bishop of Geneva, had throughout his life a special devotion to the Blessed Virgin, and never failed in his daily recital of the Rosary. Every evening it was his habit to read a portion of either The Spiritual Combat, or the Imitation of Jesus Christ; two books which he recommended to his penitents as next in usefulness to the gospels.

Following him in his Episcopal career we find that as the years rolled on his reputation passed beyond the confines of France, and reached the Vatican.

Pope Paul V., who knew him intimately, held him in high esteem, and all the Cardinals honoured him with their friendship.

Had it not been for his own firm resistance to every proposal made to him to quit his poor diocese of Belley, Mgr. Camus would assuredly have been transferred to some much more important See.

And here we may again quote the words of his panegyrist, to indicate the fruits produced by his zeal in the little corner of the vineyard of the Divine Master, which had been confided to his skilful hands.

Godeau says, "The interior sanctity which he strove to acquire for himself by prayer, by reading holy books, by the mortification of his senses, by the putting aside of all secular affairs when engaged in prayer, by humility, patience, and charity, were the inexhaustible source whence flowed all his external works, and whence they derived all their purity and vigour."

As regarded the poor and needy in his diocese, Mgr. Camus was no less generous in ministering to their temporal than to their spiritual wants. He looked upon himself as simply a steward of the goods of the Church. He, indeed, drew the revenues of his diocese, but only as rivers draw their waters from the sea, to pay them back again to it with usury.

More than once in years of famine he gave all his corn to the poor, not as Joseph did in Egypt by depriving them of their liberty, but by depriving himself of what was necessary for his support, and treating himself no better than the rest of the poor.

One day he was told that the dearness of wine was the cause of great distress among working people. He immediately gave orders that his own wine should be sold, but after a most curious and unusual fashion. He would not have any fixed price set upon it, but only desired that an open bag should be held, at the door of the cellar so that purchasers might throw in what they pleased. You may be sure that the bag was not very full and that the buyers availed themselves to the utmost of his liberality.

What, however, do you think he did with the small amount of money which he found in the bag? Even that he forthwith distributed among the poor! Surely if anything can approach the miraculous transformation of water into wine it is Bishop Camus' mode of selling it!

After having established in his diocese that order and peace which are the fruits of the knowledge and observance of the duties of religion, and having formed a body of clergy remarkable for their piety and learning, Mgr. Camus thought he ought to advance even a step further.

He felt that it was his duty to have in his Episcopal city a community of Religious men who by their example should assist both clergy and laity in their spiritual life. He did this by building, at his own expense, in 1620, a Capuchin Monastery.

For a long time he supplied these Friars with all that they needed, and finally gave them his own library, which was both choice and extensive.

He was equally cordial in his relationship with other Orders, welcoming them gladly to his own house, and often making retreats in their Monasteries.

Camus was too intimately connected with Francis de Sales not to have with him a community of spirit.

Knowing how useful the newly-formed Order of the Visitation would be to the Church, he also founded at Belley, in 1662, a Convent, to which he invited some nuns of the New Congregation. This Institution of the holy Bishop of Geneva was vigorously attacked from its very beginning. It was called in derision, the Confraternity of the Descent from the Cross, because its pious founder had excluded from this order corporal austerities, and had adapted all his rules to the reforming of the interior. The Bishop of Belley declared himself champion of this new Institution. Indeed, his ardent soul was always on fire to proclaim and to maintain the glory of the Church. At whatever point She was attacked or threatened there Camus was to be found armed cap-a-pie to defend her.

As for his own temporal interests, they were to him matters of absolute indifference when weighed in the balance of that beloved Church. His own words, however, speak best on this subject.

On one occasion, when a Minister of State wrote to ask him something contrary to those interests, backing up his request with the most liberal promises, the Bishop of Belley, after courteously excusing himself from complying with the request, wound up his answer to the statesman with these remarkable words: This is all that can be said to you by a Bishop who, as regards the past, is under no obligation to anyone; as regards the present without interest; and as regards the future has no pretentions whatever.

We have said that the Bishop of Belley was indefatigable in labouring for the sanctification of his people, but this did not in any way prevent him from bestowing due care upon the interests of his own soul.

With this object in view he considered that after long years of toil for his flock he ought to retire from the world, so as to have more time to devote to himself. To live in solitude had been the desire of his youth, as we know it was ever his desire through all the period of his Episcopate; but his spiritual guide, the holy Bishop of Geneva, always succeeded in dissuading him from laying down the pastoral staff to take refuge in the cloister.

However, after the death of his illustrious friend and counsellor, this desire returned to Camus with redoubled force. For seven years, out of respect for the advice of his dear dead friend, he abstained from carrying out his purpose, and during that time of waiting, relaxing nothing in the ardour of his love for his people and his zeal for the Church, he devoted himself to the work of repairing and restoring his Cathedral, which was accomplished in the year 1627.

When in 1837 this ancient edifice was pulled down in order to be rebuilt, an inscription was discovered stating this fact, which is not otherwise mentioned in any extant writings, probably because those in which it was recorded were among the rich archives of the Chapter destroyed by the fury of the vandals of 1793.

At last, in 1628, Camus finally decided to give up his Episcopal charge to one who was indeed worthy of such a dignity.

This was Jean de Passelaigne, Abbot of Notre Dame de Hambic, Prior of St. Victor of Nevers, and of La Charité-sur-Loire, Vicar-General of the Order of Cluny.

Then, having obtained the King's consent, Camus retired from the diocese of Belley, which he had ruled so happily and so well for twenty years, to the Cistercian Abbey of Annay, there to exercise in the calm of solitude all those virtues to the practice of which he said the stir and bustle inseparable from the episcopal functions had not allowed him to devote himself. This he did, it would seem, towards the end of 1628, or the beginning of 1629.

The Abbey of Annay, which the King gave to him on receiving his resignation of the See of Belley, was situated in Normandy, near Caen. There Camus dwelt for some time, not, however, leading an idle life, for we find that a great many of his works were printed at Caen. He also succeeded in introducing into this Religious House, and into the neighbouring one of Ardaine, that reform which it was the desire of his heart to bring back to all the Monasteries of France. It was while in Normandy that he made the acquaintance of Père Eudes, and between these two holy Priests the closest friendship sprang up, founded on a mutual zeal for the salvation of souls.

The Bishop of Belley was not long allowed to enjoy his quiet retreat at Annay. François de Harlay, Archbishop of Rouen, being unable at that time, owing to ill health, to exercise his duties as a Bishop, felt convinced that Providence had sent Mgr. Camus into his diocese on purpose that he might share his labours. His earnest entreaties prevailed upon the good Bishop to emerge from his retreat and help to bear the burden which pressed so heavily upon a sick and failing Prelate.

At Belley he had been accountable to God alone for the discharge of those duties which he had for a time laid aside; now at the call of charity he did not hesitate to take up the burden again to ease another. He was appointed Vicar-General to the Archbishop of Rouen, renouncing, like St. Paul, his liberty in order to become the servant of all men, and thus gain more souls to Jesus Christ.

Although in this new sphere Camus laboured with the utmost devotion and untiring energy, living a life of ascetic severity, fasting, sleeping on straw, or spending whole nights in prayer, while his days were given to preaching, confirming, hearing confessions, visiting the sick, consoling the afflicted, advising, exhorting, patiently listening to the crowds who flocked to consult him, yet he still felt certain that the voice of God called him to solitude and to a perpetual retreat.

Desiring to spend the rest of his days among the poor whom he loved so well, he came to Paris, and took up his abode in the Hospital for Incurables, situated in the Rue de Sèvres. He reserved for himself out of his patrimony and benefices only 500 livres, which he paid to the hospital for his board and lodging, distributing the remainder among the needy.

In this hospital he passed his time in ministering to the sick, dressing their wounds, consoling, and instructing them, and performing for them all the functions of an ordinary Chaplain.

Even if he went out to visit friends in the vicinity of Paris, he never returned later than five o'clock in the evening. Occasionally he preached in the chapel of the Duke of Orleans before His Royal Highness, and at such times denounced vehemently the luxury and indolence of Princes and courtiers.

There was at this time a diocese in a no less pitiable condition than was Belley when Mgr. Camus was, at the King's desire, placed in charge of it. This diocese was that of Arras, and on the 28th of May, 1650, he was appointed by Louis XIV., acting under the advice of the Queen-Regent, to administer all the affairs of the diocese until such time as a new Bishop should be nominated to the vacant See by His Majesty and our Holy Father the Pope. Into this laborious task of sowing, ploughing, cultivating a vast weed-grown, and unpromising field, Camus threw himself with all his old ardour and energy. He did so much in a very short time that his name will long be remembered among the descendants of those from whom the troubles of the times snatched him so suddenly, but not before he had bound them to France while leading them to God by bands of love stronger than citadels or garrisons.

Political disturbances and the calamities of war having prevented this indefatigable servant of God from carrying on his work at Arras, he withdrew again in the following year to the Hospital of the Incurables at Paris, there to await better times, and also doubtless the expected Bull from the Sovereign Pontiff. However, the great Rewarder called Camus to Himself before the Pope had sanctioned his appointment to the Bishopric of Arras.

But ere we close this slight sketch of the life of the good Bishop, and speak of its last scenes, we must say a word about the gigantic literary labours which occupied him more or less from the time of his retirement to the Abbey of Annay, in 1628, till his death, in 1652.

It was his great love for the Church which made him take pen in hand. Varied as were the subjects on which he wrote, his writings, whether controversial, dogmatic, devotional or even light and entertaining, had but one single aim and end—the instruction of mankind and the glorification of Catholicism.

If we bear this in mind we shall be ready to forgive the bitterness and harshness which we may admit characterised many of his writings. To reform the Monasteries of France, and to deal a death blow to the abuses which had crept into some of them, was the passionate desire of his heart.

This, and not a personal hatred of monks, as his enemies have averred, was the moving spring of his actions in this crusade of the pen. At the same time we do not deny that his natural impetuosity and keen sense of humour made him too often, in accordance with the bad taste of the day, present the abuses which he wished to reform, in so ridiculous and contemptible a light, as to provoke and irritate his enemies, perhaps unnecessarily.

Yet, if in this he showed the lack of judgment which he had years before lamented in himself, can anyone who knows what those times were, and who is as jealous for the honour of God as he was, blame him? There was another evil of the day which the good Bishop witnessed with grief and indignation, and set himself zealously to reform. This was the publishing of romances, or novels, which, as then written, could only poison the minds of their readers, inflame their passions, and weaken their sense of right and wrong. He pondered the matter, and having made up his mind that it would be absolutely useless to endeavour to hinder their being read, as this would only increase the obstinacy and perversity of those who took pleasure in them, he decided on adopting another method altogether, as he himself said, he "tried to make these poor diseased folk, with their depraved taste and morbid cravings, swallow his medicine under the disguise of sweetmeats."

That is to say, he himself began to write novels and romances for them; romances which, indeed, depicted the profligacy of the age, but in such odious colours as to inspire aversion and contempt. Vice, if described, was held up to ridicule and loathing. The interest of the story was so well kept up as to carry the reader on to the end, and that end often showed the hero or heroine so entirely disabused of the world's enchantment as to retire voluntarily into convents, in order, by an absolute devotion of the heart to God, to repair the injury done to Him, by giving to the creature the love due to Him alone.

These books passed from hand to hand in the gay world, were read, were enjoyed, and the fruit gathered from them by the reader was the conviction that God being Himself the Sovereign God, all other love but that of which He is the object and the end, is as contrary to the happiness of man as it is opposed to all the rules of justice.

Let us hear what Camus himself says as to his motive and conduct in the matter of novel writing.[1]

"The enterprise on which I have embarked of wrestling with, or rather contending against those idle or dangerous books, which cloak themselves under the title of novels, would surely demand the hands of Briareus to wield as many pens, and the strength of Hercules to support such a burden! But what cannot courage, zeal, charity, and confidence in God accomplish?"

He goes on to say that though he sees all the difficulties ahead, his courage will not fail, for he holds his commission from a Saint, the holy Bishop of Geneva, in whose intercessions, and in the assistance of the God of Saints, he trusts, and is confident of victory.

He tells us in several of his works, and especially in his "Unknown Traveller," that it was St. Francis de Sales who first advised him to use his pen in this manner, and that for twenty-five years the Saint had been cogitating and developing this design in his brain.

In the same little pamphlet Camus points out the methods he followed as a novel writer.

"It consists," he says, "in saying only good things, dealing only with good subjects, the single aim of which is to deter from vice, and to lead on to virtue."

He was an extraordinarily prolific and rapid writer, scarcely ever correcting or polishing up anything that he had put on paper. This was a defect, but it was the natural outcome of his temperament, which was a curious combination of lightness and solidity, gaiety and severity.

Few people really understood him. He was often taken for a mere man of the world, when in truth he was one of the stoutest champions of the Church, and in his inner life, grave and ascetic, macerating his flesh like a monk of the desert. He wrote in all about 200 volumes, 50 of these being romances.

In the latter, which drew down upon him such storms of bitter invective, owing to his freedom of language in treating of the vices against which he was warning his readers, we do not pretend to admire his work, but must remind readers that his style was that of the age in which he lived, and that Camus was essentially a Parisian. We have said that he wrote at least fifty novels; we may add that each was cleverer than that which had preceded it. Forgotten now, they were at the time of their appearance eagerly devoured, and it is morally impossible but that some good should have resulted from their production.

And now old age came upon the busy writer—old age, but not the feebleness of old age, nor its privileged inaction. As he advanced in years he seemed to increase in zeal and diligence, and it was not till suddenly stricken down by a mortal malady that his labours ceased.

Then on his death-bed in a quiet corner of the Hospital for Incurables in humility, patience, and a marvellous silence, only opening his lips to speak at the desire of his confessor, calm and peaceful, his eyes fixed upon the crucifix which he held in his hands, Jean Pierre Camus gave up his soul to God. This was on the 25th of April, 1652. He was 67 years old.

He had in his will forbidden any pomp or display at his funeral, and his wishes were strictly obeyed.

Some time after his death a stone was placed by the Administrators of the Hospital over the tomb of the good Bishop, who had been so great a benefactor to that Institution, and who rests beneath the nave of its Church in the Rue de Sèvres.

When he felt the first approach of illness, about six weeks before his death, he made his will, in which he left the greater part of his money to the Hospital, founding in it four beds for the Incurables of Belley.

And now our work is done.... The object has been to make John Peter Camus known as he really was, and to cleanse his memory from the stains cast upon it by the jarring passions of his contemporaries.

If we have succeeded in this the reader will recognise in him a pious Bishop, armed with the scourge of penance, an indefatigable writer in the defence of good morals, of religion, and of the Church—a reformer, and not an enemy of the Monastic Orders; finally a Prelate, who laboured all his life to copy the Holy Bishop of Geneva, whom he ever regarded as his father, his guide, and his oracle.

One word more. Those pious persons who wish to know better this true disciple of the Bishop of Geneva have nothing to do but to read the Spirit of Saint Francis de Sales. There they will see the Bishop of Belley as he really was. There they can admire his ardent piety, the candour of his soul, the fervour of his faith and charity; in a word, all that rich store of virtues which he acquired in the school of that great master of the spiritual life who was for fourteen years his Director.

[Footnote 1: In the preface of his book, entitled "Strange Occurrences."]

THE FRENCH PUBLISHER TO THE READER, 1639.

Since the holy death of Blessed Francis de Sales, Prince and Bishop of Geneva, which took place on December 28th, the Feast of the Holy Innocents, in the year 1622, many writers have taken up the pen to give the public the knowledge of the pious life and virtuous conversation of that holy Prelate, whom some have very fitly called the St. Charles of France.

The writer, however, with whom we are most concerned is Monseigneur Jean Pierre Camus, Bishop of Belley, whose work we are now introducing to our readers. After the death of Blessed Francis this faithful friend and devoted disciple was entreated, urged, conjured, in season and out of season, by an infinity of persons, to employ the literary faculty given to him by God in communicating to the world the many rare things which he had had the opportunity of observing in the life and conversation of Blessed Francis, under whose direction and discipline he had been for fourteen years.

M. Camus constantly excused himself under the plea that many had already taken the work in hand, and that he did not care to put his sickle into another man's crop, nor to make books by simply transcribing those of others, as is done by many writers of our day. At last, however, he allowed himself to be persuaded by some members of the Order of the Visitation, founded by the holy Bishop, to write the life, or, more properly speaking, to delineate the spirit of his beloved Master.

Having promised to do this, he considered that he had, at least partially, fulfilled his promise by publishing some pious Treatises conformable to the spirit of the holy Prelate. It was, however, afterwards thought better to gather up, and, as it were, glean from M. Camus' own sermons, exhortations, conferences, conversations, books, and letters, that Spirit of Blessed Francis which he had imbibed, in common with all the holy Bishop's disciples and spiritual children.

To make this collection was not difficult, because there was scarcely a sermon, conference, or spiritual lesson given by him in which he did not say something about the Saint, so deeply imbued was he with his instructions.

One of the most intimate and familiar friends of the Bishop of Belley, having given his attention to the matter, now lays before you as the result, this book to which he has given the title: The Spirit of Blessed Francis de Sales, represented in his most remarkable words and actions. This holy Bishop was mighty in works and in words; he was not one of those who say much that is good but who do not practise it. To say and to do was with him the same thing, or rather, his doing surpassed his saying....

In this collection offered to you, there is but little formal arrangement, the component parts were gathered up as they fell from the lips or the pen of Monseigneur Camus. It is a piece of mosaic work, a bouquet of various flowers, a salad of divers herbs, a banquet of many dishes, an orchard of different fruits, where each one can take what best suits his taste.

Note.—In this translation an endeavour has been made to group together the sections treating of the same subject. These are scattered, without order, through the three volumes of the French edition.

THE SPIRIT OF ST. FRANCIS DE SALES

UPON PERFECT VIRTUE.

Blessed Francis de Sales thought very little of any virtue unless it was animated by charity; following in this the teaching of St. Paul, who declares that without charity the greatest virtues are as nothing. Thus, even the faith which works miracles, the almsgiving which leads a man to sell all his goods to feed the poor, the spirit of martyrdom which impels him to give his body to be burned, all, if without charity, are nothing.[1]

That you may clearly understand the distinction which he drew between the natural excellence of certain virtues, and the supernatural perfection which they acquire by the infusion of charity, I will give you his exact words on the subject, as they are to be found in his Treatise on the Love of God.

He says: "The light of the sun falls equally on the violet and the rose, yet will never render the former as fair as the latter, or make a daisy as lovely as a lily. If, however, the sun should shine very clearly upon the violet, and very mistily and faintly upon the rose, then without doubt it would make the violet more fair to see than the rose. So, Theotimus, if with equal charity one should suffer death by martyrdom, and another suffer only hunger by fasting, who does not see that the value of this fasting will not, on that account, be equal to that of martyrdom? No, for who would dare to affirm that martrydom is not more excellent in itself than fasting.... Still, it is true that if love be ardent, powerful, and excellent, in a heart, it will also more enrich and perfect all the virtuous works which may proceed from it. One may suffer death and fire for God, without charity, as St. Paul supposes[2], and as I explain elsewhere. Still more then may one suffer them with little charity. Now, I say, Theotimus, that it may come to pass that a very small virtue may be of greater value in a soul where divine love fervently reigns, than martyrdom itself in a soul where love is languishing, feeble, and dull. Thus, the least virtues of our Blessed Lady of St. John, and of other great Saints, were of more worth before God than the most exalted perfections of the rest of His servants."[3]

[Footnote 1: 1 Cor. xiii. 1-3.]

[Footnote 2: 1 Cor. xiii. 3.]

[Footnote 3: Bk. xi. chap. v.]

BLESSED FRANCIS' ESTIMATE OF VARIOUS VIRTUES.

1°. He preferred those virtues the practice of which is comparatively frequent, common, and ordinary, to others which we may be called upon to exercise on rare occasions.

2°. He considered, as we have seen, that the degree of the supernatural in any virtue could not be decided by the greatness or smallness of the external act, since an act in itself altogether trivial, may be performed with much grace and charity, while a very brilliant and dazzling good work may be animated by but a very feeble spark of love of God, the intensity of which is, after all, the only rule by which to ascertain its true value in His sight.

3°. The more universal a virtue, the more, he said, it is to be preferred before all others, charity only excepted. For instance, he valued prayer as the light which illumines all other virtues; devotion, as consecrating all our actions to God; humility, which makes us set but little value on ourselves and on our doings; meekness, which yields to all; patience, which includes everything besides. He valued these, I say, more than magnanimity, or liberality, because such virtues can be more rarely practised and they affect fewer subjects.

4°. He was always on his guard against showy virtues, which of their very nature encourage vainglory, the bane of all good works.

5°. He blamed those who measure virtues by the standard set up by the world, who prefer temporal to spiritual alms; haircloth, fasting, and corporal austerities to sweetness, modesty, and the mortification of the heart; virtues by far the more excellent.

6°. He greatly condemned those who select the virtues most agreeable to their taste, and practise these alone, quite regardless of those which are specially adapted to their state of life. These people, indeed, serve God, but after a way of their own, not according to His will: a by no means uncommon mistake, which leads many, otherwise devout-minded, far out of the right path.

UPON THE LESSER VIRTUES.

He had a special affection for certain virtues which are passed over by some as trivial and insignificant. "Everyone," he used to say, "is eager to possess those brilliant, almost dazzling virtues which cluster round the summit of the Cross, so that they can be seen from afar and admired, but very few are anxious to gather those which, like wild thyme, grow at the foot of that Tree of Life and under its shade. Yet these are often the most hardy, and give out the sweetest perfume, being watered with the precious Blood of the Saviour, whose first lesson to His disciples was: Learn of Me because I am meek and humble of heart."[1]

It does not belong to every one to practise the sublime virtues of fortitude, magnanimity, endurance unto death, patience, constancy, and courage. The occasions of exercising these are rare, yet all aspire to them because they are brilliant and their names high sounding. Very often, too, people fancy that they are able, even now, to practise them. They inflate their courage with the vain opinion they have of themselves, but when put to the trial fail pitiably. They are like those children of Ephrem, who distinguished themselves wonderfully by, in the time of peace, hitting the target with every arrow, but in the battle were the first to fly before the enemy. Better had their skill been less and their courage greater.

Opportunities of acquiring offices, benefices, inheritances, large sums of money, are not to be met with every day, but at any moment we may earn farthings and halfpence. By trading well on these small profits, many have in course of time grown rich. We should become spiritually wealthy and lay up for ourselves much treasure in Heaven did we employ in the service of the holy love of God, the small opportunities which are to be met with at every hour of our lives.

It is not enough to practise great virtues; they must be practised with great charity, for that it is which in the sight of God forms the basis of and gives weight and value to all good works. An act of lesser virtue (for all virtues are not of equal importance) done out of great love to God is far more excellent than a rarer and grander one done with less love.

"Look at this good soul, she gives a cup of cold water to the thirsty with such holy love that it is changed into the water of life, life eternal. The Gospel which makes light of the weightiest sums cast into the treasury, reckons of the highest value two mites offered out of a great and fervent love."[2]

"These little homely virtues! How seldom is mention made of them! How lightly they are esteemed! Kindly concessions to the exacting temper of our neighbour, gentle tolerance of his imperfections, loving endurance of cross looks, peevish gestures, cheerfulness under contempt and small injustices, endurance of affronts, patience with importunity, doing menial actions which our social position impels us to regard as beneath us; replying amiably to some one who has given us an undeserved and sharp reproof, falling down and then bearing good humouredly the being laughed at, accepting with gentleness the refusal of a kindness, receiving a favour graciously, humbling ourselves before our equals and inferiors, keeping on kindly and considerate terms with our servants. How trivial and poor all this appears to those who have their hearts lifted up with proud aspirations. We want, they seem to say, no virtues but such as go clad in purple, and to be borne by fair winds and spreading sails towards high reputation. They forget that those who please men are not the servants of God, and that the friendship of the world and its applause are worth nothing and less than nothing in His sight."[3]

[Footnote 1: Matt. xi. 29.]

[Footnote 2: Cf. Treatise on the Love of God. Bk. iii. c. ii.]

[Footnote 3: Cf. The Devout Life. Part iii. c, i., ii., and vi.]

UPON INCREASE OF FAITH.

Lord, I believe, help my unbelief! Lord, increase the Faith in us! And how is this increase of Faith to be brought about? In the same way, assuredly, as the strength of the palm tree grows with the load it has to bear, or as the vine profits by being pruned.

A stoic philosopher remarked very truly that virtue languishes when it has nothing to overcome. What does a man know until he is tempted?

Our Blessed Father[1] when visiting the bailiwick of Gex, which adjoins the city of Geneva, in order to re-establish the Catholic religion in some parishes, declared that his Faith gained new vigour through his intercourse with the heretics of those parts, who were sitting in darkness and in the shadow of death.

He expresses his feelings on this subject in one of his letters: "Alas! in this place I see poor wandering sheep all around me; I approach them and marvel at their evident and palpable blindness. O my God! the beauty of our holy Faith then appears by comparison so entrancing that I would die for love of it, and I feel that I ought to lock up the precious gift which God has given me in the innermost recesses of a heart all perfumed with devotion. My dearest daughter, I thank the sovereign Light which shed its rays so mercifully into this heart of mine, that the more I go among those who are deprived of Faith, the more clearly and vividly I see its magnificence and its inexpressible, yet most desirable, sweetness."[2]

In order to make great progress in the spirit of Faith, which is that of Christian perfection, Blessed Francis was not satisfied with simple assent to all those truths which are divinely revealed, or with submission to the will of God as taught in them, he wanted more than this. It was his desire that we should be actuated in all our dealings by the spirit of Faith, as far at least as that is possible, so as to arrive at last at that summit of perfect charity which the Apostle calls the more excellent way, and of which he says that he who is joined to the Lord is one spirit.

[Footnote 1: St. Francis de Sales was spoken of as Our Blessed Father, not only by the Visitation Nuns, but in the whole neighbourhood of Annecy.] [Footnote 2: Cf. The Depositions of St. Chantal. Point 24th.]

UPON TEMPTATIONS AGAINST FAITH.

He who is not tempted what knows he? says Holy Scripture. God is faithful, and will not permit us to be tempted beyond our strength; nay, if we are faithful to Him, He enables us to profit by our tribulation. He not only helps us, but He makes us find our help in the tribulation itself, in which, thinking we were perishing, we cried out to Him to save us.

Those who imagine themselves to be in danger of losing the Faith, when the temptations suggested to them by the enemy against this virtue, harass and distress them, understand very little of the nature of temptations. For, besides that temptation cannot harm us, as long as it is displeasing to us, which is the teaching of one of the early Fathers, it actually, in such case, produces an absolutely contrary effect to what we fear, and to the aim of our adversary, the devil. For just as the palm tree takes deeper and stronger root, the more it is tossed and shaken by the winds and storms, so the more we are tossed by temptation, the more firmly are we settled in that virtue which the temptation was striving to overthrow.

As we see from the lives of the Saints, the most chaste are those who oppose the greatest resistance to the goad of sensuality, and the most patient are those who struggle the most earnestly against impatience. It is for this reason that Holy Scripture says: Happy is he who suffers temptation, since, after his trial, the crown of life awaits him.[1]

In this way the more violent are the temptations against Faith with which a soul is troubled, the more deeply does that virtue bury itself in the heart, and is there held all the more tightly and closely, because of our fear lest it escape.

Blessed Francis provides us in one of his letters with three excellent means of resisting and overcoming temptations against Faith. The first, is to despise all the suggestions of the Evil One. They are outside and before our heart rather than within it, for there peace maintains its hold, though in great bitterness. This so exasperates our proud enemy, who is king over all the children of pride, that, seeing himself disdained, he withdraws.

The second is not to fight against this temptation by contrary acts of the understanding, but by those of the will, darting forth a thousand protestations of fidelity to the truths which God reveals to us by His Church. These acts of Faith, supernatural as they are, soon reduce to ashes all the engines and machinations of the enemy.

Our Saint gives us his third means, the use of the discipline, saying that this bodily suffering serves as a diversion to trouble of mind, and adds that the devil, seeing the flesh, which is his partisan and confederate, thus maltreated, is terrified and flies away. This is to act like that King of Moab, who brought about the raising of the siege of his city, by sacrificing his son on the walls, in the sight of his enemies, so that, panic-stricken, with horror at a sight so appalling, they took at once to flight.

[Footnote 1: James i. 12.]

UPON THE SAME SUBJECT.

When the tempter sees that our heart is so firmly established in grace that we flee from sin as from a serpent, and that its very shadow, which is temptation, frightens us, he contents himself with disquieting us, seeing that he cannot make us yield to his will.

In order to effect this, he stirs up a heap of trivial temptations, which he throws like dust into our eyes, so as to make us unhappy, and to render the path of virtue less pleasant to us.

We must take up shield and sword to arm ourselves against great temptations; but there are many trivial and ordinary ones which are better driven away by contempt than by any other means.

We arm ourselves against wolves and bears; but who would condescend to do so against the swarms of flies which torment us in hot weather? Our Blessed Father, writing to one who was sorrowful and disquieted at finding herself assailed by temptations against Faith, though these were most hateful and tormenting to her, expresses himself thus:

"Your temptations against Faith have come back again, even though you never troubled yourself to answer them. They importune you again, but still you do not answer.

"Well, my daughter, all this is as it should be: but you think too much about them; you fear them too much; you dread them too much. Were it not for that, they would do you no harm. You are too sensitive to temptations. You love the Faith, and would not willingly suffer a single thought contrary to it to enter your mind; but the moment one so much as occurs to you you are saddened and troubled by it.

"You are too jealous of your purity of Faith. You fancy that everything that touches it must taint it.

"No, my daughter, let the wind blow, and do not think that the rustling of the leaves is the clash of arms. A little while ago I was standing near some beehives, and some of the bees settled on my face. I wanted to brush them off with my hand. 'No,' said a peasant to me, 'do not be afraid, and do not touch them, then they will not sting you at all; but if you touch them they will half devour you.' I took his advice, and not one stung me.

"Believe me, if you do not fear these temptations, they will not harm you; pass on and pay no heed to them."

UPON CONFIDENCE IN GOD.

On this subject I must relate a charming little instance of our Blessed Father's perfect confidence in God, of which he told me once with his accustomed simplicity, to the great consolation of my soul, and one which I was delighted afterwards to find related in a letter addressed to one of his most intimate friends.

"Yesterday," he said, "wishing to pay a visit to the Archbishop of Vienne, I went on the lake in a little boat, and felt very happy in the thought that my sole protection, besides a thin plank, was Divine Providence. The wind was high, and I was glad, too, to feel entirely under the command of the pilot, who made us all sit perfectly still; and, indeed, I had no wish to stir! Do not, however, my daughter, take these words of mine as proofs of my being very holy. No, they are only little imaginary virtues which I amuse myself by fancying I possess. When it comes to real earnest, I am by no means so brave."

The simplicity of the Saint's thoughts when on the water, and of his way of mentioning them, shows how childlike was his trust in God. It reminds one of the happiness with which St. John leaned upon the Saviour's breast. A saying, too, of Saint Teresa which I have read in her life comes to my mind. She declared she was never more absolutely content than when she found herself in some peril which obliged her to have recourse to God; because then it seemed to her that she was clinging more closely to His holy presence, and saying to Him, as did Jacob to the Angel, that she would not let Him go until He had blessed her.

OUR MISERY APPEALS TO GOD'S MERCY.

To a soul overwhelmed by the consideration of its infidelities and miseries he wrote these words of marvellous consolation.

"Your miseries and infirmities ought not to astonish you. God has seen many and many a one as wretched as you, and His mercy never turns away the unhappy. On the contrary, by means of their wretchedness, He seeks to do them good, making their abjection the foundation of the throne of His glory. As Job's patience was enthroned on a dung-hill, so God's mercy is raised upon the wretchedness of man; take away man's misery, and what becomes of God's mercy?"

Elsewhere he writes: "What does our Lord love to do with His gift of eternal life, but to bestow it on souls that are poor, feeble, and of little account in their own eyes? Yes, indeed, dearly beloved children, we must hope, and that with great confidence, to live throughout a happy eternity. The greater our misery the greater should be our confidence." These, indeed, are his very words in his second conference.

Again in one of his letters he says: "Why? What would this good and all-merciful God do with His mercy; this God, whom we ought so worthily to honour for His goodness? What, I say, would He do with it if He did not share it with us, miserable as we are? If our wants and imperfections did not serve as a stage for the display of His graces and favours, what use would He make of this holy and infinite perfection?"

This is the lesson left us by our Blessed Father, and we ought, indeed, to hope with that lively hope animated by love, without which none can be saved. And this lively hope, what is it, but a firm and unwavering confidence that we shall, through God's grace and God's mercy, attain to the joy of heaven, which, being infinite, is boundless and unmeasurable.

UPON SELF-DISTRUST.

Distrust of self and confidence in God are the two mystic wings of the dove; that is to say, of the soul which, having learnt to be simple, takes its flight and rests in God, the great and sovereign object of its love, of its flight, and of its repose.

The Spiritual Combat, which is an excellent epitome of the science of salvation and of heavenly teaching, makes these two things, distrust of self and confidence in God, to be, as it were, the introduction to true wisdom: they are, the author tells us, the two feet on which we walk towards it, the two arms with which we embrace it, and the two eyes with which we perceive it.

In proportion to the growth of one of these two in us is the increase of the other; the greater or the less the degree of our self-distrust, the greater or the less the degree of our confidence in God. But whence springs this salutary distrust of self? From the knowledge of our own misery and vileness, of our weakness and impotence, of our malice and levity. And whence proceeds confidence In God? From the knowledge which faith gives us of His infinite goodness, and from our assurance that He is rich in mercy to all those who call upon Him.

If distrust and confidence seem incompatible with one another, listen to what our Blessed Father says on the subject: "Not only can the soul which knows her misery have great confidence in God, but unless she has such knowledge, it is impossible for her to have true confidence in Him; for it is this very knowledge and confession of our misery which brings us to God. Thus, all the great Saints,

Job, David, and the rest, began every prayer with the confession of their own misery, and unworthiness. It is a very good thing to acknowledge ourselves to be poor, vile, abject, and unworthy to appear in the presence of God. That saying so celebrated among the ancients: Know thyself, even though it may be understood as referring to the knowledge of the greatness and excellence of the soul, which ought not to be debased or profaned by things unworthy of its nobility, may also be taken as referring to the knowledge of our personal unworthiness, imperfection, and misery. Now the greater our knowledge of our own misery the more profound will be our confidence in the goodness and mercy of God; for between mercy and misery there is so close a connection that the one cannot be exercised without the other. If God had not created man, He would still, indeed, have been perfect in goodness; but He would not have been actually merciful, since mercy can only be exercised towards the miserable. You see, then, that the more miserable we know ourselves to be the more occasion we have to confide in God, since we have nothing in ourselves in which we can trust."

He goes on to say: "It is a very good thing to mistrust ourselves, but at the same time how will that avail us, unless we put our whole confidence in God, and wait for His mercy? It is right that our daily faults and infidelities should cause us self-reproach when we would appear before our Lord; and we read of great souls, like St. Catherine of Siena and St. Teresa, who, when they had been betrayed into some fault, were overwhelmed with confusion. Again, it is reasonable that, having offended God, we should out of humility and a feeling of confusion, hold ourselves a little in the background. When we have offended even an earthly friend, we feel ashamed to meet him. Nevertheless, it is quite certain that we must not remain for long at a distance, for the virtues of humility, abjection, and confusion are intermediate virtues, or steps by which the soul ascends to union with her God.

"It would be no great gain to accept our nothingness as a fact and to strip ourselves of self (which is done by acts of self-humiliation) if the result of this were not the total surrender of ourselves to God. St. Paul teaches us this, when he says: Strip yourselves of the old man and put on the new.[1] For we must not remain unclothed; but clothe ourselves with God."

Further on our Saint says: "I ever say that the throne of God's mercy is our misery, therefore the greater our misery the greater should be our confidence."[2]

As regards the foundation of our confidence in God, he says in the same conference: "You wish further to know what foundation our confidence ought to have. Know, then, that it must be grounded on the infinite goodness of God, and on the merits of the Death and Passion of our Lord Jesus Christ with this condition on our part that we should preserve and recognise in ourselves an entire and firm resolution to belong wholly to God, and to abandon ourselves in all things and without any reserve to His Providence."

He adds that, in order to belong wholly to God, it is not necessary to feel this resolution, because feeling resides chiefly in the lower faculties of the soul; but we must recognise it in the higher part of the soul, that purer and more serene region where even in spite of our feelings we fail not to serve God in spirit and in truth.

[Footnote 1: Col. iii. 9.]

[Footnote 2: Conference ii.]

UPON THE JUSTICE AND MERCY OF GOD.

You ask me a question which would be hard for me to answer had I not the mind of our Blessed Father to guide and assist me in the matter.

You say: Whence comes it that Almighty God treated the rebel Angels with so much severity, showing them no mercy whatever, and providing for them no remedy to enable them to rise again after their fall; whereas to men He is so indulgent, patient towards their malice, waiting for them to repent, long suffering, and magnificent in His mercy, bestowing on them the copious Redemption of the Saviour?

Well, He tells us in his Treatise on the Love of God[1] that: "The angelic nature could only commit sin from positive malice, without temptation or motive to excuse, even partially. Nevertheless, the far greater part of the Angels remained constant in the service of their Saviour. Therefore God, who had so amply glorified His mercy in the work of the creation of the Angels, would also magnify His justice; and in His righteous indignation resolved for ever to abandon that accursed band of traitors, who in their rebellion had so villainously abandoned Him."

On man, however, He took pity for several reasons. First, because the tempter by his cunning had deceived our first father, Adam; secondly, because the spirit of man is encompassed by flesh and consequently by infirmity; thirdly, because his spirit, enclosed as it is in an earthly body, is frail as the vessel which enshrines it, easily overbalanced by every breath of wind, and unable to right itself again; fourthly, because the temptation in the Garden of Eden was great and over-mastering; fifthly, because He had compassion on the posterity of Adam, which otherwise would have perished with him; but the sixth, and principal cause was this: Almighty God having resolved to take on Himself our human nature in order to unite it to the Divine Person of the Word, He willed to favour very specially this nature for the sake of that hypostatic union, which was to be the masterpiece of all the communications of Almighty God to His creatures.

Do not, however, imagine that God so willed to magnify His mercy in the redemption of man that He forgot the claims of His justice. No, truly; for no severity can equal that which He displayed in the sufferings of His Son, on whose sacred Head having laid the iniquities of us all, He poured out a vengeance commensurate with His Divine wrath.

If, then, we weigh the severity displayed by God towards the rebel Angels against that with which He treated His Divine Son when redeeming mankind, we shall find His justice more abundantly satisfied in the atonement made by the One than in the rigorous punishment of the others. In fine here, as always, His mercy overrides His judgments, inasmuch as the fallen Angels are punished far less than they deserve, and the faithful are rewarded far beyond their merits.

[Footnote 1: Bk. ii c. iv.]

WAITING UPON GOD.

On this subject of waiting upon God I remember hearing from Blessed Francis two wonderful explanations. You, my dear sisters, will, I am sure, be glad to have them, and will find them of great use, seeing that your life, nailed as it is with Jesus Christ to the Cross, must be one of great long-suffering.

He thus interpreted that verse of the Psalmist: With expectation have I waited on the Lord, and He was attentive to me.[1]

"To wait, waiting," he said, "is not to fret ourselves while we are waiting. For there are some who in waiting do not wait, but are troubled and impatient."

Those who have to wait soon get weary, and from weariness springs that disturbance of mind so common amongst them. Hence the inspired saying that Hope that is deferred afflicteth the soul.[2] Of all kinds of patience there is none more fitting to tedious waiting than longanimity. Strength is developed in dangers; patience drives away the sadness caused by suffering; constancy avails for the bearing of great evils; perseverance for the carrying out a good work to its completion; but longanimity has to do with sufferings which are painful because they are long enduring.

Such pains are tedious, but not often violent, for violent sufferings are, as a rule, not lasting; either they pass away, or he on whom they are inflicted, being unable to bear them, is set free by death. To wait, indeed, for deliverance from evils quietly, but without any anguish or irritation, at least in the superior part of the soul, is to wait, waiting. Happy are those who wait in this manner, for their hope shall not be confounded. Of them the Psalmist says that God will remember them, that He will grant their prayers, and that He will deliver them from the pit of misery.[3] Those who act otherwise, and who in their adversity give themselves up to impatience, only aggravate their yoke, instead of lightening it.

They are like the bird which beats its wings against the wrist or perch on which it is poised, but cannot get free from its chain.

Wise Christians making a virtue of necessity and wishing what God wishes, make that which is necessary voluntary, and turn their suffering to their eternal advantage.

[Footnote 1: Psalm xxxix, i.]

[Footnote 2: Psalm xiii. 13.]

[Footnote 3: Psalm xxxix. 3.]

UPON THE DIFFERENCE BETWEEN A HOLY DESIRE OF REWARD AND A MERCENARY SPIRIT.

I am asked if there is not something of a mercenary spirit in these words of our Blessed Father: "Oh, how greatly to be loved is the eternity of Heaven, and how contemptible are the fleeting moments of earth! Aspire continually to this eternity, and despise heartily this decaying world."

You will observe, if you please, that there is a great deal of difference between a proper desire of reward and a mercenary habit of mind. The proper desire of recompense is one which looks principally to the glory of God, and to that glory refers its own reward. A habit of mind which, according to the teaching of the Holy Council of Trent, is most excellent.[1]

But a mercenary habit of mind is shown when we stop short voluntarily, deliberately, and maliciously at our own self-interest, neglecting and putting on one side the interests of God, and when we look forward only to the honours, satisfactions, and delights given to the faithful, and exclude, as it were, the tribute of glory and homage which they render for them to God.

As regards these words of our Blessed Father's, I am perfectly certain that, whatever they may at first sight seem to mean, they are assuredly the expression of thoughts, utterly unselfish, and totally devoid of the spirit of self-seeking. He had written just before: "Take good heed not to come to the feast of the Holy Cross, which is a million times fuller of exquisite pleasures than any wedding feast, without having on the white robe, spotless, and pure from all intentions save that of pleasing the Lamb."

Again, I should like to read to you an extract from one of his letters, in which you will see that he knew how to distinguish, even in Paradise, our interests from those of God: So pure and penetrating was his sight that it resembled that single eye of which the Gospel speaks,[2] which fills us with light and discernment in things spiritual and divine. He speaks thus in his letter: "I have not been able to think of anything this morning save of the eternity of blessings which awaits us. And yet all appear to me as little or nothing beside that unchanging and ever-present love of the great God, which reigns continually in Heaven. For truly I think that the joys of Paradise would be possible, in the midst of all the pains of hell, if the love of God could be there. And if hell-fire were a fire of love, it seems to me that its torments would be the most desirable of good things. All the delights of Heaven are in my eyes a mere nothing compared with this triumphant love. Truly, we must either die or love God. I desire that my heart should either be torn from my body or that if it remains with me it should hold nothing but this holy love. Ah! We must truly give our hearts up to our immortal King, and thus being closely united to Him, live solely for Him. Let us die to ourselves and to all that depends on ourselves. It seems to me that we ought to live only for God. The very thought of this fills my heart once more with courage and fervour. After all, that our Lord is our Lord is the one thing in the world that really concerns us."

Again, in his Theotimus,[3] he says:

"The supreme motive of our actions, which is that of heavenly love, has this sovereign property, that being most pure, it makes the actions which proceed from it most pure; so that the Angels and Saints of Heaven love absolutely nothing for any other end whatever than that of the love of the Divine goodness, and from the motive of desiring to please God. They all, indeed, love one another most ardently; they also love us, they love the virtues, but all this only to please God. They follow and practise virtues, not inasmuch as these virtues are fair and attractive to them; but inasmuch as they are agreeable to God. They love their own felicity, not because it is theirs, but because it pleases God. Yea, they love the very love with which they love God, not because it is in them, but because it tends to God; not because they have and possess it, but because God gives it to them, and takes His good pleasure in it."

[Footnote 1: De Justificat, cap. 12.]

[Footnote 2: Matt. vi. 22.]

[Footnote 3: Bk. xi. 13.]

CONTINUATION OF THE SAME SUBJECT.

There are some gloomy minds which imagine that when the motive of charity and disinterested love is insisted upon all other motives are thereby depreciated, and that it is wished to do away with them. But does he who praises one Saint blame the others? If we extol the Seraphim, do we on that account despise all the lower orders of Angels? Does the man who considers gold more precious than silver say that silver is nothing at all? Are we insulting the stars when we admire and praise the sun? And do we despise marriage because we put celibacy above it?

It is true that, as the Apostle says, charity is the greatest of all virtues, without which the others have neither life nor soul; but that does not prevent these others from being virtues, and most desirable as good habits. In doing virtuous actions the motive of charity is, indeed, the king of all motives; but blessed also are all those inferior motives which are subject to it. We may truly say of them what the Queen of Sheba said of the courtiers of Solomon: Happy are thy men who always stand before thee and hear thy wisdom.[1]

Nay, even servile and mercenary motives, although interested, may yet be good, provided they have nothing in them that cannot be referred to God. They are good in those who have not charity, preparing them for the reception of justifying grace. They are also good in the regenerate, and are compatible with charity, like servants and slaves in the service and households of the great. For it is right, however regenerate we may be, to abstain from sin, not only for fear of displeasing God, but also for fear of losing our souls. The Council of Trent tells us that we are not doing ill when we perform good works primarily in order to glorify God; and also, as an accessory, with a view to the eternal reward which God promises to those who shall do such in His love and for His love. In great temptations, for fear of succumbing, the just may with advantage call to their aid the thought of hell, thereby to save themselves from eternal damnation and the loss of Paradise. But the first principles of the doctrine of salvation teach us that, to avoid evil and do good, simply from the motive of pure and disinterested love of God, is the most perfect and meritorious mode of action.

What! say some:—Must we cease to fear God and to hope in Him? What, then, becomes of acts of holy fear, and of the virtue of hope? If a mother were to abuse the doctor who had restored her child to life, would it not excite a strong suspicion that it was she herself who had attempted to smother it? Did not she who said to Solomon: Let it be divided,[2] show herself to be the false mother? They who are so much attached to servile fear can have no real desire to attain to that holy, pure, loving, reverent fear which leads to everlasting rest, and which the Saints and Angels practise through all eternity.

Let us listen to what Blessed Francis further says on this subject.

"When we were little children, how eagerly and busily we used to collect tiny scraps of cloth, bits of wood, handfuls of clay, to build houses and make little boats! And if any one destroyed these wonderful erections, how unhappy we were; how bitterly we cried! But now we smile when we think how trivial it all was.

"Well," he goes on to say, "let us, since we are but children, be pardoned if we act as such; but, at the same time, do not let us grow cold and dull in our work. If any one knocks over our little houses, and spoils our small plans, do not let us now be unhappy or give way altogether on that account. The less so because when the evening comes, and we need a roof, I mean when death is at hand, these poor little buildings of ours will be quite unfit to shelter us. We must then be safely housed in our Father's Mansion, which is the Kingdom of His well-beloved Son."

[Footnote 1: 2 Paral. ix. 7.]

[Footnote 2: 1 Kings iii. 26.]

GOD SHOULD SUFFICE FOR US ALL.

A person of some consideration, and one who made much profession of living a devout life, was overtaken by sudden misfortune, which deprived her of almost all her wealth and left her plunged in grief. Her distress of mind was so inconsolable that it led her to complain of the Providence of God, who appeared, she said, to have forgotten her. All her faithful service and the purity of her life seemed to have been in vain.

Blessed Francis, full of compassionate sympathy for her misfortunes, and anxious to turn her thoughts from the contemplation of herself and of earthly things, to fix them on God, asked her if He was not more to her than anything; nay, if, in fact, God was not Himself everything to her; and if, having loved Him when He had given her many things, she was not now ready to love Him, though she received nothing from Him. She, however, replying that such language was more speculative than practical, and easier to speak than to carry into effect, he wound up by saying, with St. Augustine: Too avaricious is that heart to which God does not suffice. "Assuredly, he who is not satisfied with God is covetous indeed." This word covetous produced a powerful effect upon the heart of one who, in the days of her prosperity, had always hated avarice, and had been most lavish in her expenditure, both on her own needs and pleasures and on works of mercy. It seemed as if suddenly the eyes of her soul were opened, and she saw how admirable, how infinitely worthy of love God ever remained, whether with those things she had possessed or without them. So, by degrees, she forgot herself and her crosses; grace prevailed, and she knew and confessed that

God was all in all to her. Such efficacy have a Saint's words, even if unpremeditated.

CHARITY THE SHORT ROAD TO PERFECTION.

Blessed Francis, in speaking of perfection, often remarked that, although he heard very many people talking about it, he met with very few who practised it. "Many, indeed," he would say, "are so mistaken in their estimate of what perfection is, that they take effects for the cause, the rivulet for the spring, the branches for the root, the accessories for the principle, and often even the shadow for the substance."

For myself, I know of no Christian perfection other than to love God with our whole heart and our neighbour as ourselves. All other perfection is falsely so entitled: it is sham gold that does not stand testing.

Charity is the only bond between Christians, the only virtue which unites us absolutely to God, and our neighbour.

In charity lies the end of every perfection and the perfection of every end. I know that mortification, prayer, and the other exercises of virtue, are all means to perfection, provided that they are practised in charity, and from the motive of charity. But we must never regard any of these means towards attaining perfection as being in themselves perfection. This would be to stop short on the road, and in the middle of the race, instead of reaching the goal.

The Apostle exhorts us, indeed, to run, but so as to carry off the prize[1], which is for those only who have breath enough to reach the end of the course.

In a word, all our actions must be done in charity if we wish to walk in a manner, as says St. Paul, worthy of God; that is to say, to hasten on towards perfection.

Charity is the way of true life; it is the truth of the living way; it is the life of the way of truth. All virtue is dead without it: it is the very life of virtue. No one can reach the last and supreme end, God Himself, without charity; it is the way to Him. There is no true virtue without charity, says St. Thomas; it is the very truth of virtue.

In conclusion, and in answer to my repeated question as to how we were to go to work in order to attain to this perfection, this supreme love of God and of our neighbour, our Blessed Father said that we must use exactly the same method as we should in mastering any ordinary art or accomplishment. "We learn," he said, "to study by studying, to play on the lute by playing, to dance by dancing, to swim by swimming. So also we learn to love God and our neighbour by loving them, and those who attempt any other method are mistaken."

You ask me, my sisters, how we can discover whether or not we are making any progress towards perfection. I cannot do better than consult our oracle, Blessed Francis, and answer you in his own words, taken from his eighth Conference. "We can never know what perfection we have reached, for we are like those who are at sea; they do not know whether they are making progress or not, but the pilot knows, knowing the course. So we cannot estimate our own advancement, though we may that of others, for we dare not assure ourselves when we have done a good action that we have done it perfectly—humility forbids us to do so. Nay, even were we able to judge of the virtues of others, we must never determine in our minds that one person is better than another, because appearances are deceitful, and those who seem very virtuous outwardly and in the eyes of creatures, may be less so in the sight of God than others who appear much more imperfect."

I have often heard him say that the multiplicity of means proposed for advancement towards perfection frequently delays the progress of souls. They are like travellers uncertain of the way, and who seeing many roads branching off in different directions stay and waste their time by enquiring here and there which of them they ought to take in order to reach their journey's end. He advised people to confine themselves rather to some special spiritual exercise or virtue, or to some well-chosen book of piety—for example, to the exercise of the presence of God, or of submission to His will, or to purity of intention, or some similar exercise.

Among books, he recommended chiefly, The Spiritual Combat, The Imitation of Jesus Christ, The Method of Serving God, Grenada, Blosius, and such like. Among the virtues, as you know well, his favourites were gentleness and humility, charity—without which others are of no value—being always pre-supposed.

On this subject of advancement towards perfection, he speaks thus in the ninth of his Conferences:

"If you ask me, 'What can I do to acquire the love of God?' I answer, Will; i.e., try to love Him; and instead of setting to work to find out how you can unite your soul to God, put the thing in practice by a frequent application of your mind to Him. I assure you that you will arrive much more quickly at your end by this means than in any other way.

"For the more we pour ourselves out the less recollected we shall be, and the less capable of union with the Divine Majesty, who would have all we are without reserve."

He continues: "One actually finds souls who are so busy in thinking how they shall do a thing that they have no time to do it. And yet, in what concerns our perfection, which consists in the union of our soul with the Divine Goodness, there is no question of knowing much; but only of doing."

Again, in the same Conference, he says: "It seems to me that those of whom we ask the road to Heaven are very right in answering us as those do who tell us that, in order to reach such a place, we must just go on putting one foot before the other, and that by this means we shall arrive where we desire. Walk ever, we say to these souls so desirous of their perfection, walk in the way of your vocation with simplicity, more intent on doing than on desiring. That is the shortest road." "And," he adds, "in aspiring to union with the Beloved, there is no other secret than to do what we aspire to—that is, to labour faithfully in the exercise of Divine love."

[Footnote 1: 1 Cor. ix. 24.]

UPON WHAT IT IS TO LOVE GOD TRULY.

In connection with this subject of the love of God and of our neighbour, I asked our Blessed Father what loving in this sense of the word really was. He replied: "Love is the primary passion of our emotional desires, and a primary element in that emotional faculty which is the will. So that to will is nothing more than to love what is good, and love is the willing or desiring what is good. If we desire good for ourselves we have what is called self-love; if we desire good for another we have the love of friendship."

To love God and our neighbour, then, with the love of charity, which is the love of friendship, is to desire good to God for Himself, and to our neighbour in God and for the love of God. We can desire two sorts of good for God: that which He has, rejoicing that He is what He is, and that nothing can be added to the greatness and to the infinity of His inward perfection; and that which He has not, by wishing it for Him, either effectively, if it is in our power to give it to Him, or by loving and longing, if it is not in our power to give it. For, indeed, there is a good which God desires and which is not His as it should be in perfection. That external good, as it is called, is the good which proceeds from the honour and glory rendered to Him by His creatures, especially by those among them endowed with reason. This is the good which David wishes to God in so many of his Psalms. Among others, in the Praise ye the Lord from the heavens,[1] and in the Bless the Lord, O my soul.[2]

The three children also in the fiery furnace wish this good to God by their canticle: All ye works of the Lord, bless the Lord.[3]

If we truly love God we shall try to bring this good to Him through ourselves, surrendering our whole being to Him, and doing all our actions, the indifferent as well as the good, for His glory.

Not content with that, we shall also strive with all our might to make our neighbour serve and love God, so that by all and in all things God may be honoured.

To love our neighbour in God is to rejoice in the good which our neighbour possesses, provided, indeed, that he makes use of it for the divine glory; to render him in his need all the assistance which lies within our power; to be zealous for the welfare of his soul, and to work for it as we do for our own, because God wills and desires it. That is to have true and unfeigned charity, and to love God sincerely and steadfastly for His own sake and our neighbour for the love of Him.

[Footnote 1: Psalm cxlviii. 1.]

[Footnote 2: Id. ciii. 1.]

[Footnote 3: Dan. iii. 57.]

UPON THE LOVE OF GOD IN GENERAL.

A whole mountain of virtues, if destitute of this living, reigning, and triumphant love, was to Blessed Francis but as a petty heap of stones. He was never weary of inculcating love of God as the supreme motive of every action.

The whole of his Theotimus (The Treatise on the Love of God) breathes this sentiment, and he often told me that it was impossible to insist upon it too strongly in our teaching and advice to our people. "For, in fact," he used to say, "what is the use of running a race if we do not reach the goal, or of drawing the bow if we do not hit the target?" Oh! how many good works are useless as regards the glory of God and the salvation of souls, for want of this motive of charity! And yet, this is the last thing people think of, as if the intention were not the very soul of a good action, and as if God had ever promised to reward works not done for His glory, and not applied to His honour.

ALL FOR LOVE OF GOD.

You know very well how Blessed Francis valued charity, but I will give you, nevertheless, some more of his teaching on this great subject.

To a holy soul who had placed herself under his direction, he said: "We must do all things from love, and nothing from constraint. We must love obedience rather than fear disobedience. I leave you the spirit of liberty: not such as excludes obedience, for that is the liberty of the flesh, but such as excludes constraint, scruples, and over-eagerness. However much you may love obedience and submission, I wish you to suspend for the moment the work in which obedience has engaged you whenever any just or charitable occasion for so doing occurs. This omission will be a species of obedience. Fill up its measure by charity."

From this spirit of holy and Christian liberty originated the saying so often to be met with in his letters: "Keep your heart in peace." That is to say: Beware of hurry, anxiety, and bitterness of heart. These he called the ruin of devotion. He was even unwilling that people should meditate upon the great truths of Death, Judgment and Hell, unless they at the same time reassured themselves by the remembrance of God's love for them. Speaking to a holy soul, he says: "Meditation on the four last things will be useful to you provided that you always end with an act of confidence in God. Never represent to yourself Death or Hell on the one side unless the Cross is on the other; so that when your fears have been excited by the one you may with confidence turn for help to the other." The one point on which he chiefly insisted was that we must fear God from love, not love God from fear. "To love Him from fear," he used to say, "is to put gall into our food and to quench our thirst with vinegar; but to fear Him from love is to sweeten aloes and wormwood."

Assuredly, our own experience convinces us that it is difficult to love those whom we fear, and that it is impossible not to fear with a filial and reverent fear those whom we love.

You find some difficulty, it seems, my sisters, in understanding how all things, as St. Paul says,[1] whether good, bad, or indifferent, can in the end work together for good to those who love God.

To satisfy you, I quote the words of Blessed Francis on this subject in one of his letters. "Since," he says, "God can bring good out of evil, will He not surely do so for those who have given themselves unreservedly to Him? Yes; even sins, from which may God in His goodness keep us, are by His Divine Providence, when we repent of them, changed into good for those who are His. Never would David have been so bowed down with humility if he had not sinned, nor would Magdalene have loved her Saviour so fervently had He not forgiven her so many sins. But He could not have forgiven them had she not committed them."

Again: "Consider, my dear daughter, this great Artificer of mercy, who changes our miseries into graces, and out of the poison of our iniquities compounds a wholesome medicine for our souls. Tell me, then, I beseech you, if God works such wonders with our sins, what will He not effect with our afflictions, with our labours, with the persecutions which we have to endure? No matter what trouble befalls you, nor from what direction it may come, let your soul be at peace, certain that if you truly love God all will turn to good. And though you cannot see the springs which work this marvellous change, rest assured that it will take place.

"If the hand of God touches your eyes with the clay of shame and reproach, it is only to give you clearer sight, and to cause you to be honoured.

"If He should cast you to the ground, as He did St. Paul, it will only be to raise you up again to glory."[2]

[Footnote 1: Rom. viii. 28.]

[Footnote 2: Rom. viii. 28.]

THE SAME SUBJECT CONTINUED.

"All by love, nothing by constraint." This was his favourite motto, and the mainspring of his direction of others. He has often said to me that those who try to force the human will are exercising a tyranny which is hateful to God and man. This was why he had such a horror of those masterful and dominant spirits which insist on being obeyed, bon gré mal gré, and would have every one give way to them. "Those," he often said, "who love to make themselves feared, fear to make themselves loved; and they themselves are more fearful than anyone else: for others only fear them, but they are afraid of every one."

I have often heard him say these striking words: "In the royal galley of divine love there is no galley-slave; all the oarsmen are volunteers." And he expresses the same sentiment in Theotimus, when he says: "Divine love governs the soul with an incomparable sweetness; for no one of the slaves of love is made such by force, but love brings all things under its rule, with a constraint so delightful, that as nothing is so strong as love, nothing also is so sweet as its strength."[1] And in another part of the same book he makes a soul, attracted by the delicious perfume shed by the divine Bridegroom on his path, say:

"Let no one think that Thou draggest me after Thee like an unwilling slave or a lifeless load. Ah! no. Thou drawest me by the odour of Thine ointments; though I follow Thee, it is not that Thou draggest me, but that Thou enticest me. Thy drawing is mighty, but not violent, since its whole force lies in its sweetness. Perfumes draw me to follow them in virtue only of their sweetness. And sweetness, how can it attract but sweetly and pleasantly?"[2] Following out this principle, he never gave a command even to those who were bound to obey him, whether his servants or his clergy, save in the form of a request or suggestion. He held in special veneration, and often inculcated upon me the command of St. Peter: Feed the flock of God which is among you, not by constraint, but willingly, not for filthy lucre's sake, neither as lording it over the clergy, but being made a pattern of virtue to the flock.[3]

And here, my sisters, I feel that if will be for your profit, although the story is not to my own credit, to relate a circumstance which occurred in the early years of my episcopate. I was young, impetuous, and impatient; eager to reform the abuses and disorders which from time to time I met with in my pastoral visitations. Often, too, I know, I was bitter and harsh when discouraged.

Once in a despairing mood because of the many failures I noticed in myself, and others, I poured forth my lamentations and self-accusations to our Blessed Father, who said: "What a masterful spirit you have! You want to walk upon the wings of the wind. You let yourself be carried away by your zeal, which, like a will-of-the-wisp, will surely lead you over a precipice. Have you forgotten the warning of your patron, St. Peter, not to think you can walk in burning heat?[4] Would you do more than God, and restrain the liberty of the creatures whom God has made free? You decide matters, as if the wills of your subjects were all in your own hands. God, Who holds all hearts in His and Who searches the reins and the hearts, does not act thus. He puts up with resistance, rebellion against His light, kicking against the goad, opposition to His inspirations, even though His Spirit be grieved thereby. He does, indeed, suffer those to perish who through the hardness of their impenitent hearts have heaped to themselves wrath in the day of vengeance. Yet He never wearies of calling them to Him, however often they reject His offers and say to Him, Depart from us, we will not follow Thy ways.[5]

"In this our Angel Guardians follow His example, and although we may forsake God by our iniquities, they will not forsake us as long as there is breath in our body, even though we may have fallen into sin. Do you want better examples for regulating your conduct?"

[Footnote 1: Book i. 6.]

[Footnote 2: Book ii. 13.]

[Footnote 3: Peter v. 2, 3.]

[Footnote 4: 1 Peter iv. 12.]

[Footnote 5: Job xxi. 14.]

UPON THE LOVE OF GOD, CALLED LOVE OF BENEVOLENCE.

You ask me what I have to say as regards the love of benevolence towards God. What good thing can we possibly wish for God which He has not already,

What can we desire for Him which He does not possess far more fully than we can desire Him to have it?

What good can we do to Him to Whom all our goods belong, and Who has all good in Himself; or, rather, Who is Himself all good?

I reply to this question as I have done to others, that there are many spiritual persons, and some even of the most gifted, who are greatly mistaken in their view of this matter.

We must distinguish in God two sorts of good, the one interior, the other exterior. The first is Himself; for His goodness, like His other attributes, is one and the same thing with His essence or being.

Now this good, being infinite, can neither be augmented by our serving God and by our honouring Him, nor can it be diminished by our rebelling against Him and by our working against Him.

It is of it that the Psalmist speaks when he says that our goods are nothing unto Him.

But there is another kind of good which is exterior; and this, though it belongs to God, is not in Him, but in His creatures, just as the moneys of the king are, indeed, his, but they are in the coffers of his treasurers and officials.

This exterior good consists in the honours, obedience, service, and homage which His creatures owe and render to Him: creatures of whom each one has of necessity His glory as the final end and aim of its creation. And this good it is which we can, with the grace of God, desire for Him, and ourselves give to Him, and which we can either by our good works increase or by our sins take from.

In regard to this exterior good, we can practise towards God the love of benevolence by doing all things, and all good works in our power, in order to increase His honour, or by having the intention to bless, glorify, and exalt Him in all our actions; and much more by refraining from any action which might tarnish God's glory and displease Him, Whose will is our inviolable law.

The love of benevolence towards God does not stop here. For, because charity obliges us to love our neighbour as ourselves from love of God, we try to urge on our fellow-men to promote this Divine glory, each one as far as he can. We incite them to do all sorts of good, so as thereby to magnify God the more. Thus the Psalmist said to his brethren, O magnify the Lord with me, and let us extol His name together.[1]

This same ardour incites and presses us also (urget is the word used by St. Paul) to do our utmost to aid our neighbour to rise from sin, which renders him displeasing to God, and to prevent sin by which the Divine Goodness is offended. This is what is properly called zeal, the zeal which consumed the Psalmist when he saw how the wicked forget God, and which caused him to cry out: My zeal has made me pine away, because my enemies forgot thy words.[2] And again, The zeal of thy house hath eaten me up.[3]

You ask if this love of benevolence might not also be exercised towards God in respect of that interior and infinite good which He possesses and which is Himself. I reply, with our Blessed Father in his Theotimus, that we can wish Him to have this good, by rejoicing in the fact that He has it, and that He is what He is; hence that vehement outburst of David, Know ye, that the Lord he is God.[4] And again, A great King above all gods.

Moreover, the mystical elevations and the ecstasies of the Saints were acts of the love of God in which they wished Him all good and rejoiced in His possessing it. Our imagination, too, may help us, as it did St. Augustine, of whom our Blessed Father writes:

"This desire, then, of God, by imagination of impossibilities, may be sometimes profitably practised in moments of great and extraordinary feelings and fervours. We are told that the great St. Augustine often made such acts, pouring out in an excess of love these words: 'Ah! Lord, I am Augustine, and Thou art God; but still, if that which neither is nor can be were, that I were God, and thou Augustine, I would, changing my condition with Thee, become Augustine to the end that Thou mightest be God.'"[5]

We can again wish Him the same good by rejoicing in the knowledge that we could never, even by desiring it, add anything to the incomprehensible infinity and infinite incomprehensibility of His greatness and perfection. Holy, holy, holy, Lord God of Hosts. Heaven and earth are full of Thy glory: Praise to God in the highest. Amen.

[Footnote 1: Psalm xxxiii. 4.]

[Footnote 2: Psalm cxviii. 139.]

[Footnote 3: Psalm lxviii. 10.]

[Footnote 4: Psalm xciv. 3.]

[Footnote 5: Book v. c. 6.]

DISINTERESTED LOVE OF GOD.

You know that among the Saints for whom our Blessed Father had a special devotion, St. Louis of France held a very prominent position.

Now, in the life of the holy King, written by the Sieur de Joinville, there is a little story which our Blessed Father used to say contained the summary of all Christian perfection; and, indeed, its beauty and excellence have made it so well known that we find it told or alluded to in most books of devotion.

It is that of the holy woman—whose name, though written in the Book of Life, is not recorded in history—who presented herself to Brother Yves, a Breton, of the Order of St. Dominic, whom King Louis, being in the Holy Land, had sent as an ambassador to the Caliph of Syria. She was holding in one hand a lighted torch, and in the other a pitcher of water filled to the brim.

Addressing the good Dominican, she told him that her intention was to burn up Paradise with the one and to put out the fire of Hell with the other, in order that henceforth God might be served with a holy and unfeigned charity. That is to say, with a true and disinterested love, for love of Himself alone, not from a servile and mercenary spirit; i.e., from fear of punishment or hope of reward.

Our Blessed Father told me that he should have liked this story to be told on all possible occasions, and to have had engravings of the subject for distribution, so that by so beautiful an example many might be taught to love and serve God with true charity, and to have no other end in view than His Divine glory; for true charity seeks not her own advantage, but only the honour of her Beloved.

UPON THE CHARACTER OF A TRUE CHRISTIAN.

A Salamander, according to the fable, is a creature hatched in the chilling waters of Arctic regions, and is consequently by nature so cold that it delights in the burning heat of a furnace. Fire, said the ancients, cannot consume it nor even scorch it.

"Just so is it with the Christian," said Blessed Francis. "He is born in a region far away from God, and is altogether alien from Him. He is conceived in iniquity and brought forth in sin, and sin is far removed from the way of salvation. Man is condemned before his very birth. Damnatus antequam natus, says St. Bernard. He is born in the darkness of original sin and in the region of the shadow of death. But, being born again in the waters of Baptism, in which he is clothed with the habit of charity, the fire of the holy love of God is enkindled in him. Henceforth his real life, the life of grace and of spiritual growth, depends absolutely upon his abiding in that love; for he who loves not thus is dead; while, on the other hand, by this love man is called back from death to life."

"Charity," he continued, "is like a fire and a devouring flame. The little charity which we possess in this life is liable to be extinguished by the violent temptations which urge us, or, to speak more truly, precipitate us into mortal sin; but that of the life to come is a flame all-embracing and all-conquering—it can neither fail nor flicker.

"On earth charity, like fire, needs fuel to nourish it and keep it alive; but in its proper sphere, which is Heaven, it feeds upon its own inherent heat, nor needs other nourishment. It is of vital importance here below to feed our charity with the fuel of good works, for charity is a habit so disposed to action that it unceasingly urges on those in whom the Holy Spirit has shed it abroad to perform such works. This the Apostle expresses very aptly: The charity of Christ presseth us.[1]

"St. Gregory adds that the proof of true, unfeigned love is action, the doing of works seen and known to be good. For, if faith is manifested by good works, how much more charity, which is the root, the foundation, the soul, the life, and the form of every good and perfect work."

[Footnote 1: 2 Cor. v. 14.]

UPON NOT PUTTING LIMITS TO OUR LOVE OF GOD.

Blessed Francis used to say that those who narrow their charity, limiting it to the performance of certain duties and offices, beyond which they would not take a single step, are base and cowardly souls, who seem as though they wished to enclose in their own hands the mighty Spirit of God. Seeing that God is greater than our heart, what folly it is to try to shut Him up within so small a circle.

On this subject of the immeasurable greatness of the love which we should bear to God, he uttered these remarkable words: "To remain long in a settled, unchanging condition is impossible: in this traffic he who does not gain, loses; he who does not mount this ladder, steps down; he who is not conqueror in this combat, is vanquished. We live in the midst of battles in which our enemies are always engaging us. If we do not fight we perish; but we cannot fight without overcoming, nor overcome without victory, followed by a triumph and a crown."

UPON THE LAW AND THE JUST MAN.

You ask me the meaning of the Apostle's saying that the law is not made for the just man.[1] Can any man be just unless he accommodate his actions to the rule of the law? Is it not in the observance of the law that true justice consists?

Our Blessed Father explains this passage so clearly and delicately in his Theotimus that I will quote his words for you. He says: "In truth the just man is not just, save inasmuch as he has love. And if he have love, there is no need to threaten him by the rigour of the law, love being the most insistent of all teachers, and ever urging the heart which it possesses to obey the will and the intention of the beloved. Love is a magistrate who exercises his authority without noise and without police. Its instrument is mutual complacency, by which, as we find pleasure in God, so also we desire to please Him."[2]

Permit me to add to these excellent words a reminder which ought not, I think, to be unprofitable to you. Some imagine that it is enough to observe the law of God in order to save our souls, obeying the command of our Lord: Do this, that is to say, the law, and you shall live,[3] without attempting to determine the motive which impels them to observe the law.

Now the truth is that some observe the law of God from a servile spirit, and only for fear of losing their souls. Others chiefly from a mercenary spirit for the sake of the reward promised to those who keep it, and, as our Blessed Father says very happily: "Many keep the Commandments as medicines are taken, rather that they may escape eternal death than that they may live so as to please our Saviour." One of his favourite sayings was: "It is better to fear God from love than to love Him from fear."

He says also: "There are people who, however pleasant a medicament may be, feel a repugnance when required to take it, simply from the fact of its being medicine. So also there are souls which conceive an absolute antipathy to anything they are commanded to do, only because they are so commanded." As soon, however, as the love of God is shed forth in the heart by the Holy Spirit, then the burden of the law becomes sweet, and its yoke light, because of the extreme desire of that heart to please God by the observance of His precepts. "There is no labour," he goes on to say, "where love is, or if there be any, it is a labour of love. Labour mingled with love is a certain bitter-sweet, more pleasant to the palate than that which is merely sweet. Thus then does heavenly love conform us to the will of God and make us carefully observe His commandments, this being the will of His Divine Majesty, Whom we desire to please. So that this complacency with its sweet and amiable violence anticipates the necessity of obeying which the law imposes upon us, converting that necessity into the virtue of love, and every difficulty into delight."[4]

[Footnote 1: Tim. i. 9.]

[Footnote 2: Book viii. c. 1.]

[Footnote 3: Luke x. 28.]

[Footnote 4: Cf. Treatise on the Love of God. Book viii. c. 5.]

UPON DESIRES.

To desire to love God is to love to desire God, and consequently to love Him: for love is the root of all desires.

St. Paul says: The charity of God presses us.[1] And how does it press us if not by urging us to desire God. This longing for God is as a spur to the heart, causing it to leap forward on its way to God. The desire of glory incites the soldier to run all risks, and he desires glory because he loves it for its own sake, and deems it a blessing more precious than life itself.

A sick man has not always an appetite for food, however much he may wish for it as a sign of returning health. Nor can he by wishing for it obtain it, because the animal powers of our nature do not always obey the rational faculties.

Love and desire, however, being the offspring of one and the same faculty, whoever desires, loves, and whoever desires from the motive of charity is able to love from the same motive. But how, you ask, shall we know whether or not we have this true desire for the love of God, and having it, whether it proceeds from the motions of grace or from nature?

It is rather difficult, my dear sisters, to give reasons for principles which are themselves their own reason. If you ask me why the fire is hot you must not take it amiss if I simply answer because it is not cold.

But you wish to know what we have to do in order to obtain this most desirable desire to love God. Our Blessed Father tells us that we must renounce all useless, or less necessary desires, because the soul wastes her power when she spreads herself out in over many desires, like the river which when divided by the army of a Persian King into many channels lost itself altogether. "This," he said, "is why the Saints used to retire into solitary places, so that being freed from earthly cares they might with more fervour give themselves up wholly and entirely to divine love. This is why the spouse in the Canticles is represented with one eye closed, and all the power of vision concentrated in the other, thus enabling her to gaze more intently into the very depths of the heart of her Beloved, piercing it with love.

"This is why she even winds all her tresses into one single braid, using it as a chain to bind and hold captive the heart of her Bridegroom, making Him her slave by love! Souls which sincerely desire to love God, close their understanding to all worldly things, so as to employ it the more fully in meditating upon things Divine.

"All the aspirations of our nature have to be summed up in the one single intention of loving God, and Him alone: for to desire anything otherwise than for God is to desire God the less."[2]

[Footnote 1: 2 Cor. v. 14.]

[Footnote 2: Cf. Treatise on the Love of God. Book xii. 3.]

HOW CHARITY EXCELS BOTH FAITH AND HOPE.

Not only did Blessed Francis consider it intolerable that moral virtues should be held to be comparable to Charity, but he was even unwilling that Faith and Hope, excellent, supernatural, and divinely infused though they be, should be reckoned to be of value without Charity, or even when compared with it. In this he only echoed the thought and words of the great Apostle St. Paul, who in his first Epistle to the Corinthians writes: Faith, Hope, and Charity are three precious gifts, but the greatest of these is Charity.

Faith, it is true, is love, "a love of the mind for the beautiful in the divine Mysteries," as our Blessed Father says in his Treatise on the Love of God,[1] but "the motions of love which forerun the act of faith required from our justification are either not love properly speaking, or but a beginning and imperfect love," which inclines the soul to acquiesce in the truths proposed for its acceptance.

Hope, too, is love, "a love for the useful in the goods which are promised in the other life."[2] "It goes, indeed, to God but it returns to us; its sight is turned upon the divine goodness, yet with some respect to our own profit."

"In Hope love is imperfect because it does not tend to God's infinite goodness as being such in itself, but only because it is so to us.... In real truth no one is able by virtue of this love either to keep God's commandments or obtain life everlasting, because it is a love that yields more affection than effect when it is not accompanied by Charity."[3]

But the perfect love of God, which is only to be found in Charity, is a disinterested love, which loves the sovereign goodness of God in Himself and for His sake only, without any aim except that He may be that which He is, eternally loved, glorified, and adored, because He deserves to be so, as St. Thomas says. And it is in the fact that it attains more perfectly its final end that its pre-eminence consists. This is very clearly shown by Blessed Francis in the same Treatise where he tells us that Eternal life or Salvation is shown to Faith, and is prepared for Hope, but is given only to Charity. Faith points out the way to the land of promise as a pillar of cloud and of fire, that is, light and dark; Hope feeds us with its manna of sweetness, but Charity actually introduces us into it, like the Ark of the Covenant, which leads us dry-shod through the Jordan, that is, through the judgment, and which shall remain amidst the people in the heavenly land promised to the true Israelites, where neither the pillar of Faith serves as a guide, nor the manna of Hope is needed as food.[4]

That which an ancient writer said of poverty, that it was a great good, yet very little known as such, can be said with far more reason of Charity. It is a hidden treasure, a pearl shut up in its shell, and of which few know the value. The heretics of the present day profess themselves content with a dead Faith, to which they attribute all their justice and their salvation. There are also catholics who appear to limit themselves to that interested love which is in Hope, and who serve God as mercenaries, more for their own interest than for His. There are few who love God as He ought to be loved, that is to say, with the disinterested love of Charity. Yet, without this wedding garment, without this oil which fed the lamps of the wise Virgins, there is no admittance to the Marriage of the Lamb.

It is here that we may sing with the Psalmist: The Lord hath looked down from Heaven upon the children of men to see if there be any that understand and seek God, that is, to know how He wishes to be served. They are all gone aside, they are become unprofitable together: there is none that doeth good, no, not one.[5] This means that there is not one who doth good in spirit and in truth. Yet, what is serving Him in spirit and in truth but resolving to honour and obey Him, for the love of Himself, without admixture of private self-interest?

But whoever has learnt to serve God after the pattern of those His beloved ones, who worship Him in spirit and in truth, in burning Faith and Hope, animated by Charity, may be said to be of the number of the holy nation, the royal Priesthood, the chosen people, and to have entered into the sanctuary of true and Christian holiness, of which our Blessed Father speaks thus: "In the sanctuary was kept the ark of the covenant, and near it the tables of the law, manna in a golden vessel, and Aaron's rod, which in one night bore flowers and fruit. And in the highest point of the soul are found: 1°. The light of Faith, figured by the manna hidden in its vessel, by which we recognize the truth of the mysteries we do not understand. 2°. The utility of Hope, represented by Aaron's flowering and fruitful rod, by which we acquiesce in the promises of the goods which we see not. 3°. The sweetness of holy Charity, represented by God's commandments, the keeping of which it includes, by which we acquiesce in the union of our spirit with God's, though yet are hardly, if at all, conscious of this our happiness."[6]

[Footnote 1: Book ii. 13.]

[Footnote 2: Book i. c. 5.]

[Footnote 3: Book ii. 17.]

[Footnote 4: Book i. 6.]

[Footnote 5: Psalm xiii. 2, 3.]

[Footnote 6: Book i. 12.]

SOME THOUGHTS OF BLESSED FRANCIS ON THE PASSION.

Our Blessed Father considered that no thought is of such avail to urge us forward towards the perfection of divine love as the consideration of the Passion and Death of the Son of God. This he called the sweetest, and yet the most constraining of all motives of piety.

And when I asked him how he could possibly mention gentleness and constraint or violence in the same breath, he answered, "I can do so in the sense in which the Apostle says that the Charity of God presses us, constrains us, impels us, draws us, for such is the meaning of the word Urget.[1] In the same sense as that in which the Holy Ghost in the Canticle of Canticles tells us that Love is as strong as death and fierce as hell."

"We cannot deny," he added, "that love is the very essence of sweetness, and the sweetener of all bitterness, yet see how it is compared to what is most irresistible, namely, death and hell. The reason of this is that as there is nothing so strong as the sweetness of love, so also there is nothing more sweet and more lovable than its strength. Oil and honey are each smooth and sweet, but when boiling nothing is to be compared with the heat they give out.

"The bee when not interfered with is the most harmless of insects; irritated its sting is the sharpest of all.

"Jesus Crucified is the Lion of the tribe of Judah—He is the answer to Samson's riddle, for in His wounds is found the honeycomb of the strongest charity, and from this strength proceeds the sweetness of our greatest consolation. And certainly since our Lord's dying for us, as all Scripture testifies, is the climax of his love, it ought also to be the strongest of all our motives for loving Him.

"This it is which made St. Bernard exclaim: 'Oh, my Lord, I entreat Thee to grant that my whole heart may be so absorbed and, as it were, consumed in the burning strength and honeyed sweetness of Thy crucified love, that I may die for the love of Thy love, O Redeemer of my soul, as Thou hast deigned to die for the love of my love.'

"It is this excess of love, which on the hill of Calvary drained the last drop of life-blood from the Sacred Heart of the Lover of our Souls; it is of this love that Moses and Elias spoke on Mount Thabor amid the glory of the Transfiguration.

"They spoke of it to teach us that even in the glory of Heaven, of which the Transfiguration was only a glimpse, after the vision of the goodness of God contemplated and loved in itself, and for itself, there will be no more powerful incentive towards the love of our Divine Saviour than the remembrance of His Death and Passion.

"We have a signal testimony to this truth in the Apocalypse, where the Saints and Angels chant these words before the throne of Him that liveth for ever and ever: Worthy is the Lamb that was slain to receive power, and divinity, and wisdom, and strength, and honour, and glory, and benediction from every creature which is in Heaven, and on the earth."[2]

[Footnote 1: 2 Cor. v. 14.]

[Footnote 2: Apoc. v. 12, 18.]

UPON THE VANITY OF HEATHEN PHILOSOPHY.

I was speaking on one occasion of the writings of Seneca and of Plutarch, praising them highly and saying that they had been my delight when young, our Blessed Father replied: "After having tasted the manna of the Fathers and Theologians, this is to hanker for the leeks and garlic of Egypt." When I rejoined that these above mentioned writers furnished me with all that I could desire for instruction in morals, and that Seneca seemed to me more like a christian author than a pagan, he said: "There I differ from you entirely. I consider that no spirit is more absolutely opposed to the spirit of christianity than that of Seneca, and no more dangerous reading for a soul aiming at true piety can be found than his works."

Being much surprised at this opinion, and asking for an explanation, he went on to say: "This opposition between the two spirits comes from the fact that Seneca would have us look for perfection within ourselves, whereas we must seek it outside ourselves, in God, that is to say, in the grace which God pours into our souls through the Holy Ghost. Not I, but the grace of God with me.[1] By this grace we are what we are. The spirit of Seneca inflates the soul and puffs it up with pride, that of Christianity rejects the knowledge which puffs up in order to embrace the charity which edifies. In short, there is the same difference between the spirit of Seneca and the christian spirit that there is between virtues acquired by us, which are, therefore, dead, and virtues that are infused by God, which are, therefore, living. Indeed, how could this philosopher, being destitute of the true Faith, possess charity? And yet well we know that without charity all acquired virtues are unable to save us."

[Footnote 1: 1 Cor. xv. 10.]

UPON THE PURE LOVE OF OUR NEIGHBOUR.

Our Blessed Father, in his Twelfth Conference, teaches how to love one's neighbour, for whom his own love was so pure and so unfeigned.

"We must look upon all the souls of men as resting in the Heart of our Saviour. Alas! they who regard their fellow-men in any other way run the risk of not loving them with purity, constancy, or impartiality. But beholding them in that divine resting place, who can do otherwise than love them, bear with them, and be patient with their imperfections? Who dare call them irritating or troublesome? Yes, my daughters, your neighbour is there in the Heart of the Saviour, and there so beloved and lovable that the Divine Lover dies for love of him."

A truly charitable love of our neighbour is a rarer thing than one would think. It is like the few particles of gold which are found on the shores of the Tagus, among masses of sand.

Hear what he says on this subject in the eighth of his Spiritual Conferences:

"There are certain kinds of affection which appear very elevated and very perfect in the eyes of creatures, but which in the sight of God are of low degree and valueless. Such are all friendships based, not only on true charity, which is God, but only on natural inclinations and human motives.

"On the other hand, there are friendships which in the eyes of the world appear mean and despicable, but which in the sight of God have every excellence, because they are built up in God, and for God, without admixture of human interests. Now acts of charity which are performed for those whom we love in this way are truly noble in their nature, and are, indeed, perfect acts, inasmuch as they tend purely to God, while the services which we render to those whom we love from natural inclination are of far less merit. Generally speaking, we do these more for the sake of the great delight and satisfaction they cause us than for the love of God." He goes on to say: "The former kind of friendship is likewise inferior to the latter in that it is not lasting. Its motive is so weak that when slighted or not responded to it easily grows cold, and finally disappears. Far otherwise that affection which has its foundation in God, and therefore a motive which above all others is solid and abiding.

"Human affection is founded on the possession by the person we love of qualities which may be lost. It can, therefore, never be very secure. On the contrary, he who loves in God, and only in God, need fear no change, because God is always Himself." Again, speaking on this subject, our Blessed Father says: "All the other bonds which link hearts one to another are of glass, or jet; but the chain of holy charity is of gold and diamonds." In another place he remarks: "St. Catherine of Sienna illustrates the subject by means of a beautiful simile. 'If,' she says, 'you take a glass and fill it from a spring, and if while drinking from this glass you do not remove it from the spring, you may drink as much as you please without ever emptying the glass.' So it is with friendships: if we never withdraw them from their source they never dry up."

UPON BEARING WITH ONE ANOTHER.

He laid great stress at all times on the duty of bearing with our neighbour, and thus obeying the commands of Holy Scripture, Bear ye one another's burdens, and so you shall fulfil the law of Christ,[1] and the counsels of the Apostle who so emphatically recommends this mutual support. "To-day mine, to-morrow thine." If to-day we put up with the ill-temper of our brother, to-morrow he will bear with our imperfections. We must in this life do like those who, walking on ice, give their hands to one another, so that if one slips, the other who has a firm foothold may support him.

St. John the Evangelist, towards the close of his life, exhorted his brethren not to deny one another this support, but to foster mutual charity, which prompts the Christian to help his neighbour, and is one of the chiefest precepts of Jesus Christ, Who, true Lamb of God, endured, and carried on His shoulders, and on the wood of the Cross, all our sins—an infinitely heavy burden, nor to be borne by any but Him. The value set by our Blessed Father on this mutual support was marvellous, and he went so far as to look upon it as the crown of our perfection.

He says on the subject to one who was very dear to him: "It is a great part of our perfection to bear with one another in our imperfections; for there is no better way of showing our own love for our neighbour."

God will, in His mercy, bear with him who has mercifully borne with the defects of his neighbour.

Forgive, and you shall be forgiven. Give, and it shall be given to you. Good measure of blessings, and pressed down, and shaken together, and running over shall they give into your bosom.[2]

[Footnote 1: Gal. vi. 2.]

[Footnote 2: St. Luke vi. 37, 38.]

UPON FRATERNAL CORRECTION.

Speaking, my dear sisters, as he often did, on the important subject of brotherly or friendly reproof, our Blessed Father made use of words profitable to us all, but especially to those who are in authority, and have therefore to rule and guide others.

He said: "Truth which is not charitable proceeds from a charity which is not true."

When I asked him how we could feel certain that our reproofs were given out of sincere charity, he answered:

"When we speak the truth only for the love of God, and for the good of our neighbour, whom we are reproving."

He added: "We must follow the counsels of the great Apostle St. Paul, when he bids us reprove in a spirit of meekness.[1]

"Indeed gentleness is the intimate friend of charity and its inseparable companion." This is what St. Paul means when he says that charity is kind, and beareth all things, and endureth all things.[2] God, who is Charity, guides the mild in judgment and teaches the meek. His way, His Spirit, is not in the whirlwind, nor in the storm, nor in the tempest, nor in the voice of many waters; but in a gentle and whispering wind. Mildness is come upon us, says the Royal Psalmist, and we shall be corrected.[3]

Again Blessed Francis advised us to imitate the Good Samaritan, who poured oil and wine into the wounds of the poor wayfarer fallen among thieves.[4] He used to say that "to make a good salad you want more oil than either vinegar or salt."

I will give you some more of his memorable sayings on this subject. Many a time I have heard them from his own lips: "Always be as gentle as you can, and remember that more flies are caught with a spoonful of honey than with a hundred barrels of vinegar. If we must err in one direction or the other, let it be in that of gentleness. No sauce was ever spoilt by too much sugar. The human mind is so constituted that it rebels against harshness, but becomes perfectly tractable under gentle treatment. A mild word cools the heat of anger, as water extinguishes fire. There is no soil so ungrateful as not to bear fruit when a kindly hand cultivates it. To tell our neighbour wholesome truths tenderly is to throw red roses rather than red-hot coals in his face. How could we be angry with any one who pelted us with pearls or deluged us with rose water! There is nothing more bitter than a green walnut, but when preserved in sugar there is nothing sweeter or more digestible. Reproof is by nature harsh and biting, but confectioned in sweetness and warmed through and through in the fire of charity, it becomes salutary, pleasant, and even delightful. The just will correct me with mercy, and the oil of the flatterer shall not anoint my head.[5] Better are the wounds of a friend than the kisses of the hypocrite;[6] if the sharpness of the friend's tongue pierce me it is only as the lancet of the surgeon, which probes the abscess and lacerates in order to heal."
"But (I replied) truth is always truth in whatever language it may be couched, and in whatever sense it may be taken." In support of this assertion I quoted the words spoken by St. Paul to Timothy:

Preach the word; be instant in season, out of season, reprove, entreat, rebuke in all patience and doctrine; but, according to their own desires, they will heap to themselves teachers having itching ears, and will, indeed, turn away their hearing from the truth, but will be turned into fables.[7]

Our Blessed Father replied: "The whole force of that apostolic lesson lies in the phrase: In all patience and doctrine. Doctrine signifies truth, and this truth must be spoken with patience. When I use the word patience, I am trying to put before you an attitude of mind which is not one of confident expectation, that truth will always meet with a hearty welcome, and even some degree of acclamation; but an attitude of mind which is on the contrary prepared to meet with repulse, reprobation, rejection.

"Surely, seeing that the Son of God was set for a sign of contradiction, we cannot be surprised if His doctrine, which is the truth, is marked with the same seal! Surprised! Nay, of necessity it must be so.

"Consider the many false constructions and murmurings to which the sacred truths preached by our Saviour during His life on earth were exposed!

"Was not this one of the reproaches addressed by Him to the Jews: If I say the truth you believe me not.

"Was not our Lord Himself looked upon as an impostor, a seditious person, a blasphemer, one possessed by the devil? Did they not even take up stones to cast at him? Yet, He cursed not those who cursed Him; but repaid their maledictions with blessings, possessing His soul in patience."

Blessed Francis wrote to me on this same subject a letter, which has since been printed among his works, in which he expressed himself as follows:

"Everyone who wishes to instruct others in the way of holiness must be prepared to bear with their injustice and unreasonableness, and to be rewarded with ingratitude. Oh! how happy will you be when men slander you, and say all manner of evil of you, hating the truth which you offer them. Rejoice with much joy, for so much the greater is your reward in Heaven. It is a royal thing to be calumniated for having done well, and to be stoned in a good cause."

[Footnote 1: Gal. vi. 1.]

[Footnote 2: 1 Cor. xiii. 4, 7.]

[Footnote 3: Psalm lxxxix. 10]

[Footnote 4: St. Luke x. 34.]

[Footnote 5: Psalm cxl. 5.]

[Footnote 6: Prov. xxvii. 6.]

[Footnote 7: Tim. iv. 2, 4.]

UPON FINDING EXCUSES FOR THE FAULTS OF OUR FELLOW-MEN.

I was one day complaining to him of certain small landowners, who having nothing but their gentle birth to boast of, and being as poor as Job, yet set up as great noblemen, and even as princes, boasting of their high birth, of their genealogy, and of the glorious deeds of their ancestors. I quoted the saying of the wise man, that he hated, among other things, with a perfect hatred the poor proud man, adding that I entirely agreed with him.

To boast in the multitude of our riches is natural, but to be vain in our poverty is beyond understanding.

He answered me thus: "What would you have? Do you want these poor people to be doubly poor, like sick physicians, who, the more they know about their disease the more disconsolate they are? At all events, if they are rich in honours they will think the less of their poverty, and will behave perhaps like that young Athenian, who in his madness considered himself the richest person in his neighbourhood, and being cured of his mental weakness through the kind intervention of his friends, had them arraigned before the judges, and condemned to give him back his pleasant illusion. What would you have, I repeat? It is in the very nature of nobility to meet the rebuffs of fortune with a cheerful courage; like the palm-tree which lifts itself up under its burden. Would to God they had no greater failing than this! It is against that wretched and detestable habit of fighting duels that we ought to raise our voice." Saying this, he gave a profound sigh.

A certain lady had been guilty of a most serious fault, committed, indeed, through mere weakness of character, but none the less scandalous in the extreme. Our Blessed Father, being informed of what had happened, and having every kind of vehement invective against the unfortunate person poured into his ears, only said: "Human misery! human misery!" And again, "Ah! how we are encompassed with infirmity! What can we do of ourselves, but fail? We should, perhaps, do worse than this if God did not hold us by the right hand, and guide us to His will." At last, weary of fencing thus, he faced the battle, and the comments on this unhappy fall becoming ever sharper and more emphatic, exclaimed: "Oh! happy fault, of what great good will it not be the cause![1] This lady's soul would have perished with many others had she not lost herself. Her loss will be her gain, and the gain of many others."

Some of those who heard this prediction merely shrugged their shoulders.

Nevertheless, it was verified. The sinning soul returned to give glory to God, and the community which she had scandalized was greatly edified by her conversion and subsequent good example.

This story reminds me of the words used by the Church in one of her offices. Words in which she calls the sin of Adam thrice happy, since because of it the Redeemer came down to our earth—a fortunate malady, since it brought us the visit of so great a Physician.

"Even sins," says our Blessed Father, in one of his letters, "work together for good to those who truly repent of them."

[Footnote 1: Office for Holy Saturday.]

UPON NOT JUDGING OTHERS.

Men see the exterior; God alone sees the heart, and knows the inmost thoughts of all. Our Blessed Father used to say that the soul of our neighbour was that tree of the knowledge of good and evil which we are forbidden to touch under pain of severe chastisement; because God has reserved to Himself the judgment of each individual soul. Who art thou, says Sacred Scripture, who judgest thy brother? Knowest thou that wherein thou judgest another thou condemnest thyself?[1]

Who has given thee the hardihood to take upon thyself the office of Him Who has received from the Eternal Father all judgment? That is to say, all power of judging in Heaven and on earth? He observed that a want of balance of mind, very common among men, leads them to judge of what they do not know, and not to judge of what they do know. They, as St. Jude declares, blaspheme in what they know not, and corrupt themselves in what they know.[2] They are blind to what passes in their own homes, but preternaturally clear-sighted to all happening in the houses of others.

Now what is this that a man knows not at all? Surely, the heart; the secret thoughts of his neighbour. And yet how eager is he to dip the fingers of his curiosity in this covered dish reserved for the Great Master. And what is it that a man knows best of all, or at least ought to know? Surely, his own heart; his own secret thoughts. Nevertheless, he fears to enter into himself, and to stand in his own presence as a criminal before his judge. He dreads above aught besides the implacable tribunal of his own conscience, itself alone more surely convicting than a thousand witnesses.

Our Blessed Father pictures very vividly this kind of injustice in his Philothea, where he says: "It is equally necessary in order to escape being judged that we both judge ourselves, and that we refrain from judging others. Our Lord forbids the latter[3] and His Apostle commands the former. If we would judge ourselves we should not be judged.[4] Our way is the very reverse. What is forbidden to us we are continually doing. Judging our neighbour on all possible occasions, and what is commanded us, namely, to judge ourselves, that the last thing we think of."[5]

"A certain woman" (Blessed Francis continued with a smile), "all her life long had on principle done exactly the contrary to what her husband wanted her to do. In the end she fell into a river and was drowned. Her husband tried to recover the body, but was found fault with for going up the stream, since she must, necessarily, float down with the current. 'And do you really imagine,' he exclaimed, 'that even her dead body could do anything else but contradict me?' We are, most of us, very like that woman," said the Saint. "Yet it is written: Judge not, and you shall not be judged; condemn not, and you shall not be condemned."[6]

How, then, you will say, is it lawful to have judges and courts of justice, since man may not judge our neighbour? I answer this objection in Blessed Francis' own words:

"But may we, then, under no circumstances judge our neighbour? Under no circumstances whatever—for in a court of justice it is God, Philothea, not man, who judges and pronounces sentence. It is true that He makes use of the voice of the magistrate, but only to render His own sentence audible to us. Earthly judges are His spokesmen and interpreters, nor ought they to decide anything but as they have learnt from Him of Whom they are the oracles. It is when they do otherwise, and follow the lead of their own passions, that they, and not God, judge, and that consequently they themselves will be judged. In fact, it is forbidden to men, as men, to judge others.[7] This is why Scripture gives the name of gods[8] to judges, because when judging they hold the place of God, and Moses for that reason is called the god of Pharaoh."[9]

You ask if we are forbidden to entertain doubts about our neighbour when founded on good and strong reasons. I answer we are not so forbidden, because to suspend judgment is not to judge, but only to take a step towards it. We must, nevertheless, beware of being thereby hurried on to form a hasty judgment, for that is the rock on which so many make shipwreck; that is the flare of the torch in which so many thoughtless moths singe their tiny wings.

In order that we may avoid this danger he gives us an excellent maxim, one which is not only useful, but necessary to us. It is that, however many aspects an action may have, the one we should dwell upon should be that which is the best.

If it is impossible to excuse an action, we can at least modify our blame of it by excusing the intention, or we may lay the blame on the violence of the temptation, or impute it to ignorance, or to the being taken by surprise, or to human weakness, so as at least to try to lessen the scandal of it. If you are told that by doing this you are blessing the unrighteous and seeking excuses for sin, you may reply that without either praising or excusing his sin you can be merciful to the sinner.

You may add that judgment without mercy will be the lot of those who have no pity for the misfortunes or the infirmities of their brother, and who in him despise their own flesh. We all are brethren, all of one flesh. In fact, as says our Blessed Father, those who look well after their own consciences rarely fall into the sin of rash judgment. To judge rashly is proper to slothful souls, which, because they never busy themselves with their own concerns, have leisure to devote their energies to finding fault with others.

An ancient writer expresses this well. Men who are curious in their inquiries into the lives of others are mostly careless about correcting their own faults. The virtuous man is like the sky, of which the stars are, as it were, the eyes turned in upon itself.

[Footnote 1: Rom. ii. 1.]

[Footnote 2: St. Jude 10.]

[Footnote 3: St. Matt. vii. 1.]

[Footnote 4: 1 Cor. xi. 31.]

[Footnote 5: The Devout Life, Part iii. 28.]

[Footnote 6: St. Luke vi. 37.]

[Footnote 7: The Devout Life, Part iii. 28.]

[Footnote 8: Psalm lxxxi. 1, 6.]

[Footnote 9: Exod. vii. 1.]

UPON JUDGING OURSELVES.

"We do," as Blessed Francis has said, "exactly the reverse of what the Gospel bids us do. The Gospel commands us to judge ourselves severely and exactly, while it forbids us to judge our brethren. If we did judge ourselves, we should not be judged by God, because, forestalling His judgment and confessing our faults, we should escape His condemnation. On the other hand, who are we that we should judge our brethren, the servants of another? To their own Master they rise or fall.

"Let us not judge before the time until the Lord shall reveal what is hidden in darkness and pierce the wall of the temple to show what passes therein. Man judges by appearances only. God alone sees the heart; and it is by that which is within that true judgment is made of that which is without.

"So rash are we in our judgments that we as often as not seize the firebrand by the burning end; that is, we condemn ourselves while in the very act of rebuking others. The reproach of the Gospel, Physician, heal thyself,[1] we may take to ourselves. So also that other, Why seest thou the mote that is in thy brother's eye, and seest not the beam that is in thy own eye?[2] To notice which way we are going is the first condition of our walking in the right way, according to the words of David, I have thought on my ways, and turned my feet unto thy testimonies.[3] So, on the other hand, we go astray if we do not pay attention to the path we are following. Judge not others and you will not be judged; judge yourselves, and God will have mercy on you."

[Footnote 1: St. Luke iv. 23]

[Footnote 2: St. Matt. vii. 3]

[Footnote 3: Psalm cxviii. 59]

UPON SLANDER AND DETRACTION.

There is a difference between uttering a falsehood and making a mistake—for to lie is to say what one knows or believes to be false; but to mistake is to say, indeed, what is false, but what one nevertheless thinks in good faith to be true. Similarly, there is a great difference between slandering our neighbour and recounting his evil deeds. The wrong doing of our neighbour may be spoken of either with a good or with a bad intention. The intention is good when the faults of our neighbour are reported to one who can remedy them, or whose business it is to correct the wrong-doer, whether for the public good or for the sinner's own.

Again, there is no harm in speaking among friends of harm done, provided it be from friendliness, benevolence, or compassion; and this more especially when the fault is public and notorious.

We slander our neighbour, then, only when, whether true or false, we recount his misdeeds with intention to harm him, or out of hatred, envy, anger, contempt, and from a wish to take away his fair name.

We slander our neighbour when we make known his faults, though neither obliged so to do nor having in view his good nor the good of others. The sin of slander is mortal or venial according to the measure of the wrong we may thereby have done to our neighbour.

Our Blessed Father used to say that to do away with slander would be to do away with most of the sins of mankind. He was right, for of sins of thought, word, and deed, the most frequent and often the most hurtful in their effects are those committed with the tongue. And this for several reasons.

Firstly, sins of thought are only hurtful to him who commits them. They are neither occasion for scandal, nor do they annoy anyone, nor give anyone bad example. God alone knows them, and it is He alone who is offended by them. Then, too, a return to God by loving repentance effaces them in a moment, and heals the wound which they have inflicted on the heart.

Sins of the tongue, on the other hand, are not so readily got rid of. A harmful word can only be recalled by retracting it, and even then the minds of our hearers mostly remain infected with the poison we poured in through the ears; and this, in spite of our humbling ourselves to recall what we have said.

Secondly, sins of deed, when they are publicly known, are followed by punishment. This renders them rarer, because fear of the penalty acts as a curb on even the basest of mankind.

But slander (except the calumny be of the most atrocious and aggravated kind) is not, generally speaking, such as comes before the eye of the law. On the contrary, if in the guise of bantering it is ingenious and subtle it passes current for gallantry and wit.

This is why so many people fall into this evil; for, says an ancient writer: "Impunity is a dainty allurement to sin."

Thirdly, slandering finds encouragement in the very small amount of restitution and reparation made for this fault. Indeed, in my opinion, those who direct souls in the tribunal of penance are a little too indulgent, not to say lax, in this matter.

If anyone has inflicted a bodily injury on another see how severely the justice of the law punishes the outrage. In olden days the law of retaliation demanded an eye for an eye and a tooth for a tooth. If a man stole the goods of another he was condemned to the galleys, or even to the gibbet. But in the case of slander, unless, as I have said, it be of the most highly aggravated kind, there is scarcely a thought of making reparation, even by a courteous apology. Yet those who sit in high places value their reputation much more than riches, or life itself, seeing that among all natural blessings, honour undoubtedly holds the first rank. Since, then, we cannot gain admittance into heaven without having restored that which belongs to another, let the slanderer consider how he can possibly hope for an entrance there unless he re-establishes his neighbour's reputation, which he tried to destroy by detraction.

UPON HASTY JUDGMENTS.

Our Blessed Father insisted most earnestly upon the difference which exists between a vice and sin, reproving those who spoke of a person who had committed one or more grave faults as vicious.

"Virtuous habits," he would say, "not being destroyed by one act contrary to them, a man cannot be branded as intemperate because he has once been guilty of intemperance."

Thus when he heard anyone condemned as bad because he had committed a bad act, he took pains with his accustomed gentleness to modify the charge by making a distinction between vice and sin, the former being a habit, the latter an isolated act.

"Vice," he said, "is a habit, sin, the outcome of that habit; and just as one swallow does not make a summer, so one act of sin does not make a person vicious. That is to say, it does not render him a sinner in the sense of being steeped in and wholly given over to the dominion of the particular vice, the act of which he has committed once, or even more than once."

Being asked whether in conformity with this principle it would not be equally wrong to praise anyone for a single act of virtue, as if that virtue were his or her constant habit, he replied: "You must remember that we are forbidden to judge our neighbour in the matter of the evil which he may appear to do, but not in the good. On the contrary, we may and should suppose that he has the good habit from which the act seen by us naturally springs. Nor can we err in such a supposition, since the very perfection of charity consists in its excess. But when we judge evil of others, our tongue is like the lancet in the surgeon's hand, and you know how careful he must be not to pierce an artery in opening a vein. We must only judge from what we see. We may say that a man has blasphemed and sworn, if we have heard him do so; but we may not in that account alone say that he is a blasphemer; that is, that he has contracted the habit of blasphemy, substituting the vice for the sin."

The objection was raised that it would follow that we must never attempt to judge whether a person is or is not in a state of grace, however holy his life may seem to be; since no one knows whether he is worthy of love or of hate, and least of all we, who know our neighbour far less intimately than he knows himself. To this he replied, that if faith, according to St. James, is known by its works,[1] much more is charity so known, since it is a more active virtue, its works being the sparks from seeing which we learn that its fire is still burning somewhere. And though when we saw a sin, which is undoubtedly mortal, being committed, we might have said that the sinner was no longer in a state of grace, how do we know that a moment afterwards God may not have touched his heart, and that he may not have been converted from his evil ways by an act of contrition? This is why we must always fear to judge evil of others, but as regards judging well, we are free to do so as much as we please. Charity grows more and more by hoping all good of its neighbour, by thinking no evil, by rejoicing in truth and goodness, but not in iniquity.

[Footnote 1: St. James ii. 17, 26.]

UPON RIDICULING ONE'S NEIGHBOUR.

When in company he heard anyone being turned into ridicule, he always showed by his countenance that the conversation displeased him, and would try to turn the subject by introducing some other. When unsuccessful in this he would give the signal to cease, as is done in tournaments when the combatants are becoming too heated, and thus put a stop to the combat, crying: "This is too much! This is trampling too violently on the good man! This is altogether going beyond bounds! Who gives us the right to amuse ourselves thus at the expense of another? How should we like to be talked about like this, and to have our little weaknesses brought out, just to amuse anybody who may chance to hear? To put up with our neighbour and his imperfections is a great perfection, but it is a great imperfection to laugh at him and his short-comings."

He expresses himself to Philothea on the same subject as follows:

"A tendency to ridicule and mock at others is one of the worst possible conditions of mind. God hates this vice exceedingly, as He has often shown by the strange punishments which have awaited it. Nothing is so contrary to charity, and still more so to devotion, as contempt and disparagement of our neighbour. Now derision and ridicule are always simply contempt, so that the learned are justified in saying that to mock at our neighbour is the worst kind of injury that we can by mere word inflict on him; because all other words of disparagement are compatible with some degree of esteem for the person injured, but ridicule is essentially the expression of contempt and disdain."[1]

Now Holy Scripture pronounces woe upon those who despise others, and threatens them with being despised themselves. God always takes the part of the despised against the despiser. Our Lord says: He who despises you, despises Me;[2] and speaking of little children, Take heed that you despise not one of them.[3] And Almighty God in comforting Moses for an insult offered to the great law-giver by the Children of Israel, says: They have not despised you, but Me.

On one occasion when Blessed Francis was present some young lady in the company was ridiculing another who was conspicuously ill-favoured. Defects born with her were what were being laughed over. He gently reminded the speaker that it is God Who has made us and not we ourselves and that all His works are perfect. But the latter assertion only making her jeer the more, he ended by saying: "Believe me, I know for a fact her soul is more upright, more beautiful, and better formed than you can possibly have any conception of." This silenced her and sent her away abashed.

On another occasion he heard some people laughing at a poor hump-back who was absent at the time. Our Blessed Father instantly took up his defence, quoting again those words of Scripture: The works of God are perfect. "What!" exclaimed one of the company. "Perfect! and yet deformed!" Blessed Francis replied pleasantly: "And do you really think that there cannot be perfect hunchbacks, just as much as others are perfect because gracefully made and straight as a dart!" In fine, when they tried to make him explain what perfection he meant, whether outward or inward, he said: "Enough. What I tell you is true; let us talk of something better."

[Footnote 1: The Devout Life, Part iii. c. 27.]

[Footnote 2: Luke x. 16.]

[Footnote 3: Matt. xviii. 10.]

UPON CONTRADICTING OTHERS.

There is no kind of disposition more displeasing to men than one which is obstinate and contradictory. People of this sort are pests of conversation, firebrands in social intercourse, sowers of discord. Like hedgehogs and horse-chestnuts, they have prickles all over them, and cannot be handled. On the other hand, a gentle, pliable, condescending disposition, which is ready to give way to others, is a living charm. It is like the honeycomb which attracts every sort of fly; it becomes everybody's master, because it makes itself everybody's servant; being all things to all men, it wins them all.

People of a peevish, morose disposition soon find themselves left alone in a mighty solitude; they are avoided like thistles which prick whoever touches them. Our Blessed Father always spoke with the highest praise of the dictum of St. Louis, that we should never speak evil of anyone, unless when by our silence we should seem to hold with him in his wrong-doing, and so give scandal to others.

The holy King did not inculcate this from motives of worldly prudence, which he detested; nor was he following the maxim of that pagan Emperor, who declared that no one, in quitting the presence of his Sovereign, should ever be suffered to go away dissatisfied, a saying dictated by cunning and with the object of teaching his fellow-potentates to win men by fair words. No, St. Louis was travelling by a very different road, and spoke in a truly Christian spirit, desiring only to hinder disputes and contentions, and to follow the advice of St. Paul, who wishes that we should avoid contentions and strivings.[1] But if, when it is in our power to do so, we do not openly condemn the fault or error of another, will not that be a sort of connivance at, and consequently a participation in, the wrong-doing? Our Blessed Father answers that difficulty thus: "When it is a question of contradicting another, and of setting your opinion against his, it must be done with the utmost gentleness and tact, and without any desire to wound the feelings of the other; for nothing is gained by taking things ill-temperedly."

If you irritate a horse by teasing him he will, if he has any mettle, take the bit between his teeth and carry you just where he pleases. But when you slacken the rein he stops and becomes tractable.

So it is with the mind of another; if you force it to assent, you humble it; if you humble it, you irritate it; if you irritate it, you utterly lose hold of it. The mind may be persuaded; it cannot be constrained; to force it to believe is to force it from all belief. Is mildness come upon us? says David; then are we corrected.[2] The Spirit of God, gentle and sweet, is in the soft refreshing zephyrs, not in the whirlwind, nor in the tempest. It is God's enemy, the devil, who is called a spirit of contradiction; and such human beings as imitate him share his title.

[Footnote 1: Titus iii. 9.]

[Footnote 2: Psalm lxxxix. 10.]

UPON LOVING OUR ENEMIES.

Some one having complained to Blessed Francis of the difficulty he found in obeying the christian precept commanding us to love our enemies, he replied: "As for me, I know not how my heart is made, or how it happens that God seems to have been pleased to give me lately altogether a new one. Certain it is that I not only find no difficulty in practising this precept; but I take such pleasure in doing it, and experience so peculiar and delightful a sweetness in it, that if God had forbidden me to love my enemies I should have had great difficulty in obeying Him.

"It seems to me that the very contradiction and opposition we meet with from our fellow-men, ought to rouse our spirit to love them more, for they serve as a whetstone to sharpen our virtue.

"Aloes make honey seem sweeter; and wine has a more delicious flavour if we drink it after having eaten bitter almonds. It is true that mostly a little conflict and struggle goes on in our minds: but in the end it will surely come to pass with us what the Psalmist commands when he says: Be angry and sin not.[1]

"What! Shall we not bear with those whom God Himself bears with? We who have ever before our eyes the great example of Jesus Christ on the Cross praying for His enemies. And then, too, our enemies have not crucified us;

they have not persecuted us, even to death; we have not yet resisted unto blood.

"Again, who would not love this dear enemy for whom Jesus Christ prayed? For whom He died? For, mark it well, He prayed not only for those who crucified Him, but also for those who persecute us, and Him in us. As He testified to Saul when He cried out to Him: Why persecutest thou Me?[2] That is to say, Me in My members.

"We are not, indeed, obliged to love the vices of our enemy; his hatred of good, the enmity which he bears us; for all these things are displeasing to God, Whom they offend; but we must separate the sin from the sinner, the precious from the vile, if we desire to be like our Saviour."

He did not admit the maxim of the world: "We must not trust a reconciled enemy." In his opinion the exact contrary of this dictum is more in accordance with truth.

He used to say that "fallings out" in the case of friends only serve to draw the bonds of friendship closer, just as the smith makes use of water to increase the heat of his fire. He added, as a well-known fact in surgery, that the callosity which forms over a fractured bone is so dense that the limb will never break again at that particular place.

Indeed, when a reconciliation has taken place between two persons hitherto at variance, it is almost certain that each will set to work, perhaps even unconsciously, to make the newly-cemented friendship firmer. The offender by avoiding further offence, and atoning as far as possible for what is past, and the offended person by endeavouring in a truly generous spirit to bury that past in oblivion.

[Footnote 1: Psalm iv. 5.]

[Footnote 2: Acts ix. 4.]

UPON FORGIVING OUR ENEMIES.

On the subject of the forgiveness of enemies, Blessed Francis told me of an incident which occurred at Padua (possibly at the time that he was studying there). It appears that certain of the students at that university had a bad habit of prowling about the streets at night, pistol in hand, challenging passers-by with the cry of "Who goes there?" and firing if they did not receive a humble and civil answer.

One of the gang having one night challenged a fellow-student and received no answer, fired, and took such good aim that the poor young man fell dead on the pavement. Horrified and amazed at the fatal result of his mad prank, the student fled, hoping to hide from justice.

The first open door that he saw was that of the dwelling of a good widow, whose son was his friend and fellow-student. Hastily entering, he implored her to hide him in some safe place, confessing what he had done, and that, should he be taken, all was over with him.

The good woman shut him into a little room, secret and safe, and there left him. Not many minutes had elapsed before a melancholy procession approached, and the dead body of her son was brought into the house, the bearers telling the distracted mother in what manner he had been killed, and after a little questioning, giving the name of the youth who had shot her child.

Weeping and broken-hearted, she hurried to the place where she had hidden the wretched homicide, and it was from her lips that he learned who it was that he had deprived of life.

In an agony of shame and grief, tearing his hair, and calling upon death to strike him down, too, he threw himself on his knees before the poor mother; not, indeed, to ask her pardon, but to entreat her to give him up to justice, wishing to expiate publicly a crime so barbarous.

The widow, a most devout and merciful woman, was deeply touched by the youth's repentance, and saw clearly that it was thoughtlessness and not malicious intent that had been the moving spring of the deed. She then assured him that, provided he would ask pardon of God and change his way of life, she would keep her promise and help him to escape. This she did, and by so doing imitated the gentle kindness of the prophet who spared the lives of the Syrian soldiers who had come to murder him, he having them in his power in the midst of Samaria.[1]

So pleasing to God was this poor widow's clemency and forgiveness that He permitted the soul of her murdered son to appear to her, revealing to her that her pardon, granted so readily and sweetly to the man who had unintentionally been his murderer, had obtained for his soul deliverance from Purgatory, in which place he would otherwise have been long detained.

How blessed are the merciful! They shall obtain mercy both for themselves and for others!

[Footnote 1: 4 Reg. vi. 12. 23]

UPON THE VIRTUE OF CONDESCENSION.

I will give you our Blessed Father's views on this subject, first reminding you how unfailingly patient he was with the humours of others, how gentle and forbearing at all times towards his neighbour, and how perseveringly he inculcated the practice of this virtue, not only upon the Daughters of the Visitation, but upon all his spiritual children.

He often said to me: "Oh, how much better it would be to accommodate ourselves to others rather than to want to bend every one to our own ways and opinions! The human mind is like pulp, which takes readily any colour mixed with it. The great thing is to take care that it be not like the chameleon, which, one after the other, takes every colour except white. Condescension, if unaccompanied by frankness and purity, is dangerous, and much to be avoided.

"It is right to take compassion upon sinners, but it must be with the intention of extricating them from the mire, not of slothfully leaving them to rot and perish in it. It is a perverted sort of mercy to look at our neighbour, sunk in the misery of sin, and not venture to extend to him the helping hand of a gentle but out-spoken remonstrance. We must condescend in everything, but only up to the altar steps; that is to say, not beyond the point at which condescension would be a sin, and undeserving of its name.

I do not say that we must at every instant reprove the sinner. Charitable prudence demands that we rather wait the moment when he is capable of assimilating the remedies suitable for his malady, and till God shall give to his hearing joy and gladness, and the bones that have been humbled shall rejoice.[1] Turbulent zeal, zeal that is neither moderate nor wise, pulls down in place of building up. There are some who do no good at all, because they wish to do things too well, and who spoil everything they try to mend. We must make haste slowly, as the ancient proverb says. He who walks hurriedly is apt to fall. We must be prudent both in reproving others and in condescending to them. The King's honour loveth judgment."[2]

[Footnote 1: Psalm l. 10.]

[Footnote 2: Psalm xcviii. 4.]

HOW BLESSED FRANCIS ADAPTED HIMSELF TO TIMES, PLACES, AND CIRCUMSTANCES.

When the Chablais was restored to the Duke of Savoy, Bishop de Granier, the predecessor of our Holy Founder, eager to further the design of His Highness to bring back into the bosom of the Roman Church the population that had been led astray, sent to it a number of labourers to gather in the harvest. Among these, one of the first to be chosen was our Saint, at that time Provost of the Cathedral Church of St. Peter in Geneva, and consequently next in dignity to the Bishop.

With him were sent some Canons, Parish Priests, and others. Several members of various Religious Orders also presented themselves, eager to be employed in this onerous, if honourable, mission.[1]

It would be impossible to give a just idea of the labours of these missionaries, or of the obstacles which they encountered at the outset of their holy enterprise. The spirit of Blessed Francis was, however, most flexible and accommodating, and greatly tended to further the work of the people's conversion.

He was like the manna which assimilated itself to the palate of whoever tasted it: he made himself all things to all men that he might gain all for Jesus Christ.

In his ordinary mode of conversation and in his dress, which was mean and common, he produced a much less jarring effect upon the minds and eyes of these people than did the members of Religious Orders with their various habits and diversities.
He, as well as the secular Priests who worked under him, sometimes even condescended so far as to wear the short cloaks and high boots usual in the country, so as more easily to gain access to private houses, and not to offend the eyes of the people by the sight of the cassock, which they were unaccustomed to. To this pious stratagem the members of Religious Orders were unwilling to have recourse, their distinctive habit being, in their opinion, almost essential to their profession, or at least so fitting that it might never lawfully be laid aside.

Our Blessed Father went on quite a different tack, and caught more flies with a spoonful of the honey which he was so much in the habit of using, than did all the others with their harsher methods.

Everything about him, whether external or internal, breathed the spirit of conciliation; all his words, gestures, and ways were those of kindliness.

Some wished to make themselves feared; but he desired only to be loved, and to enter men's hearts through the doorway of affection. On this account, whether he spoke in public or in private, he was always more attentively listened to than anyone else.

However much the Protestants might attack him and purposely provoke him, he, on his side, ever dealt with them in a spirit absolutely free from contention, abstaining from anything likely to give offence, having often on his lips those beautiful words of the Apostle: If any man seem to be contentious, we have no such custom, nor the Church of God.[2]

To come now to the particulars which I promised you, let me tell you how our Blessed Father, having read in St. Augustine's works and in those of other ancient Fathers that in the early centuries Christian Priests, in addressing heretics and schismatics, did not hesitate to call them their brethren, inferred that he might quite lawfully follow so great an example.

By doing so he conciliated these people to such an extent that they flocked to hear him, and were charmed with the sweetness and gentleness of his discourses, the outcome of his overflowing kindliness of heart. This mode of expression was, however, so offensive to preachers who were in the habit of speaking of heretics as rebels against the light, uncircumcised of heart, etc., that they called a meeting, in which they resolved to remonstrate with the Provost (Blessed Francis), and to represent to him that, though he meant well, he was in reality ruining the cause of Catholics.

They insisted that he was flattering the pride so inherent in heresy, that he was lulling the people to sleep in their errors by sewing pillows to their elbows; that it was better to correct them in mercy and justice than to pour on their heads the oil of wheedling, as they called the kindliness of our Saint.

He received their remonstrances pleasantly, and even respectfully, without defending himself in any way, but, on the contrary, appearing to yield to their zeal, albeit somewhat sadly and unwillingly. Finding, however, that he did not begin to act upon their suggestions, as they had promised themselves he would do, some of them sent a written appeal to the Bishop, representing to him that he would have to recall the Provost and his companion missioners, who with their unwise and affected levity ruined in one day more souls than they themselves could convert in a month.

They went on to compare the labour of the missioners to Penelope's web: to say that our Saint preached more like a Huguenot pastor than a Catholic Priest, and, in fine, that he went so far as to call the heretics his brethren, a thing so scandalous that the Protestants had already conceived great hope of bringing him over to their own party.

The good Bishop, however, better informed as to the real state of the case, paid little heed to this appeal, dictated by a bitter zeal, rather than by the true science of the Saints.

He merely exhorted each one to persevere, and to remember that every spirit should praise the Lord according to the talents committed to it by God.

Our Blessed Father, being informed of these complaints made against him to his Bishop, would not defend himself, but commended his cause to the judgment of God, and, silently but hopefully, awaited the result. Nor was his expectation disappointed, for experience soon showed that the too ardent eagerness of these zealots was more likely to delay than to advance the work.

To crown all this, the preachers who had objected to his method had ere long themselves to be set aside as unfit.

On one occasion when I was talking with him and had turned the conversation on this subject, he said to me: "These good people looked through coloured spectacles. They saw all things of the same hue as their own glasses. My predecessor soon found out who were the real hindrances to the conversion of the Protestant Cantons." On my asking him how he could in reason apply the term "brethren" to persons who certainly are not such, since no one can have God for his Father who has not the Catholic Church for his mother, and since, therefore, those who are not in her bosom cannot be our brethren, he said to me: "Ah! but I never call them brethren without adding the epithet erring, a word which marks the distinction with sufficient clearness.

"Besides, they are in fact our brethren by Baptism, which they duly administer and receive. Moreover, they are our brethren according to the flesh, for are we not all children of Adam? Then, too, we are fellow citizens, and subjects of the same earthly prince. Is not that enough to constitute a kind of fraternity between us?

"Lastly, I look upon them as children of the Church, at least in disposition, since they are willing to be instructed; and as my brethren in hope, since they also are called to inherit eternal life. In the early days of the Church it was customary to give the title of brethren to catechumens, even before their baptism."

These reasons satisfied me and made me esteem highly the ingenious method suggested to him by the Holy Spirit to render these unruly and untaught souls docile and tractable.

[Footnote 1: M. Camus must have been misinformed. St. Francis had but few fellow-workers in the early years of his mission in the Chablais. [Ed.]] [Footnote 2: 1 Cor. xi. 16.]

UPON THE DEFERENCE DUE TO OUR INFERIORS AND DEPENDENTS.

Blessed Francis not only taught, but practised deference and a certain obedience towards his inferiors; towards his flock, towards his fellow citizens, and even towards his servants. He obeyed his body servant in what concerned his rising, his going to bed, and his toilet, as if he himself had been the valet and the other the master.

When he sat up far into the night either to study or to write letters, he would beg his servant to go to bed, for fear of tiring him by keeping him up. The man would grumble at his request, as if he were being taken for a lazy, sleepy-headed fellow. Our Blessed Father patiently put up with grumblings of the sort, but would complete what he had in hand as quickly as possible, so as not to keep the man waiting.

One summer morning Blessed Francis awoke very early, and, having some important matter on his mind, called this servant to bring him some necessaries for his toilet. The man, however, was too sound asleep to be roused by his master's voice. The good Prelate therefore, on rising, looked into the adjoining room, thinking that the man must have left it, but finding him fast asleep, and fearing to do him harm by waking him suddenly, dressed without his assistance and betook himself to his prayers, studies, and writing. Later the servant awoke, and dressed, and, coming to his master's room, to his surprise found him deep in his studies. The man asked him abruptly how he had managed without him. "I fetched everything myself," replied the holy Prelate. "Am I not old enough and strong enough for that?" "Would it have been too much trouble to call me?" said the man grumblingly. "No, indeed, my child," said Blessed Francis, "and I assure you that I did call you several times; but at last, thinking that you must have gone out, I got up to see where you were, and, finding you sleeping profoundly, I had not the heart to wake you." "You have the heart, it seems, to turn me into ridicule," retorted the man. "Oh, no, my friend," said Francis. "I was only telling you what happened, without a thought of either blaming you or making fun of you. Come, I promise you that for the future I will never stop calling you till you awake."

UPON THE WAY TO TREAT SERVANTS.

His opinion was that masters, as a rule, commit many grave faults with regard to their servants, by treating them with harshness and severity. Such conduct is quite unworthy of christians, and, in them, worse even than the behaviour of pagans in olden times to their slaves.

He himself never uttered an angry or threatening word to any one of his domestics. When they committed a fault, he corrected them so mildly that they were ready at once to make amends and to do better, out of love to their good master rather than from fear of him.

Once, when I was talking to him on this subject, I quoted the saying that "Familiarity breeds contempt, and contempt hatred." "Yes," he said, "improper familiarity, but never civil, cordial, kindly, virtuous familiarity; for as that proceeds from love, love engenders its like, and true love is never without esteem, nor, consequently, without respect for the object loved, seeing that love is founded wholly on the estimation in which the thing or person beloved is held. You know the saying of the ancient tyrant: Let them hate me, provided that they fear me. Speaking on this subject, we may well reverse the motto and say: Let them despise me, provided only that they love me. For if this contempt produces love, love after a while will stifle contempt, and sooner or later will in its place put respect; since there is no one that one reverences more, or has a greater fear of offending, than a person whom one loves in truth and sincerity of heart."

With regard to this, he told me a story, which he alludes to in his Philothea. Blessed Elzéar, Comte d'Arian, in

Provence, was so exceedingly gentle in his treatment of his servants that they looked upon him as a person positively deficient in understanding, and behaved in his presence with the greatest incivility and insolence, knowing well his persevering tolerance of injuries and his boundless patience. His wife, the saintly Delphina, feeling more acutely than he the disrespectful conduct of their servants, complained of it to him, saying that the menials absolutely laughed in his face. "And if they do," he answered, "why should I be put out by these little familiarities, pleasantries, and bursts of merriment, seeing that I am quite certain they do not hate me? They have not yet struck me, spat in my face, or offered me any of those indignities which Jesus Christ our Lord suffered at the hands of the high priest's servants, and not alone from those who scourged Him, derided Him, and crucified Him. Is it fitting that I, who glory in being the servant of Jesus Christ crucified, should desire to be better treated than my Master? Does it become a member to complain of any hardship under a Head wearing no crown but one of thorns? All that you tell me is but a mere jest compared with the insults heaped upon our divine Lord. The contempt of my servants—if, indeed, they do despise me—is a splendid lesson, teaching me to despise myself. How shall we practise humility if not on such occasions as these?"

Our Blessed Father went on to say: "I have proposed this example rather for your admiration than for your imitation, and that you may see of what means holy love makes use, in the hearts which are its own, in order to lead them to find rest in the very things which trouble those who are less devout. What I would say on the subject of servants is this; that, after all, they are our fellow-men and our humble brethren, whom charity obliges us to love as ourselves. Come, then, let us love them as ourselves, these dear yokefellows, who are so closely bound to us, who live under the same roof, and eat and drink of our substance. Let us treat them like ourselves, or as we should wish to be treated if we were in their place, and of their condition in life. That is the best way to deal with servants."

ANOTHER INSTANCE OF BLESSED FRANCIS' GENTLENESS WITH HIS OWN SERVANTS.

Like master, like man. Not only were all our Blessed Father's servants virtuous (he would not have suffered any who were not, to form part of his household), but, following their master's example, they were all singularly gentle and obliging in their manners and behaviour.

One of them, a young man, handsome, virtuous, and pious, was greatly sought after by many of the citizens, who thought he would prove a most desirable son-in-law, and to this end they encouraged his intercourse with their daughters. About the several advantageous matches proposed to him he always used to tell the Bishop. One day the latter said to him, "My dear son, your soul is as dear to me as my own, and there is no sort of advantage that I do not desire for you and would not procure for you if I could. That you know very well, and you know, too, that it is possibly only your youth that dazzles the eyes of certain young girls and makes them want you for their husband; but I am of opinion that more age and experience is needed before you take upon yourself the cares of a family. Think well over the matter, for when once embarked it will be too late to repent of what you have done.

"Marriage is an Order in which the profession must be made before the novitiate; if there were a year's probation, as there is in the cloister, there would be very few professions. After all, what have I done to you to make you wish to leave me? I am old, I shall soon die, and then you can dispose of yourself as you please. I shall bequeath you to my brother, who will provide for you quite as advantageously as these proposed matches would have done."

He said this with tears in his eyes, which so distressed the young man that he threw himself at the Bishop's feet, asking his pardon for having even thought of quitting him, and renewing his protestations of fidelity and of determination to serve him in life and death.

"No, no, my son," he replied; "I have no wish to interfere with your liberty. I would, on the contrary, purchase it, like St. Paul, at the cost of my own. But I am giving you friendly advice, such as I would offer to my own brother were he of your age." And in very truth he treated the members of his household; not as servants, but as his brothers and children. He was their elder brother or their father, rather than their master.

THE HOLY BISHOP NEVER REFUSED WHAT WAS ASKED OF HIM.

He practised to the letter the divine precept: Give to him who asketh of thee,[1] though, indeed, he possessed so few earthly goods that it was a standing marvel to me how he could give away as much as he did! Truly, I believe that God often multiplied the little which was really in his hands.

As regards heavenly goods, he was lavish of them to all who came to him as petitioners. He never refused spiritual consolation or advice either in public or in private, and his readiness to supply abundantly and spontaneously this mystical bread of life and wisdom was surprising. His alertness when requested to preach was also peculiarly remarkable, as his action was naturally heavy, and his habit of thought, as well as his enunciation, somewhat slow.

On one occasion, in Paris, he was asked to preach on a certain day, and readily consented to do so. One of his attendants then reminded him that he was engaged to preach elsewhere on the same day. "No matter," the Bishop replied, "God will give us grace to multiply our bread. He is rich towards all who invoke Him."[2] His servant next remarked that some care was surely due to his health. "What!" exclaimed Blessed Francis, "do you think that if God gives us the grace to find matter for preaching, He will not at the same time take care of the body, the organ by means of which His doctrine is proclaimed? Let us put our trust in Him, and He will give us all the strength we need."

"But," objected the other, "does God forbid us to take care of our health?"

"By no means," answered the Bishop; "but He does forbid a want of confidence in His goodness ... and," he added seriously and firmly, "were I requested to preach a third sermon on that same day, it would cost me less both in mind and body to consent than to refuse. Should we not be ready to sacrifice, and even, as it were, to obliterate ourselves, body and soul, for the benefit of that dear neighbour of ours whom our Lord loved so much as even to die for him?"

[Footnote 1: Matt. v. 43.]

[Footnote 2: Rom. x. 12.]

UPON ALMSGIVING.

Our Blessed Father had, as we know, so high an idea of the virtue of charity, which, indeed, he said was only christian perfection under another name, that he disliked to hear almsgiving called charity. It was, he said, like putting a royal crown on the head of a village maiden.

In answer to my objection that this was actually the case with Esther, who, though only a slave, was chosen by Assuerus to be his queen, and crowned by his royal hand, he replied: "You only strengthen my argument, for Esther would have remained in her state of servitude had she not become the spouse of Assuerus, and, queen though she was, she only wore her crown dependently on his will and pleasure. So almsgiving is only pleasing to God, and worthy of its reward, the heavenly crown of justice, in as far as it proceeds from charity, and is animated by that royal gift which converts it into an infused and supernatural virtue, which may be called either almsgiving in charity, of charitable almsgiving. But, just as the two natures, the divine and the human, were not merged in one another in the mystery of the Incarnation, although joined in the unity of the hypostasis of the Word, so this conjunction of charity with almsgiving, or this subordination of almsgiving to charity, does not change the one into the other, the object of each being as different as is the Creator from the creature. For the object of almsgiving is the misery of the needy which it tries as far as possible to relieve, and that of charity is God, Who is the sovereign Good, worthy to be loved above all things for His own sake." "But," I said, "when almsgiving is practised for the love of God, can we not then call it charity?" "No," he replied, "not any more than you can call Esther Assuerus, and Assuerus Esther. But you can, as I have said above, call it alms given in charity, or charitable almsgiving.

"Almsgiving and charity are quite different, for not only may alms be given without charity, but even against charity, as when they are given knowing they will lead to sin."

In a remarkable passage in Theotimus the Saint asks: "Were there not heretics, who, to exalt charity towards the poor, deprecated charity towards God, ascribing man's whole salvation to almsdeeds, as St. Augustine witnesses?"[1]

[Footnote 1: Love of God. B. xi. c. 14.]

OUR SAINT'S HOPEFULNESS IN REGARD TO THE CONVERSION OF SINNERS.

Our Blessed Father was always full of tenderness, compassion, and gentleness towards sinners, but he regarded and treated them in different ways according to their various dispositions.

A sinner who had grown old in evil, who clung obstinately to his wicked ways, who laughed to scorn all remonstrances, and gloried in his shame, formed a spectacle so heart-breaking and so appalling to the holy Bishop, that he shrank from contemplating it. When he had succeeded in turning his thoughts to some other subject, on their being suddenly recalled to it, he would shudder as if a secret wound had been touched, and utter some devout and fervent ejaculation such as this: "Ah! Lord, command that this blind man see! Speak the word only, and he shall be healed! Oh, my God, those who forsake Thee shall be forsaken; convert him, and he shall be converted!"

With obstinate sinners of this class his patience was unwearied. For such, he said, God Himself waited patiently, even until the eleventh hour; adding that impatience was more likely to embitter them and retard their conversion than remonstrance to edify them.

For the sinner who was more open to conviction, and was not so obstinate in his malice, for him who had, that is to say, lucid intervals in his madness, Blessed Francis had the most tender affection, regarding him as a poor paralytic waiting on the edge of the pool of healing for some helping hand to plunge him into it. To such he behaved as did the good shepherd of the Gospel, Who left the ninety-nine sheep in the desert to seek after the hundredth which had gone astray.

But towards the sinner when once converted, how describe his attitude of mind! He regarded him not as a brand snatched from the burning, not as a bruised reed, not as an extinguished taper that was still smoking, but as a sacred vessel filled with the oil of grace, as one of those trees which the ancients looked upon as holy because they had been struck by fire from Heaven. It was marvellous to observe the honour which he paid to such a one, the esteem in which he held him, the praises which he bestowed upon him.

He always considered that souls delivered by God from the mouth of the roaring lion were in consequence likely to be more vigilant, more courageous in resisting temptation, and more careful in guarding against relapses.

He did all he could to cover the faults of others, his goodness of heart being so great that he never allowed himself to think ill even of the wicked. He attributed their sinfulness to the violence of temptation and the infirmity of human nature. When faults were public and so manifest that they could not be excused, he would say: "Who knows but that the unhappy soul will be converted? The greatest sinners often become the greatest penitents, as we see in the case of David. And who are we that we should judge our brother? Were it not for the grace of God we should perhaps do worse than he."

He never allowed the conversion of a sinner to be despaired of, hoping on till death. "This life," he said, "is our pilgrim way, in which those who now stand may fall, and those who have fallen may, by grace, be set on their feet again."

Nor even after death would he tolerate an unfavourable judgment being passed on any.

His reason for this was that as the original grace of justification was not given by way of merit, so neither could the grace of final perseverance be merited.

With regard to this subject he related to me an amusing incident which occurred whilst he was a missioner in the Chablais. Amongst the Priests and Religious who were sent to help him was one of a humorous temperament, and who did not hesitate to show that he was so, even in the pulpit. One day, when preaching before our Blessed Prelate against the heresiarch[1] who had raised the standard of revolt in Geneva, he said that we should never condemn any one as lost after death, except such as are by Scripture denounced; no, not even the said heresiarch who had caused so much evil by his errors. "For," he went on to say, "who knows but that God may have touched his heart at the last moment and converted him? It is true that out of the Church and without the true faith there is no salvation; but who can say that he did not at the moment of death wish to be reunited with the Catholic Church, from which he had separated himself, and acknowledge in his heart the truth of the belief he had combated, and that thus he did not die sincerely repentant?"

After having surprised the congregation by these remarks, he most unexpectedly concluded by saying: "We must certainly entertain sentiments of boundless confidence in the goodness of God, Who is infinite in mercy to those who invoke Him. Jesus Christ even offered His peace, His love, and His salvation to the traitor Judas, who betrayed Him by a kiss. Why, then, may He not have offered the same favour to this unhappy heresiarch? Is the arm of God shortened?

"Yet, my brethren," he continued, "believe me, and I assure you I lie not, if this man is not damned he has had the narrowest escape man ever had; and if he has been saved from eternal wreck, he owes to God the handsomest votive candle that a person of his condition ever offered!"

As you may imagine, this finale did not draw many tears from the audience!

[Footnote 1: Calvin.]

BLESSED FRANCIS' SOLICITUDE FOR MALEFACTORS CONDEMNED TO DEATH.

He often went to carry consolation to prisoners, and sometimes accompanied condemned criminals to the place of execution, that he might help them to make a good death.

At such times, too, he kept to the methods we have already described as used by him in his visiting of the rest of the dying. After having made them unburden their conscience, he left them a little breathing space, and then at intervals suggested to them acts of faith, hope, and charity, of repentance, of resignation to the Will of God, and of abandonment to His mercy; not adding to their sufferings by importunity, long harangues, or endless exhortations.

So happily did the Blessed Prelate succeed in this method of treatment, that sometimes the poor criminals whom he accompanied to their execution went to it as to a marriage feast, with joy and peace, such as they had never experienced in the whole course of their lawless and sinful lives, happier far so to die than to live on as they had done. "It is," he would say to them, "by lovingly kissing the feet of God's justice that we most surely reach the embrace of His tender mercy.

"Above all things, we must be confident that they who trust in Him shall never be confounded."

UPON THE SMALL NUMBER OF THE ELECT.

Blessed Francis' extreme gentleness always led him to lean towards indulgent judgment, however slight in a particular case the apparent justification might be.

On one occasion there was a discussion in his presence as to the meaning of those terrible words in the Gospel: Many are called, but few chosen.[1] Some one said that the chosen were called a little flock, whereas the unwise or reprobates were spoken of as many in number, and so on. He replied that, in his opinion, there would be very few Christians (meaning, of course, those who are in the true Church, outside which there is no salvation) who would be lost, "because," he said, "having the root of the true faith, the tree that springs from it would sooner or later bear its fruit, which is salvation, and awakening, as it were, from death to life, they would become, through charity, active and rich in good works."

When asked what, then, was the meaning of the statement in the Gospel as to the small number of the elect, he replied that in comparison with the rest of the world, and with infidel nations, the number of Christians was very small, but that of that small number very few would be lost, in conformity to that striking text, There is no condemnation for those that are in Christ Jesus.[2] Which really means that justifying grace is always being offered them, and this grace is inseparable from a lively faith and a burning charity. Add to this that He who begins the work in us is He who likewise perfects it. We may believe that the call to christianity, which is the work of God, is always a perfect work, and therefore leads of itself to the end of all perfection, which is heavenly glory.
[Footnote 1: Matt. XX. 16.]

[Footnote 2: Rom. viii. 1.]

TO LOVE TO BE HATED, AND TO HATE TO BE LOVED.

This maxim of our Blessed Father's seems strange and altogether contrary to his sweet and affectionate nature.

If, however, we look closely into it, we shall find that it is full of the purest and most subtle love of God.

When he said that we ought to love to be hated, and hate to be loved, he was referring in the one case to the love which is in and for God alone, and in the other to that merely human love, which is full of danger, which robs God of His due, and of which, therefore, we should hate to be the object. He expresses himself thus:

"Those who have nothing naturally attractive about them are very fortunate, for they are well assured that the love which one bears them is excellent, being all for God's sake alone."

UPON OBEDIENCE.

Blessed Francis always said that the excellence of obedience consists not in doing the will of a gentle, courteous superior, who commands rather by entreaty than as one having authority, but in bowing the neck beneath the yoke of one who is harsh, stern, imperious, severe. He was, it is true, desirous that those who had to judge and direct souls should do so as fathers rather than as masters, as, indeed, he did himself, but at the same time he wished those in authority to be somewhat strict, and those subject to them to be less sensitive and selfish, and consequently less impatient, less refractory, and less given to grumbling than most men are.

He used also to say that a rough file takes off more rust and polishes iron better than a smooth and less biting one, and that very many and very heavy blows of the hammer are needed to temper a keen sword blade.

"But," I said to him, when discussing this subject, "as the most perfect obedience is that which springs from love, ought not the command to be given lovingly, so as to incite the subordinate to a loving obedience?" He answered: "There is a great deal of difference between the excellence of obedience and its perfection.

"The excellence of a virtue has to do with its nature; its perfection with the grace, or charity, in which it is clothed. Now, here I am not speaking of the supernatural perfection of obedience which emanates most assuredly from the love of God; but of its natural excellence, which is better tested by harsh than by gentle commands.

"Excessive indulgence on the part of parents and superiors is only too often the cause of many disorders.

"More than this, even as regards the supernatural perfection of obedience, it is very probable that the harshness of the command given helps its growth, and renders our love of God, which is our motive in obeying, stronger, firmer, and more generous. When a superior commands with over-much gentleness and circumspection, besides the fact that he compromises his authority and causes it to be slighted, he so attracts and attaches his inferior to himself that often unconsciously he robs God of the devotedness which is His due. The result is that the inferior obeys the man whom he loves, and because he loves him, rather than God in the man, and for the love of God alone.

"On the other hand, harshness tests far better the fidelity of a heart which loves God sincerely. For, finding nothing pleasing in the command except the sweetness of divine love, to which alone it yields obedience, the perfection of that obedience becomes the greater, since the intention is purer, more direct, and more immediately turned to God. It was in this spirit that David said that, for the sake of the words of God—that is, of His law—he had kept hard ways."[1] Our Blessed Father added this simile to explain his meaning further:

"Obeying a harsh, irritating, and vexatious superior is like drawing clear water from a spring which flows through the jaws of a lion of bronze. It is like the riddle of Samson, Out of the eater came forth meat; it is hearing God's voice, and seeing God's will alone in that of a superior, even if the command be, as in the case of St. Peter, Kill and eat;[2] it is to say with Job, Although He should kill me, I will trust in Him."[3]

[Footnote 1: Psalm xvi. 4.]

[Footnote 2: Acts x. 13.]

[Footnote 3: Job xiii. 15.]

UPON THE OBEDIENCE THAT MAY BE PRACTISED BY SUPERIORS.

Asking him one day if it was possible for persons in authority, whether in the world or in the cloister, to practise the virtue of obedience, he replied: "Certainly, and they can do so far more perfectly and more heroically than their subjects."

Then, seeing my astonishment at this apparent paradox, he went on to explain it in the following manner: "Those who are obliged, either by precept or by vow, which takes the place of precept, to practise obedience, are, as a rule, subject only to one superior. Those, on the other hand, who are in authority, are free to obey more widely, and to obey even in commanding, because if they consider that it is God Who puts them over the heads of the others, and Who commands them to command those others, who does not see that even their commanding is an act of obedience? This kind of obedience may even be practised by princes who have none but God set over them, and who have to render an account of their actions to Him alone. I may add that there is no power on earth so sublime as not to have, at least in some respects, another set over it. Christian kings render filial obedience to the Roman Pontiff, and the sovereign Pontiff himself submits to his confessor in the Sacrament of Penance. But there is a still higher degree of obedience which even Prelates and the greatest among men may practise. It is that which the Apostle counsels when he says: Be ye subject to every human creature for God's sake.[1] Who for love of us not only became subject to the Blessed Virgin and to St. Joseph, but made Himself obedient to death and to the death of the Cross, submitting Himself in His Passion to the most sinful and degraded of the earth, uttering not a cry, even as a lamb under the hand of him who shears it and slays it. It is by this universal obedience to every creature that we become all things to all men in order that we may win all to Jesus Christ. It is by this that we take our neighbour, whoever he may be, for our superior, becoming servants for our Lord's sake."

[Footnote 1: 1 Peter ii. 13.]

AN INSTANCE OF OUR SAINT'S OBEDIENCE.

On one occasion, when the Duke of Savoy, being pressed by many urgent public needs, had obtained from the Pope a Brief empowering him to levy contributions on the Church property in his dominions, Blessed Francis, finding some slackness and unwillingness on the part of the beneficed clergy of the diocese to yield obedience to this order, when he had called them together to settle what was to be done, spoke with just indignation. "What! gentlemen," he cried, "is it for us to question and reason when two sovereigns concur in issuing the same command? Is it for us, I say, to scrutinize their counsels, and ask, Why are you acting thus? Not only to the decrees of sovereign courts, but even to the sentence of the most insignificant judges appointed by God to decide differences in our affairs, we yield deference so far as not to enquire into the motive of their decisions. And here, where two oracles who have only to render account to God of what orders they give, speak, we set to work to enquire into their motives and reasons as if we were charged to investigate their conduct. Assuredly, I will take no part in such doings. Our virtue, indeed, lags sadly behind that of those christians—only lay people too—of whom St. Paul said that being wise themselves they gladly suffered bondage, stripes, every sort of ill-usage from the foolish,[1] and of whom, in another place, he says that they took with joy the being stripped of their own goods, knowing that they had a better and a lasting substance.[2] And the Apostle, as you know, is speaking to men who had been unjustly despoiled of their whole property by robbers and tyrants, whereas you will not give up a small fraction of yours to assist in the public need of our good Prince, to whose zeal we owe the re-establishment of the Catholic religion in the three divisions of the Chablais, and whose enemies are the adversaries of our faith! Is not our Order the first of the three estates in a christian kingdom? Is there anything more just than to contribute of our wealth, together with our prayers, towards the defence of our altars, of our lives, and of our peace? The people are lavishing their substance and the nobility their blood for the same cause. Remember the late wars, and tremble lest your ingratitude and disobedience should plunge you again into similar troubles."

Adding example to precept, he paid so heavy a tax upon a part of his own revenue that none could say he did not practise what he preached, and all those who had ventured to oppose him in the matter were not only effectually silenced, but covered with confusion and put to a just shame.

[Footnote 1: 2 Cor. xi. 19, 20.]

[Footnote 2: Heb. x. 34.]

UPON THE LOVE OF HOLY POVERTY.

Godliness with contentment, says Holy Scripture, is great gain.[1]

So content was the godliness of Blessed Francis that, although deprived of the greater part of his episcopal revenues, he was fully satisfied with the little that was left to him.

After all, he would say, are not twelve hundred crowns a handsome income for a Bishop? The Apostles, who were far better Bishops than we are, had nothing like that sum. It is not for us to fix our own pay for serving God.

His love of poverty was truly striking. At Annecy he lodged in a hired house, which was both handsome and roomy, and in which the apartments assigned to him as Bishop were very elegantly furnished. He, however, took up his abode in an uncomfortable little room, where there was hardly any light at all, so that he could truly say with Job: I have made my bed in darkness;[2] or with David: Night shall be my light in my pleasures;[3] or again, I am like a night raven in the house, or as a sparrow all alone on the housetop.[4]

He called this little room, or, to speak more truly, this sepulchre of a living man, Francis' chamber, while to that in which he received visitors, or gave audience, he gave the name of the Bishop's chamber.

Truly, the lover of holy poverty can always find a means of practising it, even in the midst of riches.

Blessed Francis, indeed, always welcomed poverty with a smiling countenance, though naturally it be apt to cast a gloom and melancholy upon the faces both of those who endure it and of those who only dread it.

Involuntary poverty is surly and discontented, for it is forced and against the will. Voluntary poverty, on the contrary, is joyous, free, and light-hearted. To show you how cheerfully and pleasantly he talked on this subject, I will give you one or two of his remarks.

Once, showing me a coat which had been patched up for him, and which he wore under his cassock, he said: "My people really work little miracles; for out of an old garment they have made me this perfectly new coat. Am I not well-dressed?"

Again, when his steward was complaining of down-right distress, and of there being no money left, he said: "What are you troubling yourself about? We are now more like our Master, Who had not even where to lay His head, though as yet we are not reduced to such extremity as that." "But what are we to do?" persisted the steward. "My son," the Bishop answered, "we must live as we can, on whatever goods we have, that is all." "Truly," replied the other, "it is all very well to talk of living on our goods when there are none left to live upon!" "You do not understand me," returned the Bishop; "we must sell or pledge some of our furniture in order to live. Will not that, my good M.R.,[5] be living on our goods?"

It was in this fashion that the Saint was accustomed to meet cheerfully money troubles, so unbearable to weaker characters.

On one occasion I expressed my admiration at his being able to make so good a show on his small means. "It is God," he said, "Who multiplies the five loaves." On my pressing him to tell me how it was done, "Why, it would not be a miracle," he answered, with a smile, "if we knew that. Are we not most fortunate to live on only by help of miracles? It is the mercy of God that we are not consumed." "You go quite beyond me," I said, "by taking that ground. I am not so transcendently wise."

"Listen," he replied. "Riches are truly thorns, as the Gospel teaches us. They prick us with a thousand troubles in acquiring them, with more cares in preserving them, and with yet more anxieties in spending them; and, most of all, with vexations in losing them.

"After all, we are only managers and stewards, especially if it is a question of the riches of the Church, which are the true patrimony of the poor. The important matter is to find faithful dispensers. Having sufficient to feed and clothe ourselves suitably, what more do we want? Assuredly, that which is over and above these is of evil.[6]

"Shall I tell you what my own feeling is? Well and good, but I must do so in your ear. I know very well how to spend what I have; but if I had more I should be in difficulty as to what to do with it. Am I not happy to live like a child without care? Sufficient for the day is the evil thereof. The more any one has to manage the longer the account he has to render. We must make use of this world as though we were making no use of it at all. We must possess riches as though we had them not, and deal with the things of earth like the dogs on the banks of the Nile, who, for fear of the crocodiles, lap up the water of the river as they run along its banks. If, as the wise man tells us, he that addeth knowledge addeth also labour; much more is this the case with the man who heaps up riches. He is like the giants in the fable who piled up mountains, and then buried themselves under them. Remember the miserable man who, as the Gospel tells us, thought that he had many years before him in which to live at his ease, but to whom the heavenly voice said: Thou fool, this night do they require thy soul of thee; and whose shall those things be which thou hast provided? In truth happy is he only who lays up imperishable treasures in Heaven."

He would never allow himself to be called poor; saying, that any one who had a revenue sufficient to live upon without being obliged to labour with head or hands to support himself should be called rich; and such, he said, was the case with us both.

To my objection that our revenues were nevertheless so very small that we must be really considered poor, for little, indeed, must we be working if our labour was not worth what we got from our bishoprics, he replied: "If you take it in this way you are not so far wrong, for who is there who labours in a vineyard and does not live upon its produce? What shepherd feeds his flock and does not drink its milk and clothe himself with its wool? So, too, may he who sows spiritual seed justly reap the small harvest which he needs for his temporal sustenance. If then he is poor who lives by work, and who eats the fruit of his labour, we may very well be reckoned as such; but if we regard the degree of poverty in which our Lord and His Apostles lived, we must perforce consider ourselves rich. After all, possessing honestly all that is necessary for food and clothing, ought we not to be content? Whatever is more than this is only evil, care, superfluity, wanting which we shall have less of an account to render. Happy is poverty, said a stoic, if it is cheerful poverty; and if it is that, it is really not poverty at all, or only poverty of a kind that is far preferable to the riches of the most wealthy, which are amassed with difficulty, preserved with solicitude, and lost with regret."

Our Saint used to say that, as for the cravings of nature, he who is not satisfied with what is really enough will never be satisfied. I wish that I could give any just idea of his extraordinary moderation even in the use of the necessaries of life. He told me once that when the time came for him to lay down the burden of his episcopal duties and to retire into solitude, there to pass the rest of his life in contemplation and study, he should consider five hundred crowns a year great wealth; in fact, he would not reserve more from either his patrimony or his Bishop's revenue, adding these words of St. Paul: Having food, and wherewith to be covered, let us (priests) be content.[7] He gave this as his reason. "The Church," he said, "which is the kingdom of Jesus Christ, is established on foundations directly opposed to those of the world, of which our Saviour said His kingdom was not. Now, on what is the kingdom of this world founded? Listen to St. John: All that is in the world is the concupiscence of the flesh, or of the eyes, and the pride of life; that is to say, the pleasures of the senses, avarice, and vanity. The Church then will be founded on mortification of the flesh, poverty, and humility. Pleasures and honours follow in the train of wealth; but poverty puts an axe to the roots of pride and sensual enjoyments. Some, says David, blaming them, glory in the multitude of their riches; and St. Paul exhorts the rich of this world not to be high-minded.

"It is a perilous thing for humility and mortification to take up their abode with wealth." This is why he wished for nothing but bare necessaries, fearing that superfluity might lead him into some excess.

When I reminded him that if we had this superfluity we might give alms out of it, as it is written, Of what remaineth give to the poor, he replied, that we knew well enough what: we ought to do; but that we did not know what we should do, and that it was always a species of presumption to imagine ourselves able to handle live coals without burning ourselves, seeing that even the Angel in the vision of the Prophet took them up with tongs!

[Footnote 1: 1 Tim. vi. 6.]

[Footnote 2: Job. xvii. 13.]

[Footnote 3: Ps. cxxxviii. 11.]

[Footnote 4: Ps. ci. 8.]

[Footnote 5: Georges Roland.]
[Footnote 6: Matt. v. 37.]

[Footnote 7: Tim. vi. 8.]

UPON THE SAME SUBJECT.

Our Blessed Father was so absolutely indifferent to the goods of this world that I never heard him so much as once complain of the loss of almost all his episcopal revenue, confiscated by the city of Geneva. He used to say that it was very much with the wealth of the Church as with a man's beard, the more closely it was clipped the stronger and the thicker it grew again. When the Apostles had nothing they possessed all things, and when ecclesiastics wish to possess too much, that too much is reduced to nothing.

His one hunger and thirst was for the conversion of souls, living in wilful blindness to the light of truth which shines only in the one true Church. Sometimes, he exclaimed, sighing heavily: "Give me souls, and the rest take to Thyself." Speaking of Geneva, to which city, in spite of its rebellion, he always applied terms of compassion and affection, such as "my dear Geneva," or "my poor Geneva," he said to me more than once: "Would to God that these gentlemen had taken such small remains of my revenue as they have left to me, and that we had only as small a foothold in that deplorable city as the Catholics have in La Rochelle, namely, a little chapel in which to say Mass and perform the functions of our religion! You would then soon see all these apostates come back to their senses, and we should rejoice over the return to the Church of these poor Sunamites, who are so forgetful of their duty."[1] This fond hope he always nourished in his breast.

He used to say that Henry VIII. of England, who at the beginning of his reign was so zealous for the Catholic faith, and wrote so splendidly against the errors of Luther, that he acquired for that reason the glorious title of Defender of the Faith, having, by yielding to his passion, caused so great a schism in his kingdom, even had he desired at the close of his life to return to the bosom of the Church which he had so miserably abandoned, would, on setting to work to attain this most happy end, have found the impossibility of recovering for the clergy and restoring to them the property and wealth which he had divided among his nobles, a serious difficulty.

"Alas!" our Blessed Father exclaimed, commenting upon this fact, "to think that a handful of dust should rob Heaven of so many souls! The business of every christian, and especially of the clergy, is the keeping of God's law. The Lord is the portion of their inheritance and of their cup. He would have made to them an abundant restitution of all that had been theirs, by gentle but effective means. They whose thoughts are fixed upon the Lord will be nourished by Him. The just are never forsaken nor reduced to beg their bread;

they have only to lift their eyes and their hopes to God and He will give them meat in due season; for it is He who gives food to all flesh. Moreover, it is much easier to suffer hunger with patience than to preserve virtue in the midst of plenty. It is not every one who can say with the Apostle: I know how to abound, and I know how to suffer need.[2] A thousand fall on the left hand of adversity, but ten thousand on the right hand of prosperity; for iniquity is the outcome of luxury, and the sin of the cities of the plain had its origin in a superabundance of bread; that is to say, in their wealth. To be frugal and devout is to possess a great treasure."

[Footnote 1: Cantic. vi. 12.]

[Footnote 2: Philipp. iv. 12.]

UPON POVERTY OF SPIRIT.

Three virtues, he said, were necessary to constitute poverty of spirit: simplicity, humility, and christian poverty. Simplicity consists in that singleness of aim which looks only to God, referring to Him alone those innumerable opportunities which come to us from objects other than Himself. Humility is that conviction of our own inferiority and destitution which makes the truly humble man regard himself as always an unprofitable servant. Christian poverty is of three kinds. First, that which is affective, but not effective. This can be practised in the midst of wealth, as in the case of Abraham, David, St. Louis, and many other holy persons, who, though rich in this world's goods, were ready in a moment to accept poverty with cheerfulness and thankfulness if it should please God to send it to them.

Second, effective but not affective poverty, which is a very unhappy condition. Those who are weighed down by it feel all its distressing consequences and are miserable because they cannot possess the many things which they ardently desire.

Third, affective, united with effective poverty, which is recommended in the Gospels, and which may happen to be our lot, either from birth or from some reverse of fortune.

If we are reconciled to our condition in life, however humble, and bless God Who has placed us in it, then we tread in the footsteps of Jesus Christ, of His holy Mother, and of the Apostles, who all lived a life of poverty.

Another way of practising this poverty is to follow the counsels of Jesus Christ, Who bids us sell all that we have and give it to the poor, imitating our divine Master in that poverty which He embraced for us, that we, through it, might be made rich. And never is this command more practically and worthily obeyed than when the man who has abandoned all his worldly goods for the sake of Christ, labours, not only in order to sustain his own life, but that he may have the wherewithal to give alms.

Thus did the Apostle glory when he said: For such things as were needful for me, and them that are with me, these hands have furnished.[1]

[Footnote 1: Acts xx. 34.]

FRANCIS' LOVE OF THE POOR.

To love our neighbour is not only to wish him well, but also to do him all the good that it is in our power to do. If we fall short of this, we deserve the reproach of St. James, addressed to those who, though they have ample means for giving material aid to the poor, content themselves with bare words of comfort.

The love of Blessed Francis for the poor was so intense that in their case he seemed to become a respecter of persons, preferring them to the rich, both in spiritual and in temporal matters. He was like a good physician who in visiting the sick shows the most tender solicitude for those afflicted with the most terrible diseases and lingers longest by their bedsides.

One day I had to wait my turn to go to confession to him for a very long time, he being engaged in hearing a poor blind beggar woman. When I afterwards expressed my surprise at the length of her confession, he said: "Ah! She sees far more clearly the way to go to God than many whose eyesight is otherwise perfect."

On another occasion, sailing with him on the lake of Geneva, I heard the boatman calling him "Father," and addressing him with corresponding familiarity. "Listen," he said to me, "to those good people. They are calling me their Father; and, indeed, I do believe they love me as such. Oh! how much more real happiness they give me than those who call me 'My Lord.'"

UPON THE CHRISTIAN VIEW OF POVERTY.

On one occasion I quoted that saying of Seneca: "He is truly great who dines off earthenware as contentedly as if it were silver; but he is greater still who dines off silver with as much indifference as if it were earthenware."

"The philosopher," he said, "is right in his judgment; for the first feasts on mere fancy, leading to vanity; but the second shows that he is superior to wealth, since he cares no more for a precious metal than for clay.

"Yet, Oh! how ridiculous; how empty is all mere human philosophy! This same philosopher who speaks so eloquently again and again of the contempt of riches, was all his life immersed in them; and at his death left thousands behind him. Does it not seem to you that, this being his own case, his talking about poverty makes him like a cleric expatiating on the art of war? We had far better listen to St. Paul, who speaks as a past master on the subject of poverty, since he practised it so thoroughly that he chose rather to live on what he could earn by the labour of his hands than on what the preaching of the Gospel might bring in to him, as to the other Apostles. Yes, we must needs listen to and believe St. Paul when he says that he esteems all things as dung in comparison with the service of Jesus Christ, counting as loss what he once held as gain."[1]

[Footnote 1: Philipp. iii, 8.]

UPON PROSPERITY.

Blessed Francis objected strongly to the use of the word fortune, considering it unworthy of utterance by christian lips. The expressions "fortunate," "by good fortune," "children of fortune," all common enough, were repugnant to him. "I am astonished," he said once, "that Fortune, the most pagan of idols, should have been left standing, when christianity so completely demolished all the rest! God forbid that any who ought to be the children of God's providence alone become children of fortune! and that those whose only hope should be in Him put their trust in the uncertainty of riches!"

He spoke yet more strongly of such as professing to be nailed with Jesus Christ to the Cross and to glory only in His reproaches and sufferings, yet were eager in heaping up riches, and, when amassed, in clinging fondly to them. "For," he said, "the Gospel makes christian blessedness to consist in poverty, contempt, pain, weeping, and persecutions; and even philosophy teaches us that prosperity is the stepmother of true virtue, adversity its mother!"

I asked him once how it was that we are so ready to have recourse to God when the thorn of affliction pierces us, and so eager in asking for deliverance from sickness, calumny, famine, and such like misfortunes. "It is," he said, "our weakness which thus cries out for help, and it is a proof of the infirmity which encompasses us; for as the best and firmest fish feed in the salt waters of the open sea, those which are caught in fresh water being less pleasing to the taste, so the most generous natures find their element in crosses and afflictions, while meaner spirits are only happy in prosperity.

"Moreover," he continued, "it is much easier to love God perfectly in adversity than in prosperity. For tribulation having nothing in itself that is lovable, save that it is God's gift, it is much easier to go by it straight to the will of God, and to unite ourselves to His good pleasure. Easier, I say, than by prosperity, which has attractions of its own that captivate our senses, and, like Dalila, lull them to sleep, working in us a subtle change, so that we begin insensibly to love for its own sake the prosperity which God sends us, instead of bestowing all our grateful love on God Who sends it, and to Whom all thanks and praise are due!"

UPON CHARITY AND CHASTITY.

Feeling at one time troubled and perplexed in mind as to the bearing of these two virtues upon one another, and as to the right manner of practising each, so that one should never run counter to the other, I carried my difficulties to our Blessed Father, who settled them at once in the following words; "We must," he said, "in this matter draw a careful distinction between persons who occupy positions of dignity and authority, and have the care of others, and those private individuals who have no one to look after but themselves. The former must deliver their chastity into the keeping of their charity; and if that charity is real and true it will not fail them, but will serve as a strong wall of defence, both without and within, to their chastity. On the other hand, private individual's will do better to surrender the guardianship of their charity to their chastity, and to walk with the greatest circumspection and self-restraint. The reason of this is that those in authority are obliged by the very nature of their duties, to expose themselves to the dangers inseparable from occasions: in which, however, they are assisted by grace, seeing they are not tempting God by any rashness.

"Contrariwise, those private individuals who expose themselves to danger without any legitimate excuse run great risk of tempting God and losing His grace; since it is written that he that loveth danger (still more he that seeketh it) shall perish in it."[1]

[Footnote 1: Eccles. iii. 27]

UPON PURITY OF HEART.

I can never express to you, or convey a right idea, of the high esteem in which he held purity of heart. He said that chastity of body was common enough even among unbelievers and among persons addicted to other vices; but that very few people could truly say, my heart is pure.

I do not say that by this purity of heart he meant the never being troubled by sinful desires, for that would be making the virtue of chastity to consist in insensibility; and what do those who are not tempted know about the matter?

No; he placed it in never yielding to unlawful affections. To these we should rather give the name of infections, since they infect the will, and interfere with the safe custody of the heart, which is the well-spring of the spiritual life.

UPON CHASTITY AND HUMILITY.

Speaking of the humility and chastity of the Blessed Virgin the holy Prelate said: "These two virtues, although they have to be continually practised, should be spoken of so rarely that this rarity of speech may rank as silence. The reason is that it is difficult to mention these virtues or to praise them either in themselves or in any individual who possesses them, without in some way sullying their brightness.

"1. There is, in my opinion, no human tongue which can rightly express their value, and to praise them inadequately is in a way to disparage them.

"2. To praise humility is to cause it to be desired from a secret self-love and to invite people to enter its domain through the wrong door.

"3. To praise humility in any individual is to tempt him to vanity and to flatter him dangerously; for the more he thinks himself humble the less he will really be so; and possibly when he sees that others consider him humble he will think that he must be so.

"4. As regards chastity, to praise it in itself is to leave on the mind a secret and almost imperceptible image of the contrary vice, and therefore to expose the mind to some danger of temptation. There is a sting hidden in the honey of such praise.

"5. To praise it in any individual is in a measure to expose him to the danger of falling. It is to put a stumbling-block In his way. It is to inflate that pride which under a fair disguise may lure him over a precipice.

"6. We must never be content to rely upon our hitherto untarnished purity of life, but must always fear, since innocence is a treasure which we carry in a vessel of glass, easily broken.

"7. In a word, the virtues of humility and chastity always seem to me like those subtle essences which evaporate if they are not kept very tightly corked.

"8. However, although I consider it wise very seldom to speak of these two virtues, it is wise to practise them unceasingly, humility being one of the most excellent virtues of the soul, and purity that fair white adornment of the body which is its honour, and which, like a lily growing among thorns, brings forth a wonderful flower, whose fruit is honour and riches.

"9. Nevertheless, I do not mean that we are to be so scrupulous as never to dare to speak of these virtues; not even to praise them when occasion warrants or demands our doing so. No, indeed. In one sense they can never be sufficiently praised, nor ever sufficiently valued and cultivated. What I mean is that we gain little by praising them. Our words in praise of a virtue are of little account in comparison with the smallest fruit; that is, with the least of the acts of a virtue.

"I add this because I know you attach too much importance to my words, and take them as literally as if they were oracles."

UPON MODESTY.

Our Blessed Father, speaking of the virtue of modesty, and dilating upon one of its chief properties, namely, its extraordinary sensitiveness to the slightest injurious influence, made use of two beautiful comparisons: "However pure, transparent, and polished the surface of a mirror may be, the faintest breath is sufficient to make it so dull and misty that it is unable to reflect any image. So it is with the reputation of the virtuous. However high and well established it may be, according the words of wisdom: Oh! how beautiful is the chaste generation! [1] a thoughtless, unrestrained glance or gesture is quite sufficient to give occasion to a slanderous tongue to infect that reputation with the serpent's venom, and to hide its lustre from the eyes of the world, as clouds hide the brightness of the sun.

"Again, look at this beautiful lily. It is the symbol of purity; it preserves its whiteness and sweetness, amid all the blackness and ruggedness of the encircling thorns. As long as it remains untouched its perfume is delicious and its dazzling beauty of form and colour charms every passer-by; but, as soon as it is culled, the scent is so strong as to be overpowering, and should you touch the petals they lose their satin smoothness as well as all their pure and white loveliness."

[Footnote 1: Wisd. iv. I.]

THE CONTEMPT HE FELT FOR HIS BODY.

Since our Blessed Father was not, like the martyrs, privileged to offer his body, both by living and dying, as a victim for God, he found out, with the ingenuity of love, a method of self-humiliation and self-sacrifice to be carried out after his death.

When quite young and still pursuing his studies at Padua, falling dangerously ill, and his life being despaired of, he begged his tutor to see that when he was dead his body should be given into the hands of the surgeons for dissection. "Having been of so little use to my neighbour in life," he said, "I shall thus at least, after my death, be able to render him some small service."

Happily for us, God in His great mercy spared this precious life, being contented, as in the case of the sacrifice of Isaac, with the offering of His faithful servant's will and with his generous contempt for his own flesh.

A motive which urged Blessed Francis to the above resolution, besides his desire of self-humiliation and immolation, was the hope of putting an end to the scandalous practice then prevailing among the surgical and medical students at Padua of secretly by night going to the cemeteries to disinter newly-buried bodies. This they did when they had failed to obtain those of criminals from the officers of justice. Innumerable evils, quarrels, and even murders resulted from this practice, and the indignation of the relatives and friends of the deceased persons whose corpses were stolen may be imagined. By setting the example of a voluntary surrender of his own body for dissection our Blessed Father hoped to diminish such orders.

UPON OUR SAINT'S HUMILITY.

It was of course impossible for Blessed Francis to be ignorant of the high esteem in which his piety was held, not only by his own people, but by all who knew him. This knowledge was, however, as may well be believed, a source of pain to him, and often covered him with confusion. He seldom spoke on the subject, for true humility rarely speaks, even humbly, of itself. Yet on one occasion, when more than usually worried by hearing himself praised, he allowed these words to fall from his lips: "The truth is that these good people with all their eulogiums, and expressions of esteem, are sowing the seed of a bitter fruit for me to gather in the end. When I am dead, imagining that my poor soul has gone straight to Heaven, they will not pray for it, and will leave me languishing in Purgatory. Of what avail then will this high reputation be to me? They are treating me like those animals which suffocate their young by their close pressure and caresses, or like the ivy which drags down the wall it seems to crown with verdure."

I will now give you some examples of his humility. He was sometimes told that people had spoken ill of him. Instead of excusing or defending himself, he would say cheerfully,

"Do they say no more than that? Certainly, they cannot know all, they flatter me, they spare me: I see very well that they rather pity than envy me, and that they wish me to be better than I am. Well! God be praised for this, I must correct my faults, for if I do not deserve reproof in this particular matter, I do in some other. It is really a mercy that the correction is given so kindly." If anyone took up his defence and declared that the whole accusation was false, "Ah! well," he would say, "it is a warning to make me careful not to justify it, for surely they are doing me a kindness by calling my attention to the dangers of this rock ahead."

Then, noticing how indignant we all were with the slanderers, "What," he would exclaim, "have I given you leave to fly into a passion on my account? Let them talk—it is but a storm in a teacup, a tempest of words that will die away and be forgotten. We must be sensitive indeed if we cannot bear the buzzing of a fly! Who has told us that we are blameless? Possibly these people see our faults better than we see them ourselves, and better than those who love us do. When truths displease us, we often call them slanders. What harm do others do us by having a bad opinion of us? We ought to have a bad opinion of ourselves. Such persons are not our adversaries, but rather our allies, since they enlist themselves on our side in the battle against our self-love. Why be angry with those who come to our aid against so powerful an enemy?"

It happened once that a certain simple-minded woman told our saint bluntly that what she had heard of him had caused her to loose all esteem for him. Blessed Francis replied quietly that her straightforward words only increased his fatherly affection for her, as they were an evidence of great candour, a virtue he highly respected.

The woman proceeded to declare that the reason she was so greatly disappointed in him was because she had been told that he had taken her adversary's part in a law-suit instead of acting as the father of all and siding with none. "Nay," rejoined the Saint, "do not fathers interfere in the quarrels of their children, judging between right and wrong? Besides, the verdict of the court should have convinced you that you were in the wrong, since it was given against you; and had I been one of the judges I must have decided as they did."

The woman protested that injustice had been done to her, but the Saint quietly and patiently reasoned with her and assured her that although it was natural that she should feel angry at first, yet, when the bandage of passion had fallen from her eyes, she would thank God for having deprived her of that which in justice she could not have retained.

This person finally admitted that she had been in the wrong, but enquired if Blessed Francis was really not annoyed at her having lost her high opinion of him, having formerly regarded him as a Saint. He assured her she was wrong in having done so, and that, far from being annoyed, his esteem for her was all the greater on account of this, her correct judgment. "Believe me," he went on to say, "I am speaking from a sense of truth, and not out of false humility, when I maintain that my friends over-rate me. The fact is, they try to persuade themselves that I really am what they so ardently desire me to be. They expose me to the danger of losing my soul by pride and presumption. You, on the contrary, are giving me a practical lesson in humility, and are thus leading me in the way of salvation, for it is written, God will save the humble of heart."

UPON MERE HUMBLENESS OF SPEECH.

He disliked expressions of humility unless they clearly came from the heart, and said that words of this kind were the flower, the cream, and the quintessence of the most subtle pride, subtle inasmuch as it was hidden even from him who spoke them. He compared such language to a certain sublimated and penetrating poison, which to the eye seems merely a mist.

Those who speak this language of false humility are lifted up on high, whilst in thoughts and motives they remain mean and low. He considered similar fashions of speech to be even more intolerable than the words of vain persons who are the sport of their hearers, and whose empty boasting makes them to be like balloons, the plaything of everybody. A mocking laugh is sufficient to let all the wind which puffs them out escape. Words of humility coming merely from the lips, and not from the heart, lead surely to vanity, though by what seems the wrong road. Those who utter them are like people who take their salary gladly enough, but insist on first making a show of refusing and of saying that they want nothing.

Even excuses proffered in this manner accuse and betray the person who offers them. The truly humble of heart do not wish, to appear humble, but to be humble. Humility is so delicate a virtue that it is afraid of its own shadow, and cannot hear its own name uttered without running the risk of extinction.

UPON VARIOUS DEGREES OF HUMILITY.

Blessed Francis set the highest value upon the virtue of humility, which he called the foundation of all moral virtues, and together with charity, the solid basis of true piety.

He used to say that there was no moral excellence more literally christian than humility, because it was not known even by name to the heathen of old. Even of the most renowned among ancient philosophers, such virtues as they possessed were inflated with pride and self-love.

Not every kind of humility pleased him. He was not willing to accept any as true metal until he had put it to many a test and trial.

1. He required in the first place that there should be genuine self-knowledge. To be truly humble we must recognise the fact that we come from nothing, that we are nothing, that we can do nothing, that we are worth nothing, and in fine that we are idle do-nothings, unprofitable servants, incapable of even forming a single good thought, as of ourselves. Yet self-knowledge, he said, if it stood alone, however praiseworthy in itself, would only render those who possessed it the more guilty if they did not act up to it, in order to become better; because moral virtue being in the will, and mere knowledge only in the understanding, the latter alone cannot in any way pass current as true virtue.

2. He even had some doubt of humility though residing in the will, because it is quite possible to misuse it, and to turn humility itself into vanity. Take for instance those who,

having been invited to a banquet, take at once possession of the very lowest place, or of one which they know to be inferior to that due to their rank. They may do this on purpose to be invited to go higher amidst the applause of the company, and with advantage to themselves. He called this a veritable entering into vanity, and through the wrong door: for the truly humble do not wish to appear humble, but only vile and lowly. They love to be considered as of no accounts and, as such, to be despised and rebuffed.

3. Even this did not satisfy him. He was not content with mere natural virtue, but insisted that humility must be Christian, given birth to, and animated by charity. Otherwise he held it in small esteem, refusing to admit that among christians it suffices to practise virtues in pagan fashion. But what is this infused and supernatural humility? It is to love and delight in one's own humiliation, for the reason that by its means we are able to give glory to God, Who accepts the humility of His servants, but puts far away from His heart the proud in spirit.

4. Again, our Saint taught that in striving to please God by bearing humiliations, we should aim at accepting such as are not of our own choice rather than those that are voluntary. He used to say that the crosses fashioned by us for ourselves are always of the lightest and slenderest, and that he valued an ounce of resignation to suffering above pounds' weight of painful toil, good though it might be in itself, undertaken of one's own accord.

5. Quiet endurance of reproaches, contempt, or depreciation, was, in his opinion, the true touch-stone of humility, because it renders us more like to Jesus Christ, the Prototype of all solid virtue, Who humbled and

annihilated Himself, making Himself obedient unto death, even the ignominious death of the Cross.

6. He commended voluntary seeking after humiliations, yet he insisted upon great discretion being practised in this search, since it easily happens that self-love may subtly and imperceptibly insinuate itself therein.

7. Next he considered that the highest, or more properly speaking, deepest degree of humility is that of taking pleasure and even delight in humiliations, reputing them to be in truth the greatest of honours, and of being just as much ill-content with honours as vain persons are with contempt and contumely.

In illustration of this he would quote Moses, who preferred the reproach of Israel to the glories of a kingdom offered to him by Pharaoh's daughter; of Esther, who hated the splendid ornaments with which they decked her to make her pleasing in the eyes of Assuerus; of the Apostles, whose greatest joy was to suffer shame and reproach for the name of Jesus; and of David, who danced before the Ark amid a crowd of buffoons and mountebanks, and who exulted in thus making himself appear contemptible in the eyes of Michol, his wife.

8. Blessed Francis called humility a descending charity, and charity an ascending humility. The former he compared to those streams which come down from the heights and flow down into the valleys. The latter to the slender column of smoke spoken of in the Canticle[1] which rises up towards Heaven, and is composed of all the sweet essences of the perfumer.

9. The Saint next gives a rare lesson on the measure or means of gauging humility. Obedience is to be its source

and touch-stone. This teaching he grounded on the saying of St. Paul: that our Lord humbled Himself, making Himself obedient.[2] "Do you see," he would say, "by what scale humility must be measured? By obedience. If you obey promptly, frankly, cheerfully, without murmuring, expostulating, or replying, you are truly humble. Nor without humility can one be easily and really obedient, for obedience demands submission of the heart, and only the truly humble look upon themselves as inferior to all and as subject to every creature for the love of Jesus Christ. They ever regard their fellow-men as their superiors, they consider themselves to be the scorn of men and the off-scouring of the world. Thus these two virtues, like two pieces of iron, by friction one with the other, enhance each other's brightness and polish. We are humble only in as far as we are obedient, and in fine we are pleasing to God only in as far as we have charity."

10. He recommended all to endeavour to steep their every action in the spirit of humility, as the swan steeps in water each morsel she swallows, and how can this be done except by hiding our good works as much as we can from the eyes of men, and by desiring that they may be seen only by Him to Whom all things are open, and from Whom nothing can be hid. Our Saint himself, urged by this spirit, said that he would have wished, had there been any goodness in him, that it might have been hidden from himself as well as from all others until the Judgment Day, when the secrets of all hearts will be revealed. The Gospel itself exhorts us to observe this secrecy, for it warns us to serve God in secret, and by hiding our virtues, our prayers, our almsgiving, fittingly to worship Him, Who is a hidden God.

11. Blessed Francis did not, however, desire that we should put ourselves to the constraint and discomfort of avoiding

good actions simply because of their being praiseworthy in the eyes of others. What he approved of was a noble, generous, courageous humility, not that which is mean, timid, and cowardly. True, he would not that anything should be done for so low a motive as to win the praise of men, but at the same time he would not have an undertaking abandoned for fear of its success being appreciated and applauded. "It is only very weak heads," he said, "that are made to ache by the scent of roses."

12. Above all things, he recommended people not to speak either in praise or blame of themselves save when doing so is absolutely necessary, and then with great reticence. It was his opinion (as it was Aristotle's) that both self-praise and self-blame spring from the same root of vanity and foolishness. "As for boasting, it is," he said, "so ridiculous a weakness that it is hissed down by even the vulgar crowd. Its one fitting place is in the mouth of a swaggering comedian. In like manner words of contempt spoken of ourselves by ourselves, unless they are absolutely heartfelt and come from a mind thoroughly convinced of the fact of its own misery, are truly the very acme of pride, and a flower of the most subtle vanity; for it rarely happens that he who utters them either believes them himself or really wishes others to believe them: on the contrary, the speaker is mostly only anxious rather to be considered humble, and consequently virtuous, and seeks that his self-blame should redound to his honour. Self-dispraise in general is no more than a tricky kind of boasting. It reminds me of oarsmen who turn their backs on the very place which with all the strength of their arms they are striving to reach."

The above sentiments of Blessed Francis with regard to humility are very striking, but it is much more worthy of note that he himself carried his principles strictly into practice. His actions were so many model lessons and living precepts on the subject. O God! how pleasing must the sacrifice of his humility have been in Thine eyes which look down so closely upon the humble, but regard the proud only from afar.

[Footnote 1: Cant. iii. 6.]

[Footnote 2: Philipp. ii. 8.]

UPON HUMILIATION.

The great lesson which on all possible occasions Blessed Francis inculcated on those who were fortunate enough to come into contact with him, and to treat with him concerning their soul's welfare, was that which our Saviour teaches. Learn of Me, because I am meek and humble of heart.[1] Not, however, that he attached the meaning to the words meek, and humble, often, but very erroneously, given to them.

By meekness he did not understand a kind of honeyed sweetness, too often mixed with a good deal of affectation and pretention. A wolf's heart may be hidden under the fleece and gentle seeming of a lamb, and underneath an outside covering of humility may lurk secret arrogance, such that while appearing to lie down to be trodden under men's feet, those humble after this fashion may by pride in their own pretended state of perfection be putting all men under their own feet. Our Lord's words, If any man will come after Me, let him deny himself take up his cross, and follow Me, Blessed Francis, in one of his letters, explained as follows:

"It is to walk side by side with our crucified Bridegroom, to abase ourselves, to humble ourselves, to despise ourselves even to the death of all our passions; yea, I say, even to the death of the Cross. But observe, my dear daughter, that this abasement, this humility, this contempt of ourselves, must, as I have told you before, be practised gently, quietly, persistently, and not only sweetly, but gladly and joyously."

[Footnote 1: Matt. xi. 20.]

HUMILITY WITH REGARD TO PERFECTION.

Whatever perfection the just man may recognize in himself, he is like the palm tree, which, says the Psalmist, the higher it rears its lofty head the deeper down in the earth it casts its roots.

And certainly, since all our perfection comes from God, since we have no good or perfect gift which we have not received from the Father of Lights, we have no reason to glorify ourselves.

Truly, we can do nothing of ourselves as of ourselves, all our sufficiency, in good, proceeding from God. Our vanity is such that as soon as we begin to suspect we are not guilty, we regard ourselves as innocent, forgetting that if we do not fail in one direction we do in another, and that, as St. Gregory says, our perfection, in proportion to its advancement, makes us the better perceive our imperfections.

Without purity how should we recognise impurity? It is light which makes us understand what darkness is. Many people not discerning in themselves certain particular vices think that they possess the opposite virtues, and are deceived.

Again, seeing themselves freed from some earthly passions they imagine themselves to be clothed in heavenly affections; and thus their ill-advised heart is darkened, they feed upon wind, and walk on in the vanity of their thoughts.

Our Blessed Father, reflecting one day upon the condition of his soul and feeling it to be enjoying great peace owing to its detachment from creatures, made his own the sentiments of the great Apostle, who, though not feeling himself guilty of anything, yet did not therefore consider himself justified, and who forgetting the past pressed on always farther and farther, never thinking that he had yet reached the goal of perfection.[1]

I must read you the passage in which he expresses this view of himself:—

"I find my soul a little more to my liking than usual, because I see nothing in it which keeps it attached to this world, and because it is more alive to the things of the next, to its eternal joys. Ah! if I were but as closely and consciously united to God as I am dissevered and alienated from the world, how happy I should be! And you, too, my daughter, how rejoiced you would be! But I am speaking of my feelings, and my inward self; as regards the exterior, and, worst of all, as regards my deportment and behaviour, they are full of all sorts of contradictory imperfections. The good which I wish to do, I do not do; but nevertheless I know well that truly and with no pretence, I do wish to do it, and with a most unchanging will. But, my Daughter, how can it be that out of such a will so many imperfections show themselves as are continually springing up within me? Certainly, they are not of my will, though they be in my will, and on my will. They are like the mistletoe which grows and appears on a tree and in a tree, although it is not of the tree, nor out of the tree."

[Footnote 1: Philipp. iii. 13.]

UPON EXCUSES.

Although to excuse ourselves for our faults is in many circumstances blameworthy, whilst in general to accuse ourselves of them is laudable, still when self-accusation is carried too far, it is apt to run into affectation, making us wish to pass for something different from what we really are, or, with scrupulosity, making us persuade ourselves that we are what we describe ourselves to be.

It is true that the just man is his own accuser and that, knowing his faults, he declares them simply, in order to be cured of them by wholesome corrections. It is also true that it is a bad thing to excuse oneself, an excuse being always worse than the fault committed, inasmuch as it shows that we think we were right in committing the fault; a persuasion which is contrary to truth.

If our first parents had not excused themselves, the man throwing the blame on the woman, the woman on the serpent, and if, on the contrary, confessing their sin, they had repented, they would have crushed the serpent while in the act of wounding them, and God, who had invited them to this repentance by His loving rebuke, Adam, where art thou? would in His mercy, have surely pardoned them.

This was what made David pray that God would set a watch before his mouth, and on his lips, lest he should be led to utter evil words. By evil words he means excuses which we invent to cover our sins.[1]

Our Blessed Father advises us as follows: "Be just, and without mature consideration, neither excuse nor accuse your poor soul, lest if you excuse it when you should not, you make it insolent, and if you accuse it lightly, you discourage it and make it cowardly. Walk simply and you will walk securely." I once heard him utter these striking words: "He who excuses himself unjustly, and affectedly, accuses himself openly and truly; and he who accuses himself simply and humbly, deserves to be excused kindly and to be pardoned lovingly."
There is a confession which brings confusion, and another which brings glory. Confession, says St. Ambrose, is the true medicine for sin to him who repents of wrong doing.

[Footnote 1: Psalm cxl. 3, 4.]

UPON OUR GOOD NAME.

It is hardly likely that Blessed Francis could have been ambitious of the empty honours attached to an office at court since he did not even trouble himself to keep up his own reputation, except in as far as it might serve to advance the glory of God, which was not only the great but the one passion of his heart.

When a very serious accusation against him was carried to the court, he tells us: "I remained humble and silent, not even saying what I might have said in my defence, but contenting myself with bearing my suffering in my heart. The effect of this patience has been to kindle in my soul a more ardent love of God, and also to light up the fire of meditation. I said to God: Thou art my Protector, and my Refuge in this tribulation, it is for Thee to deliver me out of it. O God of truth, redeem me from the calumny of men!"

He wrote as follows on the same subject to a holy soul who was far more keenly interested in what concerned him than in what affected herself: "After all, Providence knows the exact amount of reputation which is necessary to me, in order that I may rightly discharge the duties of the service to which I have been called, and I desire neither more nor less than it pleases that good Providence to let me have."

UPON DESPISING THE ESTEEM OF MEN.

He had no desire that we should make light of our reputation, or be careless about it, but he wished us to guard it for the service of God rather than for our own honour; and more to avoid scandal than to glorify ourselves.

He used to compare reputation to snuff, which may be beneficial if used occasionally and moderately, but which clouds and injures the brain when used in excess; and to the mandrake which is soothing when smelt at a distance, but if brought too close, induces drowsiness and lethargy.

In his Philothea he devotes one chapter to the subject of guarding our reputation, while at the same time practising humility.[1] He did not, however, content himself with teaching by precept; he went much further, and continually impressed his lesson on others by his example. On one occasion, writing to me about some slanderous reports which had been spread in Paris against him, on account of conscientious and holy advice which he had given to virtuous people who had sought counsel of him, he expressed himself in these words: "I am told that they are cutting my reputation to pieces in Paris, but I hope that God will build it up again, stronger than ever, if that is necessary for His service. Certainly I do not want it except for that purpose, for, provided that God be served, what matters whether it be by good or evil report, by the exaltation, or by the defamation of our good name?"

"Ah," he said to me one day, "what is a man's reputation, that so many should sacrifice themselves to this idol? After all,—it is nothing but a dream, a phantom, an opinion, so much smoke; praise of which the very remembrance perishes with its utterance; an estimate which is often so false that people are secretly amused to hear themselves extolled for virtues, whose contrary vices they know to be dominating them, and blamed for faults from which they are happily quite free. Surely those who complain of being slandered are over-sensitive! Their little cross, made of words, is so light that a breath of wind carries it away. The expression, 'stung me,' meaning 'abused me,' is one that I have never liked, for there is a great deal of difference between the humming of a bee, and its stinging us! We must indeed have sensitive ears, if mere buzzing stings them!

"Truly, those were clever people who invented the proverb: 'A good name is better than riches'; preferring reputation to wealth, or, in other words, vanity to avarice. Oh, my God! how far removed is this from the spirit of faith! Was there ever any reputation more torn to pieces than that of Jesus Christ? With what insults was He not overwhelmed? With what calumnies was He not loaded? And yet the Father has given Him a name which is above every name, and exalted Him the more, the more he was humbled. Did not the Apostles also come forth rejoicing from the presence of the Council where they had received affronts—for the name of Jesus?

"Oh, it is a glorious thing to suffer in so worthy a cause! But too often we will have none but open persecutions, so that our light may shine in the midst of darkness, and that our vanity may be gratified by a display of our sufferings. We should like to be crucified gloriously in the midst of an admiring crowd. What! think you that the martyrs when they were suffering their cruel tortures, were praised by the spectators for their patience? On the contrary, they were reviled and held up to execration. Ah! there are very few who are willing to trample under foot their own reputation, if so be, they may thereby advance the glory of Him Who died an ignominious death upon the Cross, to bring us to a glory which has no end."

[Footnote 1: Part iii. chap. vii.]

UPON THE VIRTUES WE SHOULD PRACTISE WHEN CALUMNIATED.

Blessed Francis was once asked if we ought not to oppose calumny with the weapons of truth, and if it was not as much our duty to keep, for God's sake, our good name, as our bodily strength. He answered that on such occasions many virtues were called into exercise, each claiming precedence over the other.

The first is truth to which the love of God and of ourselves in God, compels us to bear testimony. Nevertheless that testimony has to be calm, gentle, kindly, given without Irritation or vehemence, and with no anxiety about consequences. Our Saviour, when He was accused of having a devil, answered quite simply, "I have not a devil."[1]

If you should be blamed for any scandalous fault, of which, however, you know you are not guilty, say candidly and quietly that, by the grace of God, you are innocent of such a sin. But, if you are not believed, humility now claims her right and bids you say that you have indeed many greater faults unknown to the world, that you are in every way miserable and that if God did not sustain you in your weakness, you would commit far greater crimes than you are accused of.

This sort of humility is in no way prejudicial to truth, for was it not from the depths of true humility that David cried out saying, that if God had not aided him his soul would have dwelt in hell.[2]

Should the tempest of evil speaking continue, silence steps to the front, and offers her calm resistance to the storm, following the teaching of the Royal Prophet, who says: And I became as a dumb man not opening his mouth.[3]

Answering is the oil which feeds the lamp of calumny, silence is the water which extinguishes it. If silence is unavailing, then patience reminds you that it is her turn to act, and, coming forward; shelters you with her impenetrable shield; patience, as Holy Scripture tells us, makes our work perfect.

If we be still assailed, we must call to our aid constancy, which is a kind of double-lined buckler of patience, impervious to the most violent thrusts.

But should evil tongues, growing yet sharper and keener, cut to the very quick, longanimity, which is an unfailing, undying patience, is ready to enter the lists, and eager to help us. For when persecution, instead of yielding to our patience, is only the more irritated thereby, like a fire which burns more fiercely in frosty weather, then is the time for us to practise the virtue of longanimity.

And last of all comes perseverance, which goes with us to the very end and without which the whole network of virtues would fall to pieces; for it is the end which crowns the work, and he who perseveres to the end shall be saved.

Indeed, who can say how many more virtues claim a place in this bright choir? Prudence, gentleness, modesty of speech, and many another, circle round their queen, holy charity, who is indeed the life and soul of them all. Charity it is which bids us bless those who curse us, and pray for those who persecute us; and this same charity not unfrequently transforms our persecutors into protectors and changes slanderous tongues into trumpets to sound our praise.

[Footnote 1: John viii. 49.]

[Footnote 2: Psalm xciii. 17.]

[Footnote 3: Id. xxxvii. 14.]

UPON SOME SPIRITUAL MAXIMS.

On one occasion somebody quoted in his presence the maxims of a very great and very holy person (St. Teresa) on the way to attain perfection.

Despise the world. Despise no man.

Despise yourself. Despise being despised.

"Be it so," observed our Blessed Father, "as regards the three first sayings, but, in regard to the fourth, to my mind, the very highest degree of humility consists in loving and cherishing contempt, and in being glad to be despised. David so acted, when he showed himself pleased to be despised as a buffoon by his own wife Michol. St. Paul, too, gloried in having been scourged, stoned, and looked upon as a fool, the off-scouring and very refuse of the world. The Apostles came forth rejoicing from the presence of the Councils in which, for the love of Jesus, they had been loaded with opprobrium, contumely, and contempt. A really humble man despising himself, is only too glad to find others ready to agree with him, and to help him to humble himself. He receives reproaches as God's good gift, and deems himself unworthy of aught else."

He had something, too, to say about the first three maxims. Taking the world in the sense of the universe, it is, he said, a great stage, on which are shown the wonders of Almighty God, all of Whose works are very good—nay, are perfect. But, even taking the word "world" in the sense in which it is mostly used in Scripture, meaning the company of the wicked, he said, that we should indeed despise their vices, yet not themselves; for who knows but that they will in the end, be converted? How many vessels of contempt have been, by the change of the right hand of God, transformed into vessels of honour?

To despise no one, which is the second dictum, seems at first sight to contradict the first, if, by "the world" be meant the vicious and not merely their vices. It is certainly very right to despise no one, but it is still more reasonable and more advantageous to ourselves, who wish to advance in perfection, to value and esteem all men, because created by

God to His image, and because fitted for partaking of His grace and of His glory.

The third maxim, which tells us to despise ourselves, also needs some explanation. We ought not under pretence of humility to slight and despise the graces which God has given us. To do so would be to throw ourselves over the precipice of ingratitude in order to avoid perishing in the pitfall of vanity, "Nothing," said he, "can so humble us before the mercy of God, as the multitude of his benefits; nothing can so abase us before the throne of His justice, as the countless number of our misdeeds. We need never fear that the good things God has given us will feed our pride, as long as we remember that whatever there may be in us that is good, it is not of us."

UPON PATIENCE.

I was complaining to him one day of a great injury which had been done to me. He answered, "To anybody but you I should try to apply some soothing balm of consolation, but your circumstances, and the pure love which I bear to you, dispense me from this act of courtesy. I have no oil to pour into your wound, and, indeed, were I to affect to sympathise with you, it might only increase the pain of the wound you have received. I have nothing but vinegar and cleansing salt to pour in, and I must simply put in practice the command of the Apostle: Reprove, entreat.[1] You finished your complaint by saying that great and tried patience was needful to enable a man to bear such attacks in silence. Certainly, your patience is not of so high a stamp, since you reserve to yourself the privilege of lamentation!"

"But, Father," I replied, "you see it is only into your heart that I pour out my sorrow. When a child is troubled to whom should it turn if not to its kind father?" "You, a child, indeed; and for how long do you mean to go on clinging to your childhood? Is it right that one who is the father of others, one to whom God has given the rank of a Bishop in His Church, should play the child? When we are children, says St. Paul, we may speak as children, but not when we are become men. The lisping which pleases us in a baby is altogether unsuitable for a sturdy boy. Do you wish me to give you milk and pap instead of solid food? Am I like a nurse to breathe softly on your hurt? Are not your teeth strong enough to masticate bread, the hard bread of suffering? Have you forgotten how to eat bread? Are your teeth set on edge by eating sour grapes? It is a fine thing, indeed, for you to complain to an earthly father, you, who ought to be saying with David to your heavenly Father: I was dumb and I opened not my mouth, because thou hast done it.[2]

"'But,' you will say, 'it is not God but wicked men who have done this to me!'

"Ah, indeed! and do you forget that it is what is called the permissive will of God which makes use of the malice of men, either to correct you or to exercise you in virtue? Job says: The Lord gave and the Lord hath taken away. [3] He does not say: The devil and the thieves took my goods and my dear ones from me: he sees only the hand of God which does all these things by such instruments as it pleases Him to use. You seem unfortunately to have no wish to rank yourself with him who said that the rod and staff with which God struck him brought him consolation; [4] and that he was like a man helpless and abandoned, yet, nevertheless, free from the dead;[5] that he was as one deaf and dumb, who paid no heed to the insults poured into his ears; [6] that he was humbled in the dust, and kept silence even from good words, which might have served to justify him and to defend his innocence.

"'But, Father,' you continue, 'how is it that you have become so harsh, and have changed your gentleness, as Job says to Almighty God, into cruelty? Where is your unfailing compassion?' I answer, my compassion is as great and as sincere as ever; for God knows how much I love you, since I love you more than myself, and how I should reproach myself if I allowed my heart to be hardened against you. It is, however, too clear that the injury you have received is resented by you, since you complain of it. We do not usually complain of what pleases us, quite the reverse, we are glad and rejoice and expect to be congratulated, not pitied. Witness the great parables of the finding of the lost sheep and the lost groat.'

"'Well,' you reply, 'and do you really want me to tell you that black looks exhilarate me, and that I can bear smoke puffed in my face without even sneezing?'

"O man of little faith and of most limited patience! What then of our Gospel maxims as to giving our cheek to the smiter, and our beard to those who pluck it out; what of the beatitude of the persecuted; of the giving our coat to him who takes away our cloak; of blessing those who curse us; of a cordial and hearty love of our enemies? Are these sayings, think you, only curiosities to be put in a cabinet; are they not rather those seals of the Spouse, which He desires us to set upon our hearts and our arms, on our thoughts and on our works?

"Well, well, I pardon you from indulgence, to use the expression of the Apostle, but, on condition that you will be more courageous for the future, and that you will shut up tightly in the casket of silence all like favours which God sends to you, so as not to let their perfume escape, and that you will render thanks in your heart to our Father in Heaven, Who deigns to bestow upon you a tiny splinter from the Cross of His Son. What! you delight in wearing a heavy cross of gold upon your breast, and you cannot bear the weight of one light as is your own upon your heart, but must needs try to rid yourself of it by complaining! Then, again, even when it is gone, you must needs talk about what you have put up with, and would like me to consider you patient merely because you do not openly resent the wrong done you. As if the great virtue of patience consisted only in the not revenging yourself, and not much more, as it really does, in uttering no word of complaint.

"Moreover, it appears to me that you are quite wrong in so much as talking about being patient under injuries such as you have suffered. Patience is too distinguished a virtue to be needed for so trivial an act—the lesser good qualities of moderation, forbearance, and silence would amply suffice. In silence and In hope shall your strength be."[7] So he dismissed me, ashamed of myself, it is true, but, like the giant of fable, strengthened by having fallen. On leaving him I felt as if all the insults in the world would henceforth fail to make me utter one single word of complaint. I was much consoled afterwards by coming across, in one of his letters, the same remark about moderation and forbearance as he had then addressed to me. He writes: "Nothing can have a more tranquillizing effect upon us in this world than the frequent consideration of the afflictions, necessities, contempts, calumnies, insults, and humiliations which our Lord suffered from His birth to His most painful death. When we contemplate such a weight of bitterness as this, are we not wrong in giving to the trifling misfortunes which befall us, even the names of adversities and injuries? Are we not ashamed to ask a share of His divine patience to help us to bear such trifles as these, seeing that the smallest modicum of moderation and humility would suffice to make us bear calmly the insults offered to us?"

[Footnote 1: 2 Tim. iv. 2]

[Footnote 2: Psalm xxxviii. 10.]

[Footnote 3: Job i. 21.]

[Footnote 4: Psalm xxii. 4.]

[Footnote 5: Psalm lxxxvii. 5, 6.]

[Footnote 6: Psalm xxxvii. 15.]

[Footnote 7: Isaiah xxx. 15.]

HOW TO PROFIT BY BEARING WITH INSULTS.

He used to say that a harvest of virtues could be gathered in from a crop of affronts and injuries, because they offer us in abundance opportunities of making such acts as the following:

1. Of justice; for who is there that has not sinned and consequently has not deserved punishment? Has anyone offended you? Well, think how often you have offended God! Surely, therefore, it is meet that creatures, the instruments of His justice, should punish you.

2. But perhaps you were justly accused? Well, if so, simply acknowledge your fault, asking pardon of God as well as of men, and be grateful to those who have accused you, even though they have done it in such a manner as to add unnecessary bitterness to your suffering. Remember that medicines are none the less salutary for being nauseous.

3. But may-be you were accused falsely? If so, calmly and quietly, but without hesitation, bear witness to the truth. We owe this to our neighbours, who might, if we were silent, believe the charge brought against us, and thus be greatly disedified.

4. Yet, if, after this, people persist in blaming you, abandon any further defence of yourself, and conquer by silence, modesty, and patience.

5. Prudence has its own part to play in the conflict; for there is no better way of dealing with insults than by treating them with contempt. He who gives way to anger looks as if he acknowledged the truth of the accusation.

6. Discretion, too, comes to the aid of prudence by counselling toleration.

7. Courage in all its power and grandeur raises you above yourself.

8. Temperance bridles your passions and curbs them into submission.

9. Humility will make you love and value your humiliation.

10. Faith will, as St. Paul says, stop the mouths of lions, and more than this, it will, he says, set before our eyes for our loving contemplation and imitation Jesus Christ Himself, overwhelmed with insults and calumnies, yet silent, unmoved, as one who hears not and is dumb.

11. Hope will hold out before you an imperishable crown, the reward of your trials and sufferings which endure but for a moment.

12. Charity, last of all, will come to you and abide with you—charity, patient and sweet, benign and yielding, believing all, hoping all, enduring all, ready and willing to suffer all.

The more we value our eternal salvation the more heartily shall we welcome suffering.

UPON BEARING WITH IMPORTUNITIES.

Blessed Francis laid great stress upon the necessity of patience when we are importuned. "Yet," he would say, "patience seems almost too great a power to invoke in this matter. In reality a little gentleness, forbearance, and self-control ought to suffice. Still, when we speak of patience it must not be as if it were to be employed only in the endurance of really great evils, for, while we are waiting for these notable occasions that occur rarely in a lifetime, we neglect the lesser ones. We imagine that our patience is capable of putting up with great sufferings and affronts, and we give way to impatience under the sting or bite of an insect. We fancy that we could help, wait upon, and relieve our neighbour in long or severe sickness, and yet we cannot bear that same neighbour's ill-bred manner, and irritating moods, his awkwardness and incivility, and above all his importunity, especially if he comes just at the wrong moment to talk to us about matters which seem to us frivolous and unimportant.

"We triumphantly excuse ourselves for our impatience on these occasions by alleging our deeps sense of the value of time; that one only thing, says an ancient writer, with regard to which avarice is laudable.

"But we fail to see that we employ this precious time in doing many things far more vain and idle than in the satisfying the claims of our neighbour, and possibly less important than those about which he talks to us, occasioning what we call loss of time.

"When we are conversing with others we should try to please them and to show that their conversation is agreeable to us, and when we are alone we should take pleasure in solitude. Unfortunately, however, our minds are so inconsistent that we are always looking behind us, like Lot's wife. In company we sigh for solitude, and in solitude, instead of enjoying its sweets, we hanker after the company of others."

THAT HE WHO COMPLAINS SINS.

One of Blessed Francis' most frequent sayings was: He who complains, seldom does so without sinning. Now, you are anxious to know what exactly he meant by this, and if it is not allowable to complain to superiors of wrongs which have been done us, and when we are ill, to seek relief from suffering, by describing our pains to the physician, so that he may apply to them the proper remedies.

To put this interpretation on the words of Blessed Francis is to overstrain their meaning. The letter killeth, and needs to be interpreted by the spirit that quickeneth, that is, to be taken gently and sweetly.

Our Blessed Father condemns complaining when it borders upon murmuring. He used to say that those who thus complained sinned, because our self-love always magnifies unduly any wrongs done to ourselves, weighing them in the most deceitful of balances, and applying the most extravagant epithets to things which if done by us to others we should pass over as not worth a thought.

He did not consider it at all wrong to claim from a court of justice, quietly, calmly, and dispassionately, reparation of injuries done to our property, person, or honour. He has, indeed, devoted a whole chapter in his Philothea[1] to demonstrating that we may, without failing in humility or charity, do what is necessary for the preservation of our good name. But human weakness is such that it is difficult even in a court of justice to keep our temper and retain a proper equanimity: hence the proverb that, in a hundred-weight of law, there is not so much as an ounce of good nature.

It was also his wish that when sick we should state what ails us quite simply and straightforwardly to those who can relieve us, always remembering that God commands us to honour the physician.[2] To Philothea he says: "When you are ill offer your sufferings, pains, and weakness to the service of our Lord, and entreat Him to unite them to the torments which He endured for you. Obey the physician; take medicine, food, and other remedies for the love of God; remembering the gall which He accepted for love of you. Desire to recover your health that you may serve Him, but, if He so will, do not refuse to linger long upon your bed of pain, so as to obey Him; in fine, be ready to die if that is His pleasure, that you may praise and enjoy Him."[3]

It was his opinion that when we complain, however justly, a certain amount of self-love is always at the bottom of the complaint, and that a habit of grumbling is a positive proof of our being too tender of ourselves and too cowardly.

After all, of what use are complaints? They do but beat the air and serve to prove that if we suffer wrong it is with regret, with sadness, and not without some desire of revenging ourselves. An ungreased wheel makes the most noise in turning, and in like manner, he who has the least patience is the first to grumble.

We must remember, however, that all men deceive themselves. Those who complain do not mean to be considered impatient. On the contrary, they tell you that if it were not this particular thing, they would speak and act differently; but that, as it is, if God did not forbid vengeance they would assuredly take it in the most signal manner. Poor Israelites! really brought out of Egypt, but yet still hankering after the leeks and garlic of that miserable country! Truly such feebleness of mind is pitiable, and most unworthy of a soul avowedly consecrated to the service of the Cross of Jesus Christ.

It is not that we are absolutely forbidden to complain under great sufferings of body or mind, or under great losses. Job, the mirror of the patient, uttered many complaints, yet without prejudice to that virtue which made him so highly esteemed by God, and renders him famous in all ages. It would not only be unwise, but possibly a sin, so to conceal bodily suffering—under the pretext of being resolved not to complain—as to refuse to have recourse to either physician or remedies, and thereby to risk bringing ourselves down to the gates of the grave.

Even God, the All-Perfect, does not refrain from pouring forth His complaints against sinners, as we know from many parts of Holy Scripture. We must then in this matter preserve a just medium, and although it behoves us sometimes to suffer in silence, yet at other times we must make known our sufferings, since that suffering is truly the most wretched which, amid torments, has no voice.[4]

The Son of God, the pattern of all perfection, wept and cried aloud at the grave of Lazarus and on the Cross, showing that He pities our sufferings and shares our griefs. The measure of our complainings must be fixed by discretion, which St. Anthony calls the regent and ruler of the kingdom of virtues, appointed to guard it from the encroachments of sin, ever striving to gain dominion there.

Our Blessed Father gives us the following lesson on the subject: "We must," he says, "abstain from a but little noticed, yet most hurtful imperfection, against which few people guard themselves. This is, that when we are compelled to blame our neighbour or to complain of his conduct, which should be as seldom as possible, we never seem to get done with the matter, but go on perpetually repeating our complaints and lamentations; a sure sign of irritation and peevishness and of a heart as yet destitute of true charity. Great and powerful minds only make mourning about great matters, and even these they dismiss as quickly as possible, never giving way to passion or fretfulness."

[Footnote 1: Part iii. chap. vii.]

[Footnote 2: Eccles. xxxviii. 1, 12.]

[Footnote 3: Part iii. chap. 3.]

[Footnote 4: Virgil, Æneid I.]

BLESSED FRANCIS' CALMNESS IN TRIBULATION.

The similitude of the nest of the halcyon or kingfisher, supposed to float on the sea, which our Saint describes so well and applies so exquisitely in one of his letters, was the true picture of his own heart. The great stoic, Seneca, says that it is easy to guide a vessel on a smooth sea and aided by favourable winds, but that it is in the midst of tempests and hurricanes that the skill of the pilot is shown.[1]

So it is with the soul, whose fidelity and loyalty towards the Divine Lover is well tested by sufferings and sorrows.

The more he was crossed, the more he was upset, and, like the palm tree, the more violently the winds beat against him, the deeper and stronger roots he threw out. His own words express this truth so perfectly as to leave no doubt on the subject. He says: "For some time past the many secret contradictions and oppositions which have invaded my tranquil life have brought with them so calm and sweet a peace that nothing can be compared to it. Indeed, I cannot help thinking that they foretell the near approach of that entire union of my soul with God, which is not only the greatest but the sole ambition and passion of my heart."

Oh! blessed servant of Jesus Christ, how absolutely you practised that teaching which you impress so strongly on us in your Theotimus, in the words of blessed Brother Giles. "One to one! one soul to one only love! one heart to one only God!"

To that only God, the King eternal, Immortal, invisible, be honour and glory for ever and ever! Amen.

[Footnote 1: Senec, De Providentia, cap. iv.]

BLESSED FRANCIS' TEST OF PATIENCE IN SUFFERING.

One day he was visiting a sick person who, in the midst of intense suffering, not only showed great patience in all her words and actions, but plainly had the virtue deeply rooted in her heart. "Happy woman," said Blessed Francis, "who has found the honey-comb in the jaws of the lion!"

Wishing, however, to make more certain that the patience she showed was solid and real, rooted and grounded in Christian charity, and such as to make her endure her sufferings for the love and for the glory of God alone, he determined to try her. He began to praise her constancy, to enlarge upon her sufferings, to express admiration at her courage, her silence, her good example, knowing that in this way he would draw from her lips the true language of her heart.

Nor was he deceived, for she, sincere and absolutely patient Christian that she was, answered him: "Ah! Father, you do not see the rebellious struggles of all my senses and feelings. In the lower region of my soul everything is in confusion and disorder, and if the grace and fear of God were not to us as a tower of strength I should long ago have altogether given way and rebelled against God. Picture me to yourself as like the Prophet whom the Angel carried by one hair of his head; my patience, as it were, hangs on a single thread, and were it not for the mighty help God is to me I should long ere now have been in hell.

"It is not then my virtue but the grace of God in me which makes me show so much courage. My own part in the matter is but pretence and hypocrisy. Were I to follow my own impulses I should moan, struggle, break out into passionate and bitter words, but God restrains my lips with bit and bridle, so that I dare not murmur under the blows dealt by His hand which I have learnt through His grace to love and honour."

Our Blessed Father, on leaving her sick-room, said to those who were with him, "She has, indeed, true and Christian patience. Instead of pitying her for her sufferings we ought rather to rejoice over them, for this high virtue is only made perfect in infirmity. But do you notice how God hides from her own eyes the perfection which He is giving her? Her patience is not only courageous, but loving and humble; like pure balm, which, when unadulterated, sinks to the bottom of the water into which it is cast. Be careful, however, not to repeat to her what I have just said to you lest, by doing so, you should excite in her movements of vanity, and spoil the whole work of grace, whose waters only flow through the valley of humility.

"Let her peacefully possess her soul in patience, for she is at peace even in this extremity of bitterness."

UPON LONG ILLNESSES.

Violent sicknesses either pass quickly or they carry us to the grave; slow maladies drag wearily on and exercise the patience of the sufferers, nor less that of those who tend them.

Our Blessed Father says on the subject: "Long sicknesses are good schools of mercy for those who wait upon the sick and of loving patience for those who suffer.

"They who wait upon the sick are at the foot of the Cross with our Lady and St. John, whose compassion they imitate; the sick man himself is on the Cross with our Saviour, Whose Passion he imitates.

"But how can we imitate either this compassion or this Passion if we do not suffer from the motive of the love of God? For the Blessed Virgin and St. John, the beloved Disciple, were moved by a compassion as much more sorrowful than ours, as their love for the Crucified, their own dearest Lord, was greater than ours can be. It was at the foot of the Cross that the sword of grief pierced Mary's soul, and it was there that the beloved disciple drank that chalice of bitterness, which, after permitting him to share the glories of Thabor, the Saviour predicted should be his."

The whole life of a true Christian is one long period of suffering. Those who endure not with Jesus Christ, are not fit to reign with Him. "O soul in grace," says our Blessed Father, "thou art not yet the spouse of Jesus glorified, but of Jesus crucified. This is why the rings, necklaces, and other ornaments which He gives you, and with which He is pleased to adorn you, are crosses, nails, and thorns; and the marriage feast He sets before you gall, hyssop, and vinegar. It is in Heaven we shall possess the rubies, diamonds, and emeralds, the wine, the manna, and the honey." The world is a vast quarry in which are hewn out and shaped those living stones which are to build up the heavenly Jerusalem, as the Church sings:

Tunsionibus, pressuris,

Expoliti lapides

Suis cooptantur locis,

Per manus Artificis:

Disponuntur permansuri

Sacris ædificiis.[1]

Thou too, O Church, which here we see,

No easy task hath builded thee.

Long did the chisels ring around!

Long did the mallet's blows rebound!

Long worked the head, and toiled the hand!
Ere stood thy stones as now they stand.

[Footnote 1: Office of the Dedication of a Church.]

BLESSED FRANCIS' HOLY INDIFFERENCE IN ILLNESS.

As regards our Blessed Father's patience in time of sickness, I myself was with him in one only of his illnesses, but others, who saw him in many and were frequent witnesses of his patience, gentleness, and absolute indifference to suffering, tell us marvels on that subject.

For my part, on the one occasion when I saw him stretched upon his bed, suffering with so much endurance and sweetness, the sight at once recalled to me what St. Catherine of Genoa tells us of a certain soul in Purgatory. This poor soul she represented as so perfectly united to God by charity that it was physically unable to utter the slightest complaint, or to have the faintest shadow of a desire, which was not absolutely in conformity with the divine will. Such souls, she says, wish to be in Purgatory exactly as long as God shall please, and this, with a will so contented and so constant, that for nothing in the whole world would they be elsewhere unless it were His will. This is exactly how our Blessed Father suffered, without in any way losing heart, because of the services which he might have been able to render to God and his neighbour had he been in health. He wished to suffer because to do so was the good pleasure of God, Who held the keys of his life and of his death, of his health and of his sickness, and of his whole destiny.

If he was asked whether he would take this or that, physic or food, whether he would be bled or blistered, or the like, he had but one answer to give: "Do with the patient what you please, God has put me at the disposal of the doctors." Nothing could be more simple or obedient than his behaviour, for he honoured God in the physicians, and in their remedies, as He Himself has commanded us all to do.

He always told the doctors and attendants exactly what was the matter with him, neither exaggerating his malady by undue complaints, nor making his suffering appear less than it really was by a forced and unnatural composure. The first he said was cowardice, the second dissimulation. Even although the inferior and sensible part of his soul might be under the pressure of intense pain, there always flashed out from his face, and especially from, his eyes, rays of that calm light which illumined the superior and reasonable part of his nature, shining through the dark clouds of bodily affliction. Hence the weaker his body, the stronger became his spirit, enabling him to say with the Apostle:

Gladly, therefore, will I glory in my infirmities, That the power of Christ may dwell in me.[1]

[Footnote 1: 2 Cor. xii. 9.]

UPON THE SHAPE OF THE CROSS.

"The Cross," Blessed Francis says, "is composed of two pieces of wood, which represent to us two excellent virtues, necessary to those who desire to be fastened to it with Jesus Christ, and on it to live a dying life, and on it to die the death which is life. These two great virtues most due to Christians are humility and patience."

He wished, however, that those two virtues should be rooted and grounded in charity, that is to say, not only be practised in charity, that is, in a state of grace, without which they are of no value for Heaven, but also from the motive of charity. This is how he expresses himself:—

"Divine love will teach you that in imitation of the great Lover we must be on the Cross in company with humility, deeming ourselves unworthy to endure anything for Him Who endured so much for us; and in company with patience, so as not to wish to come down from the Cross, not even all our life long if so it pleases the Eternal Father.

"The motto of Blessed Teresa was, To suffer or to die; for divine love had attached this faithful servant of Jesus crucified so closely to the Cross that she wished not to live, save that she might have opportunities of suffering for Him.

"The great and seraphic St. Francis considered that God had forgotten him and lovingly complained when he had passed a day untouched by any suffering; and just as he called poverty his mistress, so he called pain his sister."

Our Blessed Father's motto was "To love or to die." In his Treatise on the Love of God he cries out: "To love, or to die! To die and to love! To die to all other love in order to live to Jesus' love, that we may not die eternally, but that living in Thy eternal love, O Saviour of our souls, we may eternally sing, Vive Jesus, Live Jesus. I love Jesus. Live Jesus, Whom I love! I love Jesus, Who lives and reigns for ever and ever. Amen."[1]

[Footnote 1: Book xii, c. 13.]

A DIAMOND CROSS.

It was one day reported very seriously to Blessed Francis as though it were some misdemeanor, that one of his penitents who was accustomed to wear on her breast a rich diamond ornament, had had the diamonds made up into a cross which she wore in the same manner as before, and that this was a cause of scandal to certain persons. "Ah! he cried, how true it is that the Cross is an occasion of scandal to some, and of edification to others! I do not know who advised this lady to do what she has done, but for my part I am much edified, and only wish that all the gew-gaws and trinkets worn by women could be altered in the same holy manner. That would indeed be to make vessels of the Tabernacle out of their mirrors."[1]

Among his letters I came across lately and with much pleasure, one which I think must have been written to this very lady. In it he says: "When I last had the pleasure of seeing you, dear madam, you were wearing outwardly on your heart a cross; love it fervently, I beseech you. It is all gold if you look at it with loving eyes. On one side it is true that you see the Beloved of your heart, dead, crucified amid nails and thorns; but on the other side you will find a cluster of precious stones ready to adorn the crown of glory which awaits you, if only, meanwhile, you wear lovingly the crown of thorns with your King who willed to suffer so much that He might enter into His joy."

To a lady advanced in years and distinguished by her piety, who was living in my diocese, and whom, out of reverence and affection, he used to call his mother, he wrote as follows, when the infirmities of old age were pressing heavily upon her: "I see very plainly that you must from henceforth accustom yourself to the maladies and infirmities which declining years bring with them. Ah, dear Lord! What happiness for a soul dedicated to God, to be much tried by suffering, before quitting this life! My dearest mother, how can we learn the lesson of generous and fervent love save amid thorns, crosses, languor, and faintness, and more especially when these sufferings are prolonged and lingering. Our dear Saviour showed us the measure of His boundless love by that of His labours, and of His sufferings. Show, my dear mother, your love to the Bridegroom of your heart on the bed of pain; for it was on that bed that He fashioned your heart, even before it came into existence, He beholding it as yet only in His divine plan. Ah! this Divine Saviour has reckoned up all your pains, all your sorrows, and has paid with His Precious Blood for all the patience and the love which you need in order rightly to direct your labours to His glory and to your own salvation. Content yourself with calmly desiring to be all that God wills you to be."

[Footnote 1: Exod. xxxviii. 8.]

HOLY MAGDALEN AT THE FOOT OF THE CROSS.

Our Blessed Father had a special reverence for the picture of Magdalen at the foot of the Cross, calling it sometimes the library of his thoughts. Perhaps this representation was before his mind's eye, when just before he rendered up his soul to God he murmured these words: Wash me yet more from my iniquity and cleanse me from my sin.[1] "Oh!" he exclaimed, when he was looking one day at this picture in my house at Belley, "how happy, and how profitable an exchange this penitent made! She bestowed tears on the Feet of Jesus Christ, and in return those Feet gave back to her Blood, but Blood that washed away all her sins, for Christ has cleansed us from every stain in His Blood, and by the sprinkling of this hyssop has made us, coal-black though we were, white as snow! Oh, gracious rain made by

God to fall upon His inheritance, how sweet, how much to be desired thou art!"

"Magdalen seeks our Saviour while she holds Him. She demands Him of Himself. She does not see Him in the form she looked for: therefore, unsatisfied, she seeks Him away from Himself.

"She expected to see Him in His robe of glory, not in the poor garb of a gardener; nevertheless she knew that it was He when He uttered her name Mary.[2]

"My dear sister, my daughter, it is our Lord in the clothing of a gardener whom you meet every day in one place or another, and in the various mortifications which present themselves to you.

"You wish He would offer you grander mortifications. Oh! my God! the grandest are not the best. Do you not believe that He says to you also Mary, Mary? Ah! before you see Him in His glory, He wishes to plant in your garden many flowers, small and lowly indeed, but such as He loves. That is why He wears a gardener's dress.

"May our hearts be for ever united to His Heart, and our wills to His good pleasure."

[Footnote 1: Psalm l. 4.]

[Footnote 2: John xx. 16.]

UPON THE POWER OF GENTLENESS AND PATIENCE.

An ecclesiastic in Blessed Francis' diocese, had, because of his vicious and scandalous life, been sent to prison. After a few days' sojourn there he testified the deepest repentance, and with tears and promises of amendment entreated the officers of the prison to allow him to be taken to the Holy Prelate, who had already pardoned many of his offences, that he might at his feet plead again for forgiveness.

This request was at first refused, as the officers considered that his scandalous life deserved punishment, if only as an example to others, and they knew that with Blessed Francis, to see a sinner was to pity and forgive him.

At last, however, they yielded to the priest's passionate entreaties, and he was taken before his Bishop. Throwing himself on his knees before the Holy Man, he implored mercy, declaring that he would lead a new life, and set an example of all that was edifying, whereas before he had given nothing but scandal. Blessed Francis on his part knelt down before the culprit, and with many tears, addressed these remarkable words to him; "I, too," he said, "ask you to have pity upon me, and upon all of us who are priests in this diocese, upon the Church, and upon the Catholic, Apostolic, and Roman religion, the honour of which you are ruining by your scandalous life. For that life gives occasion to the adversaries of our Faith, who are always on the watch like dragons to detect our slightest failings, to condemn us. For a priest to sin, I tell you, is to give occasion to devils to mock at the lives of our clergy, and to blaspheme our Holy Faith, I ask you also to have pity on yourself, and on your own soul which you are losing for all eternity, and to seek anew God's favour, I exhort you in the name of Jesus Christ to return to God by a true repentance, I conjure you to do this by all that is most holy, and sacred in Heaven, or on earth, by the Blood of Jesus Christ which you profane, by the loving-kindness of the Saviour, whom you crucify afresh, by the Spirit of Grace against whom you are rebelling." These remonstrances, or rather the Spirit of God speaking by the mouth of this zealous Pastor, had such effect that the guilty man was by this change of the Right Hand of the Most High converted into a perfectly different being, and became as notable an example of virtue as he had been an occasion of scandal.

Again—There was in his diocese a certain ecclesiastic who for very grave faults, and for the scandal occasioned by them, was not only imprisoned and treated while in prison with the greatest severity, but moreover, after regaining his liberty, remained for six months suspended from all ecclesiastical functions.

Our Blessed Father most unwillingly yielded to the entreaties of the officers of justice not in any way to interfere in the matter, but to let the law take its course, and to leave the offender in their hands to be treated with exceptional rigour.

So little, however, did this mode of dealing with the criminal answer, that, though while in prison he had been tractable, humble, lavish of promises of amendment, and apparently penitent, when once he had shaken off his fetters he relapsed into all his old evil habits, and passed from bad to worse. The authorities were in fine constrained to deprive him of his benefice, and to banish him from the diocese.

A few years later a very similar case occurred in which the officers showed the same unwillingness to permit the intervention of Blessed Francis, and this from no want of respect or love for him, but, as before, from a fear lest his gentleness and charity should hinder the course of justice.

In this case, however, the holy Bishop was firm. "If," he said, "you forbid him to appear before me, you will not forbid me to appear before him. You do not wish him to come out of prison, suffer me then to go to prison with him, and to be the companion of his captivity. We must comfort this poor brother, who entreats us for help. I promise you that he shall not leave the prison except with your leave."

Accompanied by the officers of justice he then proceeded to the prison. No sooner did he see the poor man kneeling humbly before his Bishop, and accusing himself of his sins, than the holy Prelate embraced him tenderly, and turning to his gaolers said: "Is it possible that you do not see that God has already pardoned this man? Is there any condemnation for one who is in Christ Jesus? If God justifies him, who shall condemn him? Certainly not I."

Then, turning to the culprit, he said: "Go in peace, my brother, and sin no more, I know that you are truly penitent."

The officials protested that the man was a hypocrite, and like that other suspended priest would himself soon show that they were right. "It is, however, possible," replied the Saint, "that had you treated that other priest with lenity, he, too, would have truly repented; beware, then, lest his soul should one day be required at your hands. For my part, if you will accept me as this man's bail, I am ready to pledge my word for his good behaviour. I am certain that he is sincerely repentant, and even if he is deceiving me, he will do more injury to himself than to me, or others."

The guilty man, bursting into tears, declared himself willing to undergo any penance that might be imposed upon him, and even to give up his benefice of his own accord, if the Bishop should judge this to be the proper course.

"I should be much grieved if you were to take that step," replied Blessed Francis, "the more so as I hope that, just as the steeple in falling crushed the church, so now being set up again it will make it more beautiful than before."

The officials gave way, the prison doors were thrown open, and after a month's suspension, a divinis, the penitent resumed all the duties of his sacred office. Thenceforth he lived so holy and exemplary a life as fully to verify the predictions of his holy Bishop, who, when these two memorable instances, one of perversion and the other of conversion, were once afterwards discussed before him, said: "It is better by gentleness to make penitents than by severity to make hypocrites."

I will now relate some other instances of Blessed Francis' extraordinary gentleness and of its softening effect upon others.

He had made himself surety for a considerable sum of money for one of his friends, who, at the time when payment was due, happened to be in Piedmont levying troops for the service of His Highness the Duke of Savoy.

The creditor becoming impatient for the discharge of the debt, applied to the good Bishop, and insisted upon his making the money good, paying no attention whatever either to his gentle remonstrances, or to his assurances that the debtor, though unable at present to leave his troops, would do so as soon as was consistent with his duty to his Prince and his country, and that meantime his regular payment of the interest, and the knowledge that he was worth a hundred times more than the sum owing, ought surely to satisfy the creditor.

Blessed Francis remained perfectly calm and unmoved amid the storm of invectives and reproaches that followed this remonstrance, and which were accompanied by furious demands reiterated again and again, that he himself as surety should repay the money.

At last, speaking with incredible gentleness, the Saint said: "Son, I am your Pastor. Can you as one of my flock, have the heart to take the bread out of my mouth in place of helping to feed me? You know that I am much straitened in circumstances, and have really only barely enough for my maintenance. I have never had in my possession the sum which you demand of me, but for which, out of charity, I made myself surety: do you wish to seize for it my goods, rather than those of the real debtor? Well, if so, I have some patrimony. I give it up to you: there is my furniture. Turn it all out into the public square, and sell it. I put myself absolutely into your hands to do as you please. I only ask of you to love me for God's sake, and not to offend Him in any way by anger, hatred, or scandal. If you will do this I am content."

The only reply to this was a fresh outburst of furious invectives and accusations, to which our Blessed Father replied with unalterable serenity: "Sir, since my indiscretion in making myself surety for my friend is the cause of your anger, I will with all the haste possible do what I can to satisfy you. At the same time, I wish you to know that had you plucked out one of my eyes, I would have looked as affectionately at you with the other, as at the dearest friend I have in the world."

The creditor retired, covered indeed with confusion, but still muttering injurious words, and calling the holy Bishop a hypocrite, a bigot, and the like. Blessed Francis immediately sent an account of the affair to the real debtor, who came as quickly as was possible and at once discharged the debt. The creditor, full of shame and repentance, hastened to ask pardon of our Blessed Father, and he, receiving the prodigal with open arms, treated him ever afterwards with special tenderness, calling him his friend regained.

Again, when he was in Paris in 1619, having gone there with the Cardinal of Savoy, who wished to be present at the marriage of his brother, the Prince of Piedmont, with Madame Christine of France, the King's sister, our Blessed Father was told that a man of tolerably good position professing the so-called Reformed Religion wished to see him.

Introduced into the Bishop's apartment, the Protestant, without the smallest sign of reverence, or even courtesy, addressed him in these words:

"Are you what they call the Bishop of Geneva?"

"Sir," replied our holy Prelate, "that is my title, though in that city I am not so much in request as I am in the other parts of the diocese committed to my charge."

"Well, I should just like to know from you, who are regarded everywhere as an apostolic man, whether the Apostles were in the habit of going about in carriages?"

Our Blessed Father, in telling me this story, owned that he was somewhat taken aback by the suddenness of this attack! Collecting his thoughts, however, and remembering the case of St. Philip the Deacon, who, though not the Apostle of that name, was undoubtedly an apostolic man, and who went up into the chariot of Queen Candace's eunuch, he answered quietly that they did so when convenience required it, and the occasion for doing so presented itself.

"I should be very glad," replied the man, scornfully, "if you could show me that in Scripture." The Bishop quoted the instance to which we have just referred. His opponent, not noticing the fact of this not being St. Philip the Apostle, retorted, "But this carriage was not his own, it belonged to the eunuch, who invited him to come up into it," "I never told you," answered Francis, "that the carriage was his own. I only said that when the occasion presented itself the first preachers of the Gospel rode in carriages." "But not in gilded coaches such as yours, sir," returned the Protestant, "nor drawn by such splendid horses, nor driven by a coachman in such superb livery. Why, the King himself has nothing better! This is what I complain of; and this it is in you which scandalizes me. And you, above all, who play the Saint, and whom the papists look upon as such. Fine Saints, forsooth, who go to Paradise so much at their ease!"

Blessed Francis, seeing at once where the shoe pinched, answered gently, "Alas, sir, the people of Geneva who have seized upon the property belonging to my See have cut me down so close as regards money that I have barely enough to live upon in the most frugal way. As to a carriage, I have never had one, nor money enough to buy one." "Then that splendid carriage, which is, so to speak, regal, in which I see you every day driving about the city is not your own?" rejoined the antagonist. "Certainly not," replied the Bishop, "and you are quite right in calling it regal, for it belongs to His Majesty, and is one of those set apart by him for people who, like myself, are mere attendants of the Princes of Savoy. The royal livery worn by the servants ought to have shown you this!" "Now, indeed," said the Protestant, "I am satisfied, and I esteem you. I see that you are in the right, and that, notwithstanding, you are humble." After some further remarks he put some questions as to the birth and manner of life of the Saint, and was so perfectly contented with his replies that he quitted him with expressions of esteem and affection, and ever afterwards held him in the highest respect.

Again, preaching during an Advent and Lent at Grenoble, not only a great concourse of Catholics flocked to hear him, but also such numbers of Protestants of the Geneva following that their ministers became alarmed and held meetings to decide what measures should be taken to avert a storm, which threatened desolation to their strongholds and was fast emptying their conventicles. They decided at last on a personal conflict with their opponent, choosing one of their most furious pastors, a man of violent temper and bitter tongue, to argue with Blessed Francis, and, as they expected, to worst him in a controversy. The holy Bishop, who had already had much practice and success in this kind of warfare at Thonon, Ternier, and Gaillard, the bailiwicks of his diocese which he had brought back into the bosom of the True Church, cheerfully agreed to the proposal. In answer to the remonstrances of his friends, and especially of one gentleman of Belley, a man of the greatest probity and piety, who painted the Protestant ministers in the blackest colours, and told the Bishop that insults would literally be heaped upon him, he replied, "Well, that is exactly what we want; this contempt is just what I ask. For how great is the glory to Himself that God will derive from my confusion!" On his friends reminding him that he would be exposing his sacred office to derision, "What of that?" replied the Bishop, "did not our Saviour suffer shame for us—were not insults heaped upon Him?"

"Oh," said the other, "you aim too high." "To tell you the truth," said our Saint, "I am hoping that God will give me the grace to endure insults without end, for when we are finely humbled He will be gloriously exalted. You will see conversion upon conversion following the train of this affair, a thousand falling on the left hand and ten thousand on the right, God is wont at all times to make our infamy redound to His honour. Did not the Apostles come forth rejoicing from those assemblies in which they had suffered contumely for the name of Jesus? Take courage, God will help us; those who hope in Him never lack any good thing and are never confounded."

Was it possible to carry patience further than this? Doubtless, had the meeting taken place, the envenomed darts of heresy would have glanced aside from the spotless, shining shield of Faith carried by Blessed Francis, but the devil, fearing to be worsted in the fight, suggested so many prudent reasons to the Protestant Minister's friends, who, in reality, had their doubts about both his virtue and his capacity for conducting the conference that they got it forbidden by the Lieutenant of the King, though himself at that time a heretic.

Another striking example of patience. A person of some influence and consideration once applied to Blessed Francis asking him to obtain an ecclesiastical preferment for a certain Priest. The Bishop replied that in the matter of conferring benefices he had, of his free will, tied his own hands, having left the choosing of fitting subjects to the decision of a board of examiners, who were to recommend the person to be appointed after due examination of the merits and talents of the candidates. As for himself, he said, he simply presided over the meeting. Should, however, the gentleman's friend present himself as a candidate, he, the Bishop, would promise to bear the recommendation in mind. The petitioner felt piqued at this answer, and quite losing his temper, replied to the Bishop in the most disrespectful and even insulting manner. The gentle firmness with which his anger was met only infuriated him the more, and he eventually lost all command over himself. It was in vain that the Bishop tried to soothe him by proposing to examine the claimant privately. This had no effect.

The Saint then said gently but gravely: "Do you then wish me to give the charge of my sheep blindfolded and to the first comer? Ask yourself if there is reasonableness in such a request as you are making?"

But not even this appeal to his reason turned the flood of the man's wrath, and he quitted the Bishop's presence in a passion of disrespect impossible to describe. A most excellent Priest who had been in the room all through the interview asked the Bishop, after the departure of his impudent visitor, how he could bear such treatment with the patience he showed. "Well," he answered, "it was not he himself that spoke, it was his passion. After all he is one of my best friends, and you will see that my silence on this occasion will only make our friendship the stronger.

"More than this. Has not God from all eternity foreseen that these insults would be offered to me to-day, and foreseen, too, that He would bestow on me such grace as would enable me to bear them joyfully? Should I not drain the chalice held to my lips by the hands of so loving a Father? Oh! how sweet is this inebriating cup, offered to me by a hand which from my infancy I have learnt to adore." "But," returned the Priest, "were not your feelings stirred at all by this treatment?"

"Well," replied the Bishop, "I tried to overcome them by fixing my thoughts on the good qualities of the man whose friendship I have so long and so happily enjoyed. Then, too, I hope that when this storm in a tea-cup has subsided and the clouds of passion have lifted, my friend will come back to me with peace in his heart and serenity on his countenance."

Nor was the Saint's expectation disappointed. His friend did come back, and with many tears begged his forgiveness; a forgiveness which was, you may be sure, granted so fully and with such loving readiness as to increase the fervour and sincerity of their old and mutual affection.

A REJOINDER BOTH STRIKING AND INSTRUCTIVE.

In the course of his long mission in the Chablais, he one day preached on that text which commands us to offer the right cheek to him who smites us on the left. As he came down from the pulpit he was accosted by a Protestant who asked him if he felt that he could practise what he had just preached, or whether he was not rather one of those who preach but do not practise.

The Saint replied: "My dear brother, I am but a weak man and beset by infirmities. At the same time, miserable though I feel myself to be, God teaches me what I ought to do. I cannot tell you what I should actually do, because though the spirit is willing, the flesh is weak. At the same time we know, that while without grace we can do nothing, with its aid we can do everything; a reed in the hand of grace becomes a mighty staff that cannot be broken. If we are told to be willing to give our life itself in defence of our faith, how much more does it behove us to endure some small affront for the maintenance of charity! Moreover, were I to be such a recreant to the grace of God as not to bear an insult of this kind patiently, let me remind you that the same Gospel which reproves those who preach but do not practise, warns us against following the example of such teachers, though it bids us do what they tell us to do."

"Yet," resumed the other, "our Saviour never presented the other cheek to the servant of the High Priest who struck Him; on the contrary He resented the act."

"What!" cried the holy Bishop, "you place our Lord on a level with those who preach but do not practise! That is blasphemy! As for us, we entertain more reverent feelings towards that Model of all perfection. It is not for us to comment on the actions of Him who, as we firmly believe, could not act otherwise than most perfectly. Neither is it for us to dare to say: 'Why hast Thou done thus?' Yet we may well remember His zeal for the salvation of that impious man's soul, and the remonstrances which He deigned to use in order to bring him to repentance. Nay, did He not offer not only His cheek to the smiter, but His whole sacred Body to the cruel scourging which covered Him with wounds from Head to Foot?"

BLESSED FRANCIS' FAVOURITE BEATITUDE.

He was once asked which, in his opinion, was the most perfect of the eight Beatitudes. It was thought that he would answer: "The second, Blessed are the meek," but it was not so; he gave the preference to the eighth: Blessed are they that suffer for justice' sake. He explained his preference by saying that "the life of those who are persecuted for justice' sake is hidden in God with Jesus Christ, and becomes conformable to His image; for was not He persecuted all through His earthly life for justice' sake, although He fulfilled it in all its perfection? Such persons are, as it were, shrouded by the veil which hides the countenance of God. They appear sinful, but they are just; dead, but they live; fools, but they are wise; in a word, though despised in the sight of men, they are dear to God with whom they live for ever.

"Should God have given me one particle of justice, enabling me thereby to do some little good, it would be my wish that in the Day of Judgment, when all secrets are revealed, God alone should know my righteousness, and that my sinful actions should be proclaimed to all creatures."

HIS GRAVITY AND AFFABILITY.

Grace produced in him that wonderful and perfectly harmonious blending of gravity and affability, which was perhaps his most distinguishing characteristic. There was in his whole demeanour and in the very expression of his face a lofty and dignified beauty which inspired reverence and even a sort of fear—that is, such fear as engenders respect and makes any undue familiarity impossible. Yet, at the same time he displayed such sweetness and gentleness as to encourage all who approached him. No one, however conscious of his own want of attractiveness, feared a repulse from the holy Bishop, and all, feeling sure of a welcome, were only eager to please and satisfy him.

For my own part I must confess that when I succeeded in doing anything which he was able to praise, and which consequently gave him pleasure, I was so happy and elated that I felt as if I were raised to the seventh heaven! Indeed, had he not taught me to refer everything to God, many of my actions would, I fear, have stopped half-way thither. People of high standing in society, accustomed even to come into close contact with royalty itself, have assured me that, in the presence of our Saint, they felt a subtle influence guarding, restraining, elevating them as no other companionship, however noble and distinguished, could ever do. It was as though in him they saw some reflection of the all-penetrating intelligence of God Himself, lighting up the inmost recesses of their heart, and laying bare its mysteries.

Yet his affability was no less marvellous, making itself felt the instant you came in contact with him. It was not like a quality or grace acquired; it was not in any way apart from his own personality, it was as if he were affability personified. Hence that power of winning over others, of making himself all things to all men, of gaining the support of so many in his plans and schemes, all of which had but one aim and object, namely, the increase of the glory of God and the promotion of the salvation of souls.

HOW BLESSED FRANCIS DEALT WITH A CRIMINAL WHO DESPAIRED OF SALVATION.

He was once asked to visit in prison a poor criminal already condemned to death, but who could not be induced to make his confession. The unhappy man had committed crimes so terrible that he despaired of the forgiveness even of God, and having often during his lifetime met death face to face in battle and in duels, he appeared to be quite ready again to meet it boldly; nay, so hardened was he by the devil that he even spoke calmly of hell, as of the abode destined for him for eternity.

Our Blessed Father finding him in this frame of mind, and altogether cold, hard, and reckless, proclaiming himself the prey of Satan and a victim prepared for hell, thus addressed him: "My brother, would you not rather be the prey of God and a victim of the Cross of Jesus Christ?" "What," cried the criminal, "do you think that God would have anything to do with a victim as repulsive as I am?"

"Oh, God!" was the silent prayer of Blessed Francis, "remember Thine ancient mercies and the promise which Thou hast made never to quench utterly the smoking flax nor wholly to break the bruised reed. Thou who wiliest not the death of the sinner, but rather that he should be converted and live, make happy the last moments of this poor soul."

Then he spoke aloud replying to the despairing words of the poor wretch, for, horrifying though they were, they had proved to the skilled workman that there was something left to work upon, that faith in God was not yet wholly dead in that poor heart. "At any rate, would you not rather abandon yourself to God than to the evil one?" "Most assuredly," replied the criminal, "but it is a likely thing indeed that' God would have anything to do with a man like me!" "It was for men like you," returned the Bishop, "that the Eternal Father sent His Son into the world, nay for worse than you, even for Judas and for the miscreants who crucified Him. Jesus Christ came to save not the just, but sinners."

"But," cried the other, "can you assure me that it would not be presumption on my part to have recourse to His mercy?" "It would be great presumption," replied our Saint, "to think that His mercy was not infinite, far above all sins not only possible but conceivable, and that His redemption was not so plentiful, but that it could make grace superabound where sin had poured forth a flood of evils. On the contrary, His mercy, which is over all His works, and which always overrides His justice, becomes so much the greater the greater the mountain of our sins.

"Upon that very mountain he sets up the throne of His mercy." With words such as these, kindling, or rather re-animating the spark of faith not yet wholly dead in the soul of the wretched man, he relighted the flame of hope, which up to that moment was quite extinguished, and little by little softened and tamed the man's natural temper, rendered savage by despair. He led him on at last to resignation, and persuaded him to cast himself into the arms of God for death and for life; to deal with him according to His own good pleasure, for his whole future in this world, or in the next.

"But He will damn me," said the man, "for He is just." "No, He will pardon you," replied Blessed Francis, "if you cry to Him for mercy, for He is merciful and has promised forgiveness to whoever implores it of Him with a humble and contrite heart." "Well," replied the criminal, "let Him damn me if he pleases—I am His. He can do with me what the potter does with his clay." "Nay," replied the holy Bishop, "say rather with David, I am Thine, O Lord, save me." Not to make the story too long, I may tell you that the holy Bishop brought this man to confession, repentance, and contrition, and that he died with great constancy, sincerely acknowledging his sins and abandoning himself entirely to the most holy will of God. The last words which our Blessed Father made him utter were these: "O Jesus, I give myself up to Thee—I abandon myself wholly to Thee."

UPON MORTIFICATION.

It is far better to mortify the body through the spirit than the spirit through the body. To deaden and beat down the body instead of trying to reduce the swelling of an inflated spirit is like pulling back a horse by its tail. It is behaving like Balaam, who beat the ass which carried him, instead of taking heed to the peril which threatened him and which the poor beast was miraculously warning him to avoid.

One of the three first Postulants who entered the Convent of the Visitation, established by me at Belley, left it before taking the novices' habit being unable to understand how Religious could be holy in an Order in which she saw so few austerities practised. She has since then, however, been disabused of her error, and has repented of it.

At that time she was under the guidance of those who considered that holiness consisted in mortifications in respect of food and clothing: as if the stings of the flesh cease to be felt when you no longer eat of it, and as if you could not be temperate over partridges and gluttonous over cabbages.

Our Blessed Father, writing to a novice in one of his convents who was perplexed on this subject, says: "The devil does not trouble himself much about us if, while macerating our bodies, we are at the same time doing our own will, for he does not fear austerity but obedience.

"What greater austerity can there be than to keep our will in subjection and In continual obedience, Reassure yourself then, O lover of voluntary penance, if, indeed, the works of self-love deserve to be called penances! When you took the habit after many prayers and much consideration, it was thought good that you should enter the school of obedience and renunciation of your own will rather than remain the sport of your own judgment and of yourself.

"Do not then let yourself be shaken, but remain where our Lord has placed you. It is true that there you suffer great mortifications of heart, seeing yourself so imperfect and so deserving of reproof and correction, but is not this the very thing you ought to seeks mortification of heart and a continual sense of your own misery? Yet, you say, you cannot do such penance as you would. My dear daughter, tell me what better penance can be given to an erring heart than to bear a continual cross and to be always renouncing self-love?"

UPON THE SAME SUBJECT.

Blessed Francis was no great friend of unusual mortifications, and did not wish them to be practised except in the pressing necessity of violent temptations.

In such cases it was his desire that those so assailed should try to repel force by force, employing that holy violence which takes heaven by storm, for, as by cutting and burning health is restored to the body, so also by these caustic remedies holiness is often preserved in the soul.

He used to say that to those who made all kinds of exterior austerities their custom, the custom in time becomes a second nature;[1] that those who had hardened their skin no longer felt any inconvenience from cold, from hard couches, or coarse garments, and that when the flame of concupiscence kindled this dry wood they possessed no remedy which they could apply to extinguish the fire.

They are like the pagan king, who had so accustomed himself to feed upon poison that when he wished to end his miseries with his life by taking it, he was obliged to live on against his will, and to serve as a sport to his enemies.

The devil cares very little about our body being laid low so long as he can hold on to us by the vices of the soul; and so cunning is he that often out of bodily mortifications, he extracts matter for vanity.

Our holy Bishop wrote as follows to a person who regretted that her health prevented her from continuing her accustomed austerities:

"Since you do not find yourself any longer able to practise corporal mortifications and the severities of penance, and since it is not at all expedient that you should think of doing so, on which point we are perfectly agreed, keep your heart calm and recollected in the presence of its Saviour; and as far as possible do what you may have to do solely to please God, and suffer whatever you may have to suffer according to His disposal of events in this life with the same intention. Thus God will possess you wholly and will graciously allow you to possess Him one day eternally."

With regard to the various kinds of mortification, that which is inward and hidden is far more excellent than that which is exterior, the former not being compatible, as is the latter, with hypocrisy, vanity, or indiscretion.

Again, those mortifications which come upon us from without, either directly from God or through men by His permission, are always superior to those which depend upon our own choice and which are the offspring of our will.

Many, however, find here a stumbling block, being very eager to embrace mortifications suggested by their own inclinations, which, after all, however apparently severe, are really easy because they are what nature itself wants.

On the other hand, mortifications which come to them from without and through others, however light they may be, they find insupportable. For example, a person will eagerly make use of disciplines, hair-shirts, and fasting, and yet will be so tender of his reputation that if once in a way laughed at or spoken against, he will become almost beside himself, robbed of his rest and even sometimes of his reason; and will perhaps in the end be driven to the most deplorable extremities.

Another will throw himself with ardour into the practice of prayer, penance, silence, and such like devotions, but will break out into a fury of impatience and complain indignantly and unrestrainedly at the loss of a law-suit, or at the slightest damage done to his property.

Another will give alms liberally and make magnificent foundations for the relief of the poor and sick, but will groan and tremble with fear when himself threatened with infirmity or sickness, however slightly; and upon experiencing the least possible bodily pain, will give vent to interminable lamentations.

In proportion as people are more or less attached to honours, gain, or mere pleasures, they bear with less or more patience the hindrances to them; nor do the majority of men seriously consider that it is the hand of God which gives and which takes away, which kills and which makes alive, which exalts and which casts down, as it pleases Him.

In order to heal this spiritual malady in a certain person our Blessed Father wrote to her: "Often and with all your heart kiss the crosses which God has laid upon your shoulders. Do not consider whether they are of precious and sweet-scented wood or not. And, indeed, they are more truly crosses when they are of coarse, common, ill-smelling wood. It is strange, but one particular chant keeps ever coming back to my mind, and it is the only one I know. It is the canticle of the divine Lamb; sad, indeed, but at the same time harmonious and beautiful—Father, not my will, but Thine be done."[2]

[Footnote 1: It is not to be inferred that Saint Francis countenanced self-indulgence. He only wished to remove the idea common in his day, that devotion must be accompanied by austerity.—[Ed.]] [Footnote 2: Luke xxii. 42.]

UPON FASTING.[1]

One day when we were talking about that holy liberty of spirit of which he thought so highly, as being one of the great aids to charity, Blessed Francis told me the following anecdote, which is a most practical illustration of his feelings on the subject.

He had been visited by a Prelate, whom, with his accustomed hospitality and kindness, he pressed to remain with him for several days. When Friday evening came, our Blessed Father went to the Prelate's room inviting him to come to supper, which was quite ready.

"Supper!" cried his guest. "This is not a day for supper! Surely, the least one can do is to fast once a week!" Our holy Bishop at once left him to do as he pleased, desiring the servants to take his collation to his room, while he himself joined the chaplains of the Prelate and his own household at the supper table.

The chaplains told him that this Prelate was so exact and punctilious in discharging all his religious exercises, of prayer, fasting, and such like, that he never abated one of them, whatever company he might have. Not that he refused to sit down to table with his visitors on fast days, but that he ate nothing but what was permitted by the rule he had imposed on himself. Our Blessed Father, after telling me this, went on to say that condescension was the daughter of charity, just as fasting is the sister of obedience; and that where obedience did not impose the sacrifice, he would have no difficulty in preferring condescension and hospitality to fasting. The lives of the Saints furnish frequent examples of this. Above all, Scripture assures us, that by hospitality some have merited to receive Angels; from which declaration St. Paul takes occasion to exhort the faithful not to forget liberality and hospitality, as sacrifices well pleasing to God.[2]

"Remember," he said, "that we must not be so deeply attached to our religious exercises, however pious, as not to be ready sometimes to give them up. For, if we cling to them too tightly, under the pretext of fidelity and steadfastness, a subtle self-love will glide in among them, making us forget the end in the means, and then, instead of pressing on, nor resting till we rest in God Himself, we shall stop short at the means which lead to Him.

"As regards the occurrence of which I have been telling you, one Friday's fast, thus interrupted, would have concealed many others; and to conceal such virtues is no less a virtue than those which are so concealed. God is a hidden God, who loves to be served, prayed to, and adored in secret, as the Gospel testifies.[3] You know what happened to that unthinking king of Israel, who, for having displayed his treasures to the ambassadors of a barbarian prince, was deprived of them all, when that same heathen king descended upon him with a powerful army.

"The practice of the virtue of condescension or affability may often with profit be substituted for fasting. I except, however, the case of a vow, for in that we must be faithful even to death, and care nothing about what men may say, provided that God is served. They that please men have been confounded, because God hath despised them."[4]

He asked me one day if it was easy for me to fast. I answered that it was perfectly easy, as it was a rare thing for me to sit down to table with any appetite. "Then," he rejoined, "do not fast at all." On my expressing great astonishment at these words, and venturing to remind our Blessed Father that it was a mortification, strongly recommended to us by God Himself.

"Yes," he replied, "but for those who have better appetites than you have. Do some other good work, and keep your body in subjection by some other mode of discipline." He went on, however, to say that fasting was, indeed, the greatest of all corporal austerities, since it puts the axe to the root of the tree. The others only touch the bark lightly; they only scrape or prune it. Whereas when the body waxes fat it often kicks, and from this sort of fatness sin is likely to proceed.

"Those who are naturally sober, temperate, and self-restrained have a great advantage over others in the matter of study and spiritual things. They are like horses that have been well broken in, horses which have a strong bridle, holding them in to their duty."

He was no friend to immoderate fasting, and never encouraged it in his penitents, as we see in his "Introduction to a Devout Life," where he gives this reason against the practice: "When the body is over-fed, the mind cannot support its weight; but when the body is weak and wasted. It cannot support the mind." He liked the one and the other to be dealt with in a well-balanced manner, and said that God wished to be served with a reasonable service; adding—that it was always easy to bring down and reduce the bodily forces, but that it was not so easy a matter to build them up again when thus brought low. It is easy to wound, but not to heal. The mind should treat the body as its child, correcting without crushing it: only when it revolts must it be treated as a rebellious subject, according to the words of the Apostle: I chastise my body and bring it into subjection.[Footnote 5]

[Footnote 1: The Saint is here speaking of fasts of devotion, not of those of obligation.—[Ed.]]

[Footnote 2: Heb. xiii. 2, 16.]

[Footnote 3: Matt. vi. 6.]

[Footnote 4: Psalm lii. 6.]

[Footnote 5: 1 Cor. ix. 27.]

DOUBTS SOLVED AS TO SOLDIERS FASTING.

I was so young when called to the episcopate that I lived in a state of continual mistrust and uncertainty; doubtful about this, scrupulous about that; ignorance being the grandmother of scruples, as servile fear is their mother.

At the time of which I am going to speak, the residences of our Blessed Father and myself were only eight leagues apart, and in all my perplexities and difficulties I had recourse to his judgment and counsel. I kept a little foot-boy in my service, almost entirely employed in running to and fro between Belley and Annecy, carrying my letters to him and bringing back his replies. These replies were to me absolute decrees; nay, I should rather say oracles, so manifestly did God speak by the mouth and pen of that holy man.

On one occasion it happened that the captains of some troops—then stationed in garrison on the borders of Savoy and France, on account of a misunderstanding which had arisen between the two countries—came to me at the beginning of Lent to ask permission for their men to eat eggs and cheese during that season. This was a permission which I had never given except to the weak and sickly. I learned from the men themselves that they were exceedingly robust and hearty, and only weak and reduced as regarded their purses, their pay being so small that it barely supplied them with food. Nevertheless, I did not consider this poor pay a sufficient reason for granting a dispensation, especially in a district where Lent is so strictly kept that the peasants are scandalized when told that on certain days they may eat butter.

In my difficulty I despatched a letter at once to our Blessed Father, whose reply was full of sweetness and kindness. He said that he honoured the faith and piety of the good centurions, who had presented this request, which, indeed, deserved to be granted, seeing that it edified, not the Synagogue, but the Church. He added that I ought not only to grant it, but to extend it, and instead of eggs, to permit them to eat oxen, and instead of cheese, the cows of whose milk it is made.

"Truly," he went on to say, "you are a wise person to consult me as to what soldiers shall eat in Lent, as if the laws of war and necessity did not over-ride all others without exception! Is it not a great thing that these good men submit themselves to the Church, and so defer to her as to ask her permission and blessing? God grant that they may do nothing worse than eat eggs, cheese, or beef; if they were guilty of nothing more heinous than that, there would not be so many complaints against them."

THE GOLDEN MEAN IN DISPENSATIONS.

"It is quite true," said our Blessed Father, on one occasion, "that there are certain matters in which we are meant to use our own judgment, and in which, if we judge ourselves, we shall not be chastised by God. But there are others in which, with the eye of our soul, that is, with our judgment, it is as with the eye of the body, which sees all things excepting itself. We need a mirror. Now, this mirror, as regards interior things, is the person to whom we manifest our conscience, and who is its judge in the place of God."

He went on to say that in the matter of granting dispensations to his flock, he had told a certain Prelate, who had consulted him on the subject, that the best rule to give to others, or to take for oneself in such questions, is to love one's neighbour as oneself, and oneself as others, in God and for God. "If," he continued, addressing the Prelate, "you now take more trouble about granting these necessary dispensations to others than in getting them for yourself, the time will come when you will be generous, easy, and indulgent towards others, and severe and rigorous towards yourself. Perhaps you imagine that this second line of conduct is better than the other. It is not, and you will find the repose and peace of your soul only in the golden mean, which is the one wholesome atmosphere for the nourishing of virtue."

UPON THE WORDS, "EAT OF ANYTHING THAT IS SET BEFORE YOU."

Our Blessed Father held in great esteem the Gospel maxim, Eat such things as are set before you.[1] He deemed it a much higher and stronger degree of mortification to accommodate the tastes and appetite to any food, whether pleasant or otherwise, which may be offered, than always to choose the most inferior and coarsest kinds. For it not seldom happens that the greatest delicacies—or those at least which are esteemed to be such by epicures—are not to our taste, and therefore to partake of them without showing the least sign of dislike is by no means so small a matter as may be thought. It incommodes no one but the person who so mortifies himself, and it is a little act of self-restraint so secret, so securely hidden from others, that the rest of the company imagine something quite different from the real truth.

He also considered that it was a species of incivility when seated at a meal to ask for some dish which was at the other end of the table, instead of taking what was close at hand. He said that such practices were evidence of a mind too keen about viands, sauces, and condiments; too much absorbed in mere eating and drinking. If, he added, this careful picking out of dishes is not done from greediness or gluttony, but from a desire to choose the worst food, it smacks of affectation, which is as inseparable from ostentation as smoke from fire. The conduct of people who do this is not unlike that of guests who take the lowest seats at the table, in order that they may, with the greater éclat, be summoned to the higher places. The following incident will show his own indifference. One day poached eggs were served to him, and when he had eaten them, he continued to dip his bread in the water in which they had been cooked, apparently without noticing what he was doing. The guests were all smiling. Upon discovering the cause of their amusement, he told them it was too bad of them to undeceive him, as he was taking the sauce with much relish, verifying the proverb that "Hunger is the best sauce"!

[Footnote 1: Luc. x. 8.]

UPON THE STATE OF PERFECTION.

The degree of perfection to which our Blessed Father brought his Religious he makes manifest to us in one of his letters.

"Do you know," he says, "what the cloister is? It is the school of exact correction, in which each individual soul must learn the lesson of allowing itself to be so disciplined, planed, and polished that at length, being quite smooth and even, it may be fit to be joined, united, and absolutely assimilated with the Will of God.

"To wish to be corrected is an evident sign of perfection, for the principal point of humility is realizing our need of it.

"A convent is a hospital for the spiritually sick. The sick wish to be cured, and, therefore, they willingly submit to be lanced, probed, cut, cauterized, and subjected to any and every pain and discomfort which medicine or surgery may suggest.

"In the early days of the Church, religious were called by a name which signifies healers. Oh! my daughter, be truly your own healer, and pay no heed to what self-love may whisper to the contrary. Say to yourself, since I do not wish to die spiritually, I will be healed, and in order to be healed I will submit to treatment and correction, and I will entreat the doctors to spare me nothing which may be required to effect my cure."

MARKS OF PROGRESS IN PERFECTION.

Our Blessed Father, who did not like people to be too introspective and self-tormenting, said that they should, however, walk as it is written of the Maccabees, Caute et ordinate;[1] that is, with circumspection and order, or, to use a common expression, "bridle in hand." And one of the best proofs of our advancement in virtue is, he said, a love of correction and reproof; for it is a sign of a good digestion easily to assimilate tough and coarse food. In the same way it is a mark of spiritual health and inward vigour to be able to say with the Psalmist, The just man shall correct me in mercy and shall reprove me.[2]

It is a great proof of our hating vice, and of the faults which we commit, proceeding rather from inadvertence and frailty, than from malice and deliberate intention, that we welcome the warnings which make us think on our ways, and turn back our feet (that is to say, our affections) into the testimonies of God, by which is meant the divine law.

An old philosopher said that to want to get well is part of the sick man's cure. The desire to keep well is a sign of health. He who loves correction necessarily desires the virtue contrary to the fault for which he is reproved, and therefore profits by the warnings given him to escape the vice from which his fault proceeded.

A sick person who is really anxious to recover his health takes without hesitation the remedies prescribed by the physician, however sharp, bitter, and painful they may be. He who aims at perfection, which is the full health, and true holiness of the soul, finds nothing difficult that helps him to arrive at that end. Justice and judgment, that is to say correction, establish in him the seat of perfect wisdom. In a word, better are the wounds of a friend (like those of a surgeon who probes only to heal) than the deceitful kisses of a flatterer, an enemy.[3]

[Footnote 1: 1 Mach. vi. 4.]

[Footnote 2: Psalm cxl. 5.]

[Footnote 3: Prov. xxvii. 6.]

UPON THE PERFECTION AIMED AT IN RELIGIOUS HOUSES.

Our Blessed Father was speaking to me one day on the subject of exterior perfection, and on the discontent expressed by certain Religions, who, in their particular order, had not found the strictness and severity of rule they desired. He said: "These good people seem to me to be knocking their heads against a stone wall. Christian perfection does not consist in eating fish, wearing serge, sleeping on straw, stripping oneself of one's possessions, keeping strict vigils, and such like austerities. For, were this so, pagans would be the more perfect than Christians, since many of them voluntarily sleep on the bare ground, do not eat a morsel of meat throughout the whole year, are ragged, naked, shivering, living for the most part only on bread and water, and on that bread of suffering, too, which is far harder and heavier than the blackest of crusts. If perfection consisted in exterior observances such as these, they would have to go back in perfection were they to enter even the most strictly reformed of our Religious Houses, for in none is a life led nearly so austere as theirs.

"The question then is in what does the essential perfection of a Christian life consist? It must surely in the first place include the assiduous practice of charity, for exterior mortifications without charity are of no account. St. Paul, we know, reckons martyrdom itself as nothing, unless quickened by charity.

"I do not exactly know what standard of perfection they who insist so much upon exterior mortification wish to set up.

"Surely the greater or lesser degree of charity is the true measure of sanctity and the measure also of the excellence of religious rule. Now, in what rule is charity, the queen of the virtues, more recommended that in that of St. Augustine? which seems to be nothing but one long discourse on charity.

"However, it is not a question of comparing one rule with another, it is rather of noticing which rule is as a matter of fact best observed. For even had other rules, in regard to the exterior perfectness of the life they prescribe, every advantage over that of St. Augustine, who does not know that it is safer to enter a community in which a rule of less excellence is exactly observed, rather than another where a higher kind of rule is preached but not kept? Of what use are laws if they are not observed?

"The consequence, in my opinion, of the mistake made by those who put over-much stress on esteem of mortification, is, that even Religious get accustomed to make use in their judgments of those lying balances of which the Psalmist speaks,[1] and that the simple-minded are forced to trust to the guidance of blind leaders. Hence it has come to pass that true and essential perfection is not what the majority of people think it to be, nor is it reached by the road along which the many travel. May God have pity on us, and bless us with the light of His countenance, so that we may know His way upon the earth, and may declare His salvation to all nations, and may He turn aside from us in this our day, that which He once threatened to those who thought themselves wise: Let them alone, they are blind leaders of the blind."[1]

[Footnote 1: Psalm lxi. 10.]

[Footnote 2: Matt. xv. 14.]

UPON FRUGALITY.

The following notable example of frugality and economy was related to me by our Blessed Father himself.

Monseigneur Vespasian Grimaldi, who was Piedmontese by birth, made a tolerably large fortune in France as an ecclesiastic, during the regency of Catherine de Medicis. He was raised to the dignity of Archbishop of Vienne in Dauphiné, and held several other benefices which brought him in a large revenue. Having amassed all these riches at court, his desire was to live there in great pomp and splendour, but whether it was that God did not bless his designs, or that he was too much addicted to extravagance and display, certain it is that he was always in difficulties, not only about money, but even about his health.

Weary at last of dragging on a life so troubled and so wretched, he resolved to quit the court, and to retire into a peaceful solitude. He had often in past days remarked the extraordinary beauty of the banks of Lake Leman, where nature seems to scatter her richest gifts with lavish hand, and there he resolved to fix his abode in a district subject to his own sovereign, the Duke of Savoy, and settling down in that quiet spot to spend the remainder of his days in peace. He selected for this purpose the little village and market town of Evian, so called because of the abundance and clearness of its lovely streams and fountains. The little town is situated on the very margin of the lake, and backed by an outlying stretch of country is as charming to, the eye as it is rich and fertile.

There, having given up his archbishopric and all his benefices, reserving only to himself a pension of two thousand crowns, he established a retreat into which he was accompanied by only three or four servants.

He was at this time sixty-five years old, but weighed down by physical infirmities much more than by the burden of his years. He had chosen this particular spot purposely because there was no approach to it from the high road, and there was little fear of visits from that great world of which he was now so weary, in the crush and tumult of which he had spent so large a portion of his life in consequence of his position at court.

Another reason for his choosing Evian was that the little township being in the diocese of Geneva, which is included in the province of Vienne in Dauphiné, in settling there he was not leaving his own province.

Living then in this calm retreat, free from all bustle and all burdens of office, with no show and state to keep up, having nothing to attend to but the sanctification of his soul and the restoration of his bodily health, a marvellous change was soon observed in him. Inward peace gave back to him health so vigorous and settled that those who had known him in the days of his infirmity declared him to be absolutely rejuvenated, and truly he did feel in his soul a renewal of strength like that of the eagle. This he attributed to exercises of the contemplative life to which he now devoted himself with fervour.

We see thus how true is the divine oracle which tells us that to those who seek first the Kingdom of God and His justice all temporal things necessary shall be given,[1] for God prospered this good Prelate in even his worldly affairs.

The small sum of money which he had reserved for himself, and which he spent in the most frugal and judicious manner possible, so increased that when he died at the age of a hundred and two or a hundred and three years, he left behind him more than 6,000 crowns.

By his will he ordered the whole to be distributed in benefactions and alms throughout the neighbourhood, and in fact it relieved every necessitous person to be found round about.

It was this very Mgr. Vespasian Grimaldi who, assisted by the Bishops of Saint-Paul-Trois-Châteaux, and of Damascus, conferred episcopal consecration upon Blessed Francis in the Church of Thorens, in the diocese of Geneva, on the feast of the Immaculate Conception of Our Lady, December 8th, 1602.

From this notable example we may easily gather:

1. That for Prelates the atmosphere of Courts is not to be recommended.

2. That it is favourable neither to the growth of holiness nor the maintenance of physical health.

3. That great fortunes entail great slavery and great anxieties.

4. A peaceful, tranquil, and hidden life, even from the point of view of common sense and of the dictates of nature, is the happiest.

5. That much more is this so when looked at in the light of grace and of the soul's welfare.

6. That the old saying is quite true that there is no surer way to increase one's income than that of frugality and judicious economy.

7. That one never has money enough to meet all the claims of worldly show and vain ostentation.

8. That he who lives in the style the world expects of him is never rich, while he who regulates his expenditure simply by his natural needs is never poor.

9. That almsdeeds is an investment which multiplies itself a hundredfold even in this present life and ensures the fruit of a blessed eternity in the next, provided only they have been given in the love, and for the love of God.

[Footnote 1: Matt. vi. 33.]

BLESSED FRANCIS' ESTEEM OF THE VIRTUE OF SIMPLICITY.

Our Blessed Father had the highest possible esteem for the virtue of simplicity. Indeed, my sisters, you know what a prominent place he gives to it in his letters, his Spiritual

Conferences, and elsewhere. Whenever he met with an example of it he rejoiced and openly expressed his delight. I will here give you one instance which he told me, as it were exulting over it. After having preached the Advent and Lent at Grenoble, he paid a visit to La Grande Chartreuse, that centre of wonderful devotion and austerity, the surroundings of which are so wild, solitary, and almost terrible in their ruggedness, that St. Bernard called it locus horroris et vastæ solitudinis.

At the time of his visit, the Prior General of the whole Order was Dom Bruno d'Affringues, a native of St. Omer, a man of profound learning and of still more profound humility and simplicity. I knew him well, and can bear witness to the beauty of his character, which in its extreme sweetness and simplicity had something in it not of this earth.

He received Blessed Francis on his arrival with his usual delightful courtesy and sincerity. After having conducted him to a guest chamber suited to his rank, and having talked with him on many lofty and sublime subjects, he suddenly remembered that it was some feast day of the Order. He therefore took leave of the Bishop, saying that he would gladly have stayed with him much longer, but that he knew his honoured guest would prefer obedience to everything else, and that he must retire to his cell to prepare for Matins, it being the feast of one of their great Saints.

Our Saint approved highly of this exact observance of rule, and they separated with mutual expressions of respect and regard.

On his way to his cell, however, the Prior was met by the Procurator of the Monastery, who asked him where he was going and where he had left his Lordship, the Bishop of Geneva. "I have left Him," the Prior answered, "in his own chamber, and I took leave of him that I might go to our cell and be ready to say Matins to-night in choir because of to-morrow's feast." "Truly, Reverend Father," said the Procurator, "you are well up in the ceremonies of the world indeed! Why, it is only a feast of our own Order! Do we, out in this desert, have every day for our guests Prelates of such distinction? Do you not know that God takes pleasure when for a sacrifice to Him we offer hospitality and kindliness? You will always have leisure to sing the praises of God; you will have plenty of other opportunities for saying Matins; but who can entertain such a Prelate better than you? What a disgrace to the house that you should leave him thus alone!" "My son," replied the Reverend Father, "I see that you are quite right and that I have certainly done wrong." So saying he at once retraced his steps to the Bishop of Geneva's apartment, and finding him, there said humbly: "My Lord, on leaving you I met one of our brethren who told me that I had been guilty of discourtesy in leaving you thus all alone; that I should have an opportunity at another time of making up for my absence from Matins, but that we do not every day have a Bishop of Geneva under our roof. I see that he is in the right and I have come back at once to ask your pardon, and to beg you to excuse my apparent rudeness, for I assure you truthfully that it was done in ignorance."

Blessed Francis was enraptured with this straightforwardness, candour, and simplicity, and told me that he was more delighted with it than if he had seen the good Prior work a miracle.

BLESSED FRANCIS' LOVE OF EXACTITUDE.

This same Dom Bruno was remarkable for his exactitude and punctuality, virtues which our Blessed Father always both admired and praised. He was so exact in the observance of the smallest monastic detail that no novice could have surpassed him in carefulness. At the same time he never allowed himself to be carried away by indiscreet fervour, beyond the line laid down in his rule, knowing how much harm would be done to his inferiors by his not preserving a calm and even tenor of life, making himself all things to men, that he might win them and keep them for Jesus Christ.

He would never allow the smallest austerities to be practised beyond those prescribed by the Constitutions of the Order. Though rigorous towards himself he was marvellously indulgent towards those whom he governed in the monastery. For himself he had the heart of a judge, for them that of a mother.

Our holy Bishop, drawing a comparison between him and his predecessor, who was addicted to such excessive austerities that it seemed as if he had either no body at all, or one of iron, said: "The late Prior was like those unskilful physicians who by their treatment fill up our cemeteries: for many who desired to imitate his mortified life, and through a zeal without knowledge, tried to do what was beyond their strength, ended by falling into the pit. On the other hand, the actual Prior of the Grand Chartreuse, by his gentleness and moderation, maintains among his monks, peace and humility of soul, together with health of body, making them preserve their strength for God, that is to say, so as to serve Him longer and with greater earnestness in those exercises which tend to His glory. In doing this he follows the example of the Patriarch Jacob, who, on his return from Mesopotamia, could have reached his father's house much sooner had he accepted the offer of camels made by his brother Esau, when he came to meet him. But Jacob preferred to accommodate his pace to that of his little ones, of his children, and even of the lambs of his flock, rather than to press on at the risk of throwing his household and followers into disorder." This example was a favourite one with our Blessed Father, and I am reminded of another of the same kind, which he valued almost as much. "Have you read," he once said to me, "the life of Blessed Aloysius Gonzaga of the Society of Jesus? If you have, perhaps you have remarked what it was that made that young prince so quickly become holy, and almost perfect. It was his extreme exactitude and punctuality, and his faithful observance of the constitutions of his Order. This was such that he refused to put one foot before the other, so to speak, or draw back a single step in order to gratify himself. This, not of course in regard to things commanded, or forbidden, for the law of God leaves us in no doubt about such, but in those indifferent matters which, being neither commanded nor forbidden, often make correct discernment difficult." There are some who imagine that this way of discerning the will of God is impracticable for persons in the world, and that it is only out of the world, as they call the cloistered life, that one can have recourse to it. Now, although we do not deny that in the well-regulated and holy life of a convent by means of obedience, and through the medium of superiors, the knowledge of God's will in things indifferent can be more perfectly ascertained, and more readily acted upon, than in any other state of life, still we venture to maintain that even in the world it is easier to ascertain God's will, even in things indifferent, than might at first sight appear."

It was one of Blessed Francis' common maxims that great fidelity towards God may be practised even in the most indifferent actions, and he considered that to be a lower degree of fidelity which is only available for great and striking occasions. He who is careful with farthings, how much more so will he be with crowns?

Not that he loved scrupulous minds, those, namely, which are troubled and anxious about every trifle. No, indeed, but he desired that God should be loved by all with a vigilant and attentive love, exact, punctual, and faithful in the smallest matters, pictured to us by the rod the Prophet used when watching the boiling caldron, to remove all the scum as it rose to the surface.[1]

And you may be sure that what he taught by word, he himself was the first to practise. He was the most punctual man I ever knew, the most exact, though without fussiness or worry. He was not only most accurate in all details of the service of the altar and of the choir, but, even when reciting his office in private, he never failed to observe all minutiæ of ceremonial in every way, bowing his head, genuflecting, etc., as if he were engaged in a solemn public function. In his intercourse with the world he was just as exact; he omitted no detail required by courtesy, he spared no pains to avoid giving inconvenience or annoyance to anyone. People who were old fashioned in their punctilious civilities, and tedious and lengthy in their ceremonious discourse, he treated with the most sweet and gracious forbearance, letting them say all they had to say, before he replied, and then answering as his duty and the laws of politeness required.

All his actions were regular as clockwork, and the holy presence of God was the loadstar of his soul. One day I was complaining to him of the too great deference which he paid me. "And for how much then do you," he answered, "account Jesus Christ, whom I honour in your person?" "Oh!" I replied, "if you take that ground, you ought to speak to me on your knees!"

Once two persons happened to be playing a game of skill when Blessed Francis was in the room. One was cheating the other. Our holy Prelate, indignant at this, remonstrated at once. "Oh," was the careless reply, "we are only playing for farthings." And "supposing you were playing for guineas," returned Francis, "how would it be then? He, who despises small faults will fall into great ones, but he who is faithful and honest in small matters will also be honest in great ones. He who fears to steal a pin will certainly not take a guinea. In fine, he who is faithful over a little shall be set over much."

I should like while I am on this subject to add a short saying which was often on the lips of this Blessed Father. "Fidelity towards God consists in abstaining from even the slightest faults, for great ones are so repulsive in themselves that often enough nature deters us from committing them."

[Footnote 1: Jer. i. 11, 13.]

A TEST OF RELIGIOUS VOCATION.

Here I will relate a pleasant little incident which befell Dom Bruno, of whom I have spoken above. Our Blessed Father often quoted it as an example for others.

The Germans, particularly those on the banks of the Rhine, have a special devotion to St. Bruno, who was a native of Cologne, in which city he is highly honoured.

A young man, a native of the same place, had a most ardent desire to enter the Carthusian Order, but his parents, influential people of the city, prevented his being received into the Chartreuse of Cologne, or into any other Carthusian monastery in the neighbourhood.

The youth, greatly distressed at this repulse, left the city in haste, and took refuge among the holy mountains where St. Bruno and his companions made their first retreat. Presenting himself at the Grande Chartreuse he asked to see the Rev. Fr. Prior, and throwing himself at his feet, entreated that he might be clothed with the habit of the Order, concealing nothing from him, neither his birth, nor his place of residence, nor the circumstances of his vocation, etc. The Prior, observing that he was fragile in appearance and of an apparently delicate constitution, remonstrated, pointing out to him how great were the austerities of the Order, and reminding him of the bleakness of the hills amidst which the monastery was situated, and of the perpetual winter which reigns there. The young man replied insisting that he knew all this, and had counted the cost, but that God would be his strength, and enable him by His grace to overcome all obstacles. "Even though," said he, "I should walk in the shadow of death I shall fear no evil provided that God be with me." Then the Prior took a more serious tone. Determined to test to the utmost the courage and resolution of the postulant, he asked him sharply if he knew all that was required of those who aspire to enter the Carthusian Order. "Are you aware," he said, "that in the first place we require him to work at least one miracle? Can you do that?" "I cannot," replied the young man, "but the power of God within me can. I trust myself entirely to His goodness. I am certain that having called me to serve Him in this vocation, and implanted in me a thorough disgust for the things of the world, He will not permit me to look back, nor to return to that corrupt society which, with all my heart and soul, I have renounced. Ask of me whatever sign you will, I am convinced that God will work a miracle, even through me, in testimony of this truth."

As he spoke the blood mounted to his forehead, his eyes shone like stars, his whole visage seemed on fire with enthusiasm.

Dom Bruno, astonished at the vehemence of his words, opened his arms, and clasping him to his heart received him at once among his children. Then turning to those who stood around him, "My brothers," he said, "his is an undeniable vocation. May God of His clemency often send such labourers into the harvest of the Chartreuse." And to the young postulant, "Have confidence, my son, God will help you, and will love you, and you will love Him, and will serve Him among us. This is the miracle we expect you to work."

You will ask me, perhaps, what use our Blessed Father could make of this example. I will tell you. When he was admitting any young girl into your congregation, my sisters, he invariably referred to it. He used to speak to her only of Calvary, of the nails, the thorns, the crosses, of inward mortification, of surrender of will, and crucifixion of private judgment, of dying wholly to self, in order to live only with God, in God, and for God: in fine, of living no longer according to natural inclinations and feelings, but absolutely according to the spirit of faith, and of your congregation.

Did anyone object that your Order was not so rigorous, or severe, as he made it out to be; but that, on the contrary, the life led by its members was easy, without many outward austerities, as was proved by the fact that even the infirm and sickly were admitted into it, and attained to the same sanctity as the rest, he replied: "Believe me, that if the body is there preserved as if it were a vessel of election, the spirit is there tested and tried in all possible ways, since the spirit that fails to stand every possible trial is no stone fit for the building up of this congregation."

He went on to quote from the life of St. Bernard. Against that holy man it was once urged that the austerities and bodily macerations practised in his Order frightened away young men, and deterred them from entering it, "Many," said the Saint, "see our crosses, but see not how well we are able to carry them. It happens to our crosses, as it does to those which are painted on the walls of a church when the Bishop in consecrating it makes a second cross upon them with holy oil. The people see the cross made by the painter, but they do not see that with which the Bishop has covered it. Our crosses, so plainly visible, are softened by very many inward consolations, which are concealed from the eyes of worldlings because they understand not the spiritual things of God, nor see how we can find peace in this bitterness which so repels those whose only thought is of themselves, and of their own pleasures. In very truth," our Blessed Father continued, "the worldling may notice in the rosebed of religion only the loveliness of the flowers, and the sweetness of their perfume, but these conceal many a thorn. The crosses of community life are hidden because the sisters of this congregation have by interior mortification to make up for what is lacking in external austerities.

"This law of your Institute has been established out of consideration for the weak and infirm, who may be admitted among you, and to whose service the stronger members have to devote themselves. This is the reason why all who purpose to enter the Order have to resolve to make war to the death against their private judgment, and still more against their self-will and self-love. This is why all ought to mortify all their passions and affections, and absolutely to bend their understanding under the yoke of obedience, to live, in short, no longer according to the old man, but entirely according to the new man, in holiness and in justice. So to live as to bear a continual cross even until death, and dying upon it, with the Son of God, to say, With Christ I am nailed to the Cross, and I live, now not I, but Christ liveth in me."[1]

[Footnote 1: Gal. ii. 19, 20.]

UPON FOLLOWING THE COMMON LIFE.

He always praised common life very highly. His exalted opinion of its merits made him refuse to allow the Sisters of the Visitation to practise extraordinary austerities in respect to dress or food. For these matters he prescribed rules such as can easily be observed by anyone who wishes to lead a christian life in the world. His spiritual daughters, following this direction, imitate the example of Jesus Christ, of His Blessed Mother, and of the disciples of our Lord, who led no other kind of life. For the rest, they have at all times to submit themselves to the discretion and judgment of their superiors, whose duty it is to decide for them on the expediency of extraordinary mortifications after hearing the circumstances of the case of any individual sister.

Our Saint himself often, indeed, practised bodily mortifications, but always with judgment and prudence, for he knew full well that the object of such austerities is the preservation of purity of soul, not the destruction of bodily health.

In one word, he practically set the life of Jesus Christ before that of St. John the Baptist.

UPON THE JUDGING OF VOCATIONS.

Although our Blessed Father has given you the fullest possible instructions on this subject, in his seventeenth

Conference, entitled, On voting in a Community, I see that you are not quite satisfied in the matter.

I know very well that your dissatisfaction does not arise from any unworthy motive, but only from a conscientious desire to do your duty to God, and to the sisters whom you have in a way to judge. To relieve your minds of doubt, I am about to supplement the teaching of that Conference with a few thoughts suggested to me at various times by Blessed Francis himself, which I put before you in words of my own.

In the first place, we must be careful never to confuse the terms vocation and avocation, for their meaning is very different.

An avocation is the condition of life in which we serve God.

A vocation is His call to that condition of life. When we call a servant to command him to do something, the calling him is one thing, his obeying and employing himself as directed quite another; and this, even if he do the work precisely as he is told, and no more. Now, there are two sorts of vocation. The first is the call to faith or grace; the second, the call to a particular avocation in life.

To follow the first vocation, viz., to Faith, is necessary for salvation, since he who refuses to listen to this call and to obey its voice risks the loss of his immortal soul. A pagan or heretic called by God to embrace Christianity or to submit to the Catholic Church, and to the end neglecting this call, must needs be lost, for out of the true Church there is no salvation. Again, if a member of the true Church who is spiritually dead in mortal sin, refuse to listen to the call, or vocation, of preventing grace which bids him return to God by confession, or by contrition of heart, he is in a state of damnation.

Not so, however, with the second kind of call or vocation. As this is only to some particular condition of life in the world or the cloister, although we must not neglect it, but must listen with respect to what it may please God to say to our heart, yet essentially it is not of vital importance to the welfare of our soul that we should follow such a call, since, at the most, it is but an inward counsel, which may be acted upon or not according to our choice.

And now remember that the counsels given in Holy Scripture are not precepts.[1] Our Blessed Father has often said that it would be not only an error, but a heresy, to maintain that there is any kind of legitimate calling or avocation in which it is impossible to save one's soul. On the contrary, in each, grace is offered, by means of which we may safely walk before God in holiness and justice all the days of our life.

To deny this would be to cut off from the hope of salvation, not thousands only, but millions of men and women, those, namely, who are engaged all their lives long in occupations which they have undertaken, not only without a vocation from God, but sometimes even against their own inclination.

This is the teaching of this Blessed Father in his Philothea, where he says, "It is an error, nay, a heresy, to wish to exclude the highest holiness of life from the soldier's barrack, the mechanic's workshop, the courts of princes, or the household of married people."

He used to say that it is not sufficient merely to love our calling, but that our most earnest endeavours as true and faithful Christians should be to strive to attain perfection in that same calling.

He remarked, too, that we do wrong to waste time in arguing as to what that perfection consists in. The glory of God should be the one aim of every devout soul.

Only by the practice of virtue can that final end be reached, and no virtue unaccompanied by charity avails to attain to it. Therefore, charity is the bond of all perfection, nay, itself is all perfection.

He attached much more importance to the spirit in which a vocation is followed out, than to the mere fact of its being embraced.

And this because the salvation of our souls, which we shall owe to God's grace, does not depend so much on the nature of our particular vocation or calling, but on our own persevering faithful submission to the will of God, which will of God is the salvation of us all.

Now, as we can save our souls, so we can also lose them in any calling whatsoever.

Would you desire a more unmistakable vocation than that of King Saul, or one more glorious than that of Judas? Yet both were lost. Where will you find one more troubled, and more interrupted by sin, than that of King David? Yet in spite of all that happened to him, how happy was its issue.

The vocation of a certain young lady who resolved upon taking the veil, but only out of a sort of despair, and because irritated against her family, was nevertheless approved by our Blessed Father, who to justify his approval gave the following explanation.

"As regards the vocation of this young lady, I consider it good, mingled though it be in her mind with imperfections and desirable though it would have been that she should have come to God simply and solely for the sake of the happiness of being wholly His. Remember that those whom God calls to Himself are not all drawn by Him with the same kind, or degree, of motives.

"There are but few who give themselves absolutely to His service from the one only desire to be His, and to serve Him alone.

"Among the women whose conversion the Gospel has made famous, Magdalen alone came through love, and with love.

"The adulteress came through public shame, the woman of Samaria from private and individual self-reproach, the woman of Canaan in order to be healed of bodily infirmity. Again, among the saints, St. Paul, the first hermit, at the age of fifteen, took refuge in his cave to escape persecution. St. Ignatius Loyola came through distress and suffering, and so on with hundreds of others. We must not expect all to begin by being perfect. It matters little how we commence, provided only that we are firmly resolved to go on well, and to end well. Certainly Leah intruded with scant courtesy into Rachel's promised place, as the wife of Jacob, yet she afterwards conducted herself so irreproachably, and behaved with such modesty and sweetness, that to her rather than to Rachel was vouchsafed the blessing of being an ancestress of our Lord.

"Those who were compelled to come into the marriage feast in the Gospel, ate, and drank of the best, nor, had they been the guests for whom the banquet was prepared, could they have fared better. If, then, we would have a pledge of their good living and perseverance, we must lock at the good dispositions of those who enter Religion rather than at the motives which impel them: for there are many souls who would not have entered the convent at all if the world had smiled upon them, and whom we nevertheless may find to be resolute in trampling under their feet the vanities of that same world."

[Footnote 1: 1 Cor. vii.]

UPON PRUDENCE AND SIMPLICITY.

"I know not," said our Blessed Father, on one occasion, "what this poor virtue of prudence has done to me that I find it so difficult to love it: if I do so at all, it is only because I have no choice in the matter, seeing that it is the very salt of life, and a light to show us the way out of its difficulties.

"On the other hand, the beauty of simplicity charms me. I would rather possess the harmlessness of one dove than the wisdom of a hundred serpents. I know that a combination of wisdom and simplicity is useful, and that the Gospel recommends it to us;[1] but I am of opinion that in this matter it should be as it is with certain medicines, in which a minute dose of poison is mixed with many wholesome drugs. If the doses, of serpent and dove were equal, I would not trust the medicine; the serpent can kill the dove, the dove cannot kill the serpent. Besides, there is a sort of prudence that is human and worldly which Scripture calls carnal wisdom,[2] as it is only used for wrong-doing, and is so dangerous and so subtle that those who possess it are unconscious of their own danger. They deceive others, yet are the first to be themselves deceived.

"I am told that in an age so crafty as our own prudence is necessary, if only to prevent our being wronged. I say nothing against this dictum, but I do believe that more in harmony with the mind of the Gospel is that which teaches us that it is great wisdom in the sight of God to suffer men to devour us, and to take away our goods,[3] bearing the loss of them joyfully, knowing that a better and a more secure substance awaits us. In a word, a good Christian should always choose rather to be the anvil than the hammer, the robbed than the robber, the victim than the murderer, the martyr than the tyrant. Let the world rage, let the prudence of so-called philosophy stand aghast, let the flesh despair; it is better to be good and simple than clever and wicked."

[Footnote 1: Matt. x. 16.]

[Footnote 2: Rom. viii. 6.]

[Footnote 3: 2 Cor. xi. 20.]

THE SAME SUBJECT CONTINUED.

Some of the friends of our Saint, actuated by this spirit of worldly prudence, having seen the flattering reception given by the public to his Philothea, which had at once been translated into various languages, advised him not to write any more books, as it was impossible that any other work from his pen should meet with equal success.

These remarks were unwelcome to our Blessed Father, who afterwards said to me: "These good people no doubt love me, and their love makes them speak as they do, out of the abundance of their hearts; but if they will only be so good as to turn their eyes for a moment from me, vile and wretched as I am, and fix them upon God, they will soon change their note; for if it has pleased Him to give His blessing to that first little book of mine, why should He deny it to my next? And if from little Philothea He made His glory to shine forth, as He brought forth the light from darkness,[1] and the sacred fire from the clay[2], is His arm thereby shortened, or His power diminished? Can He not make living and thirst-quenching water flow forth from the jaw-bone of an ass? But these good people do not dwell upon such considerations; they think solely of my personal glory, as if we ought to desire credit for ourselves, and not rather ascribe all to God, who works in us whatever good seems to emanate from us.

"Now, according to the spirit of the Gospel, so far from its being right to depend upon the applause of the world, St. Paul declares that if we please men, we are not the servants of God,[3] the friendship of the world being enmity with God. If then that little book has brought to me some vain and unmerited praise, it would be well worth my while to build upon its foundation some inferior work, so as to beat down the smoke of this incense, and earn that contempt from men which makes us so much the more pleasing to God, because we are thereby more and more crucified to the world."

[Footnote 1: Gen. i. 2, 3.]

[Footnote 2: Mach. i. 19, 22.]

[Footnote 3: Gal. i. 10.]

UPON MENTAL PRAYER.

I once asked our Blessed Father if it was not better to take one single point for mental prayer, and to draw from this point one single affection and resolution, as I thought that by taking three points and deducing from them very many affections and resolutions great confusion and perplexity of mind were occasioned. He replied that unity and simplicity in all things, but especially in spiritual exercises, must always be preferred to multiplicity and complexity, but that to beginners, and to those little skilled in this exercise, several points should be proposed so as fully to occupy their minds.

I enquired whether, supposing that a single point were taken, it would not be better to dwell likewise upon only one affection and resolution rather than upon several. He answered that when Spring is richest in flowers, bees make the least honey, because they are so delighted to flutter from flower to flower that they do not give themselves time to extract the essence and spirit of which they form their combs. Drones make a great deal of noise and produce a very small result. And to the question whether it was not better often to repeat and dwell upon the same affection and resolution, rather than to develop and expand it by thinking it out, he replied that we ought to imitate painters and sculptors, who work by repeating again and again the strokes of their brush and chisel, and that in order to make a deep impression on the heart it is often necessary to go over the same thing many times.

He added that as those sink, who in swimming move their legs and arms too rapidly, it being necessary to stretch them leisurely and easily, so also those who are too eager in mental prayer, faint away in their thoughts, their distracted meditations causing them only pain and dissatisfaction.

I am asked to explain that saying attributed by our Blessed Father to the great St. Anthony, that he who prays ought to have his mind so fixed upon God, as even to forget that he is praying. Here is the explanation in our Saint's own words. He says in one of his Conferences: "The soul must be kept steadfastly in this path (that, namely, of love and confidence in God) without allowing it to waste its powers in continually trying to ascertain what precisely it is doing and whether its work is satisfactory. Alas! our satisfactions and consolations do not always satisfy God: they only feed that miserable love and care of ourselves which has to do neither with God nor with the thought of God. Certainly, children whom our Lord has set before us as models of the perfection to be aimed at by us are, generally speaking, especially in the presence of their parents, quite untroubled about what is to happen. They cling to them without a thought of providing for themselves. The pleasures their parents procure them they accept in good faith and enjoy in simplicity, without any curiosity whatever as to their causes or effects. The love they feel for their parents and their reliance upon them is all they need. Those whose one desire is to please the Divine Lover have neither inclination nor leisure to turn back upon themselves, for their minds tend continually in the direction whither love carries them."[1]

There is a saying of Tauler's, that holy man who wrote a book on mystic theology, which our Blessed Francis held in high esteem, and was never weary of inculcating upon those of his disciples who were anxious to lead a devout life, or who, having already entered upon it, needed encouragement to make progress in it. Tauler was asked where he, who was so great a contemplative, and who held such close and familiar communication with God, had found God. He answered, "Where I found myself." On being further asked where he had found himself, he said, "Where I forgot myself in God."

He went on to say, "We must lose ourselves in order to find ourselves in God, as it is written: He that loveth his life shall lose it, and he that hateth his life in this—world keepeth it unto life eternal.[2] No man can serve two masters, God and mammon.[3] To follow one you must of necessity quit the other. There is no fellowship between light and darkness or between Christ and Belial.[4]

"The two lovers who built, one the City of Jerusalem, the other the City of Babylon, of whom St. Augustine speaks, have nothing in common. It is the struggle of Esau and Jacob over again."

[Footnote 1: Conf. xii.]

[Footnote 2: John xii. 25.]

[Footnote 3: St. Matt. 24.]

[Footnote 4: Cor. vi. 14, 15.]

UPON ASPIRATIONS.

As the Saint's own ordinary and favourite spiritual exercise was the practice of the presence of God, so he advised those whom he directed in the ways of holiness to devote themselves most earnestly to recollection, and to the use of frequent aspirations or ejaculatory prayers.

On one occasion I asked him whether there would be more spiritual loss in omitting the exercise of mental prayer or in omitting that of recollection and aspirations. He answered that the omission of mental prayer might be repaired during the day or night by frequent withdrawal of the mind into God and by aspirations to Him, but that mental prayer unaccompanied by aspirations was, in his estimation, like a bird with clipped wings. He went on to say that: "by recollection we retire into God, and draw God into ourselves, as it is written: I opened my mouth, and panted, because I longed for Thy commandments,[1] by which is meant the mouth of the heart to which God always graciously inclines His ear. In the Canticle the bride says that her Beloved led her into His cellar of wine, he set in order charity in me.[2] Or, as another version has it, He enrolled me under the banner of His love. Just as wine is stored up in vaults or cellars, and as soldiers gather under their standards or banners; so all the faculties of our soul gather together around the goodness and love of God by short spiritual retreats, made from time to time throughout the day. But when are they made, and in what place? At any moment, and in any place, and there is no meal, or company, or employment, or occupation of any sort which can hinder them, just as they on their part neither hinder nor interfere with anything that has to be done. On the contrary, this is a salt which seasons every kind of food, or rather a sugar which never spoils any sauce. It consists only in inward glances from ourselves and from God, from ourselves into God, and from God into ourselves, without pictures or speech, or any outward aid; and the simpler this recollection is the better it is. As regards aspirations, they also are short but swift dartings of the soul into God, and can be made by a simple mental glance cast towards Him. Cast thy care, or thoughts, upon the Lord,[3] says David. The more vigorously an arrow is shot from the bow the more swift is its flight. The more vehement and loving is an aspiration, the more truly is it a spiritual lightning-flash. These transports or aspirations, of which we have so many formulas, are the better the shorter they are. One of St. Bruno seems to me excellent on account of its brevity: O goodness of God; that also of St. Francis, My God and my all! and that of St. Augustine, Oh! to love, to go forward, to die to self, to reach God!"

Our Blessed Father treats excellently of these two exercises in his Philothea, and recommends them strongly, saying that they hold to one another, as did Jacob and Esau at their birth, and follow one another, as do respiration and aspiration. And just as in respiration we draw the fresh outer air into our lungs, and by aspiration drive out that into which the heat of our bodies has entered, so by the breath of recollection we draw God into ourselves, or retire into

God, and by aspirations we cast ourselves into the arms of His goodness.

Happy the soul that often thus breathes, and thus aspires, for she abides in God and God in her.

[Footnote 1: Psalm cxviii, 131.]

[Footnote 2: Cant. ii. 4.]

[Footnote 3: Psalm liv. 23.]

UPON INTERIOR RECOLLECTION AND EJACULATORY PRAYERS.

The two exercises which he especially recommended to his penitents were interior recollection and ejaculatory aspirations and prayers. By them, he said, the defects of all other spiritual exercises might be remedied, and without them those others were saltless, that is, without savour. He called interior recollection the collecting or gathering up of all the powers of the soul into the heart, there to hold communion with God, alone with Him, heart to heart.

This Blessed Francis could do in all places and at all hours without being hindered by any company or occupations. This recollection of God and of ourselves was the favourite exercise of the great St. Augustine, who so often exclaimed: "Lord, let me know Thee, and know myself!" and of the great St. Francis, who cried out: "Who art Thou, my God and my Lord? and who am I, poor dust and a worm of the earth?" This frequent looking up to God and then down upon ourselves keeps us wonderfully to our duties, and either prevents us from falling, or helps us to raise ourselves quickly from our falls, as the Psalmist says: I set the Lord always in my sight: for He is at my right hand, that I be not moved.[1]

Thou hast held me by my right hand; and by Thy will thou hast conducted me, and with Thy glory Thou hast received me.[2] He teaches us how to practise this exercise in his Philothea, where, dealing with the subject of aspirations or ejaculatory prayers, he says: "In this exercise of spiritual retreat and ejaculatory prayers lies the great work of devotion. We may make up for the deficiency of all other prayers, but failure in this can scarcely ever be repaired. Without it we cannot well lead the contemplative life, and can only lead the active life very imperfectly; without it repose is idleness, and labour only vexation. This is why I conjure you to embrace it with your whole heart, and never to lay it aside."[3]

[Footnote 1: Psalm xv. 8.]

[Footnote 2: Psalm lxxii. 24.]

[Footnote 3: Part ii. c. xii. and xiii.]

UPON DOING AND ENDURING.

His opinion was that one ounce of suffering was worth more than a pound of action; but then it must be of suffering sent by God, and not self-chosen. Indeed, to endure pain which is of our own choosing is rather to do than to suffer, and, speaking in general, our having chosen it spoils our good work, because self-love has insinuated itself into our motives. We wish to serve God in one way, while He desires to be served in another; we wish what He wishes, but not as He wishes it. We do not submit ourselves wholly and as we should do to His will.

A person who was very devout and who was accustomed to spend much time in mental prayer, being attacked with severe headache, was forbidden by her doctor to practise this devotion, as it increased her suffering and prevented her recovery. The patient much distressed at this prohibition wrote to consult our Blessed Father on the subject, and this is his reply:

"As regards meditation," he says, "the doctors are right. While you are so weak, you must abstain from it; but to make up you must double your ejaculatory prayers, and offer them all to God as an act of acquiescence in His good pleasure, which, though preventing you from meditating, in no way separates you from Himself, but, on the contrary, enables you to unite yourself more closely to Him by the practice of calm and holy resignation. What matters it how or by what means we are united to God? Truly, since we seek Him alone, and since we find Him no less in mortification than in prayer, especially when He visits us with sickness, the one ought to be as welcome to us as the other. Moreover, ejaculatory prayers and the silent lifting of the heart to God, are really a continued meditation, and the patient endurance of pain and distress is the worthiest offering we can possibly make to Him who saved us through suffering. Read also occasionally some good book that will fill up what is wanting to you of food for the spirit."

UPON MORTIFICATION AND PRAYER.

Our Blessed Father considered that mortification without prayer is like a body without a soul; and prayer without mortification like a soul without a body. He desired that the two should never be separated, but that, like Martha and Mary, they should without disputing, nay, in perfect harmony, unite in serving our Lord. He compared them to the scales in a balance, one of which goes down when the other goes up. In order to raise the soul by prayer, we must lower the body by mortification, otherwise the flesh will weigh down the soul and hinder it from rising up to God, whose spirit will not dwell with a man sunk in gross material delights or cares.

The lily and the rose of prayer and contemplation can only grow and flourish among the thorns of mortification. We cannot reach the hill of incense, the symbol of prayer, except by the steep ascent on which we find the myrrh of mortification, needed to preserve our bodies from the corruption of sin.

Just as incense, which in Scripture represents prayer, does not give forth its perfume until it is burned, neither can prayer ascend to Heaven unless it proceeds from a mortified heart. Mortification averts temptations, and prayer becomes easy when we are sheltered under the protecting wings of mortification. When we are dead to ourselves and to our passions we begin to live to God. He begins to feed us in prayer with the bread of life and understanding, and with the manna of His inspirations. In fine, we become like that pillar of aromatic smoke to which the Bride is compared, compounded of all the spices of the perfumer.[1]

Our Blessed Father's maxim on this subject was that: "We ought to live in this world as if our soul were in heaven and our body in the tomb."

[Footnote 1: Cant. iii. 6.]

UPON THE PRESENCE OF GOD.

The practice of recollection of the presence of God was so much insisted upon by our Blessed Father that, as you know, my sisters, he recommended it to your Congregation to be the daily bread and constant nourishment of your souls.

He used to say that to be recollected in God is the occupation of the blessed; nay, more, the very essence of their blessedness. Our Lord in the Gospel says that the angels see continually, without interruption or intermission, the face of their Father in heavens and is it not life eternal to see God and to be always in His most holy presence, like the angels, who are called the supporters of His throne.

You know that whenever you are gathered together for recreation, one of you is always appointed as a sort of sentinel to watch over the proper observance of this holy practice, pronouncing from time to time, aloud, these words: "Sisters, we remind your Charities of the holy presence of God," adding, if it has been a day of general communion, "and of the holy communion of to-day."

Our Blessed Father on this subject says in his Devout Life: "Begin all your prayers, whether mental or vocal, by an act of the presence of God, Adhere strictly to this rule, the value of which you will soon realize."[1]

And again: "Most of the failures of good people in the discharge of their duty come to pass because they do not keep themselves sufficiently in the presence of God."

If you desire more instruction on the matter, read again what he has written about it in the same book.

[Footnote 1: Part ii. chap. 1.]

HIS UNITY OF SPIRIT WITH GOD.

He who is joined to the Lord is one spirit,[1] says St. Paul.

Our Blessed Father had arrived at that degree of union with God which is in some sort a unity, because the will of God in it becomes the soul of our will, that is, its life and moving principle, even as our soul is the life and the moving principle of our body. Hence his rapturous ejaculation: "Oh! how good a thing it is to live only in God, to labour only in God, to rejoice only in God!"

Again, he expresses this sentiment even more forcibly in the following words: "Henceforth, with the help of God's grace, I will no longer desire to be anything to any one, or that any one be anything to me, save in God, and for God only. I hope to attain to this when I shall have abased myself utterly before Him. Blessed be God! It seems to me that all things are indeed as nothing to me now, except in Him, for whom and in whom I love every soul more and more tenderly."

Elsewhere he says: "Ah! when will this poor human love of attentions, courtesies, responsiveness, sympathy, and favours be purified and brought into perfect accordance with the all pure love of the Divine will? When will our self-love cease to desire outward tokens of God's nearness and rest content with the changeless and abiding assurance which He gives to us of His eternity? What can sensible presence add to a love which God has made, which He supports, and which He maintains? What marks can be lacking of perseverance in a unity which God has created? Neither presence nor absence can add anything to a love formed by God Himself."

[Footnote 1: 1 Cor. vi. 17.]

HIS GRATITUDE TO GOD FOR SPIRITUAL CONSOLATIONS.

In one of his letters written to a person both virtuous and honourable, in whom he had great confidence, he says: "If you only knew how God deals with my heart, you would thank Him for His goodness to me, and entreat Him to give me the spirit of counsel and of fortitude, so that I may rightly act upon the inspirations of wisdom and understanding which He communicates to me." He often expressed the same thought to me in different words. "Ah!" he would say, "how good must not the God of Israel be to such as are upright of heart, since He is so gracious to those even who have a heart like mine, miserable, heedless of His graces, and earth-bound! Oh! how sweet is His spirit to the souls that love Him and seek Him with all their might! Truly, His name is as balm, and it is no wonder that so many ardent spirits follow Him with enthusiastic devotion, eagerly and joyously hastening to Him, led by the sweetness of His attractions. Oh! what great things we are taught by the unction of divine goodness! Being at the same time illumined by so soft and calm a light that we can scarcely tell whether the sweetness is more grateful than the light, or the light than the sweetness! Truly, the breasts of the Spouse are better than wine, and sweeter than all the perfumes of Arabia.[1]

"Sometimes I tremble for fear that God may be giving me my Paradise in this world! I do not really know what adversity is; I have never looked poverty in the face; the pains which I have experienced have been mere scratches, just grazing the skin; the calumnies spoken against me are nothing but a gust of wind, and the remembrance of them dies away with the sound of the voice which utters them. It is not only that I am free from the ills of life, I am, as it were, choked with good things, both temporal and spiritual. Yet in the midst of all I remain ungrateful and insensible to His goodness. Oh! for pity's sake, help me sometimes to thank God, and to pray Him not to let me have all my reward at once!

"He, indeed, shows that He knows my weakness and my misery by treating me thus like a child, and feeding me with sweetmeats and milk, rather than with more solid food. But oh, when will He give me the grace, after having basked in the sunshine of His favours, to sigh and groan a little under the burden of His Cross, since to reign with Him, we must suffer with Him, and to live with Him, we must die together with Him? Assuredly we must either love or die, or rather we must die that we may love Him; that is to say, die to all other love to live only for His love, and live only for Him who died that we may live eternally in the embrace of His divine goodness."

[Footnote 1: Cantic. i. 1, 2.]

UPON THE SHEDDING OF TEARS.

Although he was himself very easily moved to tears, he did not set any specially high value on what is called the gift of tears, except when it proceeds, not from nature, but directly from the Father of light, who sends His rain upon the earth from the clouds. He told me once that, just as it would be contrary to physical laws for rain, in place of falling from heaven to earth, to rise from earth to heaven; so it was against all order that sensible devotion should produce that which is supernatural. For this would be for nature to produce grace. He compared tears shed, in moments of mental excitement, by persons gifted with a strong power of imagination, to hot rains which fall during the most sultry days of summer, and which scorch rather than refresh vegetation. But when supernatural devotion, seated in the higher powers of the soul, breaking down all restraining banks, spreads itself over the whole being of man, he compared the tears it causes him to shed to a mighty, irresistible and fertilising torrent, making glad the City of God. Tears of this sort, he thought much to be desired, seeing that they give great glory to God and profit to the soul. Of those who shed such tears, he said, the Gospel Beatitude speaks when it tells us that: Blessed are they that weep.[1]

In one of his letters he writes as follows: "I say nothing, my good daughter, about your imagining yourself hard of heart, because you have no tears to shed. No, my child, your heart has nothing to do with this. Your lack of tears proceeds not from any want of affectionate resolve to love, God, but from the absence of sensible devotion, which does not depend at all upon our heart, but upon our natural temperament, which we are unable to change. For just as in this world it is impossible for us to make rain to fall when we want it, or to stop it at our own good pleasure, so also it is not in our power to weep from a feeling of devotion when we want to do so, or, on the other hand, not to weep when carried away by our emotion. Our remaining unmoved at prayer and meditation proceeds, not from any fault of ours, but from the providence of God, who wishes us to travel by land, and often by desert land, rather than by water, and who wills to accustom us to labour and hardship in our spiritual life." On this same subject I once heard him make one of his delightful remarks: "What!" he cried, "are not dry sweetmeats quite as good as sweet drinks? Indeed they have one special advantage. You can carry them about with you in your pocket, whereas the sweet drink must be disposed of on the spot. It is childish to refuse to eat your food when none other is to be had, because it is quite dry. The sea is God's, for He made it, but His hands also laid the foundations of the dry land, that is to say, of the earth. We are land animals, not fish. One goes to heaven by land as easily as by water. God does not send the deluge every day. Great floods are not less to be feared than great droughts!"

[Footnote 1: Matt. v. 5.]

UPON JOY AND SADNESS.

As the blessedness of the life to come is called joy in Scripture, Good and faithful servant, enter into the joy of thy Lord, so also—it is in joy that the happiness of this present life consists. Not, however, in all kinds of joy, for the joy of the hypocrite is but for a moment,[1] that is to say, lasts but for a moment.

It is said of the wicked that they spend their days in wealth, and in a moment go down to hell,[2] and that mourning taketh hold of the end of false joy.[3]

True, joy can only proceed from inward peace, and this peace from the testimony of a good conscience, which is called a continual feast.[4]

This is that joy of the Lord, and in the Lord, which the Apostle recommends so strongly, provided it be accompanied by charity and modesty.

Our Blessed Father thought so highly of this joyous peace and peaceful joy that he looked upon it as constituting the only true happiness possible in this life. Indeed he put this belief of his into such constant practice that a great servant of God, one of his most intimate friends, declared him to be the possessor of an imperturbable and unalterable peace.

On the other hand, he was as great an enemy to sadness, trouble, and undue hurry and eagerness, as he was a friend to peace and joy. Besides all that he says on the subject in his Philothea and his Theotimus, he writes thus to a soul who, under the pretext of austerity and penance, had abandoned herself to disquietude and grief: Be at peace, and nourish your heart with the sweetness of heavenly love, without which man's heart is without life, and man's life without happiness. Never give way to sadness, that enemy of devotion. What is there that should be able to sadden the servant of Him who will be our joy through all eternity? Surely sin, and sin only, should cast us down and grieve us. If we have sinned, when once our act of sorrow at having sinned has been made, there ought to follow in its train joy and holy consolation.

[Footnote 1: Job xx. 5.]

[Footnote 2: Job xxi. 13.]

[Footnote 3: Prov. xiv. 13.]

[Footnote 4: Ibid. xv. 15.]

UPON THE DEGREES OF TRUE DEVOTION.

Loving devotion, or devout love, has three degrees, which are: 1. When we perform those exercises which relate to the service of God, but with some sluggishness. 2. When we betake ourselves to them with readiness. 3. When we run and even fly to execute them with joy and with eagerness.

Our Blessed Father illustrates this by two very apt comparisons.

"Ostriches never fly, barn door fowls fly heavily, close to the ground, and but seldom; eagles, doves, and swallows fly often, swiftly and high. Thus sinners never fly to God, but keep to the ground, nor so much as look up to Him.

"Those who are in God's grace but have not yet attained to devotion, fly to God by their good actions rarely, slowly, and very heavily; but devout souls fly to God frequently and promptly and soar high above the earth."[1] His second comparison is this:

"Just as a man when convalescent from an illness walks as much as is necessary, but slowly and wearily, so the sinner being healed from his iniquity walks as much as God commands him to do, but still only slowly and heavily, until he attains to devotion. Then, like a man in robust health, he runs and bounds along the way of God's commandments; and, more than that, he passes swiftly into the paths of the counsels and of heavenly inspirations. In fact, charity and supernatural devotion are not more different from one another than flame from fire, seeing that charity is a spiritual fire, and when its flame burns fiercely is called devotion. Thus devotion adds nothing to the fire of charity except the flame, which renders charity prompt, active, and diligent, not only in observing the commandments of God, but also in the practice of the counsels and heavenly inspirations."

[Footnote 1: The Devout Life. Part i. c. i.]

THE TEST OF TRUE DEVOTION.

It was his opinion that the touchstone of true devotion is the regulation of exercises of piety according to one's state of life. He often compared devotion to a liquid which takes the form of the vessel into which it is put. Here are his words to Philothea on the subject [1]: "Devotion," he says, "must be differently practised by a gentleman, by an artisan, by a servant, by a prince, by a widow, by a maiden, by a wife, and not only must the practice of devotion be different, but it must in measure and in degree be accommodated to the strength, occupations, and duties of each individual. I ask you, Philothea, would it be proper for a Bishop to wish to lead the solitary life of a Carthusian monk? If a father of a family were as heedless of heaping up riches as a Capuchin; if an artisan spent the whole day in church like a monk; if a monk, like a Bishop, were constantly in contact with the world in the service of his neighbour, would not the devotion of each of these be misplaced, ill-regulated, and laughable? Yet this mistake is very often made, and the world, which cannot or will not distinguish between devotion and indiscretion in those who think themselves devout, murmurs against and blames piety in general, though in reality piety has nothing to do with mistakes such as these."

He goes on to say: "When creating them, God commanded the plants to bring forth their fruits, each according to its kind; so He commands christians, who are the living plants of His Church, to produce fruits of devotion, each according to his state of life and calling."

At the close of the same chapter, our Blessed Father says: "Devotion or piety, when it is real, spoils nothing, but on the contrary perfects everything. Whenever it clashes with the legitimate calling of those who profess it, you may be quite certain that such devotion is spurious. 'The bee,' says Aristotle, 'draws her honey from a flower, without injuring that flower in the least, and leaves it fresh and intact as she found it.'"

[Footnote 1: The Devout Life. Part i. c, 3.]

WHAT IT MEANS TO BE A SERVANT OF GOD.

Some think that they are not making any progress in the service of God unless they feel sensible devotion and interior joy continually, forgetting that the road to heaven is not carpeted with rose leaves but rather bristling with thorns. Does not the divine oracle tell us that through much tribulation we must enter the Kingdom of Heaven? And that it is only taken by those who do violence to themselves? Our Blessed Father writes thus to a soul that was making the above mistake:

"Live wholly for God, and for the sake of the love which He has borne to you, do you bear with yourself in all your miseries. In fact, the being a good servant of God does not mean the being always spiritually consoled, the always feeling sweet and calm, the never feeling aversion or repugnance to what is good. If this were so, neither St. Paul, nor St. Angela, nor St. Catherine of Siena, could have served God well. To be a servant of God is to be charitable towards our neighbour, to have, in the superior part of our soul, an unswerving resolution to follow the will of God, joined to the deepest humility and a simple confidence in Him; however many times we fall, always to rise up again; in fine, to be patient with ourselves in our miseries, and with others in their imperfections."

Another error into which good people fall is that of always wanting to find out whether or not they are in a state of grace. If you tranquillize them on this point, then they begin to torment themselves as to the exact amount of progress they have made, and are actually making, in this happy state of grace, as though their progress were in any way their own work. They quite forget that though one may plant and another water, it is God who gives the increase.

In order to cure this spiritual malady, which borders very closely upon presumption, he gives in another of his letters the following wise counsel:

"Remember that all that is past is nothing, and that every day we should say with David: Now only am I beginning to love my God truly. Do much for God, and do nothing without love, let this be your aim, eat and drink for this."

THAT DEVOTION DOES NOT ALWAYS SPRING FROM CHARITY.

"Do not deceive yourself," he once said to me, "people may be very devout, and at the same time very wicked." "But," I said, "they are then surely not devout, but hypocrites!" "No, no," he answered, "I am speaking of true devotion." As I was quite unable to solve this riddle, I begged him to explain it to me, which he did most kindly, and, if I can trust my memory, more or less as follows:

"Devotion is of itself and of its own nature a moral and acquired virtue, not one that is supernatural and infused, otherwise it would be a theological virtue, which it is not. It is then a virtue, subordinate to that which is called Religion, and according to some is only one of its acts;[1] as religion again is subordinate to one of the four cardinal virtues, namely justice. Now you know that all the moral virtues, and even the theological ones of faith and hope, are compatible with mortal sin, although become, as it were, shapeless and dead, being without charity, which is their form, their soul, their very life. For, if one can have faith so great as to be able to move mountains, without charity, and yet, precisely because charity is absent, be utterly worthless and wicked; if it is possible to be a true prophet and yet a bad man, as were Saul, Balaam, and Caiphas; to work miracles as Judas is believed to have done, and yet to be sinful as he was; if we can give all our goods to the poor, and suffer martyrdom by fire, without having charity, much more may we be devout without being charitable, since devotion is a virtue less estimable in its nature than those which we have mentioned. You must not then think it strange when I tell you that it is possible to be devout and yet wicked, since we may have faith, mercy, patience, and constancy to the extent of which I have spoken, and yet, with all that be stained with many deadly vices, such as pride, envy, hatred, intemperance, and the like."

"What then," I asked, "is a truly devout man?" He answered: "I tell you again that, though in sin, one may be truly devout. But such devotion, though a virtue, is dead, not living," I rejoined: "But how can this dead devotion be real?" "In the same way," he replied, "as a dead body is a real body, soulless though it be." I rejoined: "But a dead body is not really a man." He answered: "It is not a true man, whole and perfect, but it is the true body of a man, and the body of a true man though dead. Thus, devotion without charity is true, though dead and imperfect. It is true devotion dead and shapeless, but not true devotion living and fully formed. It is only necessary to draw a distinction between the words, true, and complete or perfect, which is done so clearly by St. Thomas,[2] in order to find the solution of your difficulty. He who possesses devotion without charity has true, but not perfect or complete devotion; in him who has charity, devotion is not only true but perfect. By charity he becomes good, and by devotion devout; losing charity he loses supernatural goodness and becomes sinful or bad, but does not necessarily cease to be devout. This is why I told you that one could be devout and yet wicked. So also by mortal sin we do not necessarily lose faith or hope, except we deliberately make an act of unbelief or of despair."

He had expressed a somewhat similar idea in the first chapter of his Philothea, though I had not then noticed it. These are his words:

"Devotion is nothing more than a spiritual agility and vivacity, helped by which charity acts more readily; or better, helped by which we more readily elicit acts of charity. It belongs to charity to make us keep God's commandments, but it belongs to devotion to make us keep them promptly and diligently. This is why he who does not observe all the commandments of God cannot be considered either good or supernaturally devout, since in order to be good we must have charity, and to be devout we must have besides charity great alertness and promptitude in doing charitable actions."[3]

In another of his books, speaking to Theotimus, he says:

"All true lovers of God are equal in this, that all give their heart to God, and with all their strength; but they are unequal in this, that they give it diversely and in different manners, whence some give all their heart, with all their strength, but less perfectly than others. This one gives it all by martyrdom; this, all by virginity; this, all by the pastoral office; and whilst all give it all by the observance of the commandments, yet some give it with less perfection than others."[4]

We must remember that true devotion cannot be restricted to the practice of one virtue only; we must employ all our powers in the worship and service of God. One of the chief maxims of Blessed Francis was that the sort of devotion which is not only not a hindrance but actually a help to us in our legitimate calling is the only true one for us, and that any other is false for us. He illustrates this teaching to Philothea by saying that devotion is like a liquid which takes the shape of the vessel into which it is put. He even went further, boldly declaring that it was not simply an error but a heresy to exclude devotion from any calling whatever, provided it be a just and legitimate one. This shows the mistake of those who imagine that we cannot save our souls in the world, as if salvation were only for the Pharisee, and not for the Publican, nor for the house of Zaccheus. This error which approaches very nearly to that of Pelagius, makes salvation to be dependent on certain callings, as though the saving of our souls were the work of nature rather than of grace. Our Blessed Father supports his teaching in this matter by many examples, proving that in every condition of life we may be holy and may consequently save our souls, and arrive at a very high degree of glory.

He concludes by saying: "Some even have been known to lose perfection in solitude, which is often so helpful for its attainment, and to have regained it in a busy city life which seems to be so unfavourable to it. Wherever we are, we can and ought to aspire to the perfect life."

[Footnote 1: S. Thomas 2a, 2ae, Quaest, lxxxi., art. 2.]

[Footnote 2: 2a, 2ae, Quaest, lxxxii. to lxxxviii.]

[Footnote 3: The Devout Life, Part i., chap. 1.]

[Footnote 4: Book x., chap. 3.]

UPON PERFECT CONTENTMENT IN THE PRIVATION OF ALL CONTENT.

It is true that the devout life, which is nothing but an intense and fervent love of God, is an angelic life and full of contentment and of extraordinary consolation. It is, however, also true that those who submit themselves to the discipline of God, even while experiencing the sweetness of this divine love, must prepare their soul for temptation. The path which leads to the Land of Promise is beset with difficulties—dryness, sadness, desolation, and faint-hearted fears—and would end in bewildering discouragement, did not Faith and Hope, like Joshua and Caleb, show us the fair fruits of this much to be desired country, and thus animate us to perseverance.

But He who brings light out of darkness, and roses out of thorns, who helps us in all our tribulations, and performs wonders in heaven and earth, makes the happy souls whom He leads through His will to His glory to find perfect content in the loss of all content, both corporal and spiritual when once they recognize that it is the will of God that they should go to Him by the way of darkness, perplexity, crosses, and anguish.

In saying this I am putting into my own words the thoughts of our Blessed Father as expressed in the eleventh chapter of the sixth book of his Treatise on the Love of God.

UPON THE WILL OF GOD.

Meditating this morning on that passage of Holy Scripture which tells us that the life of man is in the good will of God,[1] I reflected that to live according to the will of the flesh, that is, according to the human will, is not really life, since the prudence of the flesh is death; but that to live according to the will of God is the true life of the soul, since the grace attached to that divine will imparts a life to our soul far higher than the life our soul imparts to our body.

The divine will is our sanctification, and this sanctification is the gate of eternal life; of that true life in comparison with which the life which we lead on earth is more truly a death. To live in God, in whom is true life, is to live according to His will.

Our life, then, is to do His will. This made St. Paul say that he lived, yet not he himself, but that Jesus Christ lived in him,[2] because he had only one will and one mind with Jesus Christ, I was rejoiced to find that unconsciously my thoughts on this subject had followed closely in the track of our Blessed Father's when he meditated on the same passage. This I discovered on reading these words in one of his letters:

"This morning, being alone for a few moments, I made an act of extraordinary resignation which I cannot put on paper, but reserve until God permits me to see you, when you shall know it by word of mouth. Oh! how blessed are the souls who live on the will of God alone. Ah! if even to taste a little of that blessedness in a passing meditation is so sweet to the heart which accepts that holy will with all the crosses it offers, what must the happiness be of a soul all steeped in that will? Oh! my God, what a blessed thing is it not to bring all our affections into a humble and absolute subjection to the divine love! This we have said, this we have resolved to do, and our hearts have taken the greatest glory of the love of God for their sovereign law. Now the glory of this holy love consists in its power of burning and consuming all that is not itself, that all may be resolved and changed into it. God exalts Himself upon our annihilation of ourselves and reigns upon the throne of our voluntary servitude."

[Footnote 1: Psalm xxix. 6.]

[Footnote 2: Gal. ii. 20.]

HIS RESIGNATION TO THE WILL OF GOD.

It happened that Blessed Francis fell ill at the very time when his predecessor in the Bishopric of Geneva was imploring the Holy See to appoint him as his coadjutor.

The illness was so serious that the physicians despaired of his life, and this our Blessed Father was told. He received the announcement quite calmly, and even joyfully, as though he saw the heavens open and ready to receive him, and being entirely resigned to the will of God both in life and in death, said only:

"I belong, to God, let Him do with me according to His good pleasure."

When someone in his presence said that he ought to wish to live if not for the service of God at least that he might do penance for his sins, he answered thus: "It is certain that sooner or later we must die, and whenever it may be, we shall always have need of the great mercy of God: we may as well fall into His pitiful hands to-day as to-morrow. He is at all times the same, full of kindness, and rich in mercy to all those who call upon Him: and we are always evil, conceived in iniquity, and subject to sin even from our mother's womb. He who finishes his course earlier than others has less of an account to render. I can see that there is a design afoot to lay upon me a burden not less formidable to me than death itself. Between the two I should find it hard to choose. It is far better to submit myself to the care of Providence: far better to sleep upon the breast of Jesus Christ than anywhere else. God loves us. He knows better than we do what is good for us. Whether we live, or whether we die, we are the Lord's.[1] He has the keys of life, and of death.[2] They who hope in Him are never confounded.[3] Let us also go, and die with Him." And when someone said it was a pity he should die in the flower of his age (he was only thirty-five), he answered: "Our Lord was still younger when He died. The number of our days is before Him, He can gather the fruits which belong to Him at any season. Do not let us waste our time and thoughts over circumstances; let us consider only His most holy will. Let that be our guiding star; it will lead us to Jesus Christ whether in the cribs or on Calvary. Whoever follows Him shall not walk in darkness but shall have the light of eternal life, and shall be no more subject to death."

These were the words, this was the perfect resignation, of our Blessed Father. Who can say we have not here the cause of the prolongation of his days, even as a like resignation led to the prolonging of those of King Ezechias.

[Footnote 1: Rom. xiv. 8]

[Footnote 2: Apoc. i. 18.]

[Footnote 3: Psalm xxiv. 3.]

THAT WE MUST ALWAYS SUBMIT OURSELVES TO GOD'S HOLY WILL.

In 1619, when our Saint was in Paris with the Prince of Savoy, a gentleman of the court fell dangerously ill. He sent for Blessed Francis, who, when visiting him, remarked with some surprise that, although he bore his physical sufferings with great patience, he fretted grievously about other troubles seemingly of very small moment. He was distressed at the thought of dying away from home, at being unable to give his family his last blessing, at not having his accustomed physician by his side, etc. Then he would begin to worry about the details of his funeral, the inscription on his tombstone, and so on. Nothing was right in his surroundings; the sky of Paris, his doctors and nurses, his servants, his bed, his rooms, all were matters of complaint. "Strange inconsistency!" exclaimed the holy Bishop. "Here is a brave soldier and a great statesman, fretted by the merest trifles, and unhappy because he cannot die in exactly the circumstances which he would have chosen for himself." I am glad to be able to add that in spite of all this the poor man made a holy and a happy end.

But Blessed Francis afterwards said to me: "It is not enough to will what God wills, we must also desire that all should be exactly, even in the minutest detail and particular, as God wills it to be. For instance, in regard to sickness we should be willing to be sick because it pleases God that we should be so; and sick of that very sickness which God sends us, not of one of a different character; and sick at such time, and in such place, and surrounded by such attendants, as it may please God to appoint. In short, we must in all things take for our law the most holy will of God."

HIS SUBLIME THOUGHTS ON HOLY INDIFFERENCE.

Many of the saints, and especially St. Catherine of Siena, St. Philip Neri, and St. Ignatius Loyola, have spoken in the most beautiful and elevated language of that holy indifference which, springing from the love of God, makes life or death and all the circumstances of the one or the other equally acceptable to the soul which realizes that all is ordered by the will of God.

Let us hear what our Blessed Father says on this subject in his Treatise on the Love of God.

"God's will is the sovereign object of the indifferent soul; wheresoever she sees it she runs after the odour of its perfumes, directing her course ever thither where it most appears, without considering anything else. She is conducted by the divine will, as by a beloved chain; which way soever it goes she follows it: she would prize hell with God's will more than heaven without it; nay, she would even prefer hell before heaven if she perceived only a little more of God's good-pleasure in that than in this, so that if—to suppose what is impossible—she should know that her damnation would be more agreeable to God than her salvation, she would quit her salvation and run to her damnation."[1]

This is, indeed, a bold and daring proposition, but to convince you how tenaciously he clung to it I would remind you of his words in the Conferences;[2] on the same subject: "The saints who are in heaven are so closely united to the will of God that if there were even a little more of His good-pleasure in hell than in paradise they would quit paradise to go there." And again in the same Conference: "Whether the malady conquers the remedies or the remedies get the better of the malady should be a matter of perfect indifference. So much so that if sickness and health were put before us and our Lord were to say to us: 'If thou choose health I will not deprive thee of a single particle of my grace, if thou choose sickness I shall not in any degree increase that grace, but in the choice of sickness there is a little more of my good-pleasure,' the soul which has wholly forsaken herself and abandoned herself into the hands of our Lord will undoubtedly choose sickness solely because it is more pleasing to God. Nay, though this might mean a whole lifetime spent on her couch in constant suffering, she would not for any earthly consideration desire to be in any other condition than this."

[Footnote 1: Bk. ix., c. 5.]

[Footnote 2: Conf. ii.]

NOTHING, SAVE SIN, HAPPENS TO US BUT BY THE WILL OF GOD.

"Nothing happens to us," Blessed Francis was accustomed to say, "whether of good or of evil, sin alone excepted, but by the will of God." Good, because God is the source of all good. Every best gift and every perfect gift is from above, coming down from the Father of lights.[1] Evil, for, Shall there be evil in the city which the Lord hath not done?[2] The evil here spoken of is that of pain or trouble, seeing that God cannot will the evil of crime, which is sin, though he permits it, allowing the human will to act according to the natural liberty which He has given to it. Properly speaking, sin cannot be said to happen to us, because what happens to us must come from without, and sin, on the contrary, comes from within, proceeding from our hearts, as holy Scripture expressly states, telling us also that iniquity comes from our fatness,[3] that is to say, from our ease and luxury.

Oh, what a happiness it would be for our souls if we accustomed ourselves to receive all things from the fatherly hand of Him who, in opening it, fills all things living with blessing! What unction should we not draw from this in our adversities! What honey from the rock, what oil from the stones! And with how much moderation should we not behave in prosperity, since God sends us both the one and the other, that we may use both to the praise and glory of His grace.

[Footnote I: St. James i. 17.]

[Footnote II: Amos iii. 6.]

[Footnote III: Psalm lxxii. 7.]

UPON THE SAME SUBJECT.

I must confess to you, my sisters, that I was astonished to read in one of our Saint's letters that our Lord Jesus Christ did not possess the quality of indifference in the sensitive part of His nature.

I will give the exact words in which this wonderful fact is stated. "This virtue of indifference," he says, "is so excellent that our old Adam, and the sensitive part of our human nature, so far as its natural powers go, is not capable of it, no, not even in our Lord, who, as a child of Adam, although exempt from all sin, and from everything pertaining to sin, yet in the sensitive part of his nature and as regards his human faculties was in no way indifferent, but desired not to die upon the Cross. Indifference, and the exercise of it, is entirely reserved for the spirit, for the supreme portion of our nature, for faculties set on fire by grace, and in fine for Himself personally, inasmuch as He is divine and human, the New Man. How, then, can we complain when as far as this lower portion of our nature is concerned we find ourselves unable to be indifferent to life, and to death, to health, and to sickness, to honour and to ignominy, to pleasure and to pain, to comfort and to discomfort, when, in a word, we feel in ourselves that conflict going on which the vessel of election experienced in such a manner as to make him exclaim: Unhappy man that I am, who shall deliver me from the body of this death?"[1]

The love of ourselves is so deeply rooted in our nature that it is impossible wholly to rid ourselves of it. Even grace does not do away with our self-love, but only reduces it to the service of divine charity.

By the love of self I mean a natural, just, and legitimate love, so legitimate indeed as to be commanded by the law of God which bids us love our neighbour as ourselves; that is to say, according to God's will, which is not only the one way in which we can rightly love our neighbour, but also the one way in which we are commanded to love ourselves.

Nevertheless, this love of ourselves, however just and reasonable it may be, turns only too easily, and too imperceptibly, into a self-love, which is unlawful and forbidden, but into which even persons the most earnest and the most spiritual are at times surprised.

We often think we love someone, or something in God, and for God, when it is really only in ourselves, and for ourselves, that we do so. We think sometimes that we have only an eye to the interests of God, which is His glory, when it is really our own glory which we are seeking in our work. This is when we stop short voluntarily at the creature to the prejudice of the Creator; as comes to pass in all sin, whether mortal or venial. We must therefore watch and be constantly on our guard lest we fall into this snare. From it we must snatch our soul as we would a bird from the snare of the fowler. We shall be safe if we remember that every just and lawful love in us is always either in actual touch with the love of God, or can be brought into such touch, whilst self-love is never in such touch, nor can ever be brought into it.

This is the test by which we can detect the false coin that is mixed up with the true.

[Footnote 1: Rom. vii. 24.]

UPON ABANDONING OURSELVES TO GOD.

I cannot tell you, my sisters, how great a point our Blessed Father made of self-abandonment, i.e., self-surrender into the hands of God. In one place he speaks of it as: "The cream of charity, the odour of humility, the flower of patience, and the fruit of perseverance. Great," he says, "is this virtue, and worthy of being practised by the best beloved children of God."[1] And again, "Our Lord loves with a most tender love those who are so happy as to abandon themselves wholly to His fatherly care, letting themselves be governed by His divine Providence without any idle speculations as to whether the workings of this Providence will be useful to them to their profit, or painful to their loss, and this because they are well assured that nothing can be sent, nothing permitted by this paternal and most loving Heart, which will not be a source of good and profit to them. All that is required is that they should place all their confidence in Him, and say from their heart, Into Thy hands I commend my spirit, my soul, my body, and all that I have, to do with them as it shall please Thee."[2]

You are inclined, my sisters, to say that we are not all of us capable of such entire self-renunciation, that so supreme an act of self-abandonment is beyond our strength. Hear then, too, what our Blessed Father goes on to say. These are his words in the same Conference: "Never are we reduced to such an extremity that we cannot pour forth before the divine majesty the perfume of a holy submission to His most holy will, and of a continual promise never wilfully to offend Him."

[Footnotes 1, 2: Conf. 2.]

UPON INTERIOR DESOLATION.

As there are, more thorns than roses in our earthly life, and more dull days than sunny ones, so also in our spiritual life our souls are more frequently clouded by a sense of desolation, dryness, and gloom, than irradiated by heavenly consolations and brightness.

Yet our Blessed Father says that "those are mistaken who think that, even in Christians, whose conscience does not accuse them of sins unconfessed, but on the contrary bears good witness for them, a heavy heart and sorrow-laden mind is a proof of God's displeasure.

"Has God not said that He is with us in tribulation, and is not His Cross the mark of the chosen? At the birth of Jesus, while the shepherds were surrounded by the light which shone from heaven and their ears filled with the songs of angels, Mary and Joseph were in the stable in the darkness of night, the silence only broken by the weeping of the Holy Child. Yet who would not rather be with Jesus, Mary, and Joseph in that shadowy gloom than with the shepherds even in their ecstasy of heavenly joy? St. Peter, indeed, amid the glories of Thabor said: It is good to be here, let us make here three tabernacles.[1] But Holy Scripture adds: Not knowing what he said.

"The faithful soul loves Jesus covered with wounds and disfigurements on Calvary, amid the darkness, the blood, the crosses, the nails, the thorns, and the horror of death: loves Him, I say, as dearly, as fervently as in His triumph, and cries out from a full heart amid all this desolation:

"Let us make here three tabernacles, one for Jesus, one for His holy Mother, and one for His beloved disciple."

[Footnote 1: Luke ix, 33.]

UPON THE PRESENCE IN OUR SOULS OF THE GRACE OF GOD.

There is, I think, no greater temptation than one which assails many good people, namely, the desire to know for certain whether or not they are in a state of grace.

To a poor soul entangled in a perfect spider's web of doubt and mistrust, our Blessed Father wrote the following consoling words: "To try and discover whether or not your heart is pleasing to God is a thing you must not do, though you may undoubtedly try to make sure that His Heart is pleasing to you. Now, if you meditate upon His Heart it will be impossible but that it should be well pleasing to you, so sweet is it, so gentle, so condescending, so loving towards those of His poor creatures who do but acknowledge their wretchedness: so gracious to the unhappy, so good to the penitent. Ah! who would not love this royal Heart, which to us is as the heart both of a father and of a mother?"

As regards interior desolation there are some souls who seem to think that no devotion is worthy of the name which is not sensible and full of emotion.

To one who complained to our Blessed Father of having lost all relish for exercises of piety, he wrote in the following words: "The love of God consists neither in consolations nor in tenderness—otherwise our Lord would not have loved His father when He was sorrowful unto death, nor when He cried out, My God, my God, why hast Thou forsaken me?[1] That is to say, then, when He performed the greatest act of love that it is possible to imagine.

"The truth is, we are always hungering after consolation, for a little sugar to be added to our spiritual food; in other words, we always want to experience our feelings of love and tenderness, and thereby to be cheered and comforted."

[Footnote 1: Matt. xxvii. 46.]

UPON OUR DESIRE TO SAVE OUR SOUL.

Faith teaches us, by means of the Holy Scriptures, that God ardently desires that we should be saved,[1] and that none should perish. His will is our sanctification, that is to say, He wishes us to be holy. Moreover, to prove that His desire is neither barren nor unhelpful, He gives us in His holy Church all the graces necessary for our salvation, so that if we are lost it will only be because of our own wilful malice.

Unfortunately, however, though it may be that all desire to save their souls, all are not willing to accept the means offered them for so doing. Hence the disorders which we see in the world around us and the truth, that, while many are called few are chosen. On this subject our Blessed Father speaks as follows in his Theotimus:

"We are," he says, "to will our salvation in such sort as God wills it; now He wills it by way of desire, and we also must incessantly desire it, in conformity with His desire. Nor does He will it only, but, in effect, gives us all necessary means to attain to it. We then, in fulfilment of the desire we have to be saved, must not only wish to be saved, but, in effect, must accept all the graces which He has provided for us, and offers us. With regard to salvation itself, it is enough to say: I desire to be saved. But, with regard to the means of salvation, it is not enough to say: I desire them. We must, with an absolute resolution, will and embrace the graces which God presents to us; for our will must correspond with God's will. And, inasmuch as He gives us the means of salvation, we ought to avail ourselves of such means, just as we ought to desire salvation in such sort as God desires it for us, and because He desires it."[2]

[Footnote 1: 1 Tim. ii. 4.]

[Footnote 2: The Love of God. Bk. viii. 4.]

UPON GOOD NATURAL INCLINATIONS.

Blessed Francis always impressed upon us the necessity of making use for the glory of God of any good inclinations natural to us. "If you possess such," he would say, "remember that they are gifts, of which you will have to render an account. Take care, then, to employ them in the service of Him who gave them to you. Engraft upon this wild stock the shoots of eternal love which God is ready to bestow upon you, if, by an act of perfect self-renunciation, you prepare yourself to receive them."

There are people who are naturally inclined to certain moral virtues, such as silence, sobriety, modesty, chastity, humility, patience, and the like, and who, however little they may cultivate these virtues, make great progress in them. This was the case with many of the great pagan philosophers as we know, and it is quite true, that with all of us, the bent and inclination of the mind towards the acquisition of any kind of excellence, whether moral or physical, is an immense assistance. Still, we must bear in mind the fact that the acquiring of every moral virtue and every physical power, nay, of the whole world itself, is nothing, if, in gaining them, we should lose our own soul. St. Paul tells us this,[1] and for the same reason, our Blessed Father warns us not to keep our talents wrapped up in a napkin, not to hide their light under the bushel of nature, but to trade with them according to the intention of Him who is their author and distributor. He reminds us that this divine Giver who bestowed them on us in order thereby to increase His exterior glory, promises us a reward if we use them as He means us to do, and threatens us with punishment if we are careless in the matter.

You ask me how we are to deal with these inclinations and manage these talents or virtues? Well, you have the answer to that question in the words of our Blessed Father which I quoted: "Engraft on the wild stock of natural inclination shoots of divine charity."

[Footnote 1: 1 Cor. xiii. 1, 3.]

HOW TO SPEAK OF GOD.

St. Francis loved those words of St. Peter: If any man speak, let him speak as the words of God. If any man minister, let him do it as of the power which God administreth,[1] and of St. Paul: All things whatsoever you do, whether in word or in work, do them in the name (that is to say, to the honour and glory) of our Lord Jesus Christ.[2]

That we may carry out this excellent precept in our actions, our Blessed Father gives us some remarkable teaching. In one of his letters he says: "We must never speak of God or of things relating to His worship, that is, of religion, carelessly, and in the way of ordinary conversation, but always with great respect, esteem, and devotion."

This advice applies to those who speak of God, and of religious matters as they would of any ordinary topics of conversation, without taking into account the circumstances of time, place, or persons. St. Jerome complained of this abuse, saying that whilst there are masters and experts in every art and science, only on matters of theology and Holy Scripture, the foundations of all arts and sciences, can few be found to speak well. Yet questions relating to them are discussed most flippantly at table, and in public places; the hare-brained youth, the uneducated labourer, and the dotard, give their opinions freely on the highest mysteries of the Faith.

Again, Blessed Francis says: "Always speak of God as of God, that is to say, reverently and devoutly, not in a self-sufficient, preaching spirit, but with gentleness, charity, and humility."[3]

In the same book he gives his advice to Philothea in the following words: "Never, then, speak of God or of religion for form's sake, or to make conversation, but always with attention and devotion. I tell you this, that you may not be guilty of an extraordinary sort of vanity, which is observable in many who profess to be devout. These people, on all possible occasions, throw in expressions of piety and fervour without the least thought of what they are saying, and, having uttered these phrases, imagine that they themselves are such, as their words would indicate, which is not at all the case."

[Footnote 1: 1 St. Peter iv. 11.]

[Footnote 2: Col. iii 17.]

[Footnote 3: Part iii., chap. 26.]

UPON ECCENTRICITIES IN DEVOTION.

Blessed Francis had a great dislike of any kind of affectation or singularity practised by devout persons, whether in Religious houses or in the world. He went so far as to say that it rendered their piety not merely offensive, but ridiculous.

He wished every one to conform as far as possible to the way of life proper to his or her calling, without affecting any peculiarity. He gave as his authority for this desire the example of our Lord, who, in the days of His flesh, condescended to make Himself like to His brethren in all things excepting sin.

The holy Bishop inculcated this lesson upon his penitents, not only by word, but much more by his example. Never during the whole fourteen years which, happily for me, I spent under his direction studying most closely all his actions, his very gestures, his words, and his teaching; never, I say, did I observe in him the faintest shadow of singularity.

I must confess to having, in order to find out exactly what he was, practised a ruse, which some might think inexcusable or impertinent. Every year he paid me a week's visit, and before he came I took care to have some holes pierced in the doors or boarding of his rooms, that I might closely observe his behaviour when quite alone. Well, I can truly say that whatever he did, whether he prayed, read, meditated, or wrote, in his lying down and in his rising up, at all times and in all circumstances, he was the same—calm, unaffected, simple—his outward demeanour corresponding with the interior beauty of his soul. Francis quite alone was the very same as Francis in company. I think, myself, that this was the result of his continual attention to the presence of God, a practice which he recommended so strongly to all who were under his direction.

When he prayed, it was as though he saw the angels and the saints gathered round him. He remained for hours calm, motionless as a statue, and changeless in expression.

Never, even when alone, did he for the sake of greater comfort sit or stand or assume attitudes other than those he permitted himself when in public. He never so much as crossed his legs, or rested his head on his hand. The unvarying but easy gravity of his demeanour naturally inspired an unfailing love and respect.

He said that our exterior deportment should be like water which, the better it is, the more is it tasteless.

I was much pleased on hearing a very famous and devout person,[1] whom I met in Paris, say this to me about our Saint. That nothing brought so vividly to his mind what the conversation of our Lord Jesus Christ must have been among men, as the presence and angelic deportment of the holy Bishop, of whom one might truly say that he was not only clothed with, but absolutely full of, Jesus Christ. Nor will this appear strange to us if we remember that the just soul, that is to say, the soul which is in a state of grace, is said to be conformed to the image of the Son of God, and is called a participator of the divine nature.

[Footnote 1: St. Vincent de Paul.]

UPON CONFRATERNITIES.

He advised devout people to give in their names boldly, and without much consultation, to the confraternities which they happened to meet with, so as to become by this means participators of grace with all those who fear God and live according to His law. He pitied the scruples of those good souls who fear to enrol themselves, lest, as they ignorantly imagine, they should sin by not fulfilling certain duties laid down in the rules given for the guidance and discipline of these confraternities, but which are rather recommended than commanded.

"For," he said, "if the rules of Religious Orders are not in themselves binding under pain of either mortal or venial sin, how much less so are the statutes of confraternities?

"The following out of the recommendations given to their members to do certain things, to recite certain prayers, to take part in certain meetings or processions, is a matter of counsel, and not of precept. To those who perform such pious actions, Indulgences are granted, which those who do not practise them fail to gain; but such failure, even if wilful, is not a sin. There is much to gain, and nothing to lose."

On this subject he speaks thus to Philothea:

"Enter readily into the confraternities of the place in which you are living, and specially into those whose exercises are the most fruitful and edifying. In doing this, you will be practising a kind of obedience which is very pleasing to God, and the more so because although the joining confraternities is not commanded, yet it is recommended by the Church, who, to show that she desires Catholics to enrol themselves therein, grants Indulgences and other privileges to their members. Then, too, it is always a charitable thing to concur and co-operate with others in their good works. And although it may be that we should make quite as good exercises by ourselves as we do in common with our fellow-members, yet we promote the glory of God better by uniting ourselves with our brethren and neighbours, and sharing our good deeds with them."[1]

[Footnote 1: Part ii., chap. 15.]

UPON INTERCOURSE WITH THE WORLD.

There are some good people whose zeal not being sufficiently tempered with knowledge, as soon as they desire to give themselves up to a devout life, fly from society and from intercourse with others as owls shun the company of birds that fly by day. Their morose and unsociable conduct causes a dislike to be taken to devotion instead of rendering it sweet and attractive to all. Our Blessed Father was altogether opposed to such moroseness, wishing His devout children to be by their example a light to the world, and the salt of the earth, so as to impart a flavour to piety which might tempt the appetite of those who would otherwise surely turn from it with disgust. To a good soul who asked him whether Christians who wished to live with some sort of perfection should see company and mix in society, he answers thus: "Perfection, my dear lady, does not lie in avoiding our fellow-men, but it does lie in not over-relishing social pleasures and in not taking undue delight in them. There is danger for us in all that we see in a sinful world, for we run the risk of fixing our affections upon things worldly; at the same time to those who are steadfast and resolute, the mere sight of the things of this world will do no harm. In a word, the perfection of charity is the perfection of life, for the life of our soul is charity. The early Christians, who were in the world in their body though not in their heart, undoubtedly were very perfect."[1]

As regards the world's opinion of us, and the estimation in which we are held by others, it is not well to be too sensitive. At the same time, to be altogether indifferent about our reputation is blameworthy. Our Blessed Prelate teaches his Philothea exactly what we have to do:

"If," he says, "the world despises us, let us rejoice, for it is right—we see for ourselves that we are very contemptible. If it esteems us, let us despise its esteem and its judgment, for it is blind. Trouble yourself very little about what the world thinks; do not ask or even care to know. Despise equally its appreciation and its contempt, and let it say what it will, good or evil. I do not approve of doing what is not right, that people may have a bad opinion of us. Transgressing is always transgressing, and we are thereby making our neighbour transgress likewise. On the contrary, I desire that, keeping our eyes always fixed upon our Lord, we do what we have to do without regarding what the world thinks of us, or its behaviour towards us. We need not endeavour to give others a good opinion of ourselves, yet neither have we to try to give a bad one, and especially must we be careful not to do wrong with this intent.

"But we can never stand quite well with the world; it is far too exacting. If out of compliance we yield to it, and play and dance with it, it will be scandalized; and if we do not, it will accuse us of hypocrisy and gloom; if we are well-dressed it will impute to us some bad motive; and if we are ill-dressed it will call us mean; it will style our gaiety dissoluteness and our mortification gloom. It will exaggerate our failings and publish our faults; and if it cannot find fault with our actions it will attack our motives. Whatever we do the world will find fault. If we spend a long time at confession it will ask what we can have to say; if we take but a short time, it will say that we do not tell everything. If one little cross word escape us it will pronounce our temper unbearable; it will denounce our prudence as avarice, our gentleness as folly. Spiders invariably spoil the bees' labour. Therefore, do not mind what opinion the world has of you, good or bad; do not distress yourself about it, whichever it be. To say that we are not what the world thinks, when it speaks well of us, is wise, for the world, like a quack doctor, always exaggerates."

You question me, regarding the contempt which we should feel for the world and the world's opinion of us; in other words you want to know exactly what St. Paul means when he says that, being crucified to the world and the world to us, we should glory only in the Cross of our Saviour Jesus Christ.[2]

This seems to you a paradox; light evolved from darkness, and glory from shame. Let me remind you that the Christian religion is full of such paradoxes, and that we belong to an all-powerful God, who has given life to us by His death; who has healed us by His wounds, and who makes us rich by His poverty. I cannot, however, explain the difficulty to you better than by quoting the words of our Blessed Father in one of his letters. He says: "In this alone lies our glory, that our divine Saviour died for us, the Master for His slaves, the just for the unjust."

[Footnote 1: Cf. The Devout Life. Part iv., c. 7.]

[Footnote 2: Galat. vi. 14.]

AGAINST OVER-EAGERNESS.

Blessed Francis advised his penitents to avoid above all things, excessive eagerness, which, in his view, is the mortal foe of true devotion. He says: "It is far better to do a few things well than to undertake many good works and leave them half done."

This was the mistake of the man in the Gospel who began to build and was not able to finish because he had not counted the cost beforehand. There are some who think they are never doing well unless they are doing much. They are like the Pharisees who considered the perfection of prayer to consist in its length. Our Lord reproves them for this and much more for devouring widows' houses with their long prayers. In one of his Conferences the Saint speaks thus: "It is not by the multiplicity of things we do that we acquire perfection, but by the perfection and purity of intention with which we do them."

And this is what he says on the subject in his Theotimus: "To do few actions but with great purity of intention and with a firm will to please God, is to do excellently. Such greatly sanctify us. Some men eat much, and yet are ever lean, thin, and delicate, because their digestive power is not good; there are others who eat little, and yet are always in excellent health and vigorous, because their stomach is good. Even so, there are some souls that do many good works and yet increase but little in charity, because they do those good works either coldly and negligently, or have undertaken them rather from natural instinct and inclination than because God so willed and with heaven-given fervour. On the contrary, others there are who get through little work, but do it with so holy a will; and inclination, that they make a wonderful advancement in charity; they have little talent, but they husband it so faithfully that the Lord largely; rewards them for it."[1]

[Footnote 1: Love of God. B. xii., c. 7.]

UPON THE SAME SUBJECT.

Our Blessed Father always insisted on the necessity of discretion as well as charity in our devotion, and warned us against that want of self-restraint and calmness, which he called eagerness. This, he said, is, indeed, the remora of true devotion, and its worst enemy, the more so because it decks itself in the livery of devotion, in order more easily to entrap the unwary and to make them mistake zeal without knowledge for genuine fervour.

He was very fond of that saying of an ancient Emperor: "Make haste slowly," and of another: "Soon enough, if well enough." He would rather have a little done thoroughly well, than a great deal undertaken with over-eagerness. One of his favourite maxims was "Little and good." In order to persuade us that he was right, he used to warn us against thinking that perfection depends on the number of our good works, exterior or interior. When asked what then became of that insatiable love of which the masters of the spiritual life speak, that love which never thinks that it has reached the goal, but is always pressing on farther and farther, spanning the whole extent of heaven with giant strides, he answered: "The tree of that love must grow at the roots, rather than by the branches." He explained his meaning thus: To grow by the branches is to wish to perform a great number of good works, of which many are imperfect, others superfluous like the useless leaves which overload the vine, and have to be nipped off before the grapes can grow to any proper size. On the other hand we grow at the roots when we do only a few good works, but those few most perfectly, that is to say, with a great love of God, in which all the perfection of the Christian consists. It is to this that the Apostle exhorts us when he bids us be rooted and grounded in charity if we would comprehend the surpassing charity of the knowledge of Jesus Christ. True devotion, he used to say, should be gentle, tranquil, and discreet, whereas eagerness is indiscreet, tempestuous, and turbulent.

Especially he found fault with the eagerness which attempts to do several things at once. He said it was like trying to thread more than one needle at a time. One of his favourite mottos was: "Sufficient to the day is the labour thereof."

When he was reproached, as he sometimes was, with bestowing such earnest and undivided attention on the most trivial concerns of the people who came to him for sympathy and advice, he answered: "These troubles appear great to them, and, therefore, they must be consoled, as if they really were so. God knows, too, that I do not want any great employment. It is perfectly indifferent to me what my occupation is so long as it is a serving of Him. To do these small works is all that is, at the time being, asked of me. Is not doing the will of God a work great enough for anyone? We turn little actions into great ones when we perform them with a supreme desire to please God, who measures our services, not by the excellence of the work we do, but by the love which accompanies it, and that love by its purity, and that purity by the singleness of its intention."

UPON LIBERTY OF SPIRIT.

He was a great enemy to every sort of spiritual restriction and constraint, and was fond of quoting the words of St. Paul: Where the spirit of God is, there is liberty.[1] And again: You are redeemed with a great price, do not make yourselves slaves again.[2] He had advised a lady of rank to work with her own hands, in order to avoid sloth, and, as she was well to do, he suggested to her to devote her manual labour to the adornment of altars or to the service of the poor, following the advice of the Apostle, who counsels us to labour with our hands to provide for the wants of the needy. This lady, who always followed his suggestions to the very letter as if they were commands, having done some little piece of work for herself, felt a scruple about the matter, as though she had failed in the exact obedience which she had resolved to yield, not only to the commands of the holy Prelate, but even to his opinions. She therefore, asked him if she ought to give in alms exactly what a piece of work she had done for herself was worth. Moreover, having been advised to fast on Fridays she wished, she said, in order to gain more merit to make a vow that she would always practise this mortification.

Here is his reply: "I approve of your Friday fasts, but not that you should make any vow to keep them, nor that you should tie yourself down, tightly in such matters. Still more do I approve of your working with your hands, spinning and so forth, at times when nothing greater or more important claims your attention, and that what you make should be destined either for the altar or for the poor, I should not, however, like you to keep to this so strictly, that if it should happen that you do something for yourself or for your family you should feel obliged to give the poor the value of your work. For, holy liberty and freedom must reign, and we must have no other law than love, which, when it bids us to do some kind of work for our own family or friends, must not be looked upon as if it had led us to do wrong. Still less does it require us to make amends, as you wished to do seeing that whatever it invites us to take in hand, whether for the rich or for the poor, is equally pleasing to our Lord." What do you think of this doctrine, you who go by rule and measure in valuing an act of virtue? Is liberality displayed towards the rich, in your opinion, worth as much as alms given to the poor? See now, this holy Bishop follows a very different rule, and measuring the one action and the other by the golden standard of charity, esteems them as equal, provided both be done with equal charity.

[Footnote 1: II. Cor. iii. 17.]

[Footnote 2: Cor. vii. 23]

UPON NATURE AND GRACE.

In certain minds there seems always to lurk some remains of Pelagianism, a hydra from which though bruised and crushed by the Church—the pillar and bulwark of the Truth—new heads are ever springing forth.

Many, as I am willing to believe, from lack of consideration, ascribe too much to nature, and too little to grace, making too great capital of the matter of moral virtues, and too little of the manner in which they are practised. These people forget that in our works God does not regard how much we do, but with how much love we do it, non quantum, sed ex quanta, in the language of the schools.

On this subject our Blessed Father gives the following excellent advice to a pious person who, because she had to devote the greater part of her time to household affairs and to mix a good deal in society was discouraged, and thought it almost impossible for her to lead a devout life.

"Do not," he says, "look at all at the substance of the things which you do, but rather, poor though they be, at the honour by which they are ennobled, that of being willed by God, ordered by His Providence, and arranged by His wisdom, in a word, that of being pleasing to God. And if they please Him, whom can they reasonably offend? Strive, my dearest daughter, to become every day more pure in heart.

"This purity of heart consists in setting on all things their true value, and in weighing them in the balance of the sanctuary, which balance is only another name for the wilt of God." In the same way in his Theotimus he teaches that acts of the lesser virtues are often more pleasing to God, and consequently more meritorious, because done with great love, than the most splendid virtues when practised with less of heavenly charity. Charity is the pure gold which makes us rich in immortal wealth.

UPON EXAGGERATED INTROSPECTION.

Blessed Francis was not at all fond of too much self-introspection, or of the habit of turning an unimportant matter over and over a hundred times in the mind. He called this pernicious hair-splitting; or, with the Psalmist: "Spinning spiders' webs."[1] People given to it he used to say are like the silkworm, which imprisons and entangles itself in its own cocoon. In his twelfth Conference he speaks further on this subject.

"The soul," he says, "which is wholly bent on pleasing its divine Lover, has neither desire nor leisure to fall back upon itself. It presses on continually (or should do so) along the one straight path which has that love for its aim, not allowing itself to waste its powers in continual self-inspection for the purpose of seeing what it is doing or if it is satisfied. Alas! our own satisfactions and consolations do not satisfy God, they only feed that miserable love and care of ourselves which is quite apart from God and the thought of Him."

A great deal of time is wasted in these useless considerations which would be far better employed in doing good works.

By over considering whether we do right, we may actually do wrong.

St. Anthony was once asked how we might know if we prayed properly. "By not knowing it at all," he answered. He certainly prays well who is so taken up with God that he does not know he is praying. The traveller who is always counting his steps will not make much headway.

[Footnote 1: Cf. Ps. lxxxix. 10.]

UPON INTERIOR REFORMATION.

Our Blessed Father used to say that, generally speaking, grace worked as nature, and not as art, does. Art only reproduces what appears outwardly as in painting and sculpture, but nature begins her work from within, so that in a living creature the internal organs are formed before the skin, whence the saying that the heart is the first living part of man.

When, therefore, he wished to lead souls on from a worldly to a devout life, he did not at first suggest changes in the exterior, in the dressing of the hair, in the fashion of garments, and so on. No, he spoke only to the heart, and of the heart, knowing that when once that stronghold is gained, nothing else can resist.

"When a house is on fire, said he, see how all the furniture is thrown out of the window! So is it when the heart is possessed by true love of God, all that is not of God seems then to it of no moment at all. If a man, says the Canticle of Canticles give all his riches for love he will think that he has done nothing."[1]

I will give you a trifling illustration of this teaching which may be useful to you. A lady of high rank, having placed herself under the direction of the holy Prelate, became more and more assiduous in attending the services of the Church, spending much time in prayer and meditation, and, in what leisure was left her from her household cares, visiting the sick and poor. Her friends and acquaintances, however, observed with surprise that she made no change at all in external matters, that her dress was as rich as ever, and that she laid aside none of her magnificent ornaments.

This so scandalized them that they began to murmur openly, not only against her, but also against her director. They even went so far as to accuse her of hypocrisy, forgetting that a hypocrite always tries to appear better in the eyes of others than he really is, whereas she, in spite of interior amendment, remained quite unchanged in her exterior.

The truth was that she did not in the least care for her ornaments, but as it was her husband's will that she should dress as before, she followed the example of Esther, who, though she detested all vain pomp and show, to please Assuerus, decked herself out with magnificence.

On one occasion some busybody told our Blessed Father that this lady, devout though she was, had not even given up wearing ear-rings, and expressed great surprise that he who was so good a confessor had not advised her to have done with the like vanities. To all this Francis replied with his accustomed gentleness, and with a touch of humour: "I assure you, I do not know that she has got ears, much less ear-rings in them. She always comes to confession with her head so completely enveloped in a great hood or scarf that I cannot see so much as its shape. Then, too, let us remember that the saintly Rebecca of old, who was quite as virtuous as this lady, lost nothing of her sanctity by wearing the ear-rings which Eleazer presented to her as the gift of his master Isaac!"

Thus did our Blessed Father deal with matters which are a stumbling-block to the weak and foolish, showing how true it is that all things work together for good to those who are good, and that to the pure all things are pure.

[Footnote 1: Cant. viii. 7.]

HIS VISION OF THE MOST HOLY TRINITY.

All Christians ought to be not only devout but absolutely devoted to the most Blessed Trinity. It is the most august and fundamental of all our mysteries; it is that to which we are consecrated by our entrance into the holy Church, for we are baptized in the name of the Father, of the Son, and of the Holy Ghost.

But you, my sisters, ought in an especial manner to be devoted to this great and ineffable mystery, remembering the wonderful vision which our Blessed Father, your founder, had on the day of his episcopal consecration. In that sublime vision Almighty God showed him most clearly and intelligibly that the three adorable Persons of the most Holy Trinity were operating in his soul, producing there special graces which were to aid him in his pastoral office, at the very moment that the three Bishops who were consecrating him, blessed him, and performed all the holy ceremonies which render this action so great and so solemn. Thenceforth he always regarded himself as consecrated to the ever-Blessed Trinity and as a vessel of honour and sanctification.

Then, too, in the year 1610, he both founded and opened your Institute on the day dedicated by the Church to the memory and adoration of that incomprehensible mystery. Trinity Sunday that year happening to fall on the Feast of St. Claude, he gave you that saint as your special intercessor with the most Holy Trinity.

Again, you Congregation began with three members only, and this of set purpose, in order to honour the Blessed Trinity as well as to accomplish what is written in the Gospel, that when two or three are gathered together in the name, that is to say, for the glory of God, He will be in the midst of them, and will animate and govern them by His spirit; the spirit of love, unity, and concord, which makes us keep the unity of the spirit in the bond of peace, and renders us one through love, as the Father, the Son, and the Holy Ghost are one only, in nature, essence, and substance. It is this peace of God, passing all understanding, which has up to the present time kept all the convents of your Order in unity. Woe to him who shall break down this defence and rampart! May the ever-Blessed Trinity avert this misery, and both regard and preserve you always, as adopted daughters of the Father, adopted sisters of the Son, and spouses of the Holy Ghost! Amen.

HIS DEVOTION TO OUR BLESSED LADY.

Astrologers, as you know, make a great point of observing what star is rising on the horizon at the moment of a person's birth. They call it the ascendant, and it forms, as it were, the apex of their horoscope. Well, this is an idle fancy, but we may draw from it a useful suggestion. It would be good for us to notice what star was in the ascendant in the heavens, that is to say, what blessed Saint's feast day illumined the heaven of the Church militant at the moment of our birth. I cannot tell you how much this knowledge has helped many a soul.

Ah! how bright and glorious an ascendant our Blessed Father had! seeing that he was born under the very sign and protection of the Mother of God, on one of the days in the Octave of her Assumption, August 21st, 1567.

No wonder that he always had a special devotion to her and showed it in every possible way; among others, in giving her name to many of the confraternities and congregations established by him in the Church. No wonder either that he had so great a love of purity, and that under the protection, and with the assistance of the Queen of Virgins, he should have consecrated himself to God in holy virginity and continence.

You know that it was on the Feast of the Immaculate Conception that he received episcopal consecration, and at the same time that inward unction which we learn so much of from the history of his life.

He also dedicated his Theotimus[1] to the Queen of Sovereign Charity, and preached continually and with extraordinary sweetness and fervour upon the perfections and greatness of that divine Mother.

Finally, my dear sisters, there was nothing that he recommended so much to his spiritual children as this devotion to the Blessed Virgin. You, indeed, more than all others, ought to bear witness to this, seeing that he made you daughters of holy Mary, under the title of the Visitation, marked thereby to distinguish you from so many other congregations consecrated to the honour and service of God under the title of Our Lady.

His devotion to our Blessed Lady was, indeed, as might have been expected from one so single-minded and sincere as he, eminently practical, From his earliest youth he sought her protection and aid in all difficulties and temptations. When he was pursuing his studies while at college in Paris, the evil spirit was permitted by God to insinuate into his mind the terrible idea that he was one of the number of the damned. This delusion took such possession of his soul that he lost his appetite, was unable to sleep, and day by day grew more and more wasted and languid. His tutor and director noticing how his health was affected and how pale, listless, and joyless he had become, often questioned him as to the cause of his dejection and evident suffering, but his tormentor who had filled his mind with this delusion, being what is called a dumb devil, the poor youth could give no explanation.

For one whole month he suffered this mental torture, this agony of soul. He had lost all the sweetness of divine love, but not, happily, his fidelity to it. He looked back with bitter tears to the happy time when he was, as it were, inebriated with that sweetness, nor did any ray of hope illumine the darkness of that night of despair.

At last, led by a divine inspiration, he entered a church to pray that this agony might pass.

On his knees before a statue of the Blessed Virgin he implored the assistance of the Mother of Mercy with tears and sighs, and the most fervent devotion.

He ended by reciting the Memorare, that devout prayer attributed to St. Augustine or St. Bernard, and which was such a favourite with our Blessed Father and taught by him to all his penitents.

I may here mention that it was from his lips that I first learnt that prayer, that I wrote it down in the beginning of my breviary, and have made constant use of it in all my necessities.

But, to return to my story. No sooner had he finished this appeal to the Mother of Mercy than he began to experience the power of her intercession.

He seemed to hear the voice of God within him saying: "I am thy salvation: Oh! man of little faith, wherefore dost thou doubt? Thou art mine and I will save thee; have confidence; I am He who has overcome the world."

Then, in a moment, the devil departed from him; the delusions with which that wicked one had filled his mind vanished; joy and consolation took their place; where darkness had reigned light assumed the empire, and Francis felt he could never sufficiently thank God for this deliverance.

Can you wonder that after such a battle and such a victory won through the intercession of the Mother of God he always advised those who were undergoing temptation to have recourse to her powerful aid? She is indeed terrible—to our foes—as an army in battle array, and a tower of strength against the face of our enemies; and what marvel seeing that it is she who has crushed the serpent's head?

[Footnote 1: The Treatise on the Love of God.]

HIS DEVOTION TO THE HOLY WINDING SHEET OF TURIN.

With regard to our Blessed Father's explanation of his special devotion to the Holy Winding Sheet, as connected with circumstances preceding his birth, I may here say a few words.

He was born, as you know, on the 21st of August, 1567. His mother was then very young, not quite fifteen, and frail and delicate in health. It happened that at that very time the Holy Winding Sheet, then in the Chapel of Chambery, was, by command of His Highness of Savoy, and at the request of the Princess Anne d'Este, wife, by her second marriage, of James of Savoy, Duke of Nemours and Prince of Geneva, brought to Annecy. Charles, Cardinal of Lorraine, and Louis, Cardinal of Guise, were at the time at Annecy, where the sacred relic was displayed with great solemnity and exposed to the veneration of the multitudes who flocked to the place from all parts.

Among these crowds came the father and mother of Blessed Francis, and we may well believe that God made use of this holy relic to imprint upon both the mother and the unborn child some special influence of grace.

There is another winding sheet at Besancon (for our Lord was buried in two, Holy Scripture itself suggesting this by the use of the word linteamina,[1] linen cloths), that city being the metropolis of the ecclesiastical province, in which the Bishopric of Belley is situated.

One day when our Blessed Father was passing by the place the authorities had the relic exposed in his honour, and begged him to preach upon the subject. He did so, with tears of emotion and such a torrent of vehement eloquence, as went straight to the hearts of all who listened to him.

In his own diocese he took care to have the feast of the Holy Winding Sheet kept in all the churches. He generally himself preached on that day, and always with much feeling and devotion.

He had a most special devotion to the Holy Winding Sheet, as it is to be seen at Turin. He had it copied or represented in all sorts of different ways, or, I should rather say, by all sorts of different arts; in embroidery, in oil painting, in copperplate, in coloured engraving, in miniature, in demi-relief, in etching. He had it in his chamber, his chapel, his oratory, his study, his refectory; in a word, everywhere.

On one occasion I asked him the reason of this. He answered: "It is the great treasure of the House of Savoy, the defence of the country; it is our great relic; more than this, it is the miraculous picture of the sufferings of Jesus Christ, traced with His own blood. And then, too, I have a special reason for my devotion to this holy relic, seeing that before I was born my mother dedicated me to our Lord, while contemplating this sacred standard of salvation.

"It is said that he who carries the standard into battle, rather than surrender it to the enemy, should wrap its folds round his body and glory in so dying. Ah! What a happiness it would he if we could thus fold round about us the Holy Winding Sheet, buried with Jesus Christ for love of Him, in whom we are buried by baptism."

[Footnote 1: Luke xxiv. 12.]

UPON MERIT.

Every good work can, as you know, have four qualities: it can be meritorious, satisfactory, consolatory, or impetratory.

In order to have the two first qualities it must be performed when we are in a state of grace; that is to say, through the motive of charity, or, at least, in charity.

But the two last it can have, although imperfectly, without charity; for how many sinners there are who feel consolation in doing works which are morally good, and how many who in praying impetrate graces and favours from the mercy of God.

Between the two first qualities of good works there is this difference, that the first abides with and belongs wholly and entirely to the person who performs the work, and cannot be communicated; that power of communication being reserved solely for the merits of Jesus Christ our Lord, which do not stop short, as it were, and end in Him, but can be, and, in fact, are, communicated to us. Neither the saints in heaven nor those on earth have power to communicate to us one tittle of their merits; not the former, because in glory they are rewarded far beyond their deserving; not the latter, because they have not yet reached the goal, and whatever sanctity they may possess, they may, through sin, fall away from it, and all have need of the grace and mercy of God to keep them from so falling.

The second quality, however, is communicable, because we can share in the necessities of one another, and can make satisfaction one for another; spiritual riches being no less communicable than temporal ones, and the abundance of some being able to relieve the starvation of others. Hear what our Blessed Father says on this subject in his eighteenth Conference: "We must never think that by going to Holy Communion for others, or by praying for them, we lose anything. We need not fear that by offering to God this communion or prayer in satisfaction for the sins of others we shall not make spiritual profit for ourselves. The merit of the communion and of the prayer will remain with us, for we cannot merit grace for one another; it is our Lord alone who can do that. We can beg for graces for others, but we can never merit them."

UPON GOOD WILL AND GOOD DESIRES.

Good will being of so great importance, you ask me of what use it is, if it does not manifest itself by its works.

And St. Gregory tells us that where there are no works there can be no love at all, or at least none that is sincere. Our Blessed Father will give the best possible answer to your question. These are his words:

"The angel who proclaimed the birth of our infant Saviour sang glory to God, announcing that he published joy, peace, and happiness to men of good will. This was done in order that no one might be ignorant that to receive this Child all that is needed is to be of good will, even though as yet one may have effected nothing of good, for Christ comes to bless all good wills, and, little by little, He will render them fruitful and of good effect, provided we allow Him to govern them.

"With regard to good desires, it is, indeed, marvellous that they should so often come to nothing, and that such magnificent blossoms should produce so little fruit.

"He gives, however, a reason for this, which pleases me very much.

"God knows, he says, why He permits so many good desires to require such length of time and such severe effort to bring them to action, nay, more than this, why sometimes they are never actuated at all.

"Yet if there were no other profit from them than that resulting from the mortification of a soul which loves God, that would be much.

"In fact, we must not desire evil things at all; good things we must desire only in moderation; but desire supremely, and in a limitless degree, that one only divine Good, God Himself."

AGAINST THE MAKING OF RASH VOWS.

A certain person of my acquaintance[1] having learnt on good authority that Blessed Francis had in his early youth made a vow to say his rosary every day, wished to imitate him in this work of piety, and yet did not like to make the vow without first consulting him.

He received the answer: "Beware of doing so." My friend replying: "Why do you refuse to others the advice which you took for yourself in your youth?" Blessed Francis continued: "The very word youth decides the question, because I made the vow at that time with less reflection, but now that I am older I say to you, Do not do it. I do not tell you not to say your rosary; on the contrary, I advise you as earnestly as I can, and even conjure you not to allow a single day to pass without reciting that prayer, which is most pleasing to God, and to the Blessed Virgin. But do it from a firm and fixed purpose, rather than from a vow, so that if you should happen to omit it either from weariness or forgetfulness, or any other circumstance, you may not be perplexed by scruples, and run the risk of offending God. For it is not enough to vow, we must also pay our vow, and that under pain of sin, which is no small matter. I assure you that this vow has often been a hindrance to me, and many a time I have been on the point of asking to be dispensed, and set free from it, or at least of having it changed into some other work of equal worth, which might interfere less with the discharge of my duties."

"But," rejoined this person, "is not what is done by vow more meritorious than what is done only from a firm and settled purpose?" "I suspected that was it," replied Blessed Francis; "in that case who do you wish should profit by what you do?" "A fine question," cried the other, "my neighbour, do you think? No, certainly, I want to gain it for myself." "Then there is nothing more to be said," replied Blessed Francis. "I see I have been making a mistake, I imagined, of course, that you wished to make your vow to God, for God, and for His sake, and so by your vow to merit or gain something for God. What! Are we to talk of our merits and graces as if He needed them, and were not

Himself absolute merit and infinite goodness and perfection?"

Our Blessed Father loved to see this bird beating its wings against the bars of its cage. At last to let him fly, he said: 'But what then is merit, but a work pleasing to God, and a work done in His grace, and by His help, and for His love—a work which He rewards with increase of grace and glory?' "Certainly," said the other, "that is how I, too, understood it." "Well, then," replied he, "if you understand it thus, why do you contend against your understanding and your conscience? Are we not meriting for God, when we do a good work in a state of grace and for the love of God? And ought not the love of God which seeks nothing but His interests, that is to say, His glory, to be the chief end and final aim of all our good works, rather than the reward we thereby merit, which is merely an accessory?"

"And of what use to God are the merits and good works of men?" continued the other. "For one thing," replied he, "God thereby saves you from taking a false step. You are standing on the brink of a precipice, and you have your eyes shut. Let me give you a helping hand."

"In very truth, no good works of ours, though done in a state of grace and for the love of God, can increase His interior and essential glory. The reason is that this glory, being God Himself and consequently infinite, can neither be increased by our good actions nor diminished by our sins; and it is in this sense that David says that God is God and has no need of our goods.[2] It is not thus, however, with the exterior glory which is rendered to Him by creatures, and for the obtaining of which He drew them forth out of nothingness into existence. This is finite, by reason of its subject, God's creature, and therefore can be increased by our good works done in and for the love of God, or, on the other hand, diminished by our evil actions, by which we dishonour God, and rob Him of His glory, though only of glory which is exterior and outside of the divine nature.

"Now that we do increase the exterior glory of God by our good works, done as I have said, is evident from the testimony of the Apostle, when he calls the man who is purified from sin by justifying grace: A vessel unto honour sanctified and profitable to the Lord prepared unto every good work.[3]

"Indeed, it is the very fact that a work done in grace increases the exterior glory of God, which makes it meritorious, His goodness being pledged by His promise to glorify those who glorify Him, and to give the crown of justice to those who fight the good fight, and who do, or endure, anything for the glory of His name. This is why I said that we must merit for God, that is to say, we should refer our actions to the glory of God, and act out of love for Him. So we shall merit eternal life, provided always we be free from mortal sin, since God is not pledged to give the glories of heaven to any but those who shall labour in His grace.

"If, on the other hand, we wish to merit for ourselves, that is to say, if we positively intend that the whole aim of our labour be the reward of grace, or glory, which we hope for: and if we do not, in performing our good works seek first and chiefly the glory of God; then we really merit nothing for ourselves, since we do nothing for God. The reason of this is that there is so close a relationship between merit and reward (the two Latin names for them, meritum and merces, having the same root and meaning), that one cannot exist without the other any more than a mountain without a valley, or paternity without sonship.

"You see now that in the theory you have unwittingly adopted you entirely destroy the nature of true merit, and are in danger of being shipwrecked on the same rock as those heretics of our day who hold that good works are unprofitable for salvation. I am convinced, as you may well believe, that you are as far from wishing to run the risk with them as you are from sharing their belief.

"Remember this, that in order to do a good work in true charity you must not make your own interest your ultimate aim, but God's interest, which is nothing else but His exterior glory. The more, too, that you think of God's interest the more He will think of yours, and the less you trouble yourself about reward, the greater will your reward be in heaven, because pure love, never mercenary, looks only to the good of the beloved one, not to its own. This is the end and aim of the sacred teaching that we must seek first the Kingdom of God, that is to say, His glory, knowing assuredly that in seeking this all good things will be added unto us.

"He who only wishes to merit for himself does nothing for God and merits nothing for himself: but, on the other hand, he who does everything for God and for His honour merits much for himself.

"In this game he who loses, wins; and he who thinks only of winning for himself, plays a losing game. His good works are, as it were, hollow, and weigh too lightly in the divine balance. He falls asleep on his pile; of imaginary spiritual wealth, and awakening finds he has nothing in his hands. He has laboured for himself, not for God, and therefore receives his reward from himself and not from God. Like a moth, he singes his wings in the flame of a merit which is truly imaginary, no work being really meritorious except that which is done in a state of grace, and with God for its last end."

"All this," replied the person, "does not at all satisfy me on the point which I brought forward, namely, as to whether work done by vow is not more meritorious than that which is done without it, seeing that to the action of the particular virtue which is vowed is added that of the virtue of religion which is the vow."

"Certainly," replied our Blessed Father, "as regards the question whether it is more meritorious to say the Rosary by vow rather than of one's free choice, it is undoubtedly, as you say, adding one act of virtue to another to do so in discharge of one's vow, for is not prayer the highest of all religious actions? Again, if I pray with devotion and fervour, am I not adding to prayer another religious action, which is devotion? If I offer to God this prayer, as incense, or a spiritual sacrifice, or as an oblation, are not sacrifice and oblation two religious actions? Moreover, if by this prayer I desire to praise God, is not divine praise a religious act? If in praying I adore God, is not adoration one also?

"And if I pray thus with devotion, adoration, sacrifice, oblation, and praise, have we not here five acts of the virtue of religion added by me to the sixth, which is prayer?"

"But," rejoined the other, "the vow is more than all that." "If," replied Blessed Francis, "you say that the act of making a vow is in itself more than all these six together, you must really bring me some proof of its being so."

"I mean," said the other, "than each of these acts taken separately," "That," returned our Blessed Father, "is not the opinion of the Angelical Doctor,[4] who, when enumerating the eleven acts of religion, places the making a vow only in the eighth rank, with seven preceding it, namely, prayer, devotion, adoration, sacrifice, oblation, the paying of tithes, and first-fruits; and three after it: the praise of God, the taking of lawful oaths, and the adjuring of creatures in God.

"It is not that the act of making a vow is not an excellent thing; but we have no right to set it above other virtues which surpass it in excellence, and other good works of greater worth. We must leave everything in its place, going neither against the order of reason nor against that of divine charity. A man who boasts too much of his noble birth provokes scrutiny into the genuineness of his claim and risks its being disallowed."

"All the same," persisted this person, "I maintain that a good work done by vow is more meritorious than one done without it, charity, of course, being taken for granted." "It is not enough," replied Francis, "to take charity for granted. We must also suppose it to be greater in the man who does the action with a vow than in the one who does it without; for if he who says some particular prayer, because bound by vow, has less charity than he who says the same without being so bound, he, doubtless, has, and you will not deny it, less merit than the other, because merit is not in proportion to the vow made, but to the charity which accompanies it, and without which it has neither life nor value."

"And supposing equal charity, vow, or no vow," resumed the person, "will not the action done by vow have greater merit than the other?" "It will only have the same eternal glory for its reward," replied our Blessed Father, "in so far as it has the same amount of charity, and thus each will receive the same reward of eternal life.

"But as regards accidental glory, supposing that there were a special halo for the vow which would add a fourth to the three of which schoolmen treat, or, if you wish, that there should be as many special and accidental halos of glory as there are kinds of virtue, they will be unequal in accidental glory.

"But then we should have to prove that this multiplicity of halos, or accidental glories, exists, in addition to the three of which the schoolmen speak. This I would ask you now to do, though I am doubtful as to the result."

"Of what then does it avail you," said the other, "to have made that vow about which I have been consulting you?"

"It renders me," replied our Blessed Father, "more careful, diligent, and attentive in keeping my word to God, in binding myself closer to Him, in strengthening me to keep my promise (for I do not deny that there is something more stable in the vow than in mere purpose and resolution), in keeping myself from the sin I might incur, if I should fail in what I have vowed, in stimulating me to do better, and to make use of this means to further my progress in the love of God," "You do not then pretend to merit more on account of it?" said the other. "I leave all that to God," replied Francis, "He knows the measure of grace which He gives, or wishes to give me. I desire no more, and only as much as it may please Him to bestow on me for His glory. Love is not eager to serve its own interests, it leaves the care of them to its Beloved, who will know how to reward those who love Him with a pure and disinterested love."

I close this subject with two extracts from the writings of our Blessed Father. In the first he says: "I do not like to hear people say, We must do this, or that, because there is more merit in it. There is more merit in saying, 'We must do all for the glory of God.' If we could serve God without merit—which cannot be done—we ought to wish to do so. It is to be feared that by always trying to discover what is most meritorious we may miss our way, like hounds, which when the scent is crossed, easily lose it altogether."

[Footnote 1: Undoubtedly M. Camus himself. Note.—It is considered by critics that M. Camus puts much of his own into the month of St. Francis in this section.—[Ed.]] [Footnote 2: Psal. xv. 2.] [Footnote 3: 2 Tim. ii. 21.] [Footnote 4: S. Thom. 2a, 2ae, Quaest, xxiii. art. vii.]

UPON THE PRO-PASSIONS OF OUR LORD.

I have been asked whether our Lord Jesus Christ had passions. I cannot do better than answer in the exact words of our Blessed Father, taken from his Theotimus. He says:

"Jesus Christ feared, desired, grieved, and rejoiced. He even wept, grew pale, trembled, and sweated blood, although in Him these effects were not caused by passions like to ours. Therefore the great St. Jerome, and, following his example, the Schools of Theology, out of reverence for the divine Person in whom they existed, do not dare to give the name of passions to them, but call them reverently pro-passions, to show that in our Lord these sensible emotions, though not passions, took the place of passions. Moreover,

He suffered nothing whatever on account of them, excepting what seemed good to Him, governing and controlling them at His will. This, we who are sinners do not do, for we suffer and groan under these disorderly emotions, which, against our will, and to the great prejudice of our spiritual peace and welfare, disturb our souls."[1]

[Footnote 1: Book I. chap. 3.]

HIS VICTORY OVER THE PASSIONS OF LOVE AND ANGER.

Blessed Francis candidly owned that the two passions which it cost him the most to conquer were "love of creatures and anger." The former overcame by skill, the latter by violence, or as he himself was wont to say, "by taking hold of his heart with both hands."

The strategy by which he conquered love of creatures was this. He gave his affections an altogether new object to feed upon and to live for, an object absolutely pure and holy, the Creator. The soul, we know, cannot live without love, therefore all depends on providing it with an object worthy of its love. Our will is like our love. "We become earthly," says St. Augustine, "if we love the earth, but heavenly if we love heaven. Nay more, if we love God, we actually, by participation, become godlike. Osee, speaking of idolaters, says: They became abominable as those things were which they loved".[1] All our Saint's writings breathe love, but a love so holy, pure, and beautiful as to justify itself in every expression of it:—Pure words ... justified in themselves ... sweeter than honey and the honeycomb.

As regards the passion of anger, which was very strong in him, he fought against it, face to face, with such persevering force and success that meekness and gentleness are considered his chief characteristics.

[Footnote 1: Osee ix. 10.]

UPON OUR PASSIONS AND EMOTIONS.

One day, at a time when I was writing a treatise on the subject of the human passions—which treatise was afterwards published among my Miscellaneous Works—I went to him to be enlightened upon several points.

After having answered my questions, and satisfied my mind, he asked me: "And what will you say about the affections?" I must confess that this question surprised me, for though I am quite aware of the distinction between the reasonable and the sensitive appetite, I had no idea that there was such a difference between the passions and the affections, as he told me existed. I imagined that when the passions were governed by reason, they were called affections, but he explained to me that this was not so at all. He said that our sensitive appetite was divided into two parts: the concupiscent and the irascible....

The reasonable appetite is also divided, like the sensitive, into the concupiscent and the irascible, but it makes use of the mind as its instrument.

The sensitive concupiscent appetite is again subdivided into six passions: 1, love; 2, hate; 3, desire; 4, aversion; 5, joy; 6, sadness. The irascible comprises five passions: 1, anger; 2, hope; 3, despair; 4, fear; 5, courage.

The reasonable appetite, which is the will, has just as many affections, and they bear the same names. There is, however, this difference between the passions and the affections. We possess the passions in common with the irrational brute creation, which, as we see, is moved by love, hate, desire, aversion, joy, sadness, anger, hope, despair, fear, and fearlessness, but without the faculty of reason to guide and regulate the impulse of the senses.

The carnal man, that is to say, he who allows himself to be carried away by the impetuosity of his feelings, is, says the Psalmist: compared to senseless beasts and is become like to them.[1]

He, however who makes use of his reason, directs his affections uprightly and well, employing them in the service of the reasonable appetite, only in as far as they are guided by the light and teaching of natural reason. As this, however, is faulty and liable to deceptions and illusions, mistakes are often made which are called by philosophers disorders of mind.

But when the regenerate, that is to say, the Christian who possesses both grace and charity, makes use of the passions of his sensitive appetite, as well as of the affections of his reason, for the glory of God, and for the love of Him alone, this does not happen. Then he loves what he ought to love, he hates what he ought to hate, he desires what God wills that he should desire, he flies from what displeases God, he is saddened by offences done against God, he rejoices and takes delight in the things which are pleasing to God. Then his zeal fills him with anger and indignation against all that detracts from the honour due to God; he hopes in God and not in the creature, he fears nothing save to offend God, he is fearless in God's service. Thus, the Psalmist, a man after God's own heart, was able to say that his flesh, that is, the passions seated in his senses, and his heart, namely, the affections rooted in his mind, rejoiced in the living God.[2]

The winds, which, as some of the ancients held, come forth from the caverns and hollows of the earth, produce two very different effects upon the sea. Without winds we cannot sail, and yet through them tempests and shipwrecks happen. The passions and affections shut up in the two caverns of the concupiscent and the irascible appetite are so many inward impulses which urge us on to evil if they are rebellious, disorderly, and irregular, but if directed by reason and charity, lead us into the haven of rest, the port of life eternal.

This is what our Blessed Father taught me, and if you desire any more information on the subject you will find it in his Treatise on the Love of God.[3] His words did indeed open my eyes! They were of the greatest assistance to me in writing the book I alluded to.

[Footnote 1: Psal. xlviii. 13.]

[Footnote 2: Psal. lxxxiii. 3.]

[Footnote 3: Book 1. chap. 5.]

HOW HE CAME TO WRITE HIS PHILOTHEA.

There is something remarkable about the origin of this book, An Introduction to the Devout Life, addressed by him to Philothea, that is, to every soul which desires to love and serve God, and especially to persons living in the world. One peculiarity about it is that it was composed two years before its author had thought of writing any book at all. He says on this subject in his preface:

"It was by no choice or desire of mine that this Introduction saw the light. Some time ago, a soul[1] richly endowed with honourable and virtuous qualities, having received from God the grace to aspire to the devout life, desired my special assistance in the matter. I, on my part, having had much to do with her in spiritual concerns, and having for a long time past observed in her a great aptitude for such a life, took great pains in instructing her. I not only led her through all the exercises suitable to her condition and aspirations, but I also gave her some written notes, to which she might refer when necessary. Later on she showed these to a learned and devout Religious man, who, considering that they might be of use to many, strongly urged me to publish them, which he easily persuaded me to do, because his friendship had great power over me, and because I valued his judgment very highly."

I am able to give some further details. This soul richly endowed with honourable and virtuous qualities, as our Blessed Father described her to be, was a lady from Normandy of good family, who had married a gentleman of note in Savoy. His estates were partly in the diocese of Geneva, where he mostly resided, and he was nearly related to our Blessed Father. The lady, who was of a most pious disposition, decided that she could not possibly choose a better guide in the devout life than our Saint, her Bishop, and her relative by marriage.

Blessed Francis instructed her carefully both by word of mouth and also by written lessons, which she not only kept and treasured up, but sorted and arranged according to their various subjects, so as to be able to find in a moment the counsel she wanted.

For two years she went on steadily collecting and amassing these precious documents as one by one he wrote them for her. At the end of that time, owing to the disturbed state of the country, a great change came over her life. Her husband served his Prince, the Duke of Savoy, in the war in Piedmont, and was obliged to leave the management of all his affairs and of his property to his wife, who was as skilful in such matters as she was devout.

The business of a great lawsuit in which her husband was concerned obliged her to take up her residence for more than six months at Chambery, where the senate or parliament was held.

During her stay in this place she took for her director Père Jean Ferrier, the Rector of the Jesuit College, and confessor to our Blessed Father. In her difficulties she applied to this Father for advice, and he willingly gave it.

Sometimes it agreed with what Blessed Francis had said to her on similar occasions, sometimes it differed. When it differed, in order to prove that she was not speaking at random, and that she had something stronger than her own memory to rely upon, she would show him some of the written memoranda of which I have spoken.

The good Priest, who was deeply versed in all spiritual matters, found so much in them that was profitable and delightful, that on one occasion he asked her if she had many more of the same sort.

"So many, Father," she replied, "that if they were arranged in proper order they would make a good-sized volume."

The Father at once expressed his wish to see them all, and after having slowly and thoughtfully perused them, begged as a further favour that he might have several copies made of them.

This being readily granted, he distributed the said copies among the Fathers of the College, who fully appreciated the gift, and treasured it most carefully.

When this lady returned to Geneva, the Father Rector wrote a letter by her to our Blessed Father, praising her many virtues and her business talents, and begging him to continue to guide and counsel a soul so rich in all Christian graces and heavenly dispositions. He then went on to extol in the highest terms the written teaching with which he (Francis) had assisted her. Our Blessed Father read Père Ferrier's first letter, he has told me, without giving a thought to the matter of his own writings. But when this was followed by letter upon letter urging and imploring him not to keep such a treasure buried, but to allow other souls to be enlightened and guided in the way of salvation by his teaching, our Blessed Father was puzzled. He wrote to Père Ferrier saying that his present charge was so onerous, and engrossing, that he had no leisure for writing, and moreover that he had no talent for it, and could not imagine why people wanted him to attempt to do so. Père Ferrier replied, saying that if his Lordship did not publish the excellent instructions which he had given in writing to this lady he would be keeping back truth unlawfully, depriving souls of great advantages, and God of great glory. Our Blessed Father, much surprised, showed the letter to the lady, begging her to explain it. She replied that Père Ferrier had made the same request to her, entreating her to have the memoranda, given her for her private direction, published.

"What memoranda?" said Blessed Francis. "Oh! Father," replied the lady, "do you not remember all those little written notes on various subjects which you gave me to help my memory?" "And pray what could be done with those notes?" he enquired. "Possibly you might make a sort of Almanack out of them, a sentence for every day in the year." "An Almanack!" cried the lady. "Why, Father, do you know that there are enough of them to fill a big book! Little by little the pile has grown larger than you would think! Many feathers make a pound, and many strokes of the pen make a book. You had better see the papers, and judge for yourself. The Father Rector has had them copied, and they make a thick volume." "What!" cried Blessed Francis, "has the good Father really had the patience to read through all these poor little compositions, put together for the use of an unenlightened woman! You have done us both a great honour, indeed, by giving the learned doctor such a trifle to amuse himself with, and by showing him these precious productions of mine!" "Yet he values them so much," replied the lady, "that he persists in assuring me that he has never come across any writings more useful, or more edifying; and he goes on to say that this is the general feeling of all the Fathers of his house, who are all eager to possess copies. If you refuse to take the matter in hand, they will themselves see that this light is not left much longer under a bushel." "Really," said our Blessed Father, "it is amazing that people should want me to believe that I have written a book without meaning it. However, let us examine these precious pearls of which so much is thought."

The lady then brought to him all the bundles of notes which she had shown to Père Ferrier. Our Blessed Father was astonished to see how many there were, and wondered at the care which the lady had taken to collect and preserve them. He asked to be allowed to look them through again, and begged Père Ferrier not to attempt to send to the press disconnected and detached fragments which he had never for a moment thought of publishing. He added, however, that if on examination he thought that what had been written for the consolation of one soul might prove useful to others, he would not fail to put them into good order, and to add what was necessary to make them acceptable to those who might take the trouble to read them.

This he did, and the result was the Introduction,[2] which we are therefore justified in saying was composed two years before its author thought of writing it!

The simplicity, beauty, and usefulness of this book is well known. It showed the possibility of living a holy life in any station, amid the tumult of worldly cares, the seductions of prosperity, or the temptations of poverty. It brought new light to devout souls, and encouragement to all, whether high or low, who were desirous of finding and following Jesus.

But, alas! there is a reverse side to the picture. I mean the misrepresentations and calumnies which our Blessed Father had to endure from those who pretended that the principles on which the book was based were absurd, and that it inculcated a degree of devotion quite impracticable in ordinary life.

I can hardly speak calmly about this matter, and so content myself with remarking that in spite of bitter opposition the book has already, in my own time, passed through thirty editions in French, and has been translated not only into Latin, but into Italian, Spanish, German, English, in short, into most European languages.

In order that you may not think, however, that I have exaggerated in what I have said of the opposition which it excited, I will close the subject with our Blessed Father's own calm and gentle words of lament. In his preface to the Treatise on the Love of God, he says:

"Three or four years afterwards I published the Introduction to a Devout Life upon the occasion, and in the manner which I have put down in the preface thereof: regarding which I have nothing to say to you, dear reader, save only that, though this little book has in general had a gracious and kind acceptance, yes, even amongst the gravest Prelates and Doctors of the Church, yet it has not escaped the rude censure of some who have not merely blamed me but bitterly and publicly attacked me, because I tell Philothea that dancing is an action indifferent in itself, and that for recreation's sake one may make puns and jokes. Knowing the quality of these censors, I praise their intention, which I think was good. I should have desired them, however, to please to consider that the first proposition is drawn from the common and true doctrine of the most holy and learned divines; that I was writing for such as live in the world, and at court; that withal I carefully point out the extreme dangers which are found in dancing; and that as to the second proposition, it is not mine but St. Louis', that admirable King, a Doctor worthy to be followed in the art of rightly conducting courtiers to a devout life. For, I believe, if they had weighed this, their charity and discretion would never have permitted their zeal, how vigorous, and austere soever, to arm their indignation against me."

[Footnote 1: Madame de Charmoisy, née Louise Dutchatel. [Ed.]] [Footnote 2: The Saint added advice given by him to his mother and others. [Ed.]]

UPON THE EXAMPLE OF THE SAINTS.

God said to Moses: Look, and make it (the tabernacle) according to the pattern that was shewn thee in the mount,[1] and he did so. The ancient philosopher was right when he described the art of imitating as the mistress of all others, because it is by making copies that we learn how to draw originals, "The way of precept is long," said the Stoics, "but example makes it short and efficacious." Seneca, treating of the best method of studying philosophy, says that it is to nourish and clothe ourselves with the maxims of eminently philosophical minds.

Blessed Francis always inculcated this practice of imitating others in virtue. Hence his choice of spiritual books to be read and followed. With respect to the Lives of the Saints, he advised the reading by preference of those of holy men and women whose vocation has either been identical with or very much like our own, in order that we may put before ourselves models we can copy more closely.

On one occasion, however, when I was telling him how I had taken him for my pattern, and how closely I watched his conduct and ways, trying thereon to model my own, and that he must be careful not to do anything less perfect, for if he did, I should certainly imitate it as a most exalted virtue, he said: "It is unfortunate that friendship, like love, should have its eyes bandaged and hinder us from distinguishing between the defects and the good qualities of the person to whom we are attached. What a pity it is that you should force me to live among you as if I were in an enemy's country, and that I have to be as suspicious of your eyes and ears as if you were spies!

"Still I am glad that you have spoken to me as you have done, for a man warned is a man armed, and I seem to hear a voice saying: 'Child of earth, be on thy guard, and always walk circumspectly, since God and men are watching thee!' Our enemies are constantly on the alert to find fault and injure us by talking against us; our friends ought to observe us just as narrowly but for a very different reason, in order, namely, that they may be able to warn us of our failings, and kindly to help us to get rid of them.

"The just man, says the Psalmist, shall correct me in mercy, and shall reprove me, but let not the oil of the sinner fatten my head. By the oil of the sinner is meant flattery. Do not be offended with me if I assure you that you are still more cruel to me, for you not only refuse to give me a helping hand to aid me in getting rid of my faults, which you might do by wholesome and charitable warnings, but you seem by your unfair copying of my faults to wish, to make me an accomplice in your own wrong doings!

"As for me, the affection God has given me for you is very different. My jealousy for God's honour makes me long so ardently to see you walk in His ways that your slightest failing is intolerable to me, and so far am I from wishing to imitate your faults, that, if I seem to overlook them for a time, I am, believe me, doing violence to myself, by waiting with patience for a fitting opportunity to warn you of them."

[Footnote 1: Exod. xxv. 40.]

UPON THE LOVE OF GOD'S WORD.

Blessed Francis considered—as indeed I have already told you in another place—that to love to listen to God, speaking to us, either by the living voice of His Priests, or in pious books, which are often the voice of His Saints, was one of the strongest marks of predestination.

But he also insisted on the folly and uselessness of listening to, or reading, without putting in practice the lessons so conveyed to us. This, he said, was like beholding our faces in a glass, then going our way, and forgetting what we are like. It is to learn the will of our Master and not to take pains to fulfil His commands.

In his Philothea he says:

"Be devoted to the word of God, whether it comes to you in familiar conversation with your spiritual friends, or in listening to sermons. Always hear it with attention and reverence, profit by it as much as possible, and never permit it to fall to the ground. Receive it into your heart as a precious balm, following the example of the Blessed Virgin, who kept carefully in her heart every word that was spoken in praise of her divine Child. Do not forget that our Lord gathers up the words which we speak to Him in our prayers, in proportion to the diligence with which we gather up those He addresses to us by the mouth of His preachers."

As regards spiritual reading, he recommended it most strongly as being food for the soul, which we could always keep at hand, at all times and in all places. He said that we might be where we could not always hear sermons, or easily have recourse to a spiritual director and guide, and that our memory might not always serve us to recall what we had been taught, either by preachers, or by those who had instructed us specially and individually in the way of salvation. He therefore desired those who aspired to lead a devout life to provide themselves with pious books which would kindle in their hearts the flame of divine love, and not to let a single day pass without using them. He wished them to be read with great respect and devotion, saying that we should regard them as missives "sent to us by the Saints from heaven, to show us the way thither, and to give us courage to persevere in it."

HIS LOVE OF RETIREMENT.

It is well known that if our Blessed Father had lived to return from Lyons, his intention was to retire from the world and its activities in which he had so long taken a part, and to lead henceforth a purely contemplative life.

With this intention he had, some years before his death, caused a little hermitage to be built in a most suitable and sequestered spot on the shores of the beautiful lake of Annecy. This, however, he had had done quite quietly without giving any idea of the real purpose for which it was destined.

On this same shore there is a Benedictine Monastery called Taloire, easily accessible, as it is built on the slope of the Hill. Into it he had introduced some salutary reforms, and he was on terms of the most affectionate intimacy with the holy men who lived a hidden life in its quiet seclusion.

At the top of a neighbouring spur of this same mountain, on a gentle and smooth rising ground, surrounded by rich vineyards and delightful shrubs of various kinds, watered by clear streams, stood an old chapel, dedicated to God, under the name of St. Germain, a Saint who had been one of the first monks in the Monastery and who is greatly honoured in that part of the country. Blessed Francis secretly gave the necessary funds for repairing and decorating this chapel, and for building round it five or six cells pleasantly enclosed. This hermitage, the Superior said, would be most useful to his monks, enabling them to make their spiritual retreats in quiet solitude. Indeed, from time to time he sent them there for this purpose, in accordance with the rule of St. Benedict, which so greatly recommends solitude, a rule practised to the letter in the hermitages of Montserrat in Spain.

Here, then, in this quiet and lonely retreat, it was the intention of Blessed Francis to spend the last years of his life, and when he spoke upon the subject in private to the good Prior, he expressed himself in these words: "When I get to our hermitage I will serve God with my breviary, my rosary, and my pen. Then I shall have plenty of happy and holy leisure, which I can spend in putting on paper, for the glory of God and the instruction of souls, thoughts which have been surging through my mind for the last thirty years and which have been useful to me in my sermons, in my instructions, and in my own private meditations. My memory is crowded with these, but I hope, besides, that God will inspire me with others, and that ideas will fall upon me from heaven thick and fast as the snowflakes which in winter whiten all our mountains. Oh! who will give me the wings of a dove, that I may fly to this holy resting place, and draw breath for a little while beneath the shadow of the Cross? I expect until my change come!"[1]

[Footnote 1: Job xiv. 14.]

HOW HE SANCTIFIED HIS RECREATIONS.

Blessed Francis, gentle and indulgent to others as regards recreation, was severe towards himself in this matter. He never had a garden in either of the two houses which he occupied during the time of his episcopate, and only took walks when the presence of guests made them necessary, or when his physician prescribed them for his health, for he obeyed him faithfully.

But he acted otherwise with his friends and neighbours. He approved of agreeable conversation after meals, never showing weariness, or making them feel ill at ease. When I went to visit him, he took pains to amuse me after the fatigue of preaching, either by a row on the beautiful lake of Annecy, or by delightful walks in the fine gardens on its banks. He did not refuse similar recreations which I offered him when he came to see me, but he never asked for or sought them for himself. Although he found no fault with those who talked enthusiastically of architecture, pictures, music, gardening, botany, and the like, and who devoted themselves to these studies or amusements, he desired that they should use them as mystical ladders by means of which the soul may rise to God, and by his own example he showed how this might be done.

If any one pointed out to him rich orchards filled with well-grown fruit trees: "We," he would say, "are the agriculture and husbandry of God." If buildings of just proportion and symmetry: "We," he would say, "are the edifice of God." If some magnificent and beautifully decorated church: "We are the living temples of the living God. Why are not our souls as richly adorned with virtues?" If flowers: "Ah! when will our flowers give fruits, and, indeed, be themselves fruits of honour and integrity?"

When there was any talk of budding and grafting, he would say: "When shall we be rightly grafted? When shall we yield fruits both plentiful and well flavoured to the heavenly Husbandman, who cultivates us with so much care and toil?" When rare and exquisite pictures were shown to him: "There is nothing," he would say, "so beautiful as the soul which is made to the image and likeness of God."

When he was taken into a garden, he would exclaim: "Ah! when will the garden of our soul be planted with flowers and plants, well cultivated, all in perfect order, sealed and shut away from all that can displease the heavenly Gardener, who appeared under that form to Magdalen!" At the sight of fountains: "When will fountains of living water spring up in our hearts to life eternal? How long shall we continue to dig for ourselves miserable cisterns, turning our backs upon the pure source of the water of life? Ah! when shall we draw freely from the Saviour's fountains! When shall we bless God for the rivers of Israel!"

And so on with mountains, lakes, and rivers. He saw God in all things and all things in God.

WHAT HE DREW FROM SOME LINES OF POETRY.

One day we went together into the cell of a certain Carthusian monk, a man whose rare beauty of mind, and extraordinary piety, drew many to visit him, and in later days have taken his candlestick from under its bushel and set it up on high as one of the lights of the French Church.

He had written in capital letters round the walls of his cell these two beautiful lines of an old Latin poet:

Tu mihi curarum requies, tu nocte vel atra

Lumen, et in solis tu mihi turba locis.[1]

Thou art my rest in grief and care,

My light in blackest gloom;

In solitude which thou dost share,

For crowds there is no room.

Our Blessed Father read and re-read these lines several times, thinking them so beautiful that he wished to engrave them on his memory, believing that they had been written by some Christian poet, perhaps Prudentius. Finding, however, that they were composedly a pagan, and on a profane subject, he said it was indeed a pity that so brilliant a burst of light should only have flashed out from the gross darkness of heathenism. "However," he continued, "this good Father has made the vessels of the Egyptians into a tabernacle, lining it with the steel mirrors which had lent themselves to feminine vanity. Thus it is that to the pure all things are pure. This, indeed, is quite a different thing from the way of acting of those who make light of the holy words of Scripture, using them carelessly and even jestingly in idle conversation, a practice intolerable among Christians who profess to reverence these oracles of salvation."

We then began to analyse these beautiful lines, taking them in the sense in which the holy monk had taken them when he wrote them on his walls, namely, as addressed to God. Our Blessed Father said that God alone was the repose of those who had quitted the world and its cares to listen to His voice speaking to their hearts in solitude, and that without this attentive hearkening, solitude would be a long martyrdom, and a source of anxiety in place of a centre of tranquillity.

At the same time he said that those who were burdened with Martha's busy anxieties would not fail to enjoy in the very midst of their hearts the deep peace of Mary's better part, provided they carried all their cares to God.

We saw afterwards another inscription containing these words of the Psalmist:

This is my rest for ever and ever:

Here will I dwell for I have chosen it.[2]

"It is in God," said our Blessed Father, "rather than in a cell, that we should choose our abode, never to change it. Oh! happy and blessed are they who dwell in that house, which is not only the house of the Lord, but the Lord Himself. Happy, indeed, for they shall praise Him for ever and ever."

Then we came upon another inscription, bearing these words: One thing I have asked of the Lord, this will I seek after; that I may see the delight of the Lord and visit His Temple.[3]

"This true dwelling of the Lord," said he, "is His holy will; which is signified by the word delight; i.e., pleasure. Since in God there is no pleasure that is not good, what difference can there be between the good pleasure and the will of God? The will of God never tends but towards goodness."

We then went back to the second part of the Latin distich: Tu nocte vel atra, lumen: my light in blackest gloom.

"Yes, truly," he said, "Jesus born in Bethlehem brought a glorious day-dawn into the midst of night; and by His Incarnation did He not come to enlighten those who were sitting in darkness and in the shadow of death? He is, indeed, our Light and our Salvation; when we walk through the valley of the shadow of death we need fear nothing if He is at our side. He is the Light of the world; He dwells in light inaccessible, light that no darkness can overtake. He alone can lighten our darkness."

Upon the last clause of the beautiful verse:

Et in solis tu mihi turba locis. In solitude which thou dost share, for crowds there is no room.

He said: "Yes, communion with God in solitude is worth a thousandfold the pleasantest converse with the gay crowds who throng the doors of the wealthy; for the rich man can only maintain his splendour by dint of much toil, and is worn out by his cares and by the importunity of others. Miserable, indeed, are riches acquired at so great cost, retained with so much trouble, and yet lost with such painful regret."

This was one of his favourite sayings: "We must find our pleasure in ourselves when we are alone, and in our neighbour as in ourselves when we are in his company. Yet, wherever we may be, we must primarily find our pleasure in God alone, who is the maker of both solitude and society. He who does otherwise will find all places wearisome and unsatisfying; for solitude without God is death, and the society of men without God is more harmful than desirable. Wherever we may be, if God is there, all is well: where He is not, nothing is well: without Him we can do nothing that has any worth."

[Footnote 1: Tibul iv., Eleg xiii. ii. 12.]

[Footnote 2: Psal. cxxxi. 14.]

[Footnote 3: Psal. xxvi. 4.]

UPON BEING CONTENT WITH OUR POSITION IN LIFE.

Perhaps there is nothing of which men are more apt to complain than of their own condition in life. This temptation to discontent and unhappiness is a favourite device of the enemy of souls. The holy Bishop used to say: "Away with such thoughts! Do not sow wishes in other people's gardens; do not desire to be what you are not, but rather try most earnestly to be the best of what you are. Try with all your might to perfect yourself in the state in which God has placed you, and bear manfully whatever crosses, heavy or light, may be laid upon your shoulders. Believe me, this is the fundamental principle of the spiritual life; and yet, of all principles it is the least well understood. Every one follows the bent of his own taste and desires; very few find their sole happiness in doing their duty according to the pleasure of our Lord. What is the use of building castles in Spain, when we have to live in France!

"This, as you remember, is old teaching of mine, and by this time you ought to have mastered it thoroughly."

UPON SELF-SUFFICIENCY AND CONTENTEDNESS.

There is one kind of self-sufficiency which is blameworthy and another which is laudable. The former is a form of pride and vanity, and those whom it dominates are termed conceited. Holy Scripture says of them that they trust in themselves. This vanity is so absurd that it seems more deserving of contempt and ridicule than of grave blame.

But to turn to good and rational contentedness. Of it the ancient stoic said that what is sufficient is always at our command, and that what we labour for is superfluous; and again, that if we live according to the laws of nature we shall never be poor, but if we want to live according to our fancies we shall never be rich.

To be contented with what really suffices, and to persuade ourselves that what is more than this Is either evil or leading to evil, is the true means of leading a tranquil, and therefore a happy, life.

This is not only my own opinion, but it is also that of our Blessed Father, who congratulates a pious soul on being contented with the sufficiency she had. "God be praised for your contentment with the sufficiency which He has given you. Persevere in thanking Him for it. It is, indeed, the beatitude of this poor earthly life to be contented with what is sufficient, because those who are not contented when they have enough will never be contented, how much soever they may acquire. In the words of your book—since you call it your book—Nothing will ever content those who are not contented when they have enough."

THE REVERENCE OF BLESSED FRANCIS FOR THE SICK.

If the poor, by reason of their poverty, are members of Jesus Christ, the sick are also such by reason of their sickness. Our Saviour Himself has told us so: I was sick, and you visited Me.[1] For if the great Apostle St. Paul said that with the weak he was weak,[2] how much more the divine Exemplar, whom he but copied?

Our Blessed Father expressed as follows his feelings of respect and honour towards a sick person to whom he was writing. "While I think of you sick and suffering in your bed, I regard you with special reverence, and as worthy of being singularly honoured as a creature visited by God, clothed in His apparel, His favoured spouse. When our Lord was on the Cross He was proclaimed King even by His enemies, and souls who are bearing the cross (of suffering) are declared to be queens. Do you know why the angels envy us? Assuredly, because we can suffer for our Lord, whilst they have never suffered anything for His sake. St. Paul, who had been raised to heaven and had tasted the joys of Paradise, considered himself happy only because of his infirmities, and of his bearing the Cross of our Lord."

Farther on he entreats her, as a person signed with the Cross, and a sharer in the sufferings of Jesus Christ, to commend to God, though in an agony of pain, an affair of much importance which concerned the glory of God. He held that in a condition such as hers was, prayer would be more readily heard, just as our Saviour, praying fervently on the Cross, was heard for His reverence. The Psalmist was of the same opinion, saying that God heard him willingly when he cried to Him in the midst of his tribulation, and that it was in his afflictions that God was nearest to him.

Our Blessed Father believed that prayers offered by those who are in suffering, though they be short, are more efficacious than any others. He says: "I entreat you to be so kind as to recommend to God a good work which I greatly desire to see accomplished, and especially to pray about it when you are suffering most acutely: for then it is that your prayers, however short, if they are heartfelt, will be infinitely well received. Ask God at that time also for the virtues which you need the most."

[Footnote 1: Matt. xxv. 36.]

[Footnote 2: Cor. xi. 29.]

UPON THE CARE OF THE SICK.

One day we went together to visit a very aged lady in her last illness. Her piety, which was of no ordinary kind, made her look forward calmly to the approach of death, for which she had prepared by the reception of the Sacraments of Penance and of the Blessed Eucharist. She only awaited the visit of her doctor before asking for that of Extreme Unction.

All her worldly affairs were in perfect order, and but one thing troubled her, namely, that her children who had all assembled round her, on hearing of her danger, were too indefatigable in their attendance upon her, and this, as she thought, to the detriment of their own health. Our Blessed Father wishing to comfort her, said tenderly: "Do you know that I, on the contrary, when I am ill, am never so happy as when I see my relatives and servants all busy about me, tiring themselves out on my behalf. You are astonished, and ask me why I feel like this. Well, it is because I know that God will repay them generously for all these services. For if a cup of cold water given to a poor man in the love and for the love of God receives such a reward as eternal life; if our least labours undertaken for the love of God work in us the weight of a supreme glory, why should we pity those whom we see thus occupied, since we are not ill-disposed towards them, nor envious of their advantages? For unto you it is given, said St. Paul to the christians of his day, not only to believe in Christ, but also to suffer for Him.

"The reapers and vintagers are never happier than when they are heavily laden, because that proves the harvest, or the vintage, to have been plentiful. In truth, if those who wait on us, whether in health or in sickness, are only considering us, and not God, and are only seeking to please us, they make so bad a use of their toil that it is right they should suffer for it. He who serves the prophet for the love of the prophet shall receive the reward of the prophet. But, if they serve us for the love of God they are more to be envied than pitied; for he who serves the prophet in consideration of Him who sends him shall receive the reward of God, a reward which passes all imagination, which is beyond price, and which no words can express."

In his visiting of the sick when on their death-bed our Blessed Father was truly an angel of peace and consolation. He treated the sick person with the utmost sweetness and gentleness, speaking from time to time a few words suited to his condition and frame of mind, sometimes uttering very short ejaculatory prayers, or aspirations for him, sometimes leading the sufferer to utter them himself, either audibly, or, if speech was painful to him, secretly in his heart; and then allowing him to struggle undisturbed with the mortal pains which were assailing him.

He could not bear to see the dying tormented with long exhortations. That was not the time, he would say, for preaching, or even for long prayers; all that was needed was to keep the soul sustained in the atmosphere of the divine will, which was to be its eternal element in heaven, to keep it up, I say, by short beatings of the wings, like birds, who in this way save themselves from falling to the earth.

UPON SPEAKING WELL OF THE DEAD.

When any of his friends or relatives died he never tired of speaking well of them nor of recommending their souls to the prayers of others. He used to say: "We do not remember our dead, our dear ones who have left us, nearly enough; and the proof that we do not remember them enough is that we speak of them too seldom. We turn away conversation from that subject as though it were a painful one; we let the dead bury their dead, their memory die out in us with the sound of the funeral knell, seeming to forget that a friendship which can end even with death can never have been a true one. Holy Scripture itself tells us that true charity, that is, divine and supernatural love, is stronger than death! It seems to me that as a burning coal not only remains alive but burns more intensely when buried under ashes, so sincere and pure love ought to be made stronger by death, and to impel us to more fervent prayers for our deceased friends and relatives than to supplications for those who are yet living.

"For thus we look upon the dead more absolutely as in God, since, having died in Him, as we piously believe, they rest upon the bosom of His mercy. Then, praise can no longer be suspected of flattery, and, as it is a kind of impiety to tear to pieces the reputation of the dead, like wild beasts digging up a corpse to devour it; so it is a mark of piety to rehearse and extol the good qualities of the departed, since our doing so incites us to imitate them: nothing affecting us so deeply and so strongly as the example of those with whom we come in close and frequent contact."

In order to encourage people to pray for the dead he used to represent to them that in this one single work of mercy all the other thirteen are included, explaining his statement in the following manner. "Are we not," he would say, "in some sort visiting the sick when we obtain by our prayers relief or refreshment for the poor Souls in purgatory?

"Are we not giving drink to the thirsty and feeding the hungry when we bestow the cool, refreshing dew of our prayers upon those who, plunged in the midst of its burning flames, are all athirst and hungering for the vision of God? When we help on their deliverance by the means which Faith suggests, are we not most truly ransoming prisoners? Are we not clothing the naked when we procure for souls a garment of light, the light of glory?

"Is it not an act of the most princely hospitality to obtain for them an entrance into the heavenly Jerusalem, and to make them fellow-citizens with the saints and servants of God in the eternal Zion?

"Then, as regards the spiritual works of mercy. Is it not the most splendid thing imaginable to counsel the doubtful, to convert the sinner, to forgive injuries, to bear wrongs patiently? And yet, what is the greatest consolation we can give to the afflicted in this life compared to the solace our prayers bring to the poor souls who are in such grievous suffering?"

UPON DEATH.

Strictly speaking, the sojourn which we make on earth, in the days of our flesh and which we call life, is rather death than life, since "every moment leads us from the cradle to the grave."

This made an ancient philosopher say that we are dying every day of our lives, that every day some portion of our being falls away, and that what we call life is truly death.[1]

Hence the beautiful saying of the wise woman of Thecua: We all die, and like waters that return no more, we fall down into the earth.[2]

Nature has imprinted in the hearts of all men a horror of death. Our Saviour, even, taking upon Himself our flesh and making Himself like to His brethren, sin only excepted, would not be exempted from this infirmity, although He knew that the passage into another world would set Him free from all miseries and transport Him into a glory which He already possessed as regarded His soul. Seneca says that death ought not to be considered an evil when it has been preceded by a good life.

What makes death so formidable is that which follows upon it. We have, however, the shield of a most blessed hope to protect us against the terrors that arise from fear of the divine judgments. This hope makes us put our trust, not in our own virtue, but solely in the mercy of God, and assures us that those who trust in His goodness are never confounded.

But, you say, I have committed many faults. True, but who is so foolish as to think that he can commit more sins than God can pardon? Who would dare to compare the greatness of his guilt with the immensity of that infinite mercy which drowns his sins in the depths of the sea of oblivion each time we repent of them for love of Him? It belongs only to those who despair like Cain to say that their sin is so great that there is no pardon for them,[3] for with God there is mercy and plentiful redemption, and He shall redeem Israel from all his iniquities.[4]

Listen to the words of holy consolation which were addressed by our Blessed Father to a soul encompassed and assaulted by the terrors of death and of the judgment to follow. They are to be found in one of his letters. "Yes," he says, "death is hideous indeed, that is most true, but the life which is beyond, and which the mercy of God will give to us, is much to be desired. There must be no mistrust in your mind, for, miserable though we may be, we are not half so miserable as God is merciful to those who desire to love

Him, and have fixed their hope in Him. When St. Charles Borromeo was at the point of death he had the crucifix brought to him, that by the contemplation of his Saviour's death he might soften the bitterness of his last agony. The best remedy of all against an unreasonable dread is meditation upon the death of Him who is our life; we should never think of our own death without going on to reflect upon that of Christ."

[Footnote 1: Senec. Epist. 24.]

[Footnote 2: Kings xiv. 14.]

[Footnote 3: Gen. iv. 13.]

[Footnote 4: Psal. cxxix. 7-8.]

UPON WISHING TO DIE.

You ask me if we are permitted to wish for death rather than offend God any more? I will tell you a thought which I believe was suggested to me by our Blessed Father, but I cannot distinctly remember on what occasion.

"It is always dangerous to wish for death, because this desire, generally speaking, is only to be met with in those who have arrived at a very high pitch of perfection, which we dare not think we have reached, or else in persons of a morose and melancholy temperament, and but seldom in those of ordinary disposition like ourselves."

It is alleged that David, St. Paul, and other saints expressed their longing to be delivered from the burden of this body so that they might appear before God and be satisfied with the vision of His glory. But we must remember that it would be presumptuous to speak the language of Saints, not having their sanctity, and to imagine that we had it would be inexcusable vanity. To entertain such a wish because of sadness, disappointment, or dejection is akin to despair.

But, you say, it is that you may no longer offend God. This, no doubt, shows great hatred of sin, but the Saints longed for death, more that they might glorify God. Whatever we may pretend, I believe it to be very difficult to have only this one end in view, in our desire to die. Usually it will be found that we are simply discontented with life. To get to heaven we must not only not sin, but we must do good. If we refrain from sin we shall escape punishment, but more is required to deserve heaven.

UPON THE SAME SUBJECT.

There are some who imagine that St. Paul desired to die in order only that he might sin no more when he said that he felt in himself a contradiction between the law of his senses and of his reason; and, feeling this, cried out: Oh! unhappy man that I am, who shall deliver me from the body of this death?[1] These people, therefore, as though they were so many little Apostles, when they are, by some trifle, goaded to impatience, instantly say that they desire to die, and pretend that their only wish is to be in a condition in which they cannot possibly offend God. This is, indeed, to cover up mere impatience and irritation with a fine cloak! But what is still worse, it is to wrench and distort the words of the Apostle and apply them in a sense of which he never thought. Our Blessed Father, in one of his letters, gives an explanation of this passage which is so clear and so excellent that I am sure if will be useful to you. He speaks thus: "Oh, unhappy man that I am, said the great Apostle, who shall deliver me from the body of this death? He felt within himself, as it were, an armed host of ill humours, antipathies, bad habits, and natural inclinations which conspired to bring about his spiritual death; and because he fears them he declares that he hates them, and because he hates them he cannot support them without pain, and his grief makes him burst out into the exclamation which he himself answers in these words: The grace of God by Jesus Christ. This will deliver him not from the death of the body with its terrors, not from the last combat, but from defeat in the struggle, and will preserve him from being overcome.

"You see how far the Apostle is from invoking death, although elsewhere he desires to be set free from the prison of the body that he may be with Jesus Christ. He calls the mass of temptations which urge and incite him to sin a body of death, sin being the true death of the soul. Grace is the death of this death and the devourer of this abortion of hell, for where sin abounded grace superabounds.

"Grace, which has been merited for us by Jesus Christ our Saviour, to whom be honour and glory for ever and ever."

[Footnote 1: Rom. vii. 24.]

UPON THE DESIRE OF HEAVEN.

Here is a little village story to show how often true and solid piety is to be found among the lowly and ignorant, of whom the world thinks not at all. I had it from the lips of our Blessed Father, who loved to tell it.

While visiting his diocese, passing through a little country town, he was told that a well-to-do inhabitant was very ill and desired to see him, and to receive his blessing before he died. Our Blessed Father hastened to his bedside and found him at the point of death, yet in full possession of all his faculties. When he saw the Bishop the good farmer exclaimed: "Oh! my Lord, I thank God for permitting me to receive your blessing before I die."

Then the room being cleared of all his relations and friends, and he being left quite alone with the holy Prelate, he made his confession and received absolution. His next question was, "My Lord, shall I die?" The Bishop, unwilling to alarm him unnecessarily, answered quietly and reassuringly that he had seen people far more ill than he recover, but that he must place all his trust in God, the Master of life and death, who knows the number of our days, which cannot be even one more than he has decreed.

"But, my Lord," returned the man, "do you really yourself think that I shall die?" "My son," replied the good Prelate, "a physician could answer that question better than I can. All I can tell you is that I know your soul to be just now in a very excellent state of preparation for death, and that perhaps were you summoned at any other time, you might not be so fit to go. The best thing you can do is to put aside all desire of living and all care about the matter, and to abandon yourself wholly to the providence and mercy of God, that He may do with you according to His good pleasure, which will be undoubtedly that very thing which is best for you."

"Oh, my Lord," cried the sick man, "it is not because I fear to die that I ask you this, but rather because I fear I shall not die, for I can't reconcile myself to the idea of recovering from this sickness."

Francis was greatly surprised at hearing him speak in this manner, for he knew that a longing to die is generally either a grace given to very perfect souls such as David, Elias, St. Paul, and the like; or, on the contrary, in sinners a prelude to despair, or an outcome of melancholy.

He therefore asked the man if he would really be sorry to live, and, if so, why such disgust for life, the love of which is natural in all men.

"My Lord," answered the good man, "this world appears to me to be of so small account that I cannot think why so many people care for nothing beyond what it has to give. If God had not commanded us to remain here below until He calls us by death I should have quitted it long ago."

The Bishop, imagining that the man had something on his mind, or that the bodily pain he was enduring was too much for him, asked him what his trouble was—perhaps something about money?

"Not at all," replied he, "I have up to the present time, and I am seventy, enjoyed excellent health, and have abundant means. Indeed, I do not, thank God, know what poverty is."

Francis questioned him as to his wife and children, asking him if any one of them was an anxiety to him. "They are each one a comfort and a delight to me," he answered, "Indeed, if I had any regret in quitting this world it would be that I shall have to part from them."

More and more surprised, and unable to understand the man's distaste for life, the Bishop said: "Then, my brother, why do you so long for death?"

"My Lord," replied he, "it is because I have heard in sermons so much about the joys of Paradise that this world seems to me a mere prison." Then, speaking out of the fullness of his heart, and giving vent to his thoughts, he uttered marvellous words concerning the Vision of God in Heaven, and the love kindled by it in the souls of the blessed.

He entered into so many details respecting the rapturous joys of Eternity that the good Bishop shed tears of delight, feeling that the good man had been taught by God in these things, and that flesh and blood had not revealed them to him, but the Holy Spirit.

After this, descending from those high and heavenly speculations, the poor farmer depicted the grandeur, the wealth, and the choicest pleasures of the world in their true colours, showing their intrinsic vileness, and how in reality they are vanity and vexation of spirit, so as to inspire Blessed Francis himself with increased contempt for them. The Saint, nevertheless, did no more than silently acquiesce in the good man's feelings, and to calm the excitement under which he saw that he was labouring, desired him to make acts of resignation, and indifference as to living or dying. He told him to follow the example set by St. Paul, and by St. Martin, and to make his own the words of the Psalmist: For what have I in heaven? And besides Thee what do I desire upon earth?[1]

A few hours later, having received Extreme Unction from the hands of the holy Bishop, the man quietly, and apparently without suffering, passed from this world. So likewise may we when our last hour comes fall gently asleep. Blessed are the dead who die in the Lord!

Another story told me by our Blessed Father relates to himself and a man with whom he came in contact.

When he was at Paris in the year 1619, this gentleman, who was not only rich in this world's goods but also in piety and charity, came to consult him on matters of conscience, and began thus: "Father, I am much afraid that I shall not save my soul, and therefore I have come to you to beg you to put me in the right way."

The Bishop asked him what was the cause of this fear. He answered: "My being too rich. You know Scripture makes the salvation of the rich a matter of such difficulty that, in my case, I fear it is an impossibility."

Francis, thinking that perhaps he had made his money dishonestly, and that on that account his conscience was now pricking him, questioned him as to this.

"Not at all," he answered, "My parents, who were excellent people, left me no ill-gotten goods, and what I have added to my inheritance has been amassed by my own frugality and honest work, God preserve me from the sin of appropriating what belongs to my neighbour! No, my conscience does not reproach me in that respect."

"Well, then," said the Bishop, "have you made a bad use of this wealth?"

"I live," he replied, "in such a manner as becomes my rank and position, but I am afraid that I do not give enough to the poor, and you know that we shall be one day judged on this point."

"Have you any children?" asked Francis.

"Yes," he replied; "but they are all well provided for, and can easily do without me."

"Really," said the Bishop, "I do not see whence your scruples can arise; you are the first man I have ever met who has complained to me of having too much money; most people never have enough."

It was easy to set this good soul at rest, so docile was he in following the Bishop's advice. The latter told me afterwards that he found upon enquiry that the man had formerly held high appointments, discharging his duties in them most faithfully, but had retired from all in order to devote himself to works of piety and mercy. Moreover, he passed all his time in churches or hospitals, or in the houses of the uncomplaining poor, upon whom he spent more than half his income. By his will, after his many pious legacies were paid, it was found that our Lord Himself was his real heir, for he gave to the town hospital a sum of money equal to that which was divided among his children. I may add that a life so holy and devoted was crowned by a most happy death. Truly, Blessed are the merciful, for they shall obtain mercy!

[Footnote 1: Psal. lxxii. 25.]

WHAT IT IS TO DIE IN GOD.

On one occasion Blessed Francis was asked what it was to die in God; what was the meaning of those words: Blessed are the dead who die in the Lord, that they may rest from their labours, for their works follow them.[1]

He replied that to die in God was to die in the grace of God, because God and His grace are as inseparable as the sun and its rays. He was asked again, if to die in God meant to die while in habitual grace, or to die in the exercise of charity, that is to say, whilst impelled by actual grace. He answered that in order to be saved it was enough to die in habitual or sanctifying grace, that is to say, in habitual charity; seeing that those who die in this state, as for instance newly-baptized infants, though they may never have performed a single act of charity, obtain Paradise by right of inheritance, habitual charity making them children of God by adoption. Those, however, who die, not only in the holy and supernatural state of habitual charity, but whilst actually engaged in works of charity, come into the possession of heaven by a double title, that of inheritance and that of reward; therefore is it written that their works follow them. The crown of justice is promised by the just Judge to those who shall have fought a good fight and finished their course with perseverance, even to the end.

Going on to explain what is meant by man's dying in actual grace, he said that it was to die while making acts of lively faith and hope, of contrition, resignation, and conformity to the will of God. He added these words, which have always remained deeply impressed on my mind: "Although God is all-powerful, it is impossible for Him to condemn to eternal perdition a soul whose will, at the moment of its leaving the body, is subject to, and united with, His own."

[Footnote 1: Apoc. xiv. 13.]

UPON LENGTH OF LIFE.

Judging from outward appearances, from the vigour of his frame, from his sound constitution, and from the temperate simplicity of his manner of life, it seemed probable that Blessed Francis would live to an advanced age.

One day I said as much to him, he being at that time about forty-two or forty-three years old. "Ah!" he replied with a sigh, "the longest life is not always the best. The best is that which has been best spent in the service of God," adding these words of David: Woe is me that my sojourning is prolonged; I have dwelt with the inhabitants of Cedar, my soul hath been long a sojourner.[1] I thought he was secretly grieving over his banishment from his See, his beloved Geneva (he always called it thus), wrapped in the darkness of error, and I quoted to him the words: Upon the rivers of Babylon there we sat, and wept.[2]

"Oh! no," he answered, "it is not that exile which troubles me. I am only too well off in our city of refuge, this dear Annecy. I meant the exile of this life on earth. As long as we are here below are we not exiled from God? While we are in the body we are absent from the Lord.[3] Unhappy man that I am! Who shall deliver me from the body of this death? The grace of God by Jesus Christ."[4]

I ventured in reply to remind him how much he had to make his life happy: how his friends esteemed him, how even the very enemies of religion honoured him, how all who came in contact with him delighted in his society.

"All that," he answered, "is beneath contempt. Those who had sung Hosanna to the Son of God three days later cried out Crucifige. Such things do not make my life any dearer to me. If I were told that I should live as long again as I have already done, and that without pain, without law-suits, without trouble, or inconveniences of any kind, but with all the content and prosperity men desire in life, I should be sadly disturbed in mind! Of what small account are not the things of time to him who is looking forward to a blessed Eternity! I have always praised the words of the Blessed Ignatius de Loyola, 'Oh! how vile and mean earth appears to me when I meditate upon and look up to heaven.'"

[Footnote 1: Psalm cxix.]

[Footnote 2: Psalm cxxxvi. 1.]

[Footnote 3: Cor. v. 6.]

[Footnote 4: Rom. vii. 24-35.]

UPON PURGATORY.

Concerning Purgatory, St. Francis used to say that in the controversy with Protestants there was no point on which the Church could support her doctrine by so many proofs, drawn both from the Scriptures and from the Fathers and Councils, as on this. He blamed those who oppose the doctrine for their lack of piety towards the dead. On the other hand, he reproved those Catholic preachers who, when speaking of Purgatory and of the pains and torments suffered there by the holy souls, do not at the same time enlarge upon their perfect love of God, and consequent entire satisfaction in the accomplishment of His will, with which their own will is so indissolubly united, that they cannot possibly feel the slightest movement of impatience or irritation. Nor can they desire to be anywhere but where they are, were it even till the consummation of all things, if such should be God's good pleasure.

On this subject he recommended the careful study of the Treatise on Purgatory, written by blessed Catherine of Genoa. By his advice I read the book with attention, and have often re-read it, always with fresh relish and profit. I have even invited Protestants to read if, and they have been quite satisfied by it. One young convert admitted that had he seen this Treatise before his conversion it would have helped him more than all the discussions into which the subject had led him.

St. Francis was of opinion that the thought of Purgatory ought rather to comfort than to terrify. "The majority of those," he used to say, "who dread Purgatory do so in view of their own interests, and out of self-love, rather than for God's interests. The cause of this is that those who preach on the subject are in the habit of depicting only the pains of that prison, and say not a word on the joy and peace which the souls therein detained enjoy. It is true that the torments of Purgatory are so great that the most acute sufferings of this life cannot be compared with them; but, then, on the other hand, the inward satisfaction of the sufferers is such that no amount of earthly prosperity or contentment can equal it. 1°. The souls who are waiting there enjoy a continual union with God. 2°. Their wills are in perfect subjection to His will; or, to speak more correctly, their wills are so absolutely transformed into the will of God that they cannot will anything but what He wills. 3°. If Paradise were open to them, they would rather cast themselves down into hell than appear before God stained and denied as they see themselves still to be. 4°. They accept their Purgatory lovingly and willingly, because it is the good pleasure of God. 5°. They wish to be there, in the manner in which it pleases God that they should be, and for as long as He wills. 6°. They cannot sin. 7°. They cannot feel the slightest movement of impatience. 8°. Nor be guilty of the smallest imperfection. 9°. They love God more than themselves and more than any other creature, and with a perfect, pure, and disinterested love, 10°. They are in Purgatory consoled by the angels. 11°. They are secure of their salvation. 12°. They are in a state of hope, which cannot but be realized. 13°. Their grief is holy and calm. 14°. In short, if Purgatory is a species of hell as regards suffering, it is a species of Paradise as regards charity. The charity which quickens those holy souls is stronger than death, more powerful than hell; its lamps are all of fire and flame. Neither servile fear nor mercenary hope has any part in their pure affection. Purgatory is a happy state, more to be desired than dreaded, for all its flames are flames of love and sweetness. Yet still it is to be dreaded, since it delays the end of all perfection, which consists in seeing God, and therefore fully loving Him, and by this sight and by this love praising and glorifying Him through all eternity."

UPON PENANCE.

He compared penance to an almond tree, not only in allusion to the word amendment and the expression, amend your ways, both of which in the French language resemble in sound the word almond, but by a very ingenious comparison.

"The almond tree," he said, "has its blossom of five petals, which as regards number bear some resemblance to the five fingers of the hand, its leaves are in the shape of a tongue, and its fruit of a heart. Thus the Sacrament of Penance has three parts which make up its whole. The first which concerns the heart is contrition, of which David says that God heals those who are contrite of heart,[1] and that He does not despise the humble and contrite heart.[2]

"The second, which concerns the tongue, is confession. The third, which regards the hand, that is to say, the doing of good works, is satisfaction. Moreover," he went on to say, "as there are almonds of two kinds, the one sweet, the other bitter, which being mixed make a pleasant flavour, agreeable to the palate, so also in penance there is a certain blending of sweetness and bitterness, of consolation and pain, of love and regret, resembling in taste the pomegranate, which has a certain sharp sweetness and a certain sweet sharpness far more agreeable than either sharpness or sweetness separately. Penance which had only the sweetness of consolation would not be a cleansing hyssop, powerful to purge away the stains of iniquity. Nor, if it had only the bitterness of regret and sorrow, without the sweetness of love, could it ever lead us to that justification which is only perfected by a loving displeasure at having offended the Eternal, Supreme, and Sovereign Goodness."

Our Blessed Father treats of this mingling of love and sorrow proper to true penitence with so much grace and gravity in his Theotimus that I think nothing grander or sweeter could be written on the subject. Here is an extract. "Amidst the tribulation and remorse of a lively repentance God often kindles at the bottom of our heart the sacred fire of His love; this love is converted into the water of tears, then by a second change into another and greater fire of love. Thus the penitent Magdalen, the great lover, first loved her Saviour; her love was converted into tears, and these tears into an excellent love; whence our Saviour told her that many sins were pardoned her because she had loved much. The beginning of perfect love not only follows upon penitence, but clings to it and knits itself to it; in one word, this beginning of love mingles itself with the end of penitence, and in this moment of mingling penitence and contrition merit life everlasting."[3]

[Footnote 1: Psalm cxlvi. 3.]

[Footnote 2: Psalm l. 19.]

[Footnote 3: Love of God, Book II, c. 20.]

UPON PENITENT CONFUSION.

Our Blessed Father had a wonderful aptitude for distinguishing between what was real and genuine and what was false in the shame manifested by his penitents. He used to say that when this confusion was full of trouble and agitation it proceeded from self-love, from vexation and shame at having to own our sins and imperfections, not from the spirit of God. This he expresses in his second Conference in these words:

"We must never suffer our confusion to be attended with sadness and disquietude; that kind of confusion proceeds from self-love, because we are troubled at not being perfect, not so; much for the love of God as for love of ourselves." An extract from Theotimus will close this subject most suitably:

"Remorse which positively excludes the love of God is infernal, it is like that of the lost. Repentance which does not regret the love of God, even though as yet it is without it, is good and desirable, but imperfect: it can never save us until it attains to love, and is mingled with it. So that, as the great Apostle said, even if he gave his body to be burned, and all his goods to the poor, and had not charity it would all be of no avail; we, too, may say with truth, that, however great our penitence may be, even though it make our eyes overflow with tears of sorrow, and our hearts to break with remorse, still if we have not the holy love of God it will serve us nothing as regards eternal life."[1]

[Footnote 1: Book ii. c. 19.]

UPON INTERIOR PEACE AMIDST ANXIETIES.

It is a great mistake when souls, in other respects good and pious, imagine that it is impossible to preserve inward peace amid bustle and turmoil. There are some even, strange to say, who though dedicated to God by their holy calling, complain if they are employed by their community in laborious and troublesome offices, calling them distracting functions and occupations. Assuredly, these good people know not what they say, any more than did St. Peter on Mount Thabor.

What do they mean by distracting occupations? Possibly those which separate us from God? I know nothing which can separate us from His love except sin, which is that labour in brick and clay in which the infernal Pharaoh, tyrant of souls, and king over the children of pride, employs his unhappy subjects. These are the strange gods who give no rest either by night or by day. But with that exception, I know of no legitimate occupation which can either separate us from God, or, still more, which cannot serve as a means to unite us to Him. This may be said of all callings, of those of soldiers, lawyers, merchants, artisans.

Our Blessed Father devotes two chapters in his Theotimus to this subject, but he speaks even more explicitly upon it in one of his letters, in which he says: "Let us all belong wholly to God, even amid the tumult and disturbance stirred up round about us by the diversity of human affairs. When can we give better proof of our fidelity than amid contrarieties, Alas! my dearest daughter, my sister, solitude has its assaults, the world has its disorder and uproar; yet in either we must be of good heart, since everywhere heaven is close to those who have confidence in God, and who with humility and gentleness implore His fatherly assistance. Beware of letting your carefulness degenerate into trouble and anxiety."

"Tossed about upon the waves and amid the winds of many a tumult, always look up to heaven, and say to our Lord: 'O God, it is for Thee that I set my sails and plough the seas; be Thou my guide and my pilot!' And then console yourself by remembering that when we are in port the joys which will be ours will blot out all remembrance of our toils and struggles to reach it. We are now voyaging thither in the midst of all these storms, and shall safely reach our harbour if only we have an upright heart, a good intention, firm courage, eyes fixed on God, and place all our confidence in Him. If the violence of the tempest makes our head dizzy, and we feel shaken and sick, do not let us be surprised, but, as quickly as we can, let us take breath again, and encourage ourselves to do better. I feel quite sure that you are not forgetful of your good resolutions as you pursue your way; do not then distress yourself about these little attacks of anxiety, and vexation, caused by the multiplicity of domestic affairs. Nay, my dear daughter, all this tumult gives you opportunities of practising the dearest and most lovable of the virtues recommended to you by our Lord. Believe me, true virtue is not nourished in external calm any more than are good fish found in the stagnant waters of the marshes."

UPON DISCOURAGEMENT.

Our Blessed Father used to say that the most cowardly of all temptations was discouragement. When the enemy of our salvation makes us lose hope of ever advancing in virtue he has gained a great advantage over us, and may very soon succeed in thrusting us down into the abyss of vice. Those who fly into a passion at the sight of their own imperfections are like people who want to strike and bruise their own faces, because they are not handsome enough to please their self-love. They only hurt themselves the more.

The holy Bishop wishing to correct this fault in one of his penitents said to her: "Have patience with every one, but especially with yourself. I mean, do not be over-troubled about your imperfections, but always have courage enough at once to rise up again when you fall into any of them. I am very glad to hear that you begin afresh every day. There is no better means for persevering in the spiritual life than continually to be beginning again, and never to think that one has done enough."

On these words we may make the following reflections:

1. How shall we patiently suffer the faults of our neighbour if we are impatient over our own?

2. How shall we reprove others in a spirit of gentleness if we correct ourselves with irritation, with disgust, and with unreasonable sharpness? What can come out of a bag but what is in it?

3. Those who fret impatiently over their own imperfections will never correct themselves of them, for correction, if it is

to be of use, must proceed from a tranquil, restful mind. Cowardice, says David, is the companion of trouble and tempest.

4. He who has lost courage has lost everything, he who has thrown up the game can never win, nor can the soldier who has thrown away his arms return to the fight, however much he may want to do.

5. David said: I waited for him that saved me from pusillanimity and a storm. He who believes himself to be far advanced in the ways of God has not yet even made a good beginning.

6. St. Paul, who had been raised to the third heaven, who had fought so many good fights, run so many splendid races, and had kept the Faith inviolate, in spite of all, never thought that he had finished his work, or reached the goal, but always pressed forward as though he had but just begun.[1]

7. This mortal life is but a road leading to heaven. It is a road to which we must steadily keep. He who stops short in it runs the risk of not reaching safely the presence of God in which it ends. He who says, I have enough, thereby shows that he has not enough; for in spiritual things sufficiency implies the desire for more.

[Footnote 1: 2 Cor. xii. 2, 4.]

UPON RISING AFTER A FALL.

Our Blessed Father was a great enemy to hurry and over-eagerness, even in rising up again after a fall.

He used to say that if our act of contrition is more hurried than humble we are very likely to fall again soon, and that this second fall will be worse than the first.

As he considered our penitence incomplete without an act of the love of God, so also he maintained recovery from a fall to be imperfect if not accompanied by tranquillity and peace. He wished us to correct ourselves, as well as others, in a spirit of sweetness. Here is the advice which he gives on the subject.

"When we happen to fall from some sudden outburst of self-love, or of passion, let us as soon as possible prostrate ourselves in spirit before God, saying, with confidence and humility: Have mercy on me, for I am weak. Let us rise again with peace and tranquillity and knot up again our network of holy indifference, then go on with our work. When we discover that our lute is out of tune, we must neither break the strings nor throw the instrument aside; but listen attentively to find out what is the cause of the discord, and then gently tighten or slacken the strings, according to what is required."

To those who replied to him that we ought to judge ourselves with severity, he said: "It is true that with regard to ourselves we ought to have the heart of a judge, but as the judge who hastily, or under the influence of passion, pronounces sentence, runs the risk of committing an injustice, but not so when reason is master of his actions and behaviour, we must, in order to judge ourselves with equity, do so with a gentle, peaceful mind, not in a fit of anger, nor when so troubled as hardly to know what we are doing."

UPON KINDLINESS TOWARDS OURSELVES.

Since the measure and the model of the love which God commands us to bear towards our neighbour ought to be the just and Christian love which we should bear towards ourselves, and as charity, which is patient and kind, obliges us to correct our neighbours' faults with gentleness and sweetness, our Blessed Father did not consider it right that we should correct ourselves in a manner different from this, nor be harsh and severe with ourselves because of our falls and ill-doings. In one of his letters he wrote as follows: "When we have committed a fault, let us at once examine our heart and ask it whether it does not still preserve living and entire the resolution to serve God. It will, I hope, answer yes, and that it would rather die a thousand deaths than give up this resolution. Let us go on to ask it further. Why, then, are you stumbling now? Why are you so cowardly? It will reply: I was taken by surprise: I know not how; but I am tolerably firm now. Ah! my dear daughter, we must pardon it; it was not from infidelity, but from infirmity that it failed. We must then correct ourselves gently and quietly, and not irritate and disturb ourselves still more. Rise up, my heart, my friend, we should say to ourselves, and lift up our thoughts to our Help, and our God.

"Yes, my dear daughter, we must be charitable to our own soul, and not rebuke it over harshly when we see that the fault it has committed was not fully wilful."

Moreover, he would not have us accuse ourselves over-vehemently and exaggerate our faults. At the same time, he had no desire that in regard to ourselves we should err on the side of leniency. He wanted us to embrace the happy medium, by humiliating without discouraging ourselves, and by encouraging ourselves with humility. In another letter he says: "Be just, neither accuse nor excuse your poor soul, except after much consideration, for fear lest if you excuse yourself when you should not, you become careless, and if you accuse yourself without cause, you discourage yourself and become cowardly. Walk simply and you will walk securely."

UPON IMPERFECTIONS.

"Some people have so high an opinion of their own perfection that should they discover any failings or imperfections in themselves they are thrown into despair. They are like people so anxious about their health that the slightest illness alarms them, and who take so many precautions to preserve this precious health that in the end they ruin it."

Our Blessed Father wished us to profit, not only by our tribulations, but also by our imperfections, and that these latter should serve to establish and settle us in a courageous humility, and make us hope, even against hope, and in spite of the most discouraging appearances. "In this way," he said, "we draw our healing and help from the very hand of our adversaries." To a person who was troubled at her imperfections, he wrote thus: "We should, indeed, like to be without imperfections, but, my dearest daughter, we must submit patiently to the trial of having a human, rather than an angelic, nature. Our imperfections ought not, indeed, to please us; on the contrary, we should say with the holy Apostle: Unhappy man, that I am, who shall deliver me from the body of this death![1] But, at the same time, they ought not to astonish us, nor to discourage us: we should draw from them submission, humility, and mistrust of ourselves; never discouragement and loss of heart, far less distrust of God's love for us; for though He loves not our imperfections and venial sins, He loves us, in spite of them.

"The weakness and backwardness of a child displeases its mother, but she does not for that reason love it less. On the contrary, she loves it more fondly, because she compassionates it. So, too, is it with God, who cannot, as I have said, love our imperfections and venial sins, but never ceases to love us, so that David with reason cries out to Him: Have mercy on me, O Lord, for I am weak."[2]

[Footnote 1: Rom. vii. 24.]

[Footnote 2: Psalm vi. 3.]

THE JUST MAN FALLS SEVEN TIMES IN THE DAY.

A good man meditating upon this passage, and taking it too literally, fell into a perfect agony, saying to himself: "Alas! how many times a day, then, must not I, who am not just, fall?" Yet during his evening examination of conscience, however closely and carefully he searched, and however much he was on the watch during the day to observe his failings and faults, he sometimes could not make up the number. Greatly troubled and perplexed about this, he carried his difficulties to our Blessed Father, who settled them in this way:

"In the passage which you have quoted," he said, "we are not told that the just man sees or feels himself fall seven times a day, but only that he does fall seven times, and that he raises himself up again without paying any heed to his so doing. Do not then distress yourself; humbly and frankly confess what you have observed of faulty in yourself, and what you do not see, leave to the sweet mercy of Him who puts out His hand to prevent those who fall without malice, from being jarred or bruised against the hard ground; and who raises them up again so quickly and gently that they never notice it nor are conscious of having so much as fallen."

The great imperfection of most of us proceeds from want of reflection, but, on the other hand, there are many who think overmuch, who fall into the mistake of too close self-inspection, and who are perpetually fretting over their failings and weaknesses.

Blessed Francis writes again on the subject: "It is quite certain that as long as we are imprisoned in this heavy and corruptible body there will always be something wanting in us. I do not know whether I have already told you that we must have patience with every one; and, first of all, with ourselves. For since we have learnt to distinguish between the old Adam and the new, between the outward man and the inward, we are really more troublesome to ourselves than any of our neighbours."

UPON THE PURGATIVE WAY.

Of the three ways leading to perfection the first is called the purgative, and consists in the purifying of the soul; from which, as from a piece of waste ground, we must take away the brambles and thorns of sin before planting there trees which shall bear good fruit. This purgation has, however, two different stages; that which precedes the justification of the soul, and that which follows it. This latter may again be subdivided into two parts. There is not only the freeing of the soul from sin, whether mortal or venial, but there is also its purgation from any inclination or attachment to either the one or the other.

It is not enough to be purged from deadly sin; we must labour incessantly to rid ourselves of any love, however slight, of the sin from which we have been cleansed, otherwise we shall be only too likely to fall back into it again. It is the same as regards venial sins. Our Blessed Father speaks of this purgative way in his Philothea as follows:

"We can never be wholly pure from venial sins, at least, never for any continuous length of time, but we can and may get rid of any sort of affection for these lesser faults. Assuredly it is one thing to tell falsehoods once or twice, lightly and thoughtlessly, and in matters of small importance; and another to take delight in lying and to cling fondly to this sort of sin."[1]

Besides venial sins, there are certain natural propensities and inclinations which are called imperfections, since they tend towards evil, and, if unchecked, lead to excesses of various kinds. They are not, properly speaking, sins, either mortal or venial; nevertheless they are true failings and defects of which we must endeavour to correct ourselves, inasmuch as they are displeasing both to God and man. Such are propensities to anger, grief, joy, excessive laughter, flattery, favouritism, self-pity, suspicion, over-eagerness, precipitancy, and vain affections. We must strive to rid ourselves of those defects which, like weeds, spring up without being sown in the soil of our corrupt nature, and incline us to evil from our birth.

The means of getting rid of all these evils, whether mortal sins, venial ones, imperfections, or attachment to any or all of these, you will find most clearly set forth by our Blessed Father in the same book.[2]

I once asked him what was the true difference between venial sin and imperfection, and I will try to recall his teaching on the subject that I may impart it to you. Every venial sin is an imperfection, but every imperfection is not a venial sin. In sin there is always malice, and malice is in the will, hence the maxim that nothing involuntary is sin; and according to the degree of this malice, whether great or small, and according to the matter on which it is exercised, the sin is either mortal or venial.

You ask me if imperfections are matters sufficient for confession, as well as venial sin. Our Blessed Father considered that it was well to accuse ourselves of them in order to learn from the confessor how to correct ourselves of and get rid of them. He did not, however, think them sufficient matter for the Sacrament, and for this reason when his penitents only told him of imperfections he would make them add some venial sin committed in the past, so as to furnish sufficient matter for absolution, I say sufficient, but not absolutely necessary matter, for it is only mortal sin that has these two qualities.

[Footnote 1: Part i. chap. 22.]

[Footnote 2: Part i. chaps. 6, 7, 22, 23, 24.]

UPON VENIAL SIN.

He compares venial sin to the diamond which was thought by its presence to prevent the loadstone from attracting iron. A soul attached to venial sin is retarded in its progress in the path of justice, but when the hindrance is removed God dilates the heart and makes it to run in the way of His commandments.

You ask me if a great number of venial sins can ever make up a mortal one, and consequently cause us to lose the grace of God.

No, indeed! Not all the venial sins which ever existed could make one mortal sin: but nevertheless, not many venial sins are needed to dispose us to commit a mortal one, as it is written that he that contemneth small things shall fall by little and little,[1] and that he who loves danger shall perish in it.[2]

For, according to the maxim of St. Bernard, received by all spiritual writers, not to advance in the way of God is to fall back, not to sow with Him is to scatter, not to gather up is to lose, not to build is to pull down, not to be for God is to be against Him, not to reap with Him is to lay waste. Now to commit a venial sin is essentially a not working with God, though it may not be a positive working against Him.

"Charity," says our Blessed Father, "being an active quality cannot be long without either acting or dying: it is, say the early Fathers, symbolized by Rachel. Give me children, she said to her husband, otherwise I shall die.[3] Thus charity urges the heart which she has espoused to make her fertile in good works; otherwise she will perish."

Venial sin, especially when the soul clings to it, makes us run the risk of losing charity, because it exposes us to the danger of committing mortal sin, by which alone charity is driven forth and banished from the soul. On this subject our Blessed Father, in the chapter from which we have already quoted, speaks as follows: "Neither venial sin, nor even the affection to it, is contrary to the essential resolution of charity, which is to prefer God before all things; because by this sin we love something outside reason but not against reason. We make too much and more than is fit of creatures, yet we do not positively prefer them before the Creator. We occupy ourselves more than we ought in earthly things; yet we do not, for all that, forsake heavenly things.

"In fine, venial sin impedes us in the way of charity, but does not put us out of it, and, therefore, venial sin, not being contrary to charity, never destroys charity either wholly or partially."

Further on he says: "However, venial sin is sin, and consequently it troubles charity, not as a thing that is contrary to charity itself, but as being contrary to its operations and progress and even to its intention. For, as this intention is that we should direct all our actions to God, it is violated by venial sin, which is the referring of an action to something outside of God and of the divine will."

[Footnote 1: Eccle. iii. 27.]

[Footnote 2: Id. iii. 27.]

[Footnote 3: The Love of God. Book iv. chap. 2.]

UPON COMPLICITY IN THE SINS OF ANOTHER.

There are some scrupulous minds which are perplexed by everything and frightened at shadows. In conversation, and in mixing with others, a faulty word which they may hear or a reprehensible action they may witness, however much they may in their secret hearts detest it, is at once charged upon their own conscience as a partaking in the sins of others.

They are also troubled with doubts, and are uncertain whether it is their duty or not to denounce the faults of their neighbour, to express their own disapproval, and to rebuke the offender. To a soul perplexed on this subject our Blessed Father gives the following wholesome advice: "As regards conversation, my dear daughter, do not worry about anything said or done by others. If good, you can praise God for it, if evil, it will furnish you with an opportunity of serving God by turning away your thoughts from it, showing neither surprise nor irritation, since you are not a person of sufficient importance to be able to put a stop to bad or idle talk. Indeed, any attempt on your part to do so would make things worse. Acting as as I bid you to do you will remain unharmed amid the hissing of serpents and, like the strawberry, will not assimilate their poison even though licked by their venomous tongues."

UPON EQUIVOCATING.

Our Saint used to say that to equivocate was, in his opinion, to canonize lying, and that simplicity was, after all, the best kind of shrewdness. The children of darkness, he said, use cunning and artifice in their dealings with one another, but the children of God should take for their motto the words: He that walketh sincerely walketh confidently.

Duplicity, simulation, insincerity always betray a low mind. If, in the language of the wise man, the lips that lie kill the soul, what can be the effect of the conversation of one who habitually speaks with a double heart?[1]

[Footnote 1: Psalm xii. 3.]

UPON SOLITUDE.

Some one was praising country life, and calling it holy and innocent.

Blessed Francis replied that country life has drawbacks just as city life has, and that as there is both good and bad company, so there is also good and bad solitude. Good, when God calls us into it, as He says by a prophet, I will lead her into the wilderness and I will speak to her heart.[1] Bad, when it is of that kind of which it is written, Woe to him that is alone.[2]

As regards holiness and innocence, he said that country folk were certainly far from being, as a matter of course, endowed with these good qualities.

As for temptations and occasions of sin, he said: "There are evil spirits who go to and fro in desert places quite as much as in cities; if grace does not hold us up everywhere, everywhere we may stumble. Lot, who in the most wicked of all cities was holy and just, when in solitude fell into the most dreadful of sins. Men carry themselves about with them and find themselves everywhere, and frailty can no more be got rid of by them than can the shadow by the body that casts it.

"Many deceive themselves greatly and become their own seducers by imagining that they possess those virtues, the sins contrary to which they do not commit. The absence of a vice and the possession of its contrary virtue are very different things.

"To be without folly is, indeed, to have the beginning of wisdom, but it is a beginning so feeble as by itself scarcely to deserve the name of wisdom.

"Abstaining from evil is a very different thing from doing good, although this abstaining is of itself a species of good: it is like the plan of a building compared with the building itself. Virtue does not consist so much in habit as in action. Habit is in itself an indolent sort of quality, which, indeed, inclines us to do good, but does no more, unless inclination be followed by action.

"How shall he who has no one in command set over him learn obedience? He who is never contradicted, patience? He who has no superior, humility? And how shall he who, like a misanthrope, flies from intercourse with other men, notwithstanding that he is obliged to love them as himself, how shall he, I say, learn brotherly love?

"There are many virtues which cannot be practised in solitude; above all, mercy, upon the exercise of which we shall be questioned and judged at the last day; and of which it is said: Blessed are the merciful, for they shall obtain mercy."[3]

[Footnote 1: Osee ii. 14.]

[Footnote 2: Eccle. iv. 10.]

[Footnote 3: Matt. v. 7.]

UPON VANITY.

It is a vanity of the understanding to think ourselves more than we really are; but it is a far more dangerous vanity of the will to aspire to a condition higher than our own, and to persuade ourselves that we are deserving of it. He who thinks himself to be more than he is has in his mind some picture of content and satisfaction, and consequently some sort of tranquillity like one who finds his peace and repose in his riches.

But he who aspires to a condition more exalted than his own is in a constant state of disquietude, like the needle of the compass which trembles incessantly until it points to the north. An ancient proverb makes the happiness of this life to consist in wishing to be what we are and nothing more.

Quod sis esse velis, nihilque malis.

Blessed Francis who, in his own opinion, had already risen too high in the hierarchy of the Church, turned his thoughts rather to giving up his dignities than to seeking promotion. He looked forward to the calm retreat of solitude rather than the dignity of illustrious offices.

He was even apprehensive of the high esteem in which he knew that he was held, dreading lest he should be less the servant of God for thus delighting men.

On one occasion some worthy soul having warned him to keep humble amid the praises and acclamations bestowed on him, he answered: "You please me greatly by recommending holy humility to me, for, do you know, when the wind gets imprisoned in our valleys, among our mountains, even the little flowers are beaten down and the trees are uprooted. I am situated rather high up and, in my post of Bishop, am tossed about most of all. O Lord! save us: command these winds of vanity to cease to blow and there will be a great calm. Stand firm, O my soul, and clasp very tightly the foot of our Saviour's holy Cross: the rain which falls there in plenteous showers on all sides stills the wind, however violent it may be.

"When I am there, O my God, as I sometimes am, how sheltered is my soul, and how refreshed by that crimson dew! but no sooner have I moved a single step away than the wind again takes me off my feet!"

UPON THE KNOWLEDGE WHICH PUFFS UP.

You wish to know what St. Paul means when he says that knowledge puffs up and that charity edifies.[1] I imagine he means by the knowledge which puffs up, that which is destitute of charity and which consequently tends only to vanity. All those are vain, say the sacred Scriptures, who have not the knowledge of God;[2] and what is this knowledge of God if not the knowledge of His ways and of His will? It is the God of knowledge who teaches this knowledge to men; the science of the saints, the science which makes saints, the science of salvation, a science without which all else is absolute ignorance. He who thinks that he knows something and does not know how to save his soul, does not yet know what it is most important to know. Those who know many things without knowing themselves, and without knowing God in the manner in which even in this present life he can be known and desires to be known, resemble the giants in the fable, who piled up mountains and then buried themselves beneath them.

Do not, however, think for a moment that, in order to save our souls, or to be truly devout, we must be ignorant; for, as sugar spoils no sauce, true knowledge is in no wise opposed to devotion. On the contrary, by enlightening the understanding it contributes much to fervour in the will. Listen to what our Blessed Father says on this subject in his Theotimus: "Knowledge is not of itself contrary, but very useful to devotion. Meeting, they should marvellously assist one another; though it too often happens through our misery that knowledge hinders the birth of devotion, because knowledge puffeth up and makes us proud, and pride, which is contrary to all virtue, ruins all devotion. Without doubt, the eminent science of a Cyprian, an Augustine, a Hilary, a Chrysostom, a Basil, a Gregory, a Bonaventure, a Thomas, not only taught these Saints to value, but greatly enhanced their devotion; as again, their devotion not only supernaturalized, but eminently perfected their knowledge."[3]

[Footnote 1: 1 Cor. viii. 1.]

[Footnote 2: Sap. xiii. 1.]

[Footnote 3: Book vi. chap. 4.]

UPON SCRUPLES.

It was Blessed Francis' opinion that scruples have their origin in a cunning self-esteem. I call it cunning because it is so subtle and crafty as to deceive even those who are troubled by it. As a proof of this assertion he evidenced the fact that "those who suffer from this malady will not acquiesce in the judgment of their directors, however discreet and enlightened in the ways of God they may be; obstinately clinging to their own opinions instead of, by humble submission, accepting the remedies and consequent peace offered to them. Who can wonder at the prolonged sufferings of the sick man who resolutely refuses every salutary remedy which he is entreated to take? Who will pity one who suffers himself to die of hunger and thirst, although everything that could satisfy the one and quench the other be placed within his reach?

"Holy Scripture teaches us that the crime of disobedience is equal in guilt to that of idolatry and witchcraft. But what shall we say of the disobedience of the scrupulous, who so idolize their own opinions as to be absolutely slaves to them, and whom no sort of remonstrance or reasoning will convince of the idleness of their unfounded fears.

"They will tell you, in answer to your judicious and soothing arguments, that you are only flattering them, that they are misunderstood, that they do not explain themselves clearly, and so on.

"This is, indeed, a malady difficult of cure, because, like jealousy, its fires are fed by everything with which it comes in contact. May God preserve you from this lingering and sad disease, which I regard as the quartan fever or jaundice of the soul."

UPON TEMPTATIONS.

"If we only knew how to make a good use of temptations," said our Blessed Father, "instead of dreading, we should welcome them—I had almost said desire them. But because our weakness and our cowardice are only too well known to us, from our long experience, and from many sorrowful falls, we have good reason to say, Lead us not into temptation.

"If to this just mistrust of ourselves we united confidence in God, who is stronger to deliver us from temptation than we are weak in falling into it, our hopes would rise in proportion to the lessening of our fears. For by Thee I shall be delivered from temptation, and through my God I shall go over a wall."[1]

With such a support can we not boldly tread upon the asp and the basilisk, and trample under foot the lion and the dragon?[2] As it is in temptation that we learn to know the greatness of our courage and of our fidelity to God, so it is by suffering temptation that we make progress in strength of heart, and that we learn to wield the weapons of our warfare, which are spiritual against the spiritual malice of our invisible enemies. Then it is that our soul, clothed in the panoply of grace, appears terrible to them as an army in battle array, and as the hosts of the Lord.

Some think that all is lost when they are tormented by thoughts of blasphemy and impiety, and fancy that their faith is gone. Yet as long as these thoughts merely distress them and they are resisted, they cannot harm them, and such stormy winds only serve to make souls become more deeply rooted in faith. As much has to be said of temptations against purity and other virtues, for the maxim is quite a general one.

There is no good Christian who is not tempted. The angel said to Tobias: Because thou wast acceptable to God it was necessary that temptation, should prove thee.[3]

[Footnote 1: Psalm xxvi. 30.]

[Footnote 2: Psalm xc. 13.]

[Footnote 3: Job xii. 13.]

UPON THE SAME SUBJECT.

You ask me why God permits the enemy of our salvation to afflict us with so many temptations, which put us into such great danger of offending God and losing our soul. I might answer you in words from Holy Scripture, but I will give you our Blessed Father's teaching on the subject, which is only an interpretation of what St. Paul and St. James tell us in their epistles: "Do you know," he says, "what God does in temptation?"

He permits the evil one to furbish up his wares and to offer them to us for sale, so that by the contempt with which we look upon them we may show our affection for divine things.

Must you then, my dear sister, my dearest daughter, because of this temptation, fret and disquiet yourself and change your manner of thought?

Oh, no! by no means, it is the devil who prowls round about your soul, peeping and prying to see if he can find an open door. He did this with Job, with St. Anthony, with St. Catherine of Siena, and with an infinity of good souls whom I know, as well as with my own, which is good-for-nothing, and which I do not know. And have you, my good daughter, to distress yourself about what the devil attempts? Let him wait outside and keep all the avenues of your soul fast shut. In the end he will be tired out, or if not God will force him to raise the siege.

Remember what I think I have told you before. It is a good sign when the devil stirs up such a tumult outside the fortress of your will, for it shows he is not inside it.

One cause of our interior trouble and mental disturbance is the difficulty we experience in discerning whether a temptation comes from within or from without, whether it is from our own heart or from the enemy, who takes up his position as a besieger before that heart? You may apply the following test in order to find out.

Does the temptation please or displease you? One of the ancient Fathers says that sins which displease us cannot harm us. How much less then displeasing temptations!

Notice that, as long as the temptation displeases you there is nothing to fear, for why should it displease if not because your will does not consent to it?"

"But," you say, "if I, as it were, dally with the temptation, either from inadvertence or torpor, or slothful unwillingness to reject and repel it, is not that in a way taking pleasure in it?" "The evil of temptation is not measured by its duration: it may be working against us all our life long, but while it displeases us it cannot make us fail into sin; on the contrary, being repulsive to us, this very antipathy not only preserves us from being infected by its venom, but adds strength to our virtue and jewels to our crown."

"But I am so much afraid of taking pleasure in it!"

"That very fear is a proof that it displeases you, for we are not afraid of that which pleases us. We are not terrified except by what displeases us, just as we can only enjoy what is good or has the appearance of being good.

"If you were able all the time to look upon temptation as an evil it cannot have pleased you."

"Still, is it wrong to find pleasure in thinking of what is sinful?" "If this pleasure is felt before we reflect that the thing is evil it is of no consequence, since voluntary malice and consent are needed to make this pleasure a sin."

"How shall we know whether or not we have yielded this consent?" "Assuredly, it is difficult to define the nature of voluntary consent. This difficulty gave rise to the saying of the Psalmist, Who can understand sins?[1]

"This, too, is why he prays to be delivered from his secret faults, that is to say, from sins which he cannot easily discern."

I will, however, on this subject give you another excellent lesson which I learned from our Blessed Father.

"When you are doubtful," he said to me, "whether or not you have consented to evil, always take the doubt for a negative, and for this reason. A true and full consent of the will is necessary to form a real grave sin, there being no sin in what is not voluntary. Now full consent is so clear that there can never be left in the mind a shadow of doubt about its having taken place."

This plain teaching surely cuts the gordian knot of our perplexities.

[Footnote 1: Psalm xviii. 13.]

THOUGHTS ON THE INCARNATION.

There are two opinions held by theologians on the subject of the Incarnation. Some hold that had Adam never sinned the Son of God would not have become incarnate, others that the Incarnation would have taken place even had our first parents remained in the state of innocence and original justice in which they were created. For, as they urge, the Word was made flesh, not to merely be a redeemer and restorer of the human race, but that through Him God might be glorified. Our Blessed Father held this second opinion, which he advanced, not only in familiar conversation and in the pulpit, but also in his writings. In his Theotimus he expresses himself thus: "God knew from all eternity that He could create an innumerable multitude of beings with divers perfections and qualities, to whom He might communicate Himself. And considering that amongst all the different communications which were possible, none was so excellent as that of uniting Himself to some created nature, in such sort that the creature might be engrafted and implanted in the Divinity, and become one single person with it: His infinite goodness, which of itself and by itself tends towards communication, resolved and determined to communicate Himself in this manner. So that, as eternally there is an essential communication in God, by which the Father communicates all His infinite and indivisible divinity to the Son in producing Him, and the Father and the Son together producing the Holy Ghost, communicate to Him also their own singular divinity; so this sovereign sweetness was so perfectly communicated externally to a creature that the created nature and the divinity retaining each of them its own properties were, notwithstanding so united together that they were but one same person. Now of all the creatures which that Sovereign Omnipotence could produce, He thought good to make choice of human nature which afterwards in effect was united to the person of God the Son, He created it, and to it He destined the incomparable honour of personal union with His divine majesty, to the end that for all eternity it might enjoy above all others the treasures of His infinite glory."[1]

This thought has always pleased me exceedingly; this thought, I mean, of the communication of God, in the worthiest manner possible, namely, through the mystery of the Incarnation. But ah! What shall we then say of the mystery of the most holy Eucharist, which is, as it were, an extension of the Incarnation! In the holy Eucharist the Son of God, in His overflowing mercy, not content with having made Himself the Son of Man, a sharer in our humanity and our Brother, has invented a wondrous way of communicating Himself to each one of us in particular. By this He incorporates Himself in us, and us in Him. He dwells in us, and makes us dwell in Him, becoming our food and support, flesh of our flesh, and bone of our bone, by a grace which surpasses every other grace, since it contains in itself the author of all grace! Truly, we possess in this divine mystery, though veiled and hidden under the sacramental species, Him whom the angels desire to see, even while they see Him continually. Nor is there any difference between their possession and ours, except in the manner in which it is effected. For if they have the advantage of sight, we have that of a closer intimacy, seeing that He is only before them as the Beatific Vision, while He is actually within us, as the living and life-giving bread, a bread strengthening our heart, or, rather, the very heart of our heart, or the soul of our heart, or the heart of our soul. And if the heart of the disciples of Emmaus burned within them when He only spoke to them on their way, what ardour should be kindled in our breasts by the receiving of Him who came to bring the fire of divine love upon earth, that it might inflame and kindle all hearts!

You ask me whether we are happier in having been redeemed from that state of original sin into which our first parents fell than had we been born in the innocence which was theirs at their creation.

At first sight it would seem that never to have been bound by the chain of misery and evil with which the first sin of Adam fettered us would surely have been more desirable than even to be loosed from it by the divine goodness!

This, however, is a merely human judgment, revealed to us by flesh and blood. The light of faith, far brighter and more ennobling, teaches us a sublimer lesson. This is what our Blessed Father says on the subject:

"Who can doubt of the abundance of the means of salvation, since we have so great a Saviour, for the sake of whom we have been made, and by whose merits we have been ransomed. For He died, for all, because all were dead, and His mercy was more far-reaching when He built up anew the race of men than Adam's misery when he ruined it.

"Indeed, Adam's sin was so far from quenching God's love for mankind, that, on the contrary, it stirred it up, and invited it. So that by a most sweet and loving re-action, love was quickened by the presence of sin, and as if re-collecting its forces for victory over evil, made grace to superabound where sin had abounded.[2] Whence, Holy Church, in an excess of devout wonder, cries out (upon Easter-eve), 'O truly necessary sin of Adam, which was blotted out by the death of Jesus Christ! O happy fault which merited to have such and so great a Redeemer!' Truly, Theotimus, we may say, as did he of old, 'We were ruined, had we not been undone; that is, ruin brought us profit, since in effect human nature, through being redeemed by its Saviour, has received more graces than ever it would have received if Adam had remained innocent.'"[3]

One of the marvels of divine Omnipotence is that it knows by a secret power, reserved to itself alone, how to draw good from evil, the contrary from the contrary; water from, fire, as in the furnace of the three children[4] and fire from water, as in the sacred fire which was found in a well, the thick water of which was changed into fire. By this secret power He makes all things work together for good to those who love Him.

"Truly," says our Blessed Father, in the same place, "as the rainbow touching the thorn aspalathus, makes it more odoriferous than the lily, so our Saviour's Redemption, touching our miseries makes them more beneficial and worthy of love than original innocence could ever have been.

"I say to you, says our Saviour, there shall be joy in Heaven upon one sinner that doth penance; more than upon ninety-nine just, who need not penance,[5] and so the state of redemption is a hundred times better than that of innocence.

"Verily, by the watering of our Saviour's Blood, made with the hyssop of the Cross, we have been re-clothed in a whiteness incomparably more excellent than the snowy robe of innocence. We come out, like Naaman, from the stream of salvation more pure and clean than if we had never been leprous, to the end that the divine majesty, as He has ordained also for us, should not be overcome by evil, but overcome evil by good,[6] that mercy (as a sacred oil) should keep itself above judgment,[7] and God's tender mercies be over all His works."[8]

[Footnote 1: Book ii. chap. 4.]

[Footnote 2: Col. i. 16.]

[Footnote 3: The Love of God. Book ii, c. 5.]

[Footnote 4: Daniel iii. 50.]

[Footnote 5: Luke xv. 7.]

[Footnote 6: Rom. xii.]

[Footnote 7: James ii. 13.]

[Footnote 8: Psalm cxliv. 9.]

UPON CONFESSION AND COMMUNION.

These two Sacraments were styled by Blessed Francis the two poles of the christian life, because around them that life ever revolves. One purifies the soul, the other sanctifies it. He greatly admired the saying of St. Bernard that all the spiritual good which we possess is derived from the frequent use of the Sacraments. He would say that those who neglect the Sacraments are not unlike the people in the Parable, who would not accept the invitation to the Marriage Feast, and who thus incurred the wrath of the Lord who had prepared it. Some plead as their excuse that they "are not good enough"; but how are they to become good if they keep aloof from the source of all goodness? Others say: "We are too weak"; but is not this the Bread of the strong? Others; "We are infirm"; but in this Sacrament have you not the Good Physician Himself? Others: "We are not worthy"; but does not the Church direct that even the holiest of men should not approach the Feast without having on his lips the words: Lord! I am not worthy that Thou shouldst enter under my roof? To those who plead that they are overwhelmed with cares and with the business of this life, He cries: Come to me all you that labour and are burdened and I will refresh you.[1] If any fear to come lest they should incur condemnation, are they not in yet greater danger of being condemned for keeping away? Indeed, the plea of humility is as false as that of Achaz, who detracted from the glory of God when he feigned to be afraid of tempting Him. What better way of learning to receive Him well can there be than receiving Him often? Is it not so with other acts which are perfected by frequent repetition?

He extolled highly the precept of St. Augustine on this subject. It was his desire that any person (he was speaking of the laity) free from mortal sin, and without any affection for it, should communicate confidently yet humbly every Sunday,[2] if not advised by his confessors to do so oftener. He does not say "anyone who is without venial sin," for from that who is exempt?

His sentiments with regard to Holy Communion were most sweet and so tempered by divine love, that reverent fear was in no way prejudicial to confidence, neither was confidence to reverence. He fervently desired that we should annihilate ourselves when receiving the Blessed Sacrament, as our Lord annihilated Himself in order to communicate Himself to us, bowing down the heaven of His greatness to accommodate and unite Himself with our lowness.

But you will be better satisfied to hear his feelings expressed in his own words.

They were addressed, not directly, but through the medium of another, to a person, who from a false idea of humility dared not approach this divine mystery, and who, in the words but not in the spirit of St. Peter, entreated her Saviour to depart from her.

"Tell her," he says, "to communicate fearlessly, calmly, yet with all humility, in order to correspond with the action of that Spouse who in order to unite Himself with us annihilated Himself and lovingly abased Himself to the extent even of becoming our food and our pasturage; condescending thus to us who are the food and pasturage of worms. Oh! my daughter, those who communicate according to the spirit of the Heavenly Bridegroom, annihilate themselves and say to our Lord: feed on me, change me, annihilate me, convert me into Thyself. There is nothing, I think, in the world of which we have more absolute possession, or over which we have more entire dominion, than over the food which, for our own self-preservation, we annihilate.

"Well, our Lord has condescended to this excess of love, namely, to give Himself to us for our food; and as for us, what ought not we to do in order that He may possess us, that He may feed on us, that He may make us what He pleases?"

Read what is said on this subject in the "Devout life" and the "Conferences."

[Footnote 1: Matt. xi. 28.] [Footnote 2: By the recent Decree of Pope Pius X., His Holiness desires that, with such dispositions, it should be daily.—[Ed.]]

UPON CONFESSION.

Our Blessed Father thought so much of frankness, candour and ingenuousness in Confession, that when he met with these virtues in his penitents he was filled with joy and satisfaction.

It happened one day that he received a letter from one of his spiritual daughters telling him that she had been betrayed into the sin of malicious envy (by which she meant jealousy) of one of her sisters. He answered her letter as follows: "I tell you with truth that your letter has filled my soul with so sweet a perfume, that I can affirm that I have not for a long time read any thing so consoling. I repeat, my dear daughter, that this letter awakens in me such fresh ardour of love towards God who is so good, and towards you whom He desires to make so good, that I can only make an act of thanksgiving for this to His divine Providence. Thus it is, my daughter, that we must always without a moment's hesitation thrust our hands into the secret recesses of our hearts to tear out the foul growths which have sprung up there, from the mingling of our self-love with our humours, inclinations, and antipathies. Oh, my God! What satisfaction for the heart of a most loving Father to hear a beloved daughter protest that she has been envious and malicious! How blessed is this envy, since it is followed by so frank a confession! Your hand in writing your letter made a stroke more valiant than ever did that of Alexander!"

UPON A CHANGE OF CONFESSOR.

I have told you by word of mouth, and now I repeat in writing, so that you may better remember it, that the scruple of scruples is not to dare to change one's Confessor. The Priest who should put this scruple into your head deserves to be left, as himself scrupulous, and unsafe. Virtue, like truth, is always to be found half way between two faulty extremes. To be always changing one's Confessor, and never to dare to do so, or sooner to omit Confession than to confess to any one but our usual Confessor, are two blameworthy extremes.

In the one case we show ourselves volatile and ill-balanced; in the other we are cowardly. If you ask me which of the two is the more to be avoided I should say the second, and this because it seems to me to indicate a low tone of mind, human respect, attachment to the creature, and in general a slavish spirit which is quite contrary to the spirit of God, who only dwells there, where there is perfect liberty.

St. Paul tells us that being redeemed by the Precious Blood of Jesus Christ we ought not to make ourselves slaves of men.

Possibly, however, you would more readily submit your judgment to that of our Blessed Father than to mine.

I remind you then how highly he thought of this holy christian liberty. You may be quite sure that he inculcated it on persons like yourself living in the world since, as I am going to show you, he made a great point of it with his Religious.

The Holy Council of Trent having decreed that three or four times a year all nuns should have extra-ordinary Confessors given to them to relieve them from the yoke and constraint which might ensue from being always under the direction of one and the same ordinary Confessor, our Blessed Father decreed that every three months, in the four Ember weeks the Sisters of the Visitation, of which Order he was the Founder, should have an Extraordinary Confessor, carefully recommending to the Superiors to ask for one even oftener for any Sisters who might desire or really need his help.

Blessed Teresa[1] was also very careful to ensure to her Sisters this holy and reasonable liberty, which renders the yoke of the Saviour sweet and light as it should be, and her daughters, the Carmelites, still value their privilege as she did.

Our Blessed Father used, moreover, to say that Religious men to whom the direction of nuns was entrusted, and all convents subject to their jurisdiction, would do well to observe the excellent rule and custom some of them have of never leaving a Confessor for more than a year in a convent.

He added that Superiors should reserve to themselves the power of withdrawing Confessors even before the time for which they were appointed had expired, and indeed whenever it may please them, and should not keep any Confessor longer than the time for which he was appointed, unless for some very urgent reason or pressing necessity.

To show you that it was not only to me that our Blessed Father expressed his opinion on this point, this is how he wrote about it to a Superior of the Visitation.

"We ought not to be so fickle as to wish without any substantial reason to change our Confessor, but, on the other hand, we should not be immovable and persistent when legitimate causes make such a change desirable, and Bishops should not so tie their own hands as to be unable to effect the change when expedient, and especially when either the Sisters or the Spiritual Father desire it."

[Footnote 1: St. Teresa was not then canonised. [Ed.]]

UPON DIFFERENT METHODS OF DIRECTION.

In the year 1619 our Blessed Father went to Paris where he remained for eight or nine months. I was there at the same time, having been summoned for the Advent and Lent sermons.

Many pious persons came to consult him on their spiritual concerns, and thus gave him the opportunity of observing the variety of methods employed by God to draw souls to Himself, and also the different ways in which His Priests guide and direct these same souls.

Among others, he told me of two priests celebrated for their preaching, and who also applied themselves most zealously to the administration of the Sacrament of Penance. Both were faithful servants of God and exemplary in the discharge of their functions, but yet so different in their methods of direction, that they almost seemed to oppose one another, though both had the one single aim in view, namely, to promote the service and the glory of God, "One of them," said the Saint, "is severe and almost terrible in his preaching. He proclaims the judgments of God like the very trump of doom. In his special devotions, too, he speaks of nothing but mortifications, austerities, constant self-examination and such like exercises. Thus, by the wholesome fears with which he fills the minds of his penitents, he leads them to an exact observance of God's law, and to an anxious solicitude for their own salvation. He does not harass them with scruples, and yet keeps them in a marvellous state of subjection.

"The effect of his direction is that God is greatly feared and dreaded by them, that they fly from sin as from a serpent, and that they earnestly practise virtue. This divine fear is coupled with a high esteem for their Director, and a friendship for him, holy indeed, but so strong and vehement that it seems to these souls as though, were they to lose their guide, they must needs go astray.

"The other Director leads souls to God by quite a different path. His sermons are always on the love of God. He inculcates the study of virtue rather than the hatred of vice. He makes his penitents love virtue more because it pleases God, than because it is itself worthy of love, and he makes them hate vice more because it displeases God than because of the sufferings which it brings upon those who are slaves to it.

"The effect of this direction is to make souls conceive a love for God that is great, pure and disinterested; also a great affection for their neighbour for the love of God; while, as for their sentiments towards their Director, they approach him with reverential awe, beholding God in him and him in God, having no affection for his person beyond that due to all our fellow-men."

Our Blessed Father never told me the name of this Director, nor even gave me the slightest hint as to who he was, and I therefore sought no further explanation, contenting myself with admiring the ways of God and His various desires for the good of the souls whom He calls to His service. I became penetrated, too, with the conviction that by many different routes we can reach one and the same goal. Let every spirit praise the Lord.

ADVICE UPON HAVING A DIRECTOR.

I asked him one day who was his Director. Taking from his pocket the Spiritual Combat, he said: "You see my Director in this book, which, from my earliest youth, has, with the help of God, taught me and been my master in spiritual matters and in the interior life. When I was a student at Padua, a Theatine Father instructed and gave me advice from it, and following its directions all has been well with me. It was written by a very holy member of that celebrated congregation, the author concealing his own name under that of his Orders which makes use of the book almost in the same way as the Jesuits make use of the Exercises of St. Ignatius Loyola."

I reminded him that in his Philothea[1] he recommends people to have a living Director. "That is true," he answered, "but have you not noticed that I say he must be chosen out of ten thousand?[2] Because there is scarcely one in a thousand to be found having all the qualities necessary for this office, or who, if he has them, displays them constantly and perseveringly; men being so variable that they never remain in one state, as Holy Scripture assures us."[3]

I asked him if we must then run uncertainly and pursue our way without guidance. He answered: "We must seek it among the dead; among those who are no longer subject to passion or change, and who have ceased to be swayed by human interests. As an Emperor of old said that his most faithful counsellors were the dead, meaning books, so we may say that our safest spiritual directors are books of piety."

"But what," I asked, "are those who cannot read to do?" "They," he replied, "must have good books read to them by people in whom they can have absolute confidence. Besides, such simple souls as these do not, as a rule, trouble themselves much about methods of devotion, or, if they do, God for the most part bestows on them such graces as to make it plain that He Himself is their Teacher, and that they are truly Theodidacts, or taught by God."

"Must we then," I asked, "give up all spiritual guides?" "By no means," he answered, "for besides the fact that we are bound to obey the law of God coming to us through our Superiors, both spiritual and temporal, we must also defer most humbly to our Confessors, to whom we lay bare the secrets of our conscience. Then, when we find difficulties in the books which we have chosen for our guidance, difficulties which, as we read, we cannot settle to our satisfaction, we must consult those who are well versed in mystic language, or rather, I should say, in spiritual matters, and listen humbly to their opinion. We must not, however, always consult the same man; for, besides the fact that Holy Scripture warns us that there is safety where there is much counsel,[4] we must remember that if we always consulted the same living oracle, he would in time become superior to the dead one; that he would make himself a supplanter, a second Jacob, pushing aside the book which we had chosen for our guide, and assuming dominion and mastery over both dead and living, that is, over the book and the reader who had chosen it for his direction. To prevent this encroachment, I had almost said this unfelt and imperceptibly increasing tyranny, it is well when we meet with difficulties to consult several persons, following the advice given by the Holy Ghost through the Apostle St. Paul not to make ourselves the slaves of men, having been delivered and redeemed at so great a price, even that of the Precious Blood of Jesus Christ."[5]

In answer to my remark that I very much preferred as a book The Imitation of Christ to the Spiritual Combat, he said that they were both the works of writers truly animated by the Spirit of God, that they were indeed different in many respects, but that it might be said of each of them as it is of the Saints: There was not found the like to him.[6]

He added that in such matters comparisons were always more or less odious; that beauty, however it might vary, was always beauty; that the book of the Imitation had in some respects great advantages over the Combat, but that the latter had also some advantages over the Imitation. Among these he mentioned with special commendation its arrangement and that it goes deeper into things and more thoroughly to the root of the matter. He concluded by saying that we should do well to read the one and not neglect the other, for that both books were so short that to do this would not put us to much expenditure of time or trouble.

He valued the Imitation, he said, greatly for its brevity and conciseness as an aid to prayer and contemplation, but the Combat as a help in active and practical life.

[Footnote 1: Book 1. c. 10.]

[Footnote 2: This hyperbole of St. Francis is sometimes pushed to excess, it is a question, too, if M. Camus always understood him rightly. [ED.]]

[Footnote 3: Job xiv. 2.]

[Footnote 4: Prov. xi. 14.]

[Footnote 5: 1 Cor. vii. 23.]

[Footnote 6: Eccle. xliv. 20.]

UPON TRUE AND MISTAKEN ZEAL.

Zeal was a virtue which Blessed Francis ever regarded with a certain amount of suspicion, "It is," he used to say, "generally speaking, impetuous, and although it strives to exterminate vice by reproving sinners, it is apt, if not guided by moderation and prudence, to produce most disastrous effects.

"There is a zeal so bitter and fierce that it pardons nothing, exaggerates the smallest faults, and, like an unskilful physician, only makes the disease of the soul more serious. There is zeal of another kind, which is so lax and weakly tender, that it forgives everything, thinking in so doing to practise charity, which is patient and kind, seeks not her own, and bears all wrongs done to her even joyfully; but such zeal, too, is quite mistaken, for true charity cannot endure without grief any wrong done to God, that is to say, anything contrary to His honour and glory.

"True zeal must be accompanied by knowledge and judgment. It pardons certain things, or, at least, winks at them, until the right time and place are come for correcting them; it reproves others when it sees there is hope of amendment, leaving no stone unturned when it thinks there is a possibility of preserving or advancing the glory of God.

"It is certain that zeal tempered with gentleness is far more efficacious than that which is turbulent and boisterous. This is why the Prophet, wishing to demonstrate the power of the Messiah to bring the whole universe under the sweet yoke of obedience to Him, does not speak of Him as the Lion of the Tribe of Juda, but as the Lamb, the Ruler of the Earth. The Psalmist says the very same thing in a few words: Mildness is come upon us, and we shall be corrected."

I was complaining one day to our Saint of injuries which I had suffered through the mistaken zeal of some persons of eminent virtue, and he replied thus: "Do you not know that the best honey is made by the bees which have the sharpest sting?" It is true, indeed, that nothing hurts us so much as wrong done by those on whose support we reckoned, as David knew well when he said: "For if my enemy had reviled me, I would verily have borne with it, and if he that hated me had spoken great things against me, I would perhaps have hidden myself from him, but thou, a man of one mind, my guide, and my familiar—who together didst take sweet meats with me: in the house of God we walked with consent."[1]

"Consider," the Saint went on to say, "by whom Jesus Christ was betrayed." Listen to the words spoken by him through the mouth of His Prophet, spoken moreover of His most sacred wounds, "With these I was wounded in the house of them that loved me."[2]

And, after all, is not hope always at the bottom of Pandora's box? Virtuous people carried away by this mistaken zeal, will, directly their eyes are opened, only too gladly recognise the truth, and will love you more than ever. Pray to God to enlighten them and to deliver you from the attacks of calumny. And if the worst comes to the worst, is it not the duty of a true Christian to bless those who curse him, to pray for those who persecute him, and to render good for evil, provided he really wishes to be a faithful child of the Heavenly Father, who makes His sun to shine, and His rain to fall, on the wicked as well as on the good.[3]

Let your sighs and lamentations be breathed softly into the ear of God alone, saying to Him:

"They will curse, and Thou wilt bless, and they that look to Thee shall not be confounded."[4]

[Footnote 1: Psalm liv. 13-16.]

[Footnote 2: Zach. xiii. 6.]

[Footnote 3: Matt. v. 44-45.]

[Footnote 4: Psalm cviii. 28.]

UPON THE INSTITUTION OF THE VISITATION ORDER.

When he instituted the Congregation of the Visitation of Holy Mary in the town of Annecy, where he resided, he had no intention either of multiplying Religious Houses or of forming a new Order or Institute with vows, of which he said there were already enough in the Church. His idea was to form an assembly of devout widows and maidens, free and unbound either by monastic vows or enclosure, who should, in their house, occupy themselves with prayer and manual labour, only going out for two objects, namely, to discharge their own domestic duties or to perform works of mercy done for their neighbour to the glory of God. Those who embraced this mode of life practised it with such success that not only the town of Annecy, but all the country round felt the influence of their holy life, and was greatly edified by their example; while the sick and poor, whom they visited in their distress, were both consoled and relieved by them.

Later on, these holy women formed a little settlement at Lyons, but not to the satisfaction of the then Archbishop, afterwards Cardinal, de Marquemont. This Prelate, although a person of much excellence, having lived the greater part of his life in Rome, where he was Auditor to the Rota, was so thoroughly imbued with all the Italian maxims as to the management of women that he could not endure their living thus without vows or enclosure. He therefore not only advised, but even urged our Blessed Father to insist upon their choosing some one of the monastic Rules approved by the Church, and upon their taking perpetual vows, and preserving an inviolable enclosure. Our Blessed Father, who was extremely pliable, condescending, and ready to yield to the will of others, allowed himself to be persuaded by this great Prelate.

The Archbishop then promised that he would submit to the approbation of Rome the Constitutions which the holy Bishop had prepared for the guidance of this simple community, provided that they were in accordance with the Rule of St. Augustine.

Our Blessed Father also induced his dear daughters to lay aside their original manner of life in order to embrace this second, which took the shape of an Order properly so called, having perpetual vows.

Since this change he has often told me that the Congregation owed its establishment simply to the providence and ordering of God, Whose Spirit breathes where He wills, and Who effects changes with His own right hand when it pleases Him; and Whose own perfection it is which makes His works admirable in our eyes.

"As for me," he once said to me, "I am filled with astonishment when I reflect that, alone and unaided, but with extraordinary calmness of mind, I have done what I wished to undo, and undone what I wished to do."

"What do you mean by that?" I asked. And he replied: "I never thought for a moment of forming a Religious Order, being of opinion that their number is already amply sufficient. No, I only intended to gather together a little company of maidens and widows without solemn vows and without enclosure, having no wealth, but that of holy charity, which is indeed all silk and gold, and is the great bond which unites all Christians, the true bond of all perfection, the bond of the Spirit of God, the spirit of holy and absolute liberty." He went on to say that their occupation had hitherto been, as I have already told you, prayer, manual labour, and visiting the sick and destitute. "I fear," he added, "that there will be quite an uproar in the little town when, under the new system, their vows and enclosure oblige them to abandon their works of mercy. Indeed, I gave their Order the title of the Visitation of Holy Mary that they might take for their pattern in their visits to the sick, that visit which the Blessed Virgin paid to her cousin St. Elizabeth, with whom she dwelt for three months, to help her and to wait upon her. Now that they are enclosed, they will be rather visited than visitors; but since the holy providence of God so orders it, may that providence be for ever blessed." All that I have just told you is clearly expressed in the letter written by him on the subject of the change to Cardinal Bellarmine, which can be seen in the volume of his letters. In remembrance, as it were, of his first design, he expresses his desire to obtain from the Holy See, through the intervention of the great Cardinal, three privileges for this Institution. The first, that it should only be obliged to recite the office of the Blessed Virgin. The second, that widows should be allowed to be received and to live there, wearing their secular dress, without taking any vows, and with power to come out if at any time the necessity of their affairs should oblige them to do so. The third, that even married women should be allowed to enter, and to remain for a short time with the permission of their husbands and of the Spiritual Father, without being either Benefactresses or Foundresses. The letter justifies all this, and is full of beautiful and sensible reasons for it. I know also that during his lifetime, when the twelve first Houses of the Order were established, he saw that in them all those rules were carried out.

I cannot here refrain from quoting for you a passage from Cardinal Bellarmine's reply to the letter written to him by our Blessed Father on this subject. It shows very plainly how highly that good and learned Prelate approved of the first design for the constitution of this Order, and how little he favoured the change of plan, which has, nevertheless, we must admit, redounded greatly to the glory of God and to the edification of the whole Church.

The Cardinal says in this letter: "I will give you the same advice as I should take for myself were I in similar circumstances. I should then keep these maidens and widows exactly as they are at present, not making any change in a state of things which is so admirable. For, before the time of Boniface VIII. there were consecrated persons in the Church, the Eastern as well as the Western, mentioned by the Fathers. Among the Latins, St. Cyprian, St. Ambrose, St. Jerome, and St. Augustine; among the Greeks, St. Athanasius, St. Chrysostom, St. Basil, and many others; but they were not enclosed in their convents in such a manner that they could not come out of them when, necessary. And your most Reverend Lordship is aware that simple vows are no less binding and are of no less merit in the sight of God than solemn ones. Indeed, the solemnizing of vows, as well as the rule of Enclosure, was originated by an ecclesiastical decree of the said Boniface VIII. Even at the present day, the convent of noble ladies, founded by St. Frances of Rome, nourishes in that city, although without any enclosure or solemn profession. Therefore, if in your country maidens and widows live in so holy a manner, without being either cloistered or enclosed, and are able thus to be of use to those in the world, I do not see why their mode of living should be changed."

What our Blessed Father dreaded for the Institute was what happens to those Institutes which fail in exactitude of observance. And he often quoted Saint Bernard's saying that though devotion had given birth to riches, these unnatural daughters had stifled their mother. Whenever he heard of any House established in his time beginning to complain of want of comforts or conveniences he would say: "One day they will have only too many." All his letters are full of exhortations to put up with discomforts, and to lean upon Providence, casting all care upon God, Who feeds the young ravens, satisfies the hunger of all flesh, and fills every living creature with blessings. Wealth, not poverty, was what he feared for his Order. This is what he says in the Constitutions: "For the more perfect observance of the holy virtue of poverty, when once the buildings of the convents are finished, the revenues shall be limited according to the place where each convent is situated, to the end that even in this a proper mean may be kept, and that there be no superfluity of goods in the Community, but only a fair sufficiency, and when this is once attained nothing further shall be taken for the reception of the Sisters coming to it, but what shall be requisite to keep up and maintain well the just competency of the convent."[1]

And in the letter which he wrote to the most Serene Infanta, Margaret of Sovoy, Dowager Duchess of Mantua, to invite her to take this Congregation under her protection, he says:

"This Congregation does not solicit alms, but is established in such a manner that the ladies who enter it give a dowry in order to maintain the buildings, the sacristy, the chaplain, and to defray the expenses of illness, etc., either by means of a regular and perpetual income, or by some other way which cannot injure anyone or interfere in any possible manner with the payment of the taxes and subsidies due to his most Serene Highness the Duke. I hope also that the above-mentioned Congregation will in a few years' time be endowed with revenues sufficient for the support of the Community, Thus widows without children, and young girls who desire to serve God in chastity, obedience, and poverty, will have every facility for entering it, since they will be received without any other payment than that of a dowry or pension provided by their family for their support."

[Footnote 1: Constitution 5.]

HIS DEFENCE OF HIS NEW CONGREGATION OF THE VISITATION.

On one occasion, some one speaking to him, my Sisters, of your "Congregation," said: "But what do you mean to do with all this crowd of women and maidens? Of what use will they be to the Church of God? Are there not already enough of such institutions into which these applicants might be drafted? Would you not be doing better if you were to establish some College for the training and education of Priests, and spend your time on them instead of on these persons to whom one must repeat a thing a hundred times before they can retain it? And then, after all, if they do, it is a treasure buried, a candlestick under a bushel. Is it not a case of painting on water and sowing on sand?"

Our Blessed Father, smiling graciously, answered with his extraordinary serenity and sweetness: "It is not for me to work with costly materials; goldsmiths handle the precious metals, potters only clay. Believe me, God is a skilled workman; with poor tools He can accomplish wonderful work. He is wont to choose weak things to confound the strong; ignorance to confound knowledge, and that which is nothing to confound that which seems to be something. What did He not do with a rod in the hand of Moses? With the jaw-bone of an ass in that of Samson? With what did He vanquish Holofernes? Was it not by the hand of a woman? When He willed to create the world, out of what did He form it, save nothingness? Believe me, great fires are often kindled from small sparks. Where was the sacred fire found when the Jews returned from their captivity among the Medes? In a little mud!

"This weaker sex is deserving of being treated with great tenderness; we must take much more care of it than we do of the stronger one. St. Bernard says that the charge of souls is for the weak far more than for the strong. Our Lord never refused His assistance to women. He was generally followed by several of them, and they did not forsake Him on the Cross, where he was abandoned by all His disciples excepting His beloved John. The Church who gives the title of devout to this sex does not hold it in such low estimation as you do.

"Besides, do you reckon as nothing the good example which they may set wherever God calls them? Is it unimportant in your opinion to be a sweet odour in Jesus Christ, an odour of life eternal? Of the two requisites for a good pastor, precept and example, which think you is the most estimable? For my part I think more of an ounce of example than of a hundred pounds' weight of precept. Without a good life doctrine turns into scandal; it is like a church bell, it calls others, but itself never goes in; hence the reproach: Physician, heal thyself.

"Even if holy women only served as perfumes for the Church they would not be useless. A great deal of incense is employed by her in her ceremonies!

"It is true that there are, as you say, a great many other Congregations already in the Church, into which some of those who are enrolled in this new one might enter; but there are, besides, many in the Visitation who, on account of their age or infirmities, or because of their feebleness of constitution, though they be young, are quite incapable of enduring the bodily austerities imposed by other Orders, and therefore cannot be admitted into them. If we receive into this one some who are strong and healthy, it is that they may wait upon the weak and delicate, for whom this Congregation has chiefly been instituted, and to put in practice that holy command: Bear ye one another's burdens, and so you shall fulfil the law of Christ.[1]

"As for your exhortation to me to think about forming a Congregation of Priests, do you not see that that is already planned by M. de Berulle, a great and faithful servant of God, who has far more capacity for the work, and much more leisure also, than I can get? Remember how heavily burdened I am with the charge of a diocese, in which is situated such a place as Geneva, the very fountain-head of the errors which are troubling the whole Church. In conclusion, let us leave great designs to great workmen. God will do what He pleases with my little plan."

[Footnote 1: Gal. vi. 2.]

UPON THE ODOUR OF SANCTITY.

Our Blessed Father held in the very highest esteem the odour of sanctity, and revered those who by their good example shed it abroad through the world, not for their own glory, but for the glory of God.

On another occasion when some morose and captious person was finding fault with the Visitation Order, and after taking exception to it because of its newness, wound up by saying to Blessed Francis, "And then of what use will it be to the Church?" The holy Prelate answered pleasantly: "To play the part of the Queen of Sheba." "And what part is that?" returned the man, "To render homage to Him who is greater than Solomon, and to fill the whole militant Jerusalem with perfumes and sweet odours."

In one of his Conferences he expresses the same thought as follows: "In my opinion the divine Majesty has made choice of you to go forth as perfume-bearers, seeing that He has commissioned you to go and scatter far and wide the sweet odours of the virtues of your Institute. And as young maidens love sweet odours (for the Bride in the Canticle of Canticles says that the name of her Beloved is as oil, or balm, shedding on all sides the sweetest perfumes, and therefore, she adds, the young maidens have followed Him, attracted by His divine perfumes), so do you, my dear sisters, as perfume-bearers of the Divine Goodness, go forth, shedding all around the incomparable sweetness of sincere humility, gentleness, and charity, so that many young maidens may be attracted thereby, and may embrace your manner of life, and that they may even in this world enjoy, like you, a holy loving peace and tranquillity of soul, and in the world to come eternal happiness."

HE REBUKES PHARISAISM.

On one occasion when the Sisters of the Visitation had made a foundation in a city famous for the piety of its inhabitants and in which there were already a number of Religious Houses highly esteemed for external austerities and severe discipline, they met with much criticism and even harsh treatment on account of their own gentler and apparently easier rule.

In the end, they made known to Blessed Francis what they had to put up with.

I ought, perhaps, to say that, among other ill-natured remarks, they had been reproached with having strewn a path of roses to lead them to Heaven, and with having brought our Saviour down from the Cross; meaning that they did not practise many corporal austerities. Those who said this quite forgot the fact that this Order of the Visitation was founded for the reception and consolation largely of women, whether young or old, weak in bodily health, though strong and healthy in mind, whose feeble frames could not support the external rigour demanded by other Communities.

Our Blessed Father, as I told you, having heard from letters addressed to him by the Superior, of the harsh treatment and sufferings of his poor daughters, wrote to her several times on the subject. The following words of his are especially remarkable for their beauty:

"Beware, my daughter, of replying in any way whatever to these good Sisters, or to their friends in the world, unless, indeed, you do so with unalterable humility, gentleness, and sweetness. Do not defend yourselves,[1] for such is the express command of the Holy Ghost. If they despise your Order because it appears to them inferior to theirs, they violate the law of charity, which does not permit the strong to despise the weak, or the great the small. Granted that they are superior to you, do the Seraphim despise the little Angels, or the great Saints in Paradise, those of inferior, nay, of the lowest rank? Oh, my dear daughter, whoever loves God the most will be the most loved by Him, and will be the most glorious up in Heaven. Do not distress yourself, the prize is awarded to those who love."

[Footnote 1: Rom. xii. 19.]

UPON RELIGIOUS SUPERIORS.

Speaking of Superiors, I may tell you that Blessed Francis divided them into four classes. "First," he said, "there are those who are very indulgent to others, and also to themselves. Secondly, there are those who are severe to others, and equally so to themselves. Thirdly, there are some who are indulgent to their subordinates and rigid to themselves. Fourthly, there are those who are indulgent to themselves and rigorous to others."

He condemned the first as careless and criminal persons, heedless of their duties: they abandon the ship they should pilot, to the mercy of the waves.

A Superior of the second kind often spoils everything precisely because he wishes to do too much, and falls into those exaggerations which have lent truth to the saying,

"Absolute right is absolute injustice." "He who would rule well," runs an ancient aphorism, "must rule with a slack hand." We must not hold our horse's bridle over tightly, for though we may save him from stumbling we hinder him even from walking.

Superiors of the third class are better because they put a kindly construction upon the faults and infirmities of others less known to them, as they necessarily are, than their own. This is the reason why they are severe to themselves and indulgent to others—a line of conduct which generally meets with the approval of their subjects. The latter are the more edified because they see their Superiors observing those very laws from which they have dispensed them. It is just so with the laity: they are mostly more anxious about the morals of their clergy than they are about their own.

Superiors of the fourth and last kind are truly unfaithful servants. They resemble those Pharisees who laid on the shoulders of other men heavy burdens which they themselves would not touch with the tip of their finger.

Our Blessed Father wished that all these four classes could be merged in a fifth, that of which the watchword should be holy equality according to that precept both of nature and of the Gospel: "Do to others as you would be done by; treat others as you would wish to be treated yourself, and treat yourself as you know you ought to be treated." In fact, since each man is to himself his nearest neighbour, we all recognise the injustice of demanding in the life of others what we do not practise in our own. To command others to do what we do not ourselves do is to be like Urias, who carried his own condemnation and death-warrant in his bosom.

One day, in his presence, I was praising a certain Superior for his extreme goodness, gentleness, patience, and condescension, which attracted all hearts to him, just as flies are attracted to a honeycomb. He answered, "Goodness is not good when it puts up with evil; on the contrary, it is bad when it allows evils to go on which it can, and should, prevent. Gentleness in such a case is not gentleness, but weakness and cowardice. Patience in such a case is not patience, but absolute stupidity.

"When we suffer evil which we could prevent, we do not merely tolerate but become accomplices in wrong-doing. I am of opinion that subjects are made good by bad, I mean, by harsh and disagreeable Superiors. The severity of a mother is more wholesome for a child than the petting of an indulgent nurse, and the firmness of a father is always more useful to his children than their mother's tenderness. The rougher the file the better it smoothes the iron, and the more rust it rubs off; the hotter the iron, the better the surface it gives to the cloth." He related with regard to this subject an anecdote which will both please and profit you.

The head of a certain Religious Order, which was at the time undergoing a vigorous reform, had, with the consent of the Provincial Chapter, established a Novitiate House which was to serve as the one only Seminary for the whole province. It was decided that no novice should be clothed until he had been examined by three Fathers of the Order appointed for that purpose. The first was to enquire into the birth and condition of those who presented themselves for examination, the second into their literary capacity, and the third into their manner of life and vocation. This last, in order to get a firm grip on the pulse of the postulants, and to sound their vocation to the very quick almost always asked them if they would have courage and patience enough to put up with bad Superiors, bad in the extreme, cruel, rude, peevish, choleric, melancholy, captious, pitiless, those, in a word, whom they would find it impossible to please or satisfy.

Some, evading the question, replied that there could be none such in the Order, or, at least, would not be suffered to remain in office, seeing that it was governed with so much gentleness and benignity, and that its yoke was so sweet and desirable. The examiner, who did not like evasive and ambiguous replies of this sort, determined to get an answer that should be straight-forward and to the point. Taking a much sterner tone, he represented a Superior to them as a sort of slave-driver: a man who would govern his subjects by blows and stripes, and who yet would expect them to drink this chalice of bitterness as if offered to their lips by the hand of God.

Some of the postulants fearing the test, became pale or crimson with agitation, and either answered nothing, showing by their silence that they could not swallow the pill, or, if they answered at all, declared that they could not believe he was speaking seriously, and that they were not galley-slaves.

These he dismissed at once as unfit to be received into the Order.

Others, however, full of courage and constancy, still answered, that they were prepared for any ill-treatment, and that nothing could deter them from carrying out their God-inspiring resolution. That no creature, however cruel and however unfeeling, could separate them from the love of Jesus Christ, nor from His service. These the examining

Father received with open arms into the bosom of the Order.

You may judge from this how skilful was this master of novices in hewing, hammering, and cutting the stones he was endeavouring to fit for the spiritual edifice of the Order. Our Blessed Father himself, in spite of all the sweetness and gentleness of his natural disposition, did not fail to follow this plan to a certain extent, representing to all who came to him, desiring to enter into religion, the interior and spiritual crosses which they must resolve to carry all their life long, not the least heavy of which, and at the same time not the least useful in helping them to make great advance in perfection would perhaps be the severity of Superiors.

UPON UNLEARNED SUPERIORS.

A certain community having had their Superior taken from them on account of their complaints of the severity of his rule, and having a new one set over them in his place, came to Blessed Francis to pour out their grievances on the subject of their recently appointed head. They declared that he was an ignorant man. "What is to be done with you?" cried our Blessed Father, "you remind me of the frogs to whom Jupiter could not give a king who was to their taste. We ought certainly to wish to have good and capable Superiors, but still whatever they may be we must put up with them." One of the complainers was so wanting in discretion as to say that their one-eyed horse had been changed into a blind one. Blessed Francis suffered this jest to pass, merely frowning slightly, but his modest silence only unchained the tongue of another scoffer who presumed to say that an ass had been given to them instead of a horse. Then Blessed Francis spoke, and, rebuking this last speech, added in a tone of gentle remonstrance, that the first remark, though far from being respectful, was more endurable because it was a proverb and implied that a Superior had been given to them who was less capable than his predecessor, and that this was expressed in figurative terms, as David speaks of himself in relation to Almighty God in one of the Psalms when he says: I am become as a beast before Thee.[1] "The second sarcasm, however," he added, "has nothing figurative in it, and is absolutely and grossly insulting. We must never speak of our Superiors in such a manner, however worthless they may be. Remember that God would have us obey even the vicious and froward,[2] and he that resisteth the power resisteth the ordinance of God."

Then taking up the defence of this much-abused Superior, "Do you imagine," he said, "that it is not within the power of God to exalt in a moment one who is poor in spirit by bestowing on him the gift of intelligence? Is not He the God of knowledge? Is it not He who imparts it to men? Are not all the faithful taught of God?

"The science of the Saints is the science of Salvation, and this is a knowledge more frequently given to those who are destitute of the knowledge which puffs up. In what condition think you was Saul when God raised him to the throne of Israel?

"He was keeping his father's asses. On what did Jesus Christ ride triumphant on Palm Sunday? Was it not upon an ass?"

Again, in his eleventh Conference, he says: "If Balaam was well instructed by an ass, we may with greater reason believe that God, Who gave you this Superior, will enable him to teach you according to His will, though it may not be according to your own."

He wound up his remarks on the subject of the new Superior by saying: "I understand that this good man is most gentle and kind, and that if he does not know much he does none the less well, so that his example makes up for any deficiency in his teaching. It is far better to have a Superior who does the good which he fails in teaching, than one who tells us what we ought to do, but does not himself practise it."

[Footnote 1: 1 Peter ii. 18.]

[Footnote 2: Rom. xiii. 2.]

UPON THE FOUNDING OF CONVENTS.

You know, my Sisters, with what circumspection and prudence our Blessed Father moved in the matter of foundations. During the last thirteen years of his life, in which he established your Congregation, he only accepted twelve convents and refused three times as many, saying, as was his wont, "Few and good." He was always very particular about the Superiors to whom he committed the charge of monastic houses, knowing the immense importance of such choice and its influence upon all the members of a Religious family.

He was fond of comparing a convent to a beehive, and in one of his Conferences applies this comparison to your own Order as follows:—"Your Congregation," he says, "is like a bee-hive which has already sent forth various swarms: but with this difference, that when bees go forth to settle in another hive and to begin a new household each swarm chooses a particular queen under whom they live and dwell apart.

"You, my dear souls, though you may go into a new hive, that is, begin a new house of your Order, have always only one and the same King, our crucified Lord, under Whose authority you will live secure and safe wherever you may be. Do not fear that anything will be wanting to you, for, as long as you do not choose any other King He will ever be with you; only take great care to grow in love and fidelity to His divine goodness, keeping as close to Him as possible. Thus all will be well with you. Learn from Him all that you will have to do; do nothing without His counsel, for He is the faithful Friend who will guide you and govern you and take care of you, as with all my heart I beseech Him to do."[1]

Very often I urged him to consent to certain foundations which it was proposed to make, but He always gave me some good reason for refusing.

It was not without trouble and difficulty that we obtained a little colony for Belley. He often said to me: "The Sisters are as yet but novices in piety, they must be left to grow a little stronger; have patience, for we shall be doing quite enough if the little we do is what pleases our divine Master.

It is better for them to grow at the roots by virtue rather than in the branches by forming new houses. Will they, do you think, be more perfect because they have more convents?"

[Footnote 1: Conf. 6.]

UPON RECEIVING THE INFIRM INTO COMMUNITIES.

Regarding the reception of the infirm, he might have exclaimed with St. Paul: Who is weak and I am not weak? Blessed Francis shared largely in this spirit, so much did he love the infirm, whether of body or of mind. He loved the poor in spirit; poor, that is, whether in earthly goods or in the wisdom of the world, and he used to say that their simplicity was a soil suitable for the planting of all sorts of virtues, that it would yield much fruit in due season. He was of opinion that during the year of Novitiate established in all communities preparatory to the embracing of religious life, too much attention was paid to the consideration of infirmities, both spiritual and corporal, just as if convents were not in reality so many hospitals for healing the diseases of body and mind. Hence, he added, came the name of Therapeutes, that is, curers, healers, or operators, formerly given to Monks.

It is true that there are certain bodily diseases which from the fact of their being infectious necessitate the separation of such as are afflicted with them from the healthy. So also there are spiritual maladies, such as incompatibility of temper and incorrigibility of defects, which may make it proper to refuse those who are thus disqualified for entering Religion, just as in former days, persons suffering from these disabilities could be dismissed even after Profession.

In one of his letters he thus expresses his feeling for the infirm: "I am," he says, "a great partisan of the infirm and am always afraid lest the inconveniences to which they must naturally put the Community should excite a spirit of human prudence in our convents and banish the spirit of charity in which our Congregation was founded, and which is our safest guide in selecting our Sisters. I take, then, the side of your infirm applicant, and provided that she be humble and ready to recognise and appreciate your charity, you must receive the poor girl; it will be a constant opportunity for the Sisters to practise the holy virtue of loving-kindness."

UPON SELF-PITY.

Gentle and compassionate as his disposition was, full of tenderness, and sympathy for the feeble and the frail, Blessed Francis was nevertheless strict and severe in his dealings with those whom he knew to be too lenient to themselves, either in temporal or spiritual matters.

He who practised so much severity in his own case, assuredly had the right to advise others to do as much, and especially, like him, to refrain from complaining at the inconveniences and sufferings endured in time of sickness. He succeeded in inspiring his Daughters of the Visitation with his spirit, teaching them that true Christian patience, which is neither apathy nor insensibility, nor the dull stupid endurance of the Stoics; but a sweet and reasonable submission to the Will of God, coupled with cheerful obedience to the physician whom He commands us to honour, and a grateful acceptance of the remedies prescribed for us.

UPON THE GOVERNMENT OF NUNS BY RELIGIOUS MEN.

It was never his opinion that nuns should be under the jurisdiction and guidance of other Religious, especially of those of their own Order.

For this he alleged several very weighty reasons, which I have been careful to bear in mind that I may impart them to you at the right time and place.

For the present, however, I will content myself with reading you one of his letters, and with afterwards making a little comment upon it.

"I observe," he says, "that many influential people are inclined to think that Religious Houses should be under the authority of the Ordinaries, according to the old rule revived lately throughout almost the whole of Italy; whilst others would have them to be under Superiors of their own Order, conformably to a custom introduced about four or five hundred years ago, and almost universally observed in France. For my own part, I confess that I cannot bring myself to adopt the view of those who desire that convents of women should be placed under the guidance of

Religious men, still less of the Fathers of their own Order. And in this I feel that I am of the same mind as the Holy See, which always, where it can be reasonably brought about, opposes itself to the government of nuns by Regulars.

"I do not say that such government is not sometimes advantageous, even at the present day, but I do say that it would be far better if in general it were done away with. And this for many reasons.

"It seems to me that it is no more difficult for the Pope to exempt the nuns of any Order from the jurisdiction of the Fathers of that same Order, than it is for him to exempt monasteries from the jurisdiction of their Ordinary, a procedure inspired no doubt by the most excellent motives, and that has been carried out successfully for so many centuries.

"The Pope has, as a matter of fact, kept our own nuns in France under the rule of the Bishops, and it appears to me that these same good nuns do not know what is good for them when they seek to be transferred to the jurisdiction of a Religious Order, seeing that Regular Superiors are apt to be a little rigorous in the exercise of their authority, and to deprive those under them of holy liberty of spirit."

I would call your attention to the fact mentioned by our Blessed Father that almost everywhere in Italy the nuns are under the guidance and jurisdiction of the Bishops. Of this I was myself an eye-witness, and I noticed at Florence, that out of fifty convents, only four are not under the jurisdiction and direction of the Archbishop.

I would also remind you that the Holy Apostolic See has, as far as possible, and for many reasons, revived this ancient form of government of nuns. That these reasons exist it is well to bear in mind, though it may not always be prudent to urge them in public.

Again, if in former times it was thought advisable to exempt nuns from the guidance and jurisdiction of their Ordinaries, or Diocesan Pastors, at the present day there are far more weighty reasons for replacing them under the authority of the Bishops, and for taking from the Regulars this exceptional jurisdiction.

This is exactly what our Blessed Father thought about the matter. Remember then always that to put convents under the Bishops is to bring things back to their first and purest state, for as regards exemption we can assuredly say that from the beginning it was not so.

It seems, too, to me, that nuns who desire the guidance of Monks, especially of Fathers of their own Order, are true daughters of Zebedee; they know not what they ask, nor what they want, nor what they are doing.

THAT WE MUST NOT BE WEDDED TO OUR OWN PLANS.

Our Blessed Father used to praise very highly the conduct of Blessed John of Avila as having been prompted by great strength of mind, and extraordinary forgetfulness of self in that his zeal made him not only love his neighbour as himself but even more than himself. I will give you an instance of this in Francis' own words, addressed to Theotimus: "The Blessed Ignatius of Loyola, having with such pains set up the company of Jesus, which he saw produced many fair fruits, and foresaw many more that would ripen in time to come, had, nevertheless, the nobleness of soul to resolve that, though he should see it dissolved (which would be the bitterest pain which could befall him) within half an hour afterwards, he would be stayed and tranquil in the Will of God. John of Avila, that holy and learned preacher of Andalusia, having a design to form a company of reformed Priests for the advancement of God's glory, and having already made good progress in the matter, as soon as he saw the Jesuits in the field, thinking they were enough for that time, immediately, with incomparable meekness and humility, renounced his own undertaking. Oh, how blessed are such souls, bold and strong in the undertakings God proposes to them, and withal tractable and facile in giving them up when God so disposes. It is a mark of a most perfect Indifference to leave off doing a good work when God pleases, and to return, our journey half accomplished when God's Will, which is our guide, so ordains."[1] I may tell you, my Sisters, that you have only to change the name of John of Avila into that of the Blessed Francis de Sales, and you can apply to an event in his life these very words. I know that he had in his mind a scheme of forming a Congregation of Priests, not bound by monastic vows, something on the pattern of your Order of the Visitation in its beginning; but, of course, conformable to the calling of the Priesthood. Hearing, however, that Pierre de Berulle, that faithful servant of God, afterwards a Cardinal, had established the Congregation of the French Oratory, now so greatly distinguished for its piety and learning, he abandoned his enterprise, rejoicing that God should have given this holy commission to one less busy than himself, and therefore more capable of ordering all things in this holy Society, and thus promoting the glory of God. I have said, that he meant to take the Visitation as a model of this projected Congregation of Priests, intending them to develop, and to prosper side by side. I must add, however, that even before the formation of your Congregation he had made an attempt in the same direction by drawing together a little company of hermits on the gloomy but holy mountain of Notre Dame de Voiron, and preparing for them laws and constitutions in the observance of which they have lived with great sanctity ever since.

You know also that his zeal was so condescending in its nature, and that he was so little wedded to his own opinions, that, though the Visitation had flourished for four or five years with great edification to others as well as to itself, yet as soon as His Grace the Archbishop of Lyons, afterwards Cardinal de Marquemont, had represented to him that it would better for it to be re-constructed with vows and enclosures like other Orders, he consented to change its whole constitution.

Speaking of great works undertaken for the glory of God, which, owing to the illness or death of their founder or head, sometimes seem in danger of falling to the ground, Blessed Francis said: "There are some undertakings which God wishes to be begun indeed by us, but completed by others. Thus David gathered together materials for the temple which his son Solomon built, St. Francis, St. Dominic, St. Ignatius Loyola, sighed for the grace of martyrdom, and sought for it by all possible means; yet God would not crown them with it, contenting Himself with the offering of their will.

"To submit ourselves simply and cheerfully to the Will of God in the failure of undertakings which concern His glory is an act of no small resignation."

[Footnote 1: Book ix. chap. 6.]

HIS VIEWS REGARDING ECCLESIASTICAL DIGNITIES.

It is certain that two great Pontiffs, Clement VIII. and Paul V., held Blessed Francis in the highest possible esteem. Paul V. more than once when speaking to me dwelt upon his merit, and said how suitable and indeed how necessary such a Bishop was for a diocese like that of Geneva.

We know, too, that the same Pope often thought of raising him to the dignity of Cardinal. Our Blessed Father was himself well aware of this, and mentioned it in letters written to his confidential friends, some of which have since been published.

It is probable that the fact that this honour was never conferred upon him was owing to the political difficulties which beset the Supreme Pontiff in these matters.

Puzzled at his not receiving the hat, I one day expressed to him my great surprise at the delay. "Why," he answered, "can you really think this dignity would in any way conduce to my serving our Lord and His Church better than I can now do? Would Rome, which would be the place of my residence, afford me more opportunities for so doing, than this post in which God has placed me? Should I have more work there, more enemies to fight against, more souls to direct, more cares, more pious exercises, more visits to make, or more pastoral functions to discharge?"

"You would enter," I replied, "into the solicitude of all the churches; and from the direction of one particular Church you would be promoted to share in the care of the Universal Church, becoming, as it were, the co-assessor of the Holy See." "Nevertheless," he replied, "you see Cardinals of our own day, who when they were Bishops and had dioceses were distinguished for their piety, quit their residence at Rome, which is only theirs by a positive and ecclesiastical law, in order to return to their flocks among which the law of God has fixed their homes, bidding them watch over these flocks and feed and guide the souls entrusted to them."

He then told me a memorable circumstance concerning the great Cardinal Bellarmine of saintly memory. That Prelate was promoted to the dignity, unknown to himself and against his will, by Clement VIII. Under the pontificate of Paul V., who succeeded Leo XI., he was promoted to the Archbishopric of Capua, again contrary to his own wishes, but by the desire of the Pope. He bowed beneath this yoke, but not until he had remonstrated with the Holy Father, who, in reply, simply commanded him to take upon himself the episcopal charge.

Immediately after his consecration he prepared to take up his residence at Capua. The Pope, who desired his services at Rome, sent for him, and asked him if he was quite resolved to live in his diocese. The Cardinal replied that he was, because unwillingly as he had accepted this charge he had done so with the conviction that his Holiness felt he could dispense with his services at Rome, nor would otherwise have placed him over the diocese of Capua. The Pope replied that he would dispense him from residing in his diocese. "Holy Father," he answered, "that is not what I have been teaching in the schools all my life. I have always held that the residence of Bishops in their diocese is commanded by the law of God, and that therefore they cannot be dispensed from observing it." "At least," returned the Pope, "give us half the year." "And during those six months," replied Bellarmine, "at whose hands will the blood of the lost sheep of my flock be required?" "Then, at least, three months," pleaded the Pope. The Cardinal gave the same answer as he had given about the six, and, in fact, soon took his departure for Capua, where he remained in uninterrupted residence for three years, in the course of which time, as a relaxation from the labours of his office, he wrote his beautiful Commentary on the Psalms.

Such was the high value set by the holy Cardinal upon the residence of a Bishop among his flock: and St. Charles Borromeo, and more recently his worthy successor, Cardinal Borromeo, have been as uncompromising as Bellarmine was. As for our Blessed Father, he only valued the Honours and dignities of the Church and of the world in proportion as they afford means for serving God and advancing His glory. This was the golden standard with which he measured the holy City of Jerusalem.

HIS PROMOTION TO THE BISHOPRIC OF GENEVA AND HIS REFUSAL OF THE ARCHBISHOPRIC OF PARIS.

Although in the life of our Blessed Father his promotion to the Bishopric of Geneva is described at great length, yet, in my opinion, the subject has been treated very superficially, and no attempt has been made to give a full account of the matter.

The truth is that the Saint had all his life but one aim in regard to the following out of his holy vocation, namely, to serve God in whatever sacred office he might be called to fill. He had passed through all the various ecclesiastical offices of Canon, Parish Priest, Provost, Dean of the Cathedral Church, Preacher, Confessor, and Missionary, when M. de Granier, at that time Bishop of Geneva, inspired by God, desired to make him his successor. In this, as in all other matters, our Saint recognised the inspiration, and with a single eye, that saw God only, committed himself entirely to His providence.

He did nothing at all either to hinder or to further the design, leaving it all to M. de Granier, who obtained the consent of the Duke of Savoy to propose Francis to his Holiness. It was, however, a condition that he should at once present himself at Rome to be examined in full Consistory. He was therefore obliged to undertake the journey thither. This journey, as we know, is fairly well described by the writers of his life. They tell also of his success, and of the approval bestowed upon him by Pope Clement, who used the inspired words: Drink water out of thine own cistern, and the streams of thine own well. Let thy fountains be conveyed abroad, and in the streets divide thy waters.[1] From so excellent a vocation what but good results could be expected? A good tree cannot bear evil fruit. We know well how worthily Blessed Francis walked in the vocation to which he had been called, and how the light of his holy life, like the dawn of morning, shone more and more unto the perfect day.

In the year 1619, having come to Paris with the Princes of Savoy, he remained there for eight months, during which time it is impossible to give any idea of all that he did for the glory of God and the good of souls. The eyes of all men in this great theatre were turned upon him, as were those of the Romans upon Cato, when one day he showed himself in their assembly.

It was not only by the people of Paris that he was thought so much of, but also by their pastor, the Cardinal de Retz (Peter de Gondi), a Prelate of incomparable gentleness, benignity, liberality, modesty, and every other delightful quality. The sweet attractive grace of Blessed Francis' manners and conversation produced such an effect upon him that he at once desired to make him his coadjutor, with right of succession.

Not expecting any opposition from the holy Bishop, and having gained the consent of the King, he thought that nothing remained to be done but to carry out the formalities prescribed by the Roman Congregations. Francis, however, with marvellous adroitness, warded off the blow, leaving the great Cardinal penetrated with admiration of his virtue if without the satisfaction of gaining his compliance.

Among the various reasons for this refusal which are to be found in his letters, one or two please me especially. For instance, he said that he did not think he ought to change a poor wife for a rich one; and again, that if he did ever quit his spouse it would not be to take another, but in order not to have one at all, following the Apostolic counsel: Art thou bound, to a wife, seek not to be loosed. Art thou loosed from a wife, seek not a wife.[2]

It is true that honours and dignities are but trifles; yet to despise and refuse them is not a trifling thing. It is easy to disdain them from a distance, but difficult to deal with them face to face, and either to quit them when we possess them, or to refuse them when they are offered. Blessed is the rich man that is found without blemish, and that hath not gone after gold nor put his trust in money, nor in treasures. Who is he? and we will praise him, for he hath done wonderful things in his life.[3]

Such a one, my Sisters, believe me, was your Father and mine, my preserver and your Founder, Blessed Francis de Sales.

[Footnote 1: Prov. v. 15, 16.]

[Footnote 2: 1 Cor. vii. 27.]

[Footnote 3: Eccle. xxxi. 8, 9.]

A BISHOP'S CARE FOR HIS FLOCK.

Good digestions assimilate all kinds of food, and convert it into wholesome nourishment, and so in like manner holy souls turn all that they meet with into material for instruction and into help towards their eternal profit. Thus, the great St. Anthony, saw the Creator on every page of the book of nature and in all living creatures. The tiniest flower, growing and blossoming at his feet, raised his thoughts to Him Who is the Flower of the Field and the Lily of the Valley, the Blossom springing from the root of Jesse.

Those who are smitten by some passionate human love are so absolutely possessed by it that they think of nothing else, and since their tongue speaks out of the abundance of their heart this is their one subject of conversation, all others being distasteful to them. They write the name of the beloved object on rocks and trees, and wherever they can they leave behind them some carved token or emblem of their affection.

Just so was it with our Blessed Father. His delight was to make all subjects of conversation, all incidents that might occur, further in one way or another the glory of God, and kindle His divine love in the hearts of others. On one occasion, when he was visiting that part of his diocese which lies among the lofty and bleak mountains of Faucigny, where it is always winter, he heard that a poor cowherd had lost his life by falling over a steep precipice while trying to save one of his herd. From this incident he drew a marvellous lesson upon the care which a Bishop ought to take of the flock entrusted to his charge by God, showing that he ought to be ready to sacrifice even life itself for its salvation. He thus relates the incident, and gives his comments on it in one of his letters.

"During the past few days I have seen mountains, terrible in their grandeur, covered with ice ten or twelve inches thick; and the inhabitants of the neighbouring valleys told me that a herdsman going out to try and recover a cow which had strayed away fell over a precipice from a height of thirty feet, and was found frozen to death at the bottom. Oh, God! I cried, and was the ardour of this poor herdsman in his search for the beast that had strayed, so burning that even the cold of those frozen heights could not chill it? Why, then, am I so slothful and lax in the quest after my wandering sheep? This thought filled my heart with grief, yet in no wise melted its frozen surface. I saw in this region many wonderful sights. The valleys were full of happy homesteads, the mountains coated with ice and snow. Like the fertile and smiling valleys, the village mothers play their homely part, while a Bishop, raised to such a lofty eminence in the Church of God, remains ice-bound as the mountains. Ah! will there never rise a sun with rays powerful enough to melt this ice which freezes me!" What zeal for souls, what humility, what holy fervour breathe in these words!

ON THE FIRST DUTY OF BISHOPS.

"Being a Bishop," he used to say to me, "you are at the same time a superintendent, sentinel, and overseer in the House of God, for this is what the word Bishop means. It is then your part to watch over and guard your whole diocese, making continual supplications, crying aloud day and night like a watchman on the walls, as the prophet bids you do, knowing that you have to render an account to the great Father of the family of all the souls committed to your care.

"But especially you ought to watch over two classes of people who are the heads of all the others, namely, the Parish Priests and the fathers of families, for they are the source of most of the good and of most of the evil which is to be found in parishes or households.

"From the instruction and good example given by Parish Priests, who are the shepherds of the flock, proceeds all the advance of that flock in knowledge and virtue. They are like the rods of which Jacob made use to give the colours he wanted to the fleeces of the lambs. Teaching does much, but example does incomparably more. It is the same with fathers and mothers of families: on their words, but still more on their conduct, depends all the welfare of their households.

"As Bishop you are the master-builder, the superintendent. It is your duty then to watch over the leaders of your flock and over those who, like Saul, are a head taller than the rest. Through them healing and blessing flows down upon others, even as Aaron's ointment descended from his head to the very hem of his garment.

"This is why you ought continually to exhort and instruct, in season and out of season, for you are the Parish Priest of all Parish Priests, and the Father of all Fathers of families."

UPON THE PASTORAL CHARGE.

On one occasion I was complaining to him of the difficulties which I met with in the discharge; of my episcopal duties. He replied that on entering the service of God we must prepare ourselves for temptation, since no one could follow Jesus Christ or be of the number of His true disciples except by bearing His Cross, nor could anyone enter Heaven except by the path and through the gate of suffering. "Remember," he said, "that our first father even in the state of innocence was put into the earthly Paradise to work in it and to keep it. Do you imagine that he was banished from it in order to do nothing? Consider how God condemned him and all his posterity to labour, and to till an ungrateful earth which produced of itself nothing but thorns and thistles. There is much more toil and difficulty in weeding and cultivating souls than any earthly soil, rough, stony, and barren though it may be. The art of arts is the direction of souls, it is of no use to undertake it unless we have made up our minds to innumerable labours and disappointments.

"The Son of God being a sign of contradiction, can we wonder if His work is exposed to the same; and if He had so much difficulty in winning souls, is it likely that his coadjutors and those who labour with Him will have less?"

Then fearing to depress me by the enumeration of so many difficulties, he went on to cheer me with the example of the Prince of Pastors, the Bishop of our souls, the Author and Finisher of our faith, who preferred shame and toil to joy, that He might further the work of oar salvation.

He added that of the Apostles, and other Pastors of the Church, reminding me that if we think much of the honour of being their successors we must, with the inheritance, accept its burdens, nor shelter ourselves by, in legal phrase, disclaiming liability for debts beyond the assets inherited. Otherwise, he said, we should be like that kinsman of Ruth who wished to have the inheritance of the first husband, but not to marry the widow and raise up to him an heir.

He generally wound up his remarks with some reminder of that love which makes all that is bitter to be sweet: sometimes quoting to me those words of St. Augustine, "Where we love, there is no labour, or if there is any we love the labour itself, for he who labours in loving, loves to labour for the beloved object."

UPON THE CARE OF SOULS.

A Priest once complained to Blessed Francis of the thorns besetting his path in life, of the difficulties of his holy calling, of the anxieties inseparable from it, but chiefly of the intractableness of stiff-necked Christians, who refuse to submit to the easy yoke of Jesus Christ, and to do what their duty requires. The Bishop replied that their obstinacy was not so much to be wondered at as the weakness of their Pastors who were so easily discouraged and impatient, just because they saw that the seed sown by their labours did not forthwith produce the plentiful harvest they desired.

"The peasant is not blamed for failing to reap an abundant harvest, but only for not carefully cultivating his field, and for not doing all that is necessary to make his land productive. Discouragement is a mark of excessive love of self and of zeal unaccompanied by knowledge.

"The best lesson for those who have the care of souls, is that which the Apostle gives to all in the person of one:

Preach the word: be instant in season and out of season: reprove, entreat, rebuke in all patience and doctrine.[1]

"In this text the word patience is the key to the whole mystery, for patience has its perfect work when it is accompanied by charity, which is patient, kind, and is the virtue by which we possess our souls in peace."

The charge of souls means having to bear with the weak, for the strong are able to go on by themselves in their progress towards what is good. Our holy Bishop explained this by two beautiful similitudes: "The plumage of birds is heavy, and yet without this load they could neither raise themselves from the ground nor hover in the air. The burden borne by holy souls is like a load of cinnamon, which, by its perfume invigorates him who carries it. So souls which are weak serve to make their Pastors, who bear the burden of them, rise on wings towards Heaven, and on earth to run in the way of God's commandments."

The other comparison Is this: "Notice," he said, "a shepherd driving a flock of sheep: if one of them breaks a leg the shepherd at once takes it on his shoulders to carry it back to the fold, and this single one is certainly a heavier load than all the rest together, who go along of themselves. In like manner souls which of themselves advance in the way of God afford little occasion for their Pastors to exercise care and vigilance. It is of the faulty and intractable they have chiefly to think, St. Bernard says that the care of souls is not a care of the strong, but of the infirm, for if any one helps thee more than he is helped by thee, know that thou art not his father but his equal."

Even the prophets complain of men of obstinate and rebellious hearts. To work among them is to go down to the sea in ships and to do our business in great waters, for these waters are God's people with whom we have to deal.

[Footnote 1: 2 Tim. iv. 2.]

UPON LEARNING AND PIETY.

By rights, the more learned a man becomes the more pious should he be. This does not, however, always happen, and if we must choose between the two, there is no doubt that it is better to be uneducated but pious, rather than to be learned without being religious-minded.

Blessed Francis remarked one day when we were speaking of a Parish Priest whose holy life was highly praised, but with whose defects as a teacher great fault was found: "It is quite true that knowledge and piety are, as it were, the two eyes of a Priest; still, as a man can, by dispensation, receive Holy Orders even though he has only one eye, so also it is quite possible for a Parish Priest to be a most faithful servant in his ministry by simply leading a zealous, exemplary, and well-regulated life. The function of teaching may be discharged by others, who, as St. Paul says, are instructors but not fathers.[1] But no one can be a pattern to others except by giving good example, and this cannot be done by proxy."

Besides, the Gospel tells us that we are to pluck out the eye which offends. It is better to enter heaven with one eye, than to be cast into hell-fire with two.[2] "There is, indeed," he continued, "a degree of ignorance so gross as to be inexcusable and to render him who is plunged into it in very truth a blind leader of the blind. When, however, a man is in good repute for his piety he surely has within him that true light which leads him to Jesus Christ and enables him to show light to others. It is as though he said to them, like Gideon, Do as I do, or with St. Paul, Be ye followers of me, as I also am of Christ.[3] Such a one does not walk in darkness and those who follow him are sure to reach the haven. Though he has not talents of learning and erudition such as would make him shine in the pulpit, yet he has enough if he can, as the Apostle says, exhort in sound doctrine and convince the gainsayers.[4] Remark," he added, "how God taught Balaam by the mouth of his ass." Thus, his charity dexterously covered the defects of his neighbour, and by this lesson he taught us to value an ounce of piety more than many pounds of empty learning.

[Footnote 1: 1 Cor. iv. 15.]

[Footnote 2: Matt. xviii. 9.]

[Footnote 3: 1 Cor. iv. 16.]

[Footnote 4: Tit. i. 9.]

ADVICE TO BISHOP CAMUS AS TO RESIGNING HIS SEE.

When I was consulting him once as to whether or not I should follow the bent of my own inclination in the matter of retiring into a private and solitary life, he, wishing to ascertain by what spirit I was led, answered me in the beautiful words of St. Augustine: Otium sanctum diligit charitas veritatis, et negotium justum suscipit veritas charitatis.[1] Charity, the holy love of eternal truth, draws us into retirement, that we may in that calm leisure contemplate things divine; but when our hearts are filled with true charity we are none the less urged to undertake good works in order to advance the glory of God by serving our neighbour.

Although he esteemed Mary's part—called in the Gospel "the better part"—much more highly than Martha's, yet it was his opinion that Martha's, undertaken purely for the love of God, was more suitable to this present life, and that Mary's had more in common with that of a blessed eternity. He only made an exception as regards some special and extraordinary vocations, some irresistible and most powerful attractions, acting upon the soul, and in the case of those who do not possess the talents requisite for serving as Martha served, and have only those suitable for a purely contemplative life. Also those who, having expended, all their physical strength in the service of the Church, withdraw into solitude towards the close of their life, there to prepare for that last journey which is ordained for all flesh.

For this reason he repulsed and silenced me—not indeed harshly, for his incomparable sweetness was incompatible with harshness—but firmly and decidedly whenever I spoke to him of quitting my post and of resigning the helm into the hand of some more skilful pilot. He called my desire to do so a temptation, and in the end closed the discussion so peremptorily that, during his lifetime, I never ventured to revive it with anyone.

He dealt in almost exactly the same manner with that virtuous soul[2] the corner-stone of the spiritual edifice of the Congregation of the Visitation which he founded, for he kept her in the world for more than seven years, bringing up and educating the children whom God had given her and affording spiritual help to her father and father-in-law. He kept her back, I say, for this long period, before permitting her to retire into the solitude of the cloister; so exact was he in himself following, and in leading those who were under his direction to follow, the holy light of faith rather than the false and lurid glimmers of their natural inclinations.

On a previous occasion a certain Bishop whom I knew well asked him whether in his opinion it would be allowable for him to give up his Bishopric with its heavy burdens and retire into private life, bringing forward as an example St. Gregory of Nazianzen, surnamed the Theologian, the oracle of his time, who gave up the charge of three Bishoprics, Sozima, Nazianzen, and the Patriarchate of Constantinople, that he might go and end his days In rural life, on his paternal estate of Arianzen.

Our Blessed Father replied that we must presume that these great Saints never did anything without being moved to do it by the Spirit of God, and that we must not judge of their actions by outward appearances. He added that St. Gregory in quitting Constantinople was only yielding to pressure and violence, as is proved by the manner in which he said his last Mass in public, and which brought tears into the eyes of all who heard him.

This same Bishop replying that the greatness of his own charge terrified him, and that he was overpowered by the thought of having to answer for so many souls: "Alas!" said Blessed Francis, "what would you say, or do, if you had such a burden as mine on your shoulders? And yet that must not lessen my confidence in the mercy of God."

The Bishop still complaining and declaring that he was like a candle which consumes itself in order to give light to others, and that he was so much taken up with the service of his neighbour that he had scarcely any leisure to think of himself and to look after the welfare of his own soul, our Blessed Father replied: "Well, considering that the eternal welfare of your neighbour is a part, and so large a part, of your own, are you not securing the latter by attending to the former? And how, indeed, could you possibly work out your own salvation except by furthering that of others, seeing that you have been called to do so precisely in this manner?"

The Bishop still objecting and saying that he was like a whetstone which is worn out by the mere sharpening of blades, and that while trying to lead others to holiness he ran the risk of losing his own soul, our Holy Prelate rejoined: "Read the history of the Church and the lives of the Saints, and you will find more Saints among Bishops than in any other Order or avocation, there being no other position in the Church of God which furnishes such abundant means of sanctification and perfection. For remember that the best means of making progress in perfection is the teaching others both by word and example. Bishops are by their very office compelled to do this and to strive with all their heart and soul to be a pattern and model to their flocks. The whole life of a Christian on earth is a warfare, and should be one unceasing progress towards the goal of perfection. Were you to do as you propose it would be in a manner to look behind you, and to imitate the children of Ephraim, who turned back when they should have faced the enemy. You were going on so well, who is it who is holding you back? Stay in the ship in which God has placed you to make the voyage of life; the passage is so short that it is not worth while changing the boat. For, indeed, if you feel giddy in a large vessel, how much more so will you in a slight skiff tossed by every motion of the waves! A lower condition of life, though less busy and apparently more tranquil, is none the less equally subject to temptation."

This reasoning so convinced the Bishop[3] that he remained faithful to his post in the army of Holy Church.

[Footnote 1: De Civit. Dei. Lib. 19. cap 19.]

[Footnote 2: St. Jane Frances de Chantal.]

[Footnote 3: This Bishop was evidently M. Camus himself. [Ed.]]

THE JOYOUS SPIRIT OF BLESSED FRANCIS.

So light-hearted and gay was he, so truly did his happy face express the serenity and peace of his soul that it was almost impossible to remain for any time in his company without catching something of this joyous spirit.

I feel sure that only those of dull and gloomy temperament can take exception to what I am going to relate in order to illustrate our Blessed Father's delightful gift of pleasantry in conversation.

On one occasion when I was paying a visit to him at Annecy two young girls, sisters, and both most virtuous and most devout, were professed in one of the convents, he performing the ceremony, and I, by his desire, giving the exhortation. While preaching, although I said nothing to my mind very heart-stirring, I noticed that a venerable Priest who was present was so much affected as to attract the attention of everyone. After the ceremony, when we were breakfasting with the holy Bishop, the Priest being also at table, I asked Blessed Francis what had been the cause of such emotion. He replied that it was not to be wondered at seeing that this good Priest had lost his aureola, and had been reduced from the high rank of a martyr to the lowly one of a Confessor!

He went on to explain that the Priest had been married, but that on the death of his wife, who was a most saintly woman, he had become a Priest, and that all the children of that happy marriage had been so piously brought up that every one of them had devoted himself or herself to the service of the Altar, the young girls just professed being of the number.

The tears shed by the Priest were therefore of joy, not of sorrow, for he saw his most ardent desire fulfilled, and that his daughters were now the Brides of the Lamb. "But," I cried, "what did you mean by saying that a man married to such a wife as that was a Martyr? That may be the case when a man has a bad wife, but it cannot be true in his case."

Our Blessed Father's manner changed at once from gaiety to seriousness. "Take care," he said to me in a low voice, "that the same thing does not happen to you; I will tell you how, by-and-by, in private."

When we were alone afterwards I reminded him of his promise. "Take care," he said again with some severity of aspect, "lest if you yield to the temptation which is now assailing you something worse does not befall you." He was alluding to my desire to give up the burden of my Bishopric and to retire into more private life.

"Your wife," he went on to say, meaning the Church, whose ring when he consecrated me he had put on my finger, "is far more holy, far more able to make you holy than was that good man's faithful wife, whose memory is blessed. It is true that the many spiritual children whom she lays in your arms are a cause of so much anxiety that your whole life is a species of martyrdom, but remember that in this most bitter bitterness you will find peace for your soul, the peace of God which is beyond all thought or imagination. If you quit your place in order to seek repose, possibly God will permit your pretended tranquillity to be disturbed by as many vexations as the good brother Leone's, who, amid all his household cares in the monastery, was often visited by heavenly consolations. Of these he was deprived when, by permission extorted from his Superior, he had retired into his cell in order, as he said, to give himself up more absolutely to contemplation. Know (Oh! how deeply these words are engraven on my memory) that God hates the peace of those whom He had destined for war.

"He is the God of armies and of battles, as well as of peace, and he compares the Sulamite, the peaceful soul, to an army drawn up in battle array and in that formation terrible to its enemies." I may add that our Blessed Father's predictions were perfectly verified, and after his death when the very things he had spoken of happened to me I remembered his words with tears.

As I write I call to mind another instance of his delightful manner which you will like to hear.

Young as I was when consecrated a Bishop, it was his desire that I should discharge all the duties of my holy office without leaving out any single one of them, although I was inclined to make one exception, that of hearing confessions. I considered myself too young for this most responsible work, and wanting in that prudence and wisdom which are born of experience.

Our Blessed Father, however, thought differently in the matter, and I, holding this judgment in so much higher esteem than my own, gave way, bent my neck under the yokes and took my place in the confessional. There I was besieged by penitents, who scarcely allowed me any time for rest or refreshment.

One day, worn out with this labour, I wrote to St. Francis, saying, among other things, that intending to make a Confessor he had really made a Martyr.

In answering my letter he said that he knew well that the vehemence of my spirit suffered the pangs of a woman in travail, but then I must take courage and remember that it is written, a woman when she is in labour hath sorrow because her hour is come; but when she hath brought forth the child she remembereth no more the anguish for joy that a man is born into the world.[1]

[Footnote 1: John xvi. 21.]

UPON DAILY MASS. HIS ADVICE TO A YOUNG PRIEST.[1]

To a Priest whom I know well, and whom our Blessed Father loved much in Our Lord, he gave most excellent advice, and in a very kindly manner, conveyed it to him by means of an ingenious artifice.

The Priest was young, and owing to his extreme youth, although he was a Parish Priest, he dreaded saying Mass often, contenting himself with doing so on Sundays and holidays.

Our Blessed Father, wishing to lead him to say his Mass every day, devised this plan. He presented him with a little box covered with crimson satin, embroidered in gold and silver and studded with pearls and garnets. Before he actually put it into his hands, however, he said to him, "I have a favour to ask of you which I am sure you will not refuse me, since it only concerns the glory of God, which I know you have so much at heart." "I am at your command," replied the Priest. "Oh, no," said the Bishop, "I am not speaking to you as one who commands, but as one who requests, and I make this request in the name and for the love of God, which is our common watchword." After that, what could the Priest possibly refuse him? His silence testified his readiness to obey, better than any words could have done.

Blessed Francis then opening the box showed him that it was quite full of unconsecrated hosts, and said, "You are a Priest, God has called you to that vocation, and also to the Pastoral Office in His Church. Would it be the right thing if an artisan, a magistrate, or a doctor only worked at his profession one or two days in the week? You have the power to say Holy Mass every day. Why do you not avail yourself of it?

"Consider that the action of saying Mass is the loftiest, the most august, of all the functions of religion, the one which renders more glory to God and more solace to the living and the dead than any other.

"I conjure you, then, by the glory of Him in whom we live and move and have our being, to approach the Altar every day, and never, except under extreme necessity, to fail to do so.

"There is nothing, thank God, to prevent your doing this. I know your soul as well as a soul can be known, and of this you are yourself quite aware, you who have so frankly unfolded to me the inmost recesses of your conscience. Far from seeing any impediment, I see that everything invites you to do what I ask, and that you may so use the daily and supersubstantial Bread I make you this present, entreating you not to forget at the holy Altar him who makes you this prayer on the part of God Himself."

The young Priest was somewhat surprised, and without attempting to evade the implied rebuke contented himself with submitting to the judgment of the holy Bishop his secret unworthiness, his youth, his unmortified passions, his fear of misusing so divine a mystery by not living as they should live who each day offer it up.

"All this excusing yourself, replied our Blessed Father, is only so much self-accusing as would appear if I chose to examine your reasons in detail and weigh them in the scales of the sanctuary. But without entering into any discussion of them let it suffice that you refer the matter to my judgment. I tell you then, and in this I think that I have the Spirit of God, that all the reasons which you bring forward to dispense yourself from so profitable an exercise of piety are really those which oblige you to practise it. This holy exercise will ripen your youth, moderate your passions, weaken your temptations, strengthen your weakness, illuminate your path, and the very act of practising it will teach you to do so with greater perfection. Moreover, if the sense of your unworthiness would make you abstain from it out of humility, as happened to St. Bonaventure, and if your own unfitness makes the custom of daily celebrating productive in your soul of less fruit than it should, consider that you are a public person, and that your flock and your Church have need of your daily Mass. More than that, you ought to be stimulated and spurred on by the thought that every day on which you refrain from celebrating you deprive the exterior glory of God of increase, the Angels of their delight, and the Blessed of a most special happiness."

The young Priest deferred to this counsel, saying "Fiat, fiat," and from that time for a space of thirty years has never failed to say Mass daily, even when on long journeys through France, Italy, Spain, Germany, and in heretical countries. He never failed, I repeat, even under conditions which seemed to make the saying of Mass impossible.

Such power have remonstrances when tempered with kindness and prudence.

[Footnote 1: Possibly M. Camus himself. [Ed.]]

A PRIEST SAYING MASS SHOULD BE CONSIDERATE OF OTHERS.

He was told that I was very lengthy in my preparation for saying Holy Mass, and that this was a cause of inconvenience to many who either wished to be present at it or to speak to me afterwards. I was accustomed, by his orders, to say daily Mass at a fixed hour, and not in the private chapel of the Bishop's house, unless I happened to be ill, but in a large chapel adjoining the Cathedral Church, where synods, ordinations, and similar pastoral functions were held. The bell rang for this Mass always at a few minutes before the appointed hour, but those who knew the length of my preparation in the sacristy did not hurry to come to it, and those who did not know lost patience, and in winter time often got chilled to the bone.

Our Blessed Father, wishing to correct this fault in me, waited quietly till the right moment came for doing so. He was paying me one of his annual visits at Belley, when it chanced that one morning he was detained very late in his room writing some letters which he had to send off without loss of time. When eleven o'clock drew near, his servants, knowing that he never failed to say Mass unless hindered by illness or some real impediment, came to remind him that he had not yet done so.

The Altar in the private Chapel had been prepared for him. He came out of his room, wearing as usual his rochet and mosetta, and after saluting those who had come to see him and to hear his Mass, said a short prayer at the foot of the Altar, then vested and celebrated the holy sacrifice. Mass ended, he knelt down again, and, after another short prayer, joined us with a face of angelic serenity. Having greeted each of us affectionately, he entered into conversation with us, until we were called, as we soon were, to table. I, who watched his actions most closely and ever found them regular and harmonious as a stave of music, was amazed at the brevity of this preparation and thanksgiving. In the evening, therefore, when we were alone together, I said, using the filial privilege which I knew was mine, "Father, it seemed to me this morning that your preparation for Mass and your thanksgiving were very hasty and short."

He turned suddenly, and, embracing me, exclaimed, "Oh, how delighted I am that you are so straightforward in telling me home truths! For three or four days I have been wanting to do the same thing to you, but did not know how to begin! Now, tell me what do you say as to that lengthiness of yours which inconveniences everybody? All complain, and quite openly, though possibly these complaints have not yet reached your ears, so few dare speak the truth to Bishops. Doubtless it is because no one loves you as I do that I have been asked to speak about this. My commission is quite authentic, though I do not show you the signatures. A little of your superfluity handed over to me would do us both good, by making you go more quickly and, me more slowly.

"Do you think," he continued, "that the people who are so anxious to assist at your Mass have any sympathy with your long preparation before-hand in the sacristy? Still less those who are waiting to speak to you after Mass, with your interminable thanksgiving.

"Many of these people come from a distance, and have business engagements in the town."

"But, Father," I said, "how ought we to make our preparation? Scripture says, Before prayer prepare thy soul, and be not as a man that tempteth God.[1] How much more, then, must we prepare with all care for the stupendous act of celebrating Mass, before which, in the words of the Preface, the powers of Heaven tremble? How can one play on a lute without tuning it?" "Why do you not make this preparation earlier, in your morning exercise, which I know, or at least I think, you never neglect?" "I rise at four o'clock in the summer, sometimes sooner," I replied, "and I do not go to the Altar till about nine or ten o'clock." "And do you suppose," he returned, "that the interval from four to nine is very great to Him, in Whose sight a thousand years are as yesterday?"[2]

This passage, so well applied, was like a sudden illumination to me. "And what about the thanksgiving?" I said. "Wait till your evening exercise to make it," he answered; "you make your examination of conscience, surely so great an act will have its weight; and is not thanksgiving one of the points of self-examination? Both these acts can be made more at leisure and more calmly in the morning and evening: no one will be inconvenienced by them, and they will interfere with none of your ordinary duties." "But," I objected, "will it not be a cause of disedification to others to see me so quick over things? God should not be adored hurriedly." "We may hurry as much as we like," he replied; "God goes faster than we do. He is as the lightning which comes forth from the east and the next moment flashes in the west. All things are present to Him; with Him there is neither past nor future. How can we escape from His spirit?" I acquiesced, and since then all has gone well in this matter.

[Footnote 1: Eccle. xviii. 23.]

[Footnote 2: Psalm lxxxix. 4.]

BLESSED FRANCIS ENCOURAGES THE BISHOP OF BELLEY.

Owing to the fact that the See of Belley had been vacant for four years, a dispensation was obtained from the Bishop enabling me, at the age of twenty-five, to be consecrated Bishop, and at the same time to be put in possession of that See to which the King, Henry IV., had already appointed me.

Blessed Francis Himself consecrated me, in my own Cathedral Church of Belley, August 30th, 1609.

After a while scruples began to disturb my mind on account of this consecration, seemingly so premature. I had, as it were, been made a captain when I had scarcely enlisted as a soldier. I carried my troubles to the director of my conscience, this Blessed Father who consoled and cheered me by suggesting many excellent reasons for this unusual state of things. The necessities of the diocese, the testimony to my character of so many persons of dignity and piety, the judgment of Henry the Great, whose memory he held in high honour, and, last of all, and above all, the command of His Holiness. He concluded by urging me not to look back, but rather to stretch forward to the things which were before me, following the advice of St. Paul.

"You have come to the vineyard," he went on to say, "in the first hour of your day. Beware lest you labour there so slothfully, that those who enter at the eleventh hour outstrip you both in the work and in reward."

One day I said jestingly to him: "Father, virtuous and exemplary as you are considered to be, you have committed one fault in your life, that of having consecrated me too early."

He answered me with a laugh which opened a heaven of joy to me. "It is certainly true," he said, "that I have committed that sin, but I am much afraid God will never forgive me for it, for up to the present moment I have never been able to repent of it. I conjure you by the bowels of our common Master to live in such a manner that you may never give me cause for regret in this matter and rather, often to stir up in yourself the grace which was bestowed upon you from on high by the imposition of my hands. I have, you must know, been called to the consecration of other Bishops, but only as assistant. I have never consecrated any one but you: you are my only one, my apprenticeship work.

"Take courage. God will help us.

"He is our light and our salvation, whom shall we fear? He is the Protector of our life, of whom shall we be afraid?"

UPON A COMPASSIONATE MIND.

Although his soul was one of the strongest and most well-balanced possible, yet it was capable of the tenderest and most compassionate feelings for the sorrows of others. He did not repine over the miseries and infirmities of human nature, he only desired that all souls should be strengthened by grace.

To a lady who was heart-broken at the death of a sister whom she passionately loved, he wrote:

"I will not say to you, do not weep, for, on the contrary, it is just and reasonable that you should weep a little—but only a little—my dear daughter, as a proof of the sincere affection which you bore her, following the example of our dear Master, who shed a few tears over His friend Lazarus, but not many, as do those whose thoughts, being bounded by the moments of this miserable life, forget that we, too, are on our way to Eternity, in which if we live well in this life we shall be reunited to our beloved dead, nor ever be parted from them again. We cannot prevent our poor hearts from being affected by the changes of this life, and by the loss of those who have been our pleasant companions in it. Still never must we be false to our solemn promise to unite our will inseparably to the Will of God."

Again, let me remind you how tenderly he expresses himself on the sorrowful occasions of the death of his dearest relatives and friends. "Indeed," he says, "at times like these I myself weep much. Then my heart, hard as a stone with regard to heavenly things, breaks and pours forth rivers of tears. But God be praised! They are always gentle tears, and, speaking to you as to my own dear daughter, I never shed them without a loving grateful thought of the providence of God. For, since our Saviour loved death and gave His death to be the object of our love, I cannot feel any bitterness, or grudge against it, whether it be that of my sisters or of anyone else, provided it be in union with the holy death of my Saviour."

And in another place he says:

"I must say just one word in confidence to you. There is not a man living who has a heart more tender and more open to friendship than mine, or who feels more keenly than I do the pain of separation from those I love; nevertheless. I hold so cheap this poor earthly life which we lead that I never turn back to God with a more ardent affection than when He has dealt me some blow of the kind or permitted one to be dealt me."

UPON DOING ONE'S DUTY, WITHOUT RESPECT OF PERSONS.

After I had preached several Advents and Lents in various towns of my diocese of Belley, he thought it well that I should do so in my own native city, Paris.

Well knowing, as he did, the various views and judgments of the great world which rules there, he wished to teach me to care very little what people said about me, and he impressed the lesson upon me by relating to me the following story of an aged Priest and the college clock.

A good Father being incapacitated by infirmities even more than by age from fulfilling the duty of teaching binding on his Order, and yet being anxious to have some little useful employment, was entrusted by his Superior with the winding and regulating the college clock.

Very soon, however, he came to complain of the difficulty and almost impossibility of his work; not, he said, that it was at all beyond his strength, but that it was quite beyond him to satisfy everyone. When the clock was a little slow, he said, the young men who had difficult and troublesome work to do indoors, complained, declaring that the town clocks were much faster, and to please them he would put it on a little. As soon as this was done complaints burst forth from those whose work lay outside the college, in visiting the sick and prisoners, or providing for the needs of the household in the city. They came back declaring that the town clocks were much slower, and reproaching me for having put theirs on.

The Superior settled the matter by telling the good Father to let the clock take its own course, but always to use soft words to those who might complain, and to assure each one of them that he would do his best to keep the clock right if possible. "So let it be with you," concluded our Blessed Father. "You are going to be exposed to the criticism of many; if you attend to all that they say of you, your work, like Penelope's, will never be done, but every day you will have to begin it over again.

"Even some of your friends will in perfect good faith give you suggestions on matters which seem to them important, but which in reality are not so at all.

"One will tell you that you speak too fast, another that you gesticulate too much, a third that you speak too slowly, and don't move enough—one will want quotations, another will dislike them; one will prefer doctrinal, another moral lessons; some one thing, some another.

"They will be like drones who do nothing but disturb the working bees, and who, though they can sting, yet make no honey."

"Well! what is to be done in all this?"

"Why, you must always answer gently, promising to try and correct yourself of your faults whatever they may be, for there is nothing which pleases these counsellors so much as to see that their suggestions are accepted as judicious, and, at least, worthy of consideration. In the meantime go your own way, follow the best of your own character, pay no heed to such criticisms, which are often contradictory one of the other.

"Keep God before your eyes, abandon yourself to the guidance of the spirit of grace, and say often with the Apostle, 'If I yet pleased men I should not be the servant of Christ,' who said of Himself that He was not of this world. Neither, indeed, were His Apostles, for the friendship of the world is enmity with God.

"It is no small matter for a steersman in the midst of a storm to keep the rudder straight. Of little consequence ought it to be to us that we are judged by men. God is our only true judge, and it is He Who sees the secrets of our hearts, and all that is hidden in darkness."

THE HONOUR DUE TO VIRTUE.

Honour is like thyme which the pagans thought ought only to be burnt on the Altar of Virtue. In ancient Rome the Temple of Honour could only be entered through the Temple of Virtue.

The virtue of Blessed Francis de Sales was so generally recognized by both Catholics and Protestants that he may be truly said to have been universally reverenced.

A remarkable instance of this occurred at Grenoble, the chief town of Dauphiné, in the year in which he went there to preach during Advent and Lent. Monsieur de Lesdigiuères, the King's Viceroy at Grenoble, and Marshal of France, was not yet converted to the Catholic Faith. He, however, received the Bishop with affectionate warmth, and paid him extraordinary honours. He frequently invited him to his table, and often visited him in his house, sometimes even being present at his sermons, for he really valued the teaching of the holy Bishop, and thought most highly of his virtue. The Protestants of Grenoble took fright at this, more particularly because of the long, private interviews which took place between the Magistrate and the holy Bishop.

Wherever he went the King's representative spoke of Blessed Francis in the highest terms, and invariably made a point of giving him his title, Bishop of Geneva. In short, he paid him such deference as excited universal astonishment.

In vain did the Huguenot clergy storm and rage, in vain did they threaten to excommunicate anyone having dealings with the Bishop. They could not prevent the majority of their congregations from pressing every day to hear the Saint's sermons, which created a great sensation amongst them.

The Huguenot preachers, far from gaining fresh adherents, saw their flock steadily dwindling away.

At last, in despair, the Consistory determined to send a deputation to remonstrate with M. de Lesdigiuères on the warm welcome he was giving the holy Bishop, and on his own behaviour in scandalizing the whole Protestant party by attending Blessed Francis' sermons.

The deputation, formed of the elders and most notable men of the sect, reached the Marshal's house early in the morning, so that he was not even dressed when their request for an interview was brought to him.

Being a man who would not be dictated to, he sent down word to the Huguenots that if they came to visit him as friends, or to communicate any matter of business to him, he would receive them gladly, but if they meant to remonstrate with him, in the name of the Consistory or ministers, on the politeness he was showing to the Bishop of Geneva, they might rest assured that they would go out through the window faster than they had come in by the door!

This message was enough. The deputation broke up at once; but with how many lamentations over this unexpected reception, given by one whom they had reckoned upon as the chief stay and prop of their sect.

Their next plan was to send one of the principal noblemen of the province, a Protestant like themselves, upon the same errand as before. He, however, fared no better than the deputation.

Tell those gentlemen (said M. de Lesdigiuères) that I am old enough to know the rules of politeness.

Up to the age of thirty I was myself a Roman Catholic. I know how Roman Catholics treat their Bishops, and with what respect these Bishops are treated by Kings and Princes. They hold a rank altogether different from that of our ministers, who, even the highest among them, are only Parish Priests, since they themselves deny the very existence of the order of Bishop, however good a foundation for it there may seem to be in the teaching of Holy Scripture. As for me, my belief is that they will in the end be sorry they have given up this distinction of rank. "Tell M. B. (he was a minister of low birth, had formerly been M. de Lesdigiuères' servant, and owed to him his actual position in the so-called Reformed Church of Grenoble) that when I see among Huguenot ministers, sons and brothers of sovereign Princes, as I do among Roman Catholic Bishops, Archbishops, and Cardinals, I will perhaps change my mind as to how to treat them socially.

"As regards the Bishop of Geneva, I can only say that if I were in his place and were, as he is, sovereign Prince of this city, I would see that I was properly obeyed, and that my authority was duly recognised. I know what are his rights and titles better than B … or any of his colleagues can possibly do; it is for me to give them a lesson on the subject, and for them, if they are wise, to listen. It is not for young, uneducated men to presume to show a man of my age and rank how to behave himself."

After this the Viceroy redoubled his attentions to the holy Bishop, to whom he paid every honour in his power.

On the other hand, he himself received such good impressions of our religion from what he saw of the Bishop that they greatly facilitated his conversion, which took place after he had been promoted to the rank of Constable.

He died an excellent Catholic, and most happily.

UPON MEMORY AND JUDGMENT.

On one occasion Blessed Francis was complaining to me of the shortness of his memory. I tried to console him by reminding him that even if it were true, there was no lack in him of judgment, for in that he always excelled.

In reply, he said that it was certainly unusual to find a good memory and excellent judgment united, although the two qualities might be possessed together by some in a moderate degree. He added that there were of course exceptions to the rule, but such exceptions were mostly of rare and extraordinary merit.

He gave as an instance one of his most intimate friends, the great Anthony Favre, first President of Savoy, and one of the most celebrated lawyers of his time, who united in his own person remarkable keenness of judgment with a marvellous memory. "In truth," he went on to say, "these two qualities are so different in their nature, that it is not difficult for one to push the other out. One is the outcome of vivacity and alertness, the other is not unfrequently characteristic of the slow and leaden-footed."

After some more conversation with me on this subject, in which I deplored my want of judgment, he concluded with these words: "It is a common thing for people to complain of their defective memory, and even of the malice and worthlessness of their will, but nobody ever deplores his poverty of spirit, i.e., of judgment. In spite of the Beatitude, everyone rejects such a thought as a doing an injustice to themselves. Well, courage! advancing years will bring you plenty of judgment: it is one of the fruits of experience and old age.

"But as for memory, its failure is one of the undoubted defects of old people. That is why I have little hope of the improvement of my own; but provided I have enough to remember God that is all I want.[1] I remembered, O Lord, Thy judgments of old: and I was comforted."

[Footnote 1: Psalm cxviii. 52.]

A PRIEST SHOULD NOT AIM AT IMITATING IN HIS SERMONS ANY PARTICULAR PREACHER.

I esteemed him so highly, and not without reason, that all his ways delighted me. Among others, I thought that I should like to imitate his style of preaching. Can it be said that I chose a bad model or was wanting in taste?

Do not, however, imagine for a moment that I have ever aimed at reproducing his lofty and deep thoughts and teaching, the eloquent sweetness of his language, the marvellous power which swayed the hearts of his audience. No, I have always felt that to be beyond my powers, and I have only tried to mould my action, gestures, and intonation after the pattern set by him. Now, as it happened, that owing to his constitution and temperament his speech was always slow and deliberate, not to say prosy, and my own quite the opposite, I became so strangely changed that my dear people at Belley (where the above incident occurred) almost failed to recognise me. They thought a changeling had been foisted upon them in the place of their own Bishop, whose vehement action and passionate words they dearly loved, even though sometimes they had found his discourses hard to follow. In fact, I had ceased to be myself; I was now nothing more than a wretched copy with nothing in it really recalling the original.

Our Blessed Father heard of this, and being eager to apply a remedy chose his opportunity, and one day, when we were talking about sermons, quietly remarked that he was told I had taken it into my head to imitate the Bishop of Geneva in my preaching. I replied that it was so, and asked if I had chosen a bad model, and if he did not preach better than I did.

"Ah," he replied, "this is a chance for attacking his reputation! But, no, he does not preach so badly, only the worst of it is that they tell me you imitate him so badly that his style is not recognisable: that you have spoiled the Bishop of Belley yet have not at all succeeded in reproducing the Bishop of Geneva. You had better, like the artist who was forced to put the name of his subject under every portrait he painted, give out that you are only copying me." "Well, be it so," I replied, "in good time you will see that little by little from being a pupil I have become a master, and in the end my copies will be taken for originals."

"Jesting apart," he continued, "you are spoiling yourself, ruining your preaching, and pulling down a splendid building to re-fashion it into one which sins against the rules of nature and art. You must remember, too, that if at your age, like a piece of cloth, you have taken a wrong fold, it will not be easy to smooth it out."

"Ah! if manners could be changed, what would I not give for such as yours? I do what I can to stir myself up, I do not spare the spur, but the more I urge myself on, the less I advance. I have difficulty in getting my words out, and still more in pronouncing them. I am heavier than a block, I can neither excite my own emotions, nor those of others. You have more fire in the tip of your fingers than I have in my whole body. Where you fly like a bird, I crawl like a tortoise. And now they tell me that you, who are naturally so rapid, so lively, so powerful in your preaching, are weighing your words, counting your periods, drooping your wings, dragging yourself on, and making your audience as tired as yourself. Is this the beautiful Noemi of bygone days? the city of perfect loveliness, the joy of the whole earth?"

Why should I dwell more on his reproof? Sufficient to say that he cured me of my error, and I returned to my former style of preaching, God grant that it may be for His glory!

UPON SHORT SERMONS.

He highly approved of brevity in preaching, and used to say that the chief fault of the preachers of the day was lengthiness.

I ventured to ask how that could be a fault, and how he could speak of abundance as if it were famine?

He answered: "When the vine is thick in leaves it always bears less fruit, multiplicity of words does not produce great results. You will find that a powerful and spirited horse will always start off promptly, and as promptly pull up. A poor post hack, on the contrary, will go on several paces after his rider has reined him in. Why is that? Because he is weak. So it is with the mind and intellect. He who is strong leaves off speaking when he pleases, because he has great control over himself, and readiness of judgment. A weak-minded man speaks much, but loses himself in his own thoughts, nor thinks of finishing what he has to say. Look at all the homilies and sermons of the ancient Fathers and observe how short they were, yet how much more efficacious than our lengthy ones! Wise St. Francis of Assisi, in his Rule, prescribes that the preachers of his Order shall preach the Gospel with brevity, and gives an excellent reason: 'Remembering,' he says, 'that: a short word shall the Lord make upon the earth.'[1] The more you say, the less your hearers will retain. The less you say, the more they will profit. Believe me in this, for I speak from experience. By overloading the memory of a hearer we destroy it, just as lamps are put out when they are filled too full of oil, and plants are spoilt by being too abundantly watered. When a discourse is too long, by the time the end is reached, the middle is forgotten, and by the time the middle is reached the beginning has been lost. Moderately good preachers are accepted, provided they are brief, and the best become tiresome when they are too lengthy. There is no more disagreeable quality in a preacher than prolixity."

Our Blessed Father sometimes surprised me by saying that we ought to be pleased if, when going up into the pulpit to preach, we saw before us a small and scattered audience. "Thirty years of experience," he said, "have made me speak thus: I have always seen greater results from the sermons which I have preached to small congregations than from those which I have delivered in crowded churches. An occurrence which I am going to relate will justify what I say.

"When I was Provost, or rather Dean, of my church, my predecessor in this diocese, sent me, in company with some other Priests, to instruct in the Faith the inhabitants of the three bailiwicks of the Chablais, namely, Thonon, Ternier, and Gaillard. The towns being full at that time of Huguenots, we had no access to them, and could only say Mass and give instruction in some scattered and rather distant chapels.

"One Sunday, when the weather was very bad, there were only seven persons at my Mass, and these few suggested to some one to tell me that I ought not to take the trouble of preaching after Mass, as it was the custom then to do, the number of hearers being so small. I replied that neither did a large audience encourage me, nor a scanty one discourage me; provided only that I could edify one single person, that would be enough for me.

"I went up; therefore, into the pulpit, and I remember that the subject of my sermon was praying to the Saints, I treated it very simply and catechetically, not at all controversially, as you know that is neither my style nor is the doing so to my taste. I said nothing pathetic, and put nothing very forcibly, yet one of my small audience began to weep bitterly, sobbing and giving vent to audible sighs. I thought that he was ill, and begged him not to put any constraint upon himself, as I was quite ready to break off my sermon, and to give him any help he needed. He replied that he was perfectly well in body, and he begged me to go on speaking boldly, for so I should be administering the needful healing to the wound.

"The sermon, which was very short, being ended, he hurried up to me, and throwing himself at my feet cried out: 'Reverend sir, you have given me life, you have saved my soul to-day. Oh, blessed the hour in which I came here and listened to your words! This hour will be worth a whole eternity to me.'

"And then, being asked to do so, he related openly before the little congregation, that, having conferred with some ministers on this very same subject of praying to the Saints, which they made out to be sheer idolatry, he had decided on the following Thursday to return to their ranks (he was a recent convert to Catholicism), and to abjure the Catholic religion. But, he added, that the sermon which he had just heard had instructed him so well, and had so fully dispersed all his doubts, that he took back with his whole heart the promise he had given them, and vowed new obedience to the Roman Church.

"I cannot tell you what an impression this great example, taking place in so small a congregation, made throughout the country, or how docile and responsive to the words of life and of truth it made all hearts. I could allege other similar instances, some even more remarkable."

For myself I now prefer small congregations, and am never so well pleased as when I see only a little group of people listening to my preaching. Seneca once said to his friend Lucillus that they themselves formed a theatre wide enough for the communication of their philosophy, and, speaking of those who came to hear his teaching, he says: Satis sunt pauci, satis est alter, satis est unus. A few are enough—two are enough—nay, one is enough. Why should not a Christian Philosopher be content with what was enough for this Stoic?

[Footnote 1: Rom. ix. 28.]

UPON PREACHING AND PREACHERS.

On the subject of preaching, Blessed Francis had very definite and weighty thoughts. He considered that it was not sufficient for a preacher to teach the ways of God to the unrighteous, and by converting the wicked, to build up by his words the walls of Jerusalem, that is, of holy Church, while making known to God's people the ways of divine providence. He wanted more than this, and said that every sermon ought to have some special plan, with always for its end the giving glory to God and the converting and instructing of those who were to hear it. Sometimes this would be the setting forth of a mystery, sometimes the clearing up of some point of faith, sometimes the denouncing of a particular vice, sometimes the endeavouring to plant some virtue in the hearts of the hearers.

"No one," he said, "can sufficiently lay to heart the importance of having a definite aim in preaching; for want of it many carefully studied sermons are without fruit. Some preachers are content to explain their text with all the painstaking and mental effort that they can bring to bear upon the subject. Others give themselves up to elaborate and exhaustive research and excite the admiration of their hearers, either by their scientific reasonings, their eloquence, the studied grace of their gestures, or by their perfect diction. Others add to all this beautiful and useful teaching, but so that it only slips in here and there, as it were, by chance, and is not expressly dwelt upon. But when we have only one aim, and when all our reasonings and all our movements tend towards it and gather round it, as the radii of a circle round the unity of its centre, then the impression made is infinitely more powerful. Such speaking has the force of a mighty river which leaves its mark upon the hardest of the stones it flows over.

"Drones visit every flower, yet gather no honey from any. The working bee does otherwise: it settles down upon each flower just as long as is necessary for it to suck in enough sweetness to make its one honeycomb. So those who follow my method will preach profitable sermons, and will deserve to be accounted faithful dispensers of the divine mysteries; prudent administrators of the word of life and of eternal life."

When our Blessed Father heard a certain preacher praised up to the skies, he asked in what virtues he excelled; whether in humility, mortification, gentleness, courage, devotion or what? When told that he was said to preach very well, he replied: "That is speaking, not acting: the former is far easier than the latter. There are many who speak and yet act not, and who destroy by their bad example what they build up with their tongue. A man whose tongue is longer than his arm, is he not a monstrosity?"

On one occasion, of some one who had delighted all his hearers by a sermon he had preached, it was said: "To-day he literally did wonders." The Saint replied: "If he did that he must be one of those absolutely blameless men of whom Scripture says 'they have not sought after gold, nor hoped for treasures of gold and silver.'" Another time he was told that this same preacher had on a particular day surpassed himself. "Ah!" he said, "what new act of self-renunciation has he made? What injury has he borne? For it is only after overcoming ourselves in this way that we surpass ourselves."

"Do you wish to know," he continued, "how I test the excellence and value of a preacher? It is by assuring myself that those who have been listening to him come away striking their breasts and saying: 'I will, do better'; not by their saying: 'Oh how well he spoke, what beautiful things he said!' For to say beautiful things in fluent and well-chosen words shows indeed the learning and eloquence of a man; but the conversion of sinners and their departing from their evil ways is the sure sign that God has spoken by the mouth of the preacher, that he possesses the true power of speech, which is inspired by the science of the Saints, and that he proclaims worthily in the name of Almighty God that perfect law which is the salvation of souls.

"The true fruit of preaching is the destruction of sin and the establishment of the kingdom of justice upon earth.[1] By this justice, of which the prophet speaks, is meant justification and sanctification. For this, God sends his preachers, as Jesus Christ sent His Apostles, that they may bring forth fruit, and that this fruit may remain,[2] and by consequence that they may labour for a meat which perishes not, but which endures unto life everlasting."[3]

When I was in residence in my diocese I never failed to preach on every possible day in Advent and Lent, besides doing so on all Sundays and holidays. Some good people who set themselves up as judges in such matters, full of worldly prudence said that I was making myself too common, and bringing the holy function of preaching into contempt.

This came to the ears of our Blessed Father, and he, despising such poor earthly wisdom, observed, that to blame a husbandman or vinedresser for cultivating his land too well was really to praise him. Speaking to me on the subject, and fearing that all that had been said might discourage me, he related to me what follows: "I had," he said, the best father in the world, but as he had spent a great part of his life at court and in the camp, he knew the maxims that hold in those conditions of life far better than he did the principles of holy living.

"While I was Provost," he continued, "I preached on all possible occasions, whether in the Chablais, where I was busy for many years uprooting heresy, or, on my return, in the Cathedral, in parish churches, and even in the chapels of the most obscure Confraternities. While at Annecy I never refused any invitation whencesoever it came to preach. One day my good father took me aside and said to me: 'Provost, you preach too often. Even on week days I am always hearing the bell ringing for sermons, and when I ask who is preaching I invariably get the same answer: "The Provost, the Provost." In my time, it was not so; sermons were rare, but then they were sermons! They were learned and well studied, more Greek and Latin was quoted in one of them than in ten of yours; people were delighted and edified, they crowded to hear them, just as they would have crowded to gather up manna. Now, you make preaching so common that no one thinks much of it, and you yourself are held in far less esteem.'

"You see my good father spoke according to his lights and quite sincerely. You may be sure he was not wishing me ill, but he was guided by the maxims of the world in which he had been brought up.

"Yet what folly in the sight of God are all the principles of human wisdom! If we pleased men we should not be the servants of Jesus Christ, He Himself, the model of all preachers, did not use all this circumspection, neither did the Apostles who followed in His footsteps. Preach the word: be instant in season out of season.[4]

"Believe me, we can never preach enough, especially in this border-land of heresy, heresy which is only kept alive by sermons, and which will never be destroyed except by that very breath of God which is holy preaching.

"If you will take my advice, therefore, you will shut your eyes against the counsels of your worldly-wise monitors and listen rather to St. Paul, who says to you: But be thou vigilant, labour in all things, do the work of an evangelist, fulfil thy ministry.[5]

"Moreover, when the Apostle continues, Be sober, he refers to temperance in eating and drinking, not to sobriety or restraint in the discharge of pastoral duties. Blessed is the pastor who shall be found watching and feeding his flock! I tell you that the divine Master will set him over all his goods. And when the Prince of Pastors shall come he will receive from His hand a crown of glory which can never fade."

[Footnote 1: Dan. ix 24.]

[Footnote 2: John xv. 16.]

[Footnote 3: Id. vi. 27.]

[Footnote 4: 2 Tim. iv. 2, 3.]

[Footnote 5: 2 Tim. iv. 5.]

BLESSED FRANCIS AND THE BISHOP OF BELLEY'S SERMON.

One day I was to preach at the Visitation Convent at Annecy, the first established convent of the Order, and I knew that our Blessed Father, as well as a great congregation, would be present. I had, to tell the truth, taken extra pains in the consideration of my subject, and intended to do my very best. I had chosen for text a passage in the Canticle of Canticles, and this I turned and twisted into every possible form, applying it to the Visitation vocation which I extolled far too extravagantly to please the good Bishop.

When he and I were alone together afterwards, he told me that, though my hearers had been delighted with me, and could not say enough in praise of my sermon, there was one solitary exception, one individual who was not pleased with it. On my expressing surprise and much curiosity to know whom I could have hurt or distressed by my words, he answered quietly that I saw the person now before me. I looked around—there was no one present but himself. "Alas!" I cried, "this is indeed a wet blanket thrown upon my success. I had rather have had your approbation than that of a whole province! However, God be praised! I have fallen into the hands of a surgeon who wounds only to heal.

"What more have you to say, for I know you do not intend to spare me?"

"I love you too much," he replied, "either to spare or to flatter you, and had you loved our Sisters in the same way, you would not have wasted words in puffing them up in place of edifying them, and in praising their vocation, of which they have already quite a sufficiently high opinion.

"You would have dealt out to them more salutary doctrine, in proportion as it would have been more humiliating. Always remember that the whole object of preaching is to root out sin, and to plant justice in its stead."

On my replying to this that those whom I addressed were already delivered from the hands of their enemies, the world, the flesh, and the devil, and were serving God securely in holiness and justice, "Then," he said, "since they are standing, you should teach them to take heed lest they fall, and to work out their salvation with fear and trembling.

"It is right, indeed, for you to encourage them to persevere in their holy undertaking, but you must do so without exposing them to the danger of presumption and vanity. Enough said; I know that for the future you will be careful in this matter."

The next day he sent me to preach in a convent of Poor Clares, an Order renowned for the exemplary life of its members and for their extraordinary austerities. I took good care to avoid the rock on which I had struck the day before, and against which he had warned me. There was as large a congregation as before, but I confined myself to plain and simple language, without a thought of studied rhetoric.

I did not praise the austerities of the good nuns, nor did I labour to please any of my hearers, their edification was my sole object.

On our return to the house, our Blessed Father said, embracing me tenderly, that though most of those present were dissatisfied, and compared my sermon most unfavourably with that of the preceding day, yet, that he, on the contrary, who had then found fault with me, was now perfectly contented and pleased, and that he believed that God was pleased also. "As for your past faults," he continued, "I give you a plenary indulgence for them all.

"If you continue to preach as you have just done, whatever the world may say, you will be doing much service for the Master of the Vineyard, and will become a fitting servant of His Testament."

One day I was preaching before him at Annecy in the church which he used as his cathedral. He was surrounded by all his canons, who, with the whole Chapter, attended him to the bench where he was in the habit of sitting to hear sermons.

This particular one of mine pleased him as regarded its matter and delivery, but I suffered an allusion to escape me referring to his own name of Sales, and implying, or rather affirming, that he was the salt (Sal es) with which the whole mass of the people was seasoned.

This praise was so distasteful to him that, on our return from the church, he took me to task for it, in a tone and with a manner as severe as was possible to his gentle nature. "You were going on so well," he said. "What could have induced you to play these pranks? Do you know that you spoilt your sermon by them? Truly, I am a fine sort of salt, fit only to be thrown into the street and trampled under foot by the people. For certainly you must have said what you did say in order to put me to shame—you have found out the right way to do that—but, at least, spare your own friends."

I tried to excuse myself, alleging that what the Bishop of Saluces once said to him had suddenly come into my heads and that, quite without premeditation, the very same words escaped my lips, "But," he replied, "in the pulpit such things must not escape our lips. I am quite aware that this time they really did escape you, but you must not allow it to happen again."

I may here explain, for your benefit, what I meant by this reference to a saying of the Bishop of Saluces. That holy prelate, who died in the odour of sanctity, and who was a disciple of Sr. Philip Neri, was an intimate friend of our Blessed Father's.

On one occasion, when the latter was passing through Saluces on his way to the shrine of Our Lady of Montdeay, the good Bishop received him with every mark of respect, and begged him to preach in his cathedral. After the sermon, he said to him, "My Lord, truly tu Sal es; at ego, neque sal, neque lux." That is to say, "You are a true salt (Sal es), and I am neither salt nor light," alluding to the word Saluces (Sal lux), his diocese.[1]

[Footnote 1: NOTE.—Another version says that it was St. Francis who answered: "On the contrary, tu sal et lux." See "Vies de S. F. de Sales." by his nephew, Charles Auguste de Sales and Hamon. Also the life of Blessed Juvenal Ancina, the said Bishop of Saluces. [Ed.]]

UPON CONTROVERSY.

The gentleness of his disposition made Blessed Francis averse to disputing, either in private or public, in matters of religion. Rather, he loved to hold informal and kindly conferences with any who had wandered from the right way; and by this means he brought back countless souls into the Catholic Church. His usual method of proceeding was this. He first of all listened readily to all that his opponents had to say about their religion, not showing any sign of weariness or contempt, however tired he might be of the subject. By this means he sought to incline them to give him in his turn some little attention. When, if only out of mere civility, he was given in his turn an opportunity of speaking, he did not lose a moment of the precious time, but at once took up the subject treated by the heretic, or perhaps another which he considered more useful, and deduced from it briefly, clearly, and very simply the truth of the Catholic belief, and this without any air of contending, without a word which breathed of controversy, but neither more nor less than as if dealing in a catechetical instruction with an Article of the Faith.

If interrupted by outcries and contemptuous expressions, he bore the annoyance with incredible patience, and, without showing himself disturbed in the least, continued his discourse as soon as ever an opportunity was given to him.

"You would never believe," he said, "how beautiful the truths of our holy Faith appear to those who consider them calmly. We smother them when we try to dress them up, and we hide them when we aim at rendering them too conspicuous. Faith is an infused, not a natural, knowledge; it is not a human science, but a divine light, by means of which we see things which, in the natural order, art invisible to us. If we try to teach it as human sciences are taught, by ocular demonstrations and by natural evidence, we deceive ourselves; Faith is not to be found where human reason tries only to support itself by the experience of the senses.

"All the external proofs which can be brought to bear upon our opponents are weak, unless the Holy Spirit is at work in their soul's, teaching them to recognise the ways of God. All that has to be done is to propose to them simply the truths of our Faith. To propose these truths is to compel men to accept them, unless, indeed, they resist the Holy Spirit, either through dullness of understanding, or through uncircumcision of the heart. The attaching over much importance to the light of natural reason is a quenching of the Spirit of God. Faith is not an acquired, but an infused virtue; it must be treated with accordingly, and in instructing heretics we must beware of taking to ourselves any part of the glory which belongs to God alone.

"One of the greatest misfortunes of heretics is that their ministers in their discourses travesty our Faith, representing it as something quite different from what it really is. For example, they pretend that we have no regard for Holy Scripture; that we worship the Pope as God; that we regard the Saints as divinities; that we hold the Blessed Virgin as being more than Jesus Christ; that we pay divine worship to images and pictures; that we believe souls in Purgatory to be suffering the selfsame agony and despair as those in Hell; that we deprive the laity of participation in the Blood of Jesus Christ; that we adore bread in the Eucharist; that we despise the merits of Jesus Christ, attributing our salvation solely to the merit of our good works; that auricular confession is mental torture; and so on, endeavouring by calumnies of this sort to discredit our religion and to render the very thought of it odious to those who are so thoroughly misinformed as to its nature. When, on the contrary, they are made acquainted with our real belief on any of these points, the scales fall from their eyes, and they see that the fascination and cajolery of their preachers has hidden from them the truth as to God's goodness and the beauty of God's truth, and has put darkness before them in the place of light.

"It is true that at first they may shrug their shoulders, and laugh us to scorn; but when they have left us, and, being alone, reflect a little on what we have told them, you will see them flutter back like decoyed birds, saying to us, 'We should like to hear you speak again about those things which you brought before us the other day.' Then they fall, some on the right hand, others on the left, and Truth, victorious on all sides, brings them by different paths to know it as it really is."

He gave me many instances of conversions he had himself made in this manner during his five years' mission in the Chablais.

He gave them to show how useful this mode of proceeding was, and how far more helpful to souls than mere controversy can be.

THE SAME SUBJECT CONTINUED.

Blessed Francis did not approve of controversial sermons,[1] "The Christian pulpit," he used to say, "is a place for improving of morals, not for wrangling about them, for instructing the faithful in the truth of their belief, rather than for convincing of their error those who have separated themselves from the Church. An experience of thirty years in the work of evangelising makes me speak thus. We made some trial of the controversial method, when God through us led back the Chablais to the Catholic Faith, but when I attempted to throw my treating of controversial subjects in the pulpit into the form of a discussion, it was never successful. In place of reclaiming our separated brethren, this method scares them away; when they see that we are of set purpose attacking them, they instantly put themselves on their guard; when we bring the lamp too close to their eyes, they start back from the light. Nor have I ever observed that any of my fellow labourers in this work of the Lord were more successful in following out this plan, of fencing, as I may more justly call it, even though they engaged in it with the utmost enthusiasm, and in a place where the congregation all sang hymns together, and each one in his turn acted the preacher, each saying exactly what he liked, and no one taking any kind of official lead among them.

"But, in truth, this fencing was what St. Paul calls beating the air.[2] I do not mean that we must not prove Catholic truths, and refute the contrary errors; for the weapons of the spiritual armoury and of the Word of God are powerful to destroy all false teaching which rears itself up against the truth, and to condemn disobedience to God; but we must not slash with our words as desperate fencers do, but rather manage them dexterously, as does a surgeon when using his lancet—he probes skilfully, so as to wound the patient as little as possible."

And, indeed, Blessed Francis' way of dealing with this branch of theology, bristling with thorns as it does at every point, was so sweet and pleasant as to make it, as it were, blossom into roses. I could relate many instances of the success of his preaching, without employing controversy, in bringing back wanderers from the fold, equally with other sinners, into the Church.

He accomplished this by simply stating great truths, and bringing them home to his hearers. One of the most remarkable instances, perhaps, is that of the Protestant lady, who hearing him preach on the Last Judgment at Paris in the year 1619, having been attracted more by curiosity than by any good motive to listen to the sermon, there received that first flash of light which afterwards guided her into the bosom of the true Church, into which later she was followed by all the members of her noble family, one that has since given us many celebrated divines and preachers. This incident, however, with many more of the same kind, is fully related in the life of our Blessed Father. So successful was he with Protestants that Cardinal du Perron used to say that if it were only a question of confounding the heretics, he thought he had found out the secret, but to convert them he felt obliged to send for the Bishop of Geneva.

[Footnote 1: Note.—It is more correct to say that St. Francis preferred moral sermons to controversy.] [Footnote 2: 1 Cor. ix. 26.]

UPON REASON AND REASONING.

He used to say that reason never deceives, but reasoning often does. When a person went to him with some complaint, or about some troublesome business, he would always listen most patiently and attentively to any reasons which were put before him, and, being full of prudence and good judgment, he could always discern between what had any bearing on the matter and what was foreign to it. When, therefore, people began obstinately to defend their opinions by reasons, which, plausible though they might appear, really carried no weight sufficient to secure a judgment, he would sometimes say very gently, "Yes, I know quite well that these are your reasons, but do you know that all reasons are not reasonable?" Someone on one occasion having retorted that he might as well assert that heat was not warm, he replied seriously, "Reason and reasoning are two different things: reasoning is only the path leading to reason." Thus he would endeavour to bring the person who had strayed away from truth back to it. Truth and reason can never be separated, because they are one and the same thing.

UPON QUOTING HOLY SCRIPTURE.

St. Charles Borromeo never read the Scriptures except on his knees, just as if he were listening to God speaking on Mount Sinai in thunder and lightning.

Blessed Francis also would not allow the Bible to be treated with anything but the most extreme reverence, whether in public speaking, in writing, or in private reading.

He was especially averse to that habit which some preachers have of plunging into the mystical meaning of a passage, whether allegorical or figurative, before they have explained its literal sense. "To do this," he said, "is to build the roof of a house before laying the foundation. Holy Scripture must be treated with more reverence and more consistency—it is not material to be cut according to our fancy, and made into ornamental garments such as fashion suggests."

UPON POLITICAL DIPLOMACY.

On one occasion I expressed my surprise to our Blessed Father that his Serene Highness Charles Emanuel, Duke of Savoy, who was one of the most excellent Princes and foremost politicians of his age, should never have employed him in his affairs, especially in those which regarded France, where they did not prosper.

As may be supposed, I explained the reason of my surprise, insisting that his gentleness, patience, skill, and probity were certain to bring about the desired result.

He listened in silence, and then answered with a seriousness and earnestness which put me to shame, "You say too much, you exaggerate: you imagine that others esteem me as you do, you who are always looking at me through a magnifying glass. However, let us put that aside. As regards our Prince, my feeling is very different from yours, for in this very matter I consider that he shows the excellence of his judgment.

"I will tell you why I speak and think this. In the first place, I have not all that skill and prudence in the management of affairs with which you credit me. Is it likely I should have? The mere words, human prudence, business, politics, terrify me. That is not all. To speak frankly, I know nothing of the art of lying, dissimulating, or pretence, which latter is the chief instrument and the mainspring of political manoeuvring; the art of arts in all matters of human prudence and of civil administration.

"Not for all the provinces of Savoy, of France, nay, not for the whole empire, would I connive at deceit. I deal with others frankly, in good faith, and very simply; the words of my lips are the outcome of the thoughts of my heart. I cannot carry two faces under one hood; I hate duplicity with a mortal hatred, knowing that God holds the deceitful man in abomination. There are very few who, knowing me, do not at least discern this much of my character. They therefore judge very wisely that I am by no means fit for an office in which you have to speak peace to your neighbour whilst you are plotting mischief against him in your heart. Moreover, I have always followed, as a heavenly, supreme, and divine maxim, those great words of the Apostle: No man being a soldier to God entangleth himself with secular business that he may please Him to whom he hath engaged himself."[1]

[Footnote 1: Tim. ii, 4.]

UPON AMBITION.

St. Francis was truly like Aaron called to the pastoral charge by God alone, without his having used artifices or other means to procure himself such honour. This plainly appears from his life written by so many worthy persons.

His Bishopric was, indeed, no sinecure, being a most onerous burden. He says of it himself in one of his letters:

"The affairs of this diocese are not streams, they are torrents which cannot be forded." Alluding to the words of the prophet: And, it was a torrent which I could not pass over.[1]

Towards the close of his life, when Madame Christina of France, the King's sister,[2] married His Serene Highness the Prince of Piedmont, heir to the Duke of Savoy, she wished to have Blessed Francis in some official position close to her person, and, to effect this, proposed to make him her Grand Almoner. Certain prelates who had been themselves hoping to obtain this office, seeing their design thus frustrated, murmured bitterly, bursting forth into angry invectives against the Saint, as if by cabals, and intrigue, according to the custom of the world, he had succeeded in gaining the post for himself. St. Francis, however, was merely amused by what he called the buzzing of flies, and wrote to one in whom he could confide:

"Her Highness and the Prince of Piedmont wish me to become the Princess's Grand Almoner, but you will believe me readily enough, I am sure, when I tell you that I neither, directly nor indirectly, have shown any wish to obtain this office. No, truly, my dearest Mother, I have no ambition save that of being able to employ the remainder of my days usefully in the service and to the honour of our Lord. Indeed, I hold courts in sovereign contempt, because they are centres of the power of this world, which I abhor each day more and more—itself, its spirit, its maxims, and all its follies."

[Footnote 1: Ezech. xlvii. 5.]

[Footnote 2: Louis XIII.]

UPON COURTS AND COURTIERS.

Blessed Francis did not hold the opinion of many that the courts of Princes are places the very atmosphere of which is so tainted as to infect all who frequent them, and to be invariably prejudicial to the health and holiness of the soul.

Those who describe a court in terms of this sort are usually very ignorant on the subject. They speak of what they have never seen nor heard about from competent witnesses. A soul which has received the grace of God, and preserves it, can work out its salvation anywhere, nor is there any harmful intercourse so disease-laden that it cannot be overcome by this heavenly antidote, "David, and after him St. Louis," says our Holy Bishop, "in the press of the perils, toils, and travails which they endured, as well in peace as in war, did not cease to sing in truth: 'What have I in Heaven, and, besides Thee, what do I desire upon earth?'"[1]

"St. Bernard lost none of the ground which he desired to gain in this holy love by passing much time in the courts and armies of great Princes where he laboured to guide matters of state to the advancement of God's glory. He changed his habitation, but he changed not his heart, nor did his heart change its love, nor his love its object; in fine, to speak his own language, changes were made round about him, but not in him.

"His employments were different, yet he was indifferent to all employment, and different from them all, his soul not taking its colour from his affairs and conversations, as the chameleon does from the places where it is, but remaining ever wholly united to God, ever white in purity, ever red with charity, and ever full of humility.

"I am not ignorant, Theotimus, of that wise man's counsel,

He ever flies the Court and legal strife

Who seeks to sow the seeds of holy life:

Rarely do camps effect the soul's increase,

Virtue and faith are daughters unto peace.

"And the Israelites had good reason to excuse themselves to the Babylonians, who urged them to sing the sacred Canticles of Sion: How shall we sing the song of the Lord in a strange land?[2] But do not forget that those poor people were not only among the Babylonians, but were also their captives, and whoever is intent only on winning the favours of princes, dignities, military honours, alas! he is lost, he cannot sing the hymn of heavenly love. But he who is at Court, in the army, at the bar, only because it is his duty, God helps him, and heavenly sweetness is an Epithem on his heart, to preserve him from the plague which rages round about him.

"There are some kinds of fish, such as salmon, and the like, which, instead of losing their flavour, become better and more agreeable to the taste when they forsake the salt water of the sea for the sweet water of rivers.

"Roses smell sweeter when planted near garlic, and in like manner there are souls which grow more fervent in places where libertinism and irreligion seem to drag all virtue at their chariot wheels."[3]

Our Blessed Father's piety was of this sort, for, knowing that he who is consecrated to God should not entangle himself in the intrigues of the world.[4] he speaks thus to one in whom he confided: "I must confess that, as regards business, especially that of a worldly nature, I feel myself more than ever to be nothing but a poor priest, having, thank God, learnt at court to be more simple and less worldly."

Truly, we may say here with the wise man: Who is he and we will praise him? for he hath done wonderful things in his life.[5]

[Footnote 1: Psalm lxxii. 25.]

[Footnote 2: Psalm cxxxvi. 4.]

[Footnote 3: Love of God. Book xii. c. 4.]

[Footnote 4: 2 Tim. ii. 4.]

[Footnote 5: Eccles. xxxi. 9.]

UPON THE CARNIVAL.

His sad time each year was the Carnival, those days of disorder and licence which, like a torrent, carry away into excesses of one sort or another even the staunchest and most fervent in their piety. He felt, indeed, like Job of old, who offered sacrifices and prayers, and afflicted both body and soul with fasts and mortifications, while his children were passing their time in revellings and banquetings.

As our Blessed Father was all things to all men, and weak with the weak, so he also burned with the scandalised; and who would not be scandalised to see the Pagan festival of the Bacchanalia celebrated among Christians? For this very reason, as we know, the name of God is blasphemed by many, and the Catholic religion unjustly blamed, as if it permitted what it cannot prevent, as if it commanded what it tolerates with reluctance, as if it ordered what it detests and declaims against by the mouth of its preachers. Perhaps you would like to hear the words in which our Blessed Father pours forth his lamentations over this period of the year, so full of disorder and confusion.

"I must tell you," he says, "that now I have come to my sorrowful time. From the Epiphany even to Lent my heart is full of strange sensations. Miserable and detestable as I am, I am weighed down with grief to see the loss of so much devotion, I mean the falling off of so many souls. These two last Sundays I have found our communions diminished by one-half. That has grieved me very much, for even if those who made them do not give way to sin, why, and for what, do they now omit them? For nothing at all—out of mere vanity, it is that which grieves me."

AN INSTANCE OF HIS COMPASSION FOR ANIMALS.

The Church inculcates on the Clergy perfect gentleness and kindness. This is why they may never take any part in anything involving bloodshed. His having shed the blood of a fellow man, even when required by the interests of justice, is considered a canonical irregularity, and deprives a Priest of the right to celebrate Holy Mass.

Blessed Francis was remarkable for his gentleness and tender-heartedness towards all creatures. I will give you a little instance of this.

One day he was at my house, when a nobleman of distinction called upon us. This gentleman was at the head of a hunting party, and seeing in my orchard a roebuck which had been given to me and which was peacefully feeding, he proposed, as he said, to amuse our Blessed Father by setting his dogs upon the poor animal, and to confine the hunt to my orchard.

The good Bishop's remonstrances were in vain. But though he refused to go to the orchard, he could not avoid being a witness, however unwillingly, of what took place, as his room overlooked the ground. Great numbers of people came to enjoy the spectacle; the horns were blown, the dogs barked, while the poor roebuck, as if it knew who would fain have been its deliverer, bounding towards the window near which the Bishop was seated, seemed, like a suppliant, to be imploring his help.

Blessed Francis drew back, and begged as earnestly that the hunt might be given up as if he had been asking pardon for a criminal.

He did not see the end, for the animal was at once brought to bay and despatched. They wanted him to see it when dead, but he did not deign so much as to look at it, and when the venison was served at table, he most unwillingly partook of the dish. "Alas," he exclaimed, "what hellish pleasure! This is just how infuriated demons pursue poor souls by temptations to sin, so as to precipitate them into the abyss of everlasting death, yet of that no one thinks."

UPON HUNTING.

Blessed Francis was sometimes taxed with over much good nature and gentleness, and was told that this was the cause of many disorders which would not have occurred had he been more wholesomely severe. He, however, answered calmly and sweetly that he had always in his mind the words of the great St. Anselm, the glory of our Alps, among which he was born. That Saint, he observed, was in the habit of saying that if he had to be punished either for being too indulgent or being over-rigorous, he would far rather it should be for the former. He gave as his reason that judgment with mercy would be meted out to the merciful, and that God would always have more pity on the pitiful than on the rigorous. He went on to recall that most sound maxim: Sovereign right is only sovereign injustice, and remarked that in Holy Scripture those pastors who were over-severe were invariably blamed.

Our Saint used always to say that sugar never yet spoilt any sauce, but that too much salt or vinegar often did.

His speaking of St. Anselm's gentleness reminds me of the story told of the same Saint by Blessed Francis in his Philothea. "One day," he says, "as he, St. Anselm, was travelling, a hare, being closely run by the hounds which pursued it, took refuge between his horse's feet, and the dogs remained yelping around unable to molest their prey in this its strange sanctuary. His followers were highly entertained at so novel a spectacle, but Saint Anselm groaned and wept. 'Even thus,' said he, 'do the enemies of the soul pursue it and drive it into all manner of sins, until at the last they can kill and devour it, and whilst the terrified soul seeks for some refuge and help, its enemies mock and laugh if it finds none.'"[1]

Our Blessed Father, following the example of the holy Archbishop, was invariably kind and gentle, even with the brute creation. He not only himself never did them harm, but he prevented, as far as he could, any being done to them by others, for he believed that those who thus inflict pain on innocent creatures often, even at the risk of their own lives, display a cruel and malevolent kind of courage. He went so far as to regard it as a venial sin to injure creatures for the sole pleasure of harming them where no advantage of any sort would accrue to ourselves; his reason being that we in this way deprive them of the joy to be found in mere existence bestowed upon them by God.

"What, then," he was asked, "do you say to the chase, and to the killing of animals for the food of man?" "As regards the food of man," he replied, "the very words you use justify the act, and it is that end which justifies the chase." From this we may conclude that the mere pleasure of the chase was not sufficient, in his opinion, to render lawful the indulging in it.

Although he blamed the superstition of the Turks, who think that they acquire merit in the sight of God by lavishing kindness on senseless brutes, even the most savage and cruel, such as wolves and lions, still he used to say that this pity had a good natural source, and that those who were so compassionate to animals were likely to be no otherwise to men, nature teaching us not to despise our own flesh. In spite of these feelings, he was very far from falling into those mistakes which casuists enumerate as the result of excess in gentleness and kindness.

The various writers of the life of Blessed Francis tell us how it was commonly remarked that all animals by natural instinct seemed to recognise his tender, compassionate feelings for them, and that when hunted and pursued, they at once took refuge with him, witness the pigeons, which at different times when he was saying the Divine Office, flew for safety and shelter into his very hands.

[Footnote 1: Devout Life. Part II. c. 13.]

UPON THE FEAR OF GHOSTS.

Fear is a natural passion, which, like all the others, is in itself neither bad nor good, but bad when it is excessive and disquieting, good when it is subordinate to reason. There are some who, because naturally timid and apprehensive, would never dare to speak in public. Others are so afraid of thunder and lightning that they faint in a storm. Others are afraid of noises at night, and have a horror of darkness and solitude. Others, again, have so great a fear of ghosts and apparitions that they dare not sleep alone in a room.

I have been told, on good authority, that one of our Bravest and most distinguished Generals, who went to battle as gaily and confidently as he would go to a marriage, declared that he could never suffer his valet, after settling him for the night, to leave his sleeping apartment, it being quite impossible for him to sleep when left alone at night. Our Blessed Father writes in the following consoling manner to a pious person who suffered from the weakness of being afraid of ghosts:

"I am told," he says, "that you are afraid of spirits. The Sovereign Spirit of our God is everywhere, and without His Will or permission no other spirit dare stir. Those who fear this Divine Spirit ought not to fear any other. You are beneath His wings, like a little chicken under those of its mother; what do you fear? In my youth I, too, was a prey to these imaginations, and in order to get the better of them I forced myself when quite a child to go alone into places which my fancy had peopled with fantastic terrors. I went alone, I say, but my heart was armed with confidence in God. Now I am grown so strong in this confidence that darkness and the solitude of the night are delightful to me, since in solitude I realise better the all-embracing Presence of God. The good angels are there round about us like a company of soldiers on guard. The truth of God, says the Psalmist, shall compass thee with a shield; thou shall not be afraid of the terror of night.[1]

"This feeling of safety you will acquire little by little, in proportion as the grace of God grows in you: for grace engenders confidence, and confidence is never confounded."

See how, with this timid, fearful soul, he makes himself weak and infirm. If I may be permitted to add to this great example my own poor and worthless experience, I would say that when I was young I was greatly afflicted with this weakness. It was indeed, perhaps, the chief impediment to my entering the Order of St. Bruno, which is, in my opinion, the holiest, as it certainly is the most retired and the most steadfast of all the religious orders. I, however, lost this infirmity as soon as I had received the imposition of hands from the Blessed Francis de Sales, and I may add that Almighty God permitted me to succeed, in the episcopal chair, three Saints of that order which I revered so much, namely, Saints Artauld, Audace, and Anthelme.[2]

[Footnote 1: Psalm xi. 5.]

[Footnote 2: Six Carthusians occupied the See of Belley: Ponce de Balmay, St. Anthelme, Raynauld, St. Arthaut, Bernard, and Bd. Boniface of Savoy. (Trésor de Chronologie, Chez Palmé, Paris, 1880). Audace, first Bp. of Belley, was not canonised, nor was he a Carthusian.]

HIS PORTRAIT.

I have known great servants of God who would not on any account allow their portraits to be painted, imagining that their doing so must involve some degree of vanity and dangerous self-complacency. Our Blessed Father was not of this opinion, but, making himself all things to all men that he might win all to Jesus Christ, he made no objection to having his portrait taken when asked to do so. He gave as his reason that since we are obliged by the law of holy charity to communicate to our neighbour the representation of our mind, imparting to him without dissimulation or jealousy what we have learnt concerning the science of salvation, so we ought to be still less niggardly in pleasing our friends by placing before their eyes the picture of our outward self which they so earnestly desire to have.

If we see, not only without annoyance, but even with pleasure, our books, which are the portraits of our minds, in the hands of our fellow men, why grudge them the picture of our countenance, if it contribute anything to their satisfaction. On this subject he expresses himself as follows in one of his letters: "Here, then, is the picture of the earthly man, for I am unwilling to refuse you anything which you desire.

"I am told that my portrait has never been really well painted. That, I think, matters very little, surely man passeth as an image. Yea, and he is disquieted in vain.[1]

"I borrowed it in order to send it to you, for I have not myself got my own portrait. Ah! if the image of my Creator were imprinted in all its splendour on my soul, how gladly would I let you see it!

"O Jesu, tuo lumine, luo redemptos sanguine,

sana, refove, perfice, tibi conformes, effice. Amen."

Thus did he turn every subject into an occasion of elevating the soul to God.

[Footnote 1: Psalm xxxviii. 7]

UPON BLESSED FRANCIS' TRUE CHARITY.

Since charity was the animating motive of all that our Holy Bishop thought, said, or did, and since it was in truth his very spirit, we cannot better close these reminiscences of that saintly spirit than by quoting the words of the Prince of the Apostles: Before all things have a constant charity among yourselves, for charity covers a multitude of sins. Let every one behave himself according to the dispensation of grace. If any man speak, let him speak as the words of God. If any man minister, let him do it as of the power which God administers, that in all things God may be honoured through Jesus Christ, to whom is glory and empire for ever and ever. Amen.[1]

[Footnote 1: 1 Peter iv. 8, 10, 11.]

Printed in Great Britain
by Amazon

22979304R10297